WORKING WOMEN AND CHILDREN

WORKING WOMEN AND CHILDREN

Volume - 3

Child Labour: A Reality

Editor-in-Chief

C. P. RAI

LAXMI SHIKSHAN SANSTHAN
LUCKNOW

&

ANMOL PUBLICATIONS PVT. LTD.
NEW DELHI - 110 002 (INDIA)

ANMOL PUBLICATIONS PVT. LTD.
4374/4B, Ansari Road, Daryaganj
New Delhi - 110 002

Working Women and Children

First Edition, 2000

ISBN 81-261-0658-1 (Set)

PRINTED IN INDIA

Published by J.L. Kumar for Anmol Publications Pvt. Ltd., New Delhi -110 002 and Printed at Mehra Offset Press, Delhi.

CONTENTS

PREFACE

Conventionally labour force consists of persons in the age group 15 to 59 years. However, there are about 52 million child workers in the world. More than 50 million working children are from under-developed countries, where Asia alone accounts for 38 million, with concentration in South and South East Asia of 29 million. The child labour is a symptom of poverty, unemployment and illiteracy. The child labour is normally found in unorganised sectors where he is highly vulnerable to exploitation.

A common observation in India, as in many developing countries, is that a large number of children are engaged in economically productive work. Children are often employed in the rural areas, for example, to graze cattle and on the farm. In urban areas, children are engaged in, among other things, construction, automobile repairs, restaurants and domestic work. According to the 1971 Census of India, the total work of participation rate for males up to 14 years of age was 6.6 per cent; for females of the same age the rate was 2.5 per cent (Office of the Registrar General and Census Commissioner, 1977). The corresponding percentages for 1981 were 5.5 and 2.9 which, in absolute numbers, works out to be 10.7 and 11.2 million child workers in 1971 and 1981 respectively. Although the census data for the two years are not comparable, the data, nevertheless, give in idea about the magnitude of children who are working. The census data also indicate that the participation rate of children as workers in rural areas is nearly three times the rate in urban areas; whereas in 1971 the rural and urban rates were 5.3 and 1.8 per cent, in 1981 the rates for these areas were 5.0 and 1.7 per cent respectively. And the actual situation in the year 2000 A.D., has much worsened.

This book focusses on two main themes. First, Child labour: a real Position; and the second Exploitation of child labour and welfare measures.

Derived from the writings of eminent scholars in the field, this work portrays all aspects of and issues pertaining to working children and their plight and suggestions for welfare measures. We are grateful to these scholars. We also owe deep sense of gratitude to Mr. J.L.Kumar, Managing Director, Anmol Publications Pvt. Ltd., New Delhi for bringing out the work in record time.

— C. P. Rai

1

CHILD LABOUR: CONCEPT, REASONS AND REPERCUSSIONS

Concept of Child Labour

The definition of child labour varies from one act to another depending upon the seriousness of the problems of children working in a particular employment (Govil, 1975: 73-78). The precise age of what constitutes child labour has not been laid down anywhere because of variations in the age of child as given under different legislative enactments. Article 24 of the Constitution of India maintains: "No child below the age of 14 years shall be employed to work in any factory or mine or employed in any hazardous employment." Section 82 of the Indian Penal Code, 1860 reads: "Nothing is an offence which is done by a child under 7 years of age." Section 83 of the Indian Penal Code 1860, provides: "Nothing is an offence which is done by a child above 7 years and under 12 who has not attained sufficient maturity of understanding to judge the nature and consequence of his conduct on the occasion." Section 105 of the Indian Evidence Act, 1872 lays down:" When a person is accused of any offence, the burden of proving the existence of circumstances bringing the case within any of the general or special exception including that of childhood of the Indian penal code or any concerning law is upon him". Under the Indian Majority Act, 1874 the age of majority has been fixed at 18 years. Under the Vaccination Act, 1880, children have been defined as persons "who have not attained the age of 14 years in case of boys and 18 years in case of girls". Under the Reformatory Schools Act, 1887, "youth offender" means any boy who has been convicted of any offence punishable with imprisonment for life or death and who at the time of such conviction, was under the age of 15 years. "The Child Marriage Restraint Act, 1929 (Sharda Act) defines child as "a male below twenty one years and a female below eighteen years of age." Under the Motor Vehicles Act, 1939, child has been defined as a person under the age of 18 years. According to the U.P. children Act, 1951, "child" means a person under the age of 16 years. The Young Persons Harmful Publication Act, 1956 defines young person as "a person under the age of 20 years." Under the Suppression of Immoral Traffic in Women and Girls Act, 1956, "Girl" means a female who has not completed the age of 21 years." According to the Orphanages and Charitable Homes (Supervision and Control) Act, 1960, "Child" means a boy or girl who has not completed the age of eighteen years." As per provisions of the Children Act, 1960, "Child" means a boy who has attained the age of 16 years or a girl who has not attained the age of 18 years. Section 27 of the Code of Criminal Procedure, 1973 reads: "any offence not punishable with death or imprisonment for life, committed by any person who at the date when he appears or is brought before the count in under the age of Sixteen years, may be tried by the court of a Chief Judicial Magistrate, or by any court specially empowered under the Children Act, 1960 or any other law for the time being enforced providing for the treatment, training and rehabilitation of youthful offenders." According to Section 3 of the Employment of Children Act, 1938, "No child who has not completed his fifteenth year shall be employed or permitted to work in any occupation......... No child who has completed his fifteenth year but has not completed his seventeenth year shall be employed or permitted to work in any occupation unless the periods of work of such child for any day are so fixed as to allow an interval of rest for at least twelve consecutive hours which shall include at least such seven consecutive hours between 10 p.m. and 7 a.m. as may be prescribed...... No child who has not completed his fourteenth year shall be employed or permitted to work in any workshop wherein any of the processes set forth in the schedule is carried on. "Under Section 2(C) of the Factories Act, 1948, "Child means a person who has not completed his fifteenth year of age." Section 67 of the Act provides: "No child who has not completed his fourteenth year shall be required or allowed to work in any factory." Section 68 of the Act further lays down: "A child who has completed his fourteenth year or an adolescent shall not be required or allowed to work in any factory unless—(a) certificate of fitness granted with reference to him......is in the custody of the manager of the factory, and (b) such child or adolescent carries while he is at work a token giving a reference to such certificate." "Adjacent", according to the Act, "means a person who has completed his fifteenth year of age but has not completed his eighteenth year." As per section 2 (c) of the Plantation Labour Act, 1951, "Child" means a person who has not completed his fifteenth year." Section 24 of the Act lays down: "No child who has not completed his twelfth year shall be required or allowed to work in any plantation." According to section 2 (e) of the Mines Act, "Child" means a person who has not completed his fifteenth year." Section 45 of the Act stipulates: "No child shall be employed in any mine, nor shall any child be allowed to be present in any part of a mine which is below ground or in any open cast working in which any mining operation is being carried on." In the Merchant Shipping Act, 1958, employment of children below 15 years as seamen has ordinarily been prohibited. Persons below eighteen years cannot be employed as trimmers and stokers. According to section 2 (c) of the Motor Transport Workers' Act, 1961, "child" means a person who has not completed his fifteenth year." Section 21 of the Act provides: "No adolescent shall be required or allowed to work as a motor transport worker in any motor transport undertaking unless—(a) a certificate of fitness granted with reference to him.........is in the custody of the employer, and (b) such adolescent carries with him while he is at work, a token giving a reference to such certificate." "Adolescent", according to section 2 (a) of the Act. "means a person who has completed his fifteenth year but has not completed his eighteenth year." According to section 2 (b) of the Bidi and Cigar Workers (Conditions of Employment) Act, 1966, "child" means a person who has not completed fourteenth years of age." Section 24 of the Act provides" "No child shall be required or allowed to work in any industrial premises." Under the Radiation Protection Rules, 1971 framed under the Atomic Energy Act, 1962, "A child has been defined as a person below eighteen years of age." According to Section 2 (2) of the U.P. Dookan Aur Vanijya Adhishthan Adhiniyam, 1962, "Child" means a person who has not completed his fourteenth years." Section 1 of the Act clearly says. "No child shall be required or allowed to work in any shop or commercial establishment except as an apprentice in such employment as may be notified by the State Government in the Gazette." In Shops and Commercial Establishment Acts passed by other States and Union Territories, child has been defined as a person between 12 and 14 years. It is because of this variation in age of a child in different laws that child labour will have to be defined in the context of a vocation in which a child is employed (Madan, 1975: 92). Since children employed in agriculture are not covered under any statutory provision, the age of child labour in agriculture has to be defined keeping in view the nature of agricultural work. In this regard an observation made by Mendelievich (1979: 4) seems to be pertinent: "Agriculture is one of the most hazardous sectors for the physical safety and health of workers for several reasons: the prevalence of dangerous modern machinery; prolonged exposure to heat, sunlight, dust, wind and insects; the almost constant physical effort that agricultural work demands; contact with various chemical products such as fertilisers and pesticides whose long-term effects on man may be completely unknown and for the majority of which, in cases of poisoning, no specific antidotes exist. Children are particularly at risk from endemic and parasitic diseases, diseases of the respiratory tract, dermatosis and fatal accidents." The Convention concerning the Minimum Age of Employment, 1973 lays down that as regards work which is likely to adversely affect health, or morals of young persons, minimum age for admission to any type of employment or work of this kind shall not be less than 18 years. This is why the minimum age in the context of child labour in agriculture with which the present study has been concerned, has been fixed at 18 years.

Child labour has been differently defined in various studies. According to the Committee on Child Labour (1979: 8), "Child labour, however, can broadly be defined as that segment of the child population which participates in work either paid or unpaid" In their study of Working Children in Bombay, Singh *et al.* (1980: 23) have held the view: "Child labour means a working child who is between 6 and 15 years of age' is not attending school during the day, is working under an employer or is learning some trade as an apprentice.' In the study titled as Working Children in Urban Delhi conducted by the Indian Council of Child Welfare (1977: 125). "Every child below 14 years, who contributed to the family income or was gainfully employed including those marginally working was treated as a worker." V.V. Giri (1958: 360) has expressed the view: "The term "child labour" is commonly interpreted in two different ways: first, as an economic practice an second, as a social evil. In the first context it signifies employment of children in gainful occupations with a view to adding to the total income of the family. It is in the second sense that the term child labour is now more generally used. In assessing the nature and extent of social evil, it is necessary to take into account the character of the jobs on which children are engaged, the dangers to which they are exposed and the opportunities of development which they have been denied." Hommerfolks, Chairman of the United National Child Labour Committee, has defined child labour as "any work by children that interferes with their full physical development, their opportunities for a desirable level of education or their needed recreation." (in Stein and Deavis, 1940: 112-113). Kulshretha (1978: 2) is of the view that "Child labour in a restricted sense means the employment of child in gainful occupations which are dangerous to their health and deny them the opportunities of development,......... The term child labour not only applied to the children working in the industries but also to the children in all forms of non-industrial occupations which are injurious to their physical, mental, moral and social development." According to Alakh Narayan Sharma (1979: 9), "Child labour means the employment of children in gainful occupations (in industrial as well as non-industrial occupations) which are injurious to their physical, mental, moral and social development. Thus, the term includes wage-labour as well as self-employed children working independently as well as in family enterprises." Child labour therefore, can be defined here as any work undertaken by children below 18 years in agriculture and allied works injurious to their health and harmful to their proper development.

Age at Which the Child Workers Started Working

Information gathered regarding age at which the child workers started working and analysed in relation to their nature of employment on the assumption that the age of starting work may be different in case of children working on their own land, on land owned by others and on own as well as others' land, reveals that the largest single group of child workers (25.00%) had started work between 7-9 years followed by those who had started work between 9-11 years. (19.00%), below 5 years (13.60%), 5-7 years (12.40%), 11-13 years and 13-15 years (9.00%) each and 15-17 years (3.00%). It is noteworthy that as many as 9.00% of the child workers did not remember their age of starting work. The average age of starting work has been 8.57 years. Singh *et al.* (1980: 75) have found in their study: "Thus one out of every four working children, joined the workforce before completing 9 years of age and a little less than of half before completing 12 years of age and again a little more than one fourth as soon as they entered their thirteenth year of life". Gangrade (in Mendelievich, 1979: 82) has concluded that "children only 6 years old have been found working, although the usual age of entry into employment seems to be 8 to 9 years. Boys of 10 to 12 have been found working on regular term contracts of several years duration."

Khandekar and Naik (1972: 369) have found that "a fairly large number of children below what is considered to be the working age, are called upon to supplement the economic activity of their elders."

An analysis in terms of nature of employment reveals that in the case of the child workers working on their own land, the largest single group (27.14%) has started work between 7-9 years of age, followed by those who had begun working between 9-11 years (20.48%), below 5 years (16.19%), 5-7 years (14.05), 11-13 years (9.05%), 13-15 years (5.00%) and 15-17 year (0.48%). As many as 7.61% of the child workers did not remember the age of starting work. The average age of starting work on own land has been 7.93 years. In case of the child workers working on land owned by others, the largest single group (42.86%) had started working between 13-15 years of age, followed by those who had started doing so between 7-9 and 11-13 years (14.29% each) and 5-7, 9-11 and 15-17 years (7.14)% each). There have been 7.14 per cent children working on land owned by others who did not remember the age of starting work. The average age of starting work on land owned by others has been 12 years. As for children working on their own land as also on land owned by others, the largest single group (27.27%) had started work between 13-15 years of age followed by those who had started doing so between 15-17 years (18.18%), 7-9 years (13.64%) 9-11 years (12.12%), 11-13 years (7.58) and 5-7 years (3.03%). As many as 18.18% children working on their own land as well as on land owned by others did not remember the age of starting work. The mean age of starting work on own land as also on land owned by other has been 12.33 years. It is noteworthy that none of the child workers working exclusively on land owned by others or on own land as well as on land owned by others had started working below 5 years of age because in wage employment, efforts are made by inconsiderate employers to take maximum work within minimum time which children are not in a position to physically bear. To conclude, the child workers had started working between 7-9 years of age. Average age of starting work on own land has been lower than that of taking up work on land owned by others as also on own as well as others' land.

Persons for Whom the Child Workers Work

Children are forced to take up work out of necessity to fulfil the basic unmet needs of their own as also of their family members. Information gathered regarding persons for whom the child workers might have been forced to work and analysed in relation to their age on the assumption that child workers in different age-groups might have been working for the fulfilment of the needs of different categories of persons, reveals that an overwhelming majority of the child workers (68.70%) have been working for satisfaction of their own as well as family members' needs followed by those who have been working for the sake of their family members only (10.20%) and those who have engaged in work for their own sake (9.00%). As many as 12.20% have not given any response in this regard. In the age-group of 8-12 years, majority of the child workers (61.07%) have been working with a view to satisfying their own as well as family members' needs followed by those who have been involved in work for the sake of their family members (8.05%) and their own sake (4.70%) only. 19.46% of the child workers in this age-group have not given any response. In the age-group of 13-18 years, an overwhelming majority of the child workers (71.79%) have been participating in work in order to fulfil their own as well as family members' needs followed by those who have been engaged in work for the sake of their family members (11.11%) and for their own sake (7.98). As many as 9.12% of the child workers in this age-group also did not give any response. Thus the child workers, irrespective of their age composition, have, by and large, been working to satisfy their own as well as family followed by those who have been engaged in work for the sake of their family members' needs. However, results of chi-square [Chi-square (cal.) = 10.67, chi-square (tab.) 9.49, d.f. = 4, =.05)] show that there is significant association between persons whose needs child workers want to fulfil and their age.

Persons Motivating Children to Work

Children may get motivation to work from different sources. They may themselves decide to work when they see that even basic needs of their own as also of their family members are not properly et despite the best possible efforts made by their parents. They may be motivated by their parents to take up work out of sheer compulsion of family circumstances. Other members of their family, and even those outside their family, may suggest children to share the burden of their parents unable to afford the family expenses. Data gathered regarding persons who have motivated the child whokers to take up work reveal that in a majority of cases (54.8%) motivation to work has been provided by child workers themselves and their parents followed by those where such motivation has come from self (21.80%), parents (14.20%), self and brothers (3.60%), self and guardians (0.80%), brothers (0.40%) and guardians (0.20%). It has not been possible for 4.20% of the child workers to spell out the persons who motivated them to take up the work.

Reasons Why Children Work

A number of reasons with different types of combinations have been held responsible for work by Children. Labour Bureau (In NIPCCD, 177:179), the first to undertake a detailed survey of child labour in India, had come to the conclusion: "The major reason for the prevalence of child labour in a developing country like India is not far to seek. In these countries, the poverty of the parents compels them to send their children to work at an early age......the existence of child labour in differential degrees in almost all sectors of economy-organised or unorganised—can mainly be attributed to economic causes." George (in NIPCCD, 1977: 166-167) has cited these reasons for seeking employment: "To supplement family income (72.50%); death of father (23.00%) do not like to depend on others (19.00%); parents asked to search for job (17.00%); for out-of-pocket expenses (10.00%); no one to look after (7.00%); no other earning member (5.00%); to earn for education (5.00%); to learn the job (4.00%); parents asked to assist in occupation (3.00%), interested in the job (3.00%); just to escape attending school (0.50%)." Punekar (in NIPCCD, 1977: 129) has maintained: "In the rural area, employment of children (i.e., persons below the age of 15) as wage-paid labour is mainly to supplement the meagre income of chronically poverty-stricken households" Govil (in NIPCCD, 1977: 82) has pointed out that "poverty is the root cause for child labour" Kulshrestha (1978: 12-19) has mentioned poverty, absence of scheme of family allowance, large family, cheaper rates of child labour, absence of compulsory education, illiteracy and ignorance, slow process of protective labour legislation and inadequate inspecting machinery as the causes of child labour. Jain and Chand (1979: 322) have observed: "Children work not because their parents are wicked or those that employ them are wicked but because their income is essential for the survival of the family or themselves, if they have left their home for lack of means of survival." Mendelievich, while detailing the reasons, (1979: 8-9) has made a mention of (1) need to reduce to the greatest possible extent the poverty, (2) parents' wish to keep their children occupied and off the streets, (3) poor performance at school, (4) situation at home characterised by tension and uncertainty absence of one of the or both the parents etc. and (5) instability and insecurity caused by migration from rural to urban areas. Citing a study undertaken in Bangkok, Mendelievich has made a pointed reference of these reasons: poverty (23.40%) need to assist parents in household economic activity (32.90%), parents want them to work (26.30%), need to earn their own living (7.90%), better than doing nothing (6.90%) and other reasons (2.60%). Gangrade (in Mendelivich, 1979: 81) has maintained: "The poverty of many families forces the parents to put their children to work instead of sending them to school." Singh *et al.* (1980: 9-12) have thrown light on tradition and poverty as the main causes of child labour. Ministry of Labour, Government of India (1979: 10-13 and 70) has maintained tradition, poverty, lack of adequate awareness among parents for educating children, illiteracy, large size of family, inadequate schooling facility, loss of parents or breadwinner of the family, unemployment and lack of land as the causes of child labour. Sharma (1979: 67) has come to the conclusion that "child labour originates due to the prevalence of poverty in the society......non-realisation on the part of parents of the important role of education, and their preference for work to education might have contributed to social evil". Smt. Kusum (Government of India; 1978: 16) has expressed the view that "it their children to seek employment. Inadequate income of the adult bread-earner of the family, unemployment absence of any family allowance or subsistence allowance on one side, and the large family on the other, death of the adult bread-earner, drinking habits and other social evils in adults and absence of school and provision of compulsory education, illiteracy and ignorance of parents etc. are the main reasons of the child labour." Pichholiya (1980: 99) has held the view that "children's participation in labour force for wages is mainly due to the need to supplement household income." Nadeem Mohshin (1980: 27) has held that "the supply of child labour is governed mainly by two factors: (1) non-availability of adult labour in the family, (2) inadequate income of the family......in India where a large section of population suffers from acute poverty; child labour, by and large, is a product of unemployment, under employment of the adult wage earners." The Labour Bureau Simla (1981: 53), on the basis of survey of child labour in Indian industries, has observed; "Extreme poverty, lack of opportunity for gainful employment and intermitancy of income and low standards of living are the main reasons for the wide prevalence of child labour."

It is thus sufficiently clear that poverty is the main reason for children's employment in India Facts relating to poverty in India reveal that 48.13% of the population in 1977-78 has been living below poverty line of Rs. 65.00 per capita per month on 1977-78 prices corresponding to daily calorie requirement of 2400 per person in rural areas and Rs. 75.00 per capita per month on 1977-78 prices corresponding to minimum daily calorie requirement of 2100 in urban areas (Indian Worker, 1980: 2). Assuming that the poverty line is drawn at consumption level of Rs. 65.00 per capita per month for rural areas and Rs. 75.00 per capita per month for urban areas, children below the poverty line would the about 18 million, embracing 55% of the rural children and 45% of the urban ones (Majumdar: 1981).

There are certain circumstances which compel the children to take up work at an early age. Data collected regarding such circumstances and analysed in relation to age of the child workers on the assumption that such circumstances may be different in case of children of different age-composition, reveal that majority of the child workers (64.67%) have been compelled to take up work by poor economic condition followed by apathy in studies (22.60%), preference fro work (21.15%), need for extra working hands (12.98%), weakness in studies (11.45), no other employment opportunity (10.34) and parents' desire (9.38). Further analysis in terms of age indicates that in both the age-groups of 8-12 (62.96%) and 13-18 (62.26%), majority of the child workers have reported poor economic condition as the factor which has compelled them to take up work.

Analysis of data relating to such circumstances in relation to sex reveals that in case of the male child workers, poor economic condition (67.22%) followed by apathy towards studies (21.74%), preference for work (16.72%), weakness in studies and need for extra working hands (13.04%) each), no other employment opportunity (7.36%) and parents' desire (3.01%) have been the reasons behind taking up work whereas in case of female child workers, poor economic condition (58.12%), preference for work and parents desire (32.48% each), apathy towards studies (24.79%), no other employment opportunity (17.95%), need for extra working hands (12.82%) and weakness in studies (7.69%) have been the compelling factors. This shows that poor economic condition has been the main factor compelling the child workers to take up work, irrespective of their sex differences.

Further analysis in relation to state of education unravels that in case of the child workers without any education, poor economic condition (70.40%) followed by preference for work (32.80%), need for extra working hands (8.80%), no other employment opportunity (7.20%) and parents' desire (5.60%) have been the compelling circumstances. As for the child workers who have discontinued their education, poor economic condition (67.02%) followed by apathy towards studies (38.46%), preference for work (27.47%), need for extra working hands (19.78%), weakness in studies (13.29%), no other employment opportunity (12.08%) and parents' desire (9.89%) have been the reasons. In so far as the child workers who have been able to continue their education are concerned, poor economic condition (60.00%) followed by apathy towards studies (22.50%), weakness in studies (18.00%), need for extra working hands (12.50%), parents' desire and no other employment opportunity (11.50% each) and preference for work (11.00%) have been the forcing factors.

In a nutshell, it has been the poor economic condition of child workers that has compelled them to take-up work irrespective of their age, sex and state of education.

Reasons of Employers' Preference for Children in Work

There are a number of reasons due to which children are preferred by employers. Reasons stated in the Report of the Committee on Child Labour (Government of India, 1980: 11-12) are: (1) less developed ego and status consciousness; (2) lesser affliction by feeling of guild and shame; (3) no hesitation to do non-status, even demeaning, jobs; (4) activeness, agility and quickness and lesser feeling of tiredness; (5) greater discipline and control; (6) less expensive to maintain; (7) superior adaptive abilities; (8) lack of organisation; (9) moral consideration of the employers to help and to provide succour to the destitute or forsaken children; and (10) acquisition of fineness through initiation in the early age. Singh et al. (1980: 12-13) have made a mention of (1) hesitation among adults to perform certain jobs; (2) cheapness of child giving larger surplus value to the employed (3) superior adaptability of children; (4) absence of many negative qualities among children; (5) lack of organisation; (6) religiosity of the employer to provide succour to destitute and forsaken children; and (7) acquisition of fineness as reasons behind employers' preference for children in work. The National Commission on Labour (1969: 386) has also pointed out that "quite often it is the feeling of sympathy rather than the desire to exploit which weighs with employers in employing child workers........ We have been told by some employers that unless the fingers were thus trained at very early age, their adaptation later would be difficult." Information gathered regarding reasons of preference for employment of children by employers and analysed in relation to age of the child workers on the assumption that reasons given by the child workers in different age-groups may be varied, unreavels that the largest single group of child workers (36.25%) has given shortage of working hands and high economic status of employers followed by more land (20.00%), and high economic status of employers (16.25), more land and high economic status of employers (13.75%), shortage of working hands (8.75%) and intensive cultivation (5.00%). An analysis in terms of age reveals that in case of the child workers in the age-group of 8-12 years, shortage of working hands and high economic status of employer (56.25%) followed by more land and high economic status of employer (18.57% each) and shortage of working hand (6.25%) have been spelt out as reasons for preference. As for the child workers in the age-group of 13-18 years, shortage of working hands and high economic status of employer (31.25%) followed by more land and high economic status (21.31% each) more land and high economic status of employer (12.5%), shortage of working hands (9.38%) and intensive cultivation (6.25%) have been put foward as reasons for preference.

In a nutshell, shortage of working hands coupled with high economic status, of the employer has been given by the child workers irrespective of age composition, as the main reason behind employer's, preference for children in work.

Reasons Why Child Workers Like Agricultural Work

There may be a number of reasons responsible for a person's liking for any kind of work. Information gathered from the child workers regarding reasons for their liking for agricultural work and analysed in relation to their age on the assumption that reasons may differ according to age-composition, clearly indicates that apathy towards studies (28.63%) followed by a combination of apathy towards studies and desire to stay at home (27.35), no other employment opportunity (11.56%), desire to stay at home (19.68%), no other employment opportunity and desire to stay at home (8.55%), apathy towards studies and poor economic status of family (5.56%), relatively more economic benefit (4,79%), and poor economic status of family (2.99%), have been given as reasons for liking agricultural work. Age-wise analysis shows that in both the age-groups of 8-12and 13-18 years, the largest single group has given apathy towards studies followed by a combination of apathy towards studies and desire to stay at home as the reasons. It can, therefore, be concluded that it has been mainly because of apathy towards studies coupled with desire to stay at home that the child workers have developed liking for agricultural work.

Repercussions of Child Labour

It is beyond doubt that children are forced by circumstances to do labour in the tender age when they should have been at schools. The mere fact that it is not the work but labour that children are coerced to do has manifold repercussions for them, for their family and for the society as a whole. In the context of child workers themselves, harmful effects of child labour can be seen in the form of their improper physical development, varied kinds of illness and physical deformities, damage to central nervous system, impoverishment of the entire mental world, lack of capacity to adjust with other persons in society, inability to express views, indulgence in various social vices etc. Khandekar and Naik (1972: 369) have observed: "Since the early years are meant to equip oneself with knowledge, techniques and skills for one's different adult roles in the society, having to take up a job at a young age to earn a living, is bound to affect the very process of growing up."

Initiation of children in work from the early stage deprives them of opportunities for acquiring various abilities and skills through education and training which are necessary for getting important positions in the contemporary competitive society; and thus they become unable to contribute their mite to their families which they would otherwise have done, had they been sent to educational and training institutions in their formative period. Participation of children in work outside the family dissociates them from their family members and creates a physical distance between them and thereby reduces the degree of intimacy, love and affection towards the family among them. The incidence of earning money from childhood generates a feeling of independence among children due to which they like to behave freely and promiscuously and do not like to be subjected to control and discipline by other family members and are seen, in many cases, adopting many a bad habit and separating from their families immediately after their marriage, and in some cases, even before marriage. Thus the family not only suffers the economic loss in the long run but also becomes subjected to loose social bonds and ties within the family, and at times, even family disorganistion.

Ultimately it is the society which suffers a great deal because of incidence of child labour. Work by children means not only decrease in opportunities for adult employment but also reduction in the wages of adult workers. It is estimated (Chaturvedi, 1979: 9-27) that if workers under 18 years of age in India could be taken out of the labour force and provided educational and vocational training, some 15 to 20 million unemployed adults would be able to find jobs on standard wages. In the long run, child labour means prevalence of unskilled and incompetent labour force in society. Thus the society not only suffers the economic loss but also has to bear the blame of having child labour in a welfare state despite whose commitment to ensure a minimum desirable standard of living, children are forced, out of necessity, to take up employment in their tender age.

Mendelievich (1979: 46) has vividly described the social repercussions of child labour in these worlds: "As a general rule, however, when a child performs stultifying, precarious and insignificant work from an early age, this prevents (or at least considerably hinders) his acquiring genuine qualifications for more skilled work. This, together with the lack of inclination to learn that stems from his immaturity, effectively puts an end to his chances of better employment, higher pay and social advancement. It is, therefore, very likely that a man who has been at work from an early age will spend his whole life at the bottom of the social ladder, performing routine, unskilled jobs, when he is not out of work altogether."

Dwelling on the harmful effects of child labour, T.N. Chaturvedi (1977: 369) has observed: "Child labour deprives children of educational opportunities, minimises their chances for vocational training, hampers their intellectual development and by forcing them into the army of unskilled labours, condemns them to low wages all their lives."

The Committee on Child Labour (Government of India, 1979: 5) has summed up the stultifying effects of child labour in these words: "To conclude, child labour is economically unsound, psychologically disastrous and physically as well as morally dangerous and harmful."

2

CONCEPTS AND MEASURES OF CHILD LABOUR

The Backdrop

> "The result of buying children and young persons of under-age by the capitalist is physical deterioration and moral degradation."
>
> —Karl Mark in *Das Capital*

In Orissa, without any statistical report, one may find small children at the back-yard of hotels and home-steads either cleaning utensils or gathering remnants. Instead of "self-help", there still exists a tinge of aristocracy "to be served".

So the question of child labour in the face of growing industrialisation and urbanisation, needs serious attention.

In Delhi alone, it is estimated that about 20000 children are employed as domestic servants by the more affluent citizens. The I.L.O. made a survey of domestic service in private households in 1965 and said that India as compared with advanced countries, had not even touched the fringe of rights and status which domestic servants should enjoy.

Census figures reveals that, Greater Bombay has the largest number of working children, among metropolitan towns. This is because, Bombay is highly industrialised and offers larger number of job opportunities to children in *tertiary sector.*

Since the organised sector of industry demands a minimal technical skill, the small scale sector attracts child labour relatively to a larger extent. Hence such factories can never dream of any regulated wage system or other welfare schemes that the organised sector is statutorily compelled to adopt.

With the collapse of the rural economy and the disintegration of joint family system, and large scale industrialisation and the consequent erosion of agricultural economy, compel the rural families and the children to participate in the collective task of finding monetary resource to maintain the family. Thus, the unregulated industries take advantage of the situation and employ large number of children at very low wages.

The National Institute of Public Co-operation and Child Development in study of the children in Bombay came out with some startling facts: 30 per cent of the children employed had started work between the age of six and nine; 27 per cent between 13 and 15. A large percentage of these children of different age group had to work at an average 10 to 11 hours a day. According to a different study nearly 80 per cent of these working children in Bombay came from the families of migrant labour and 19 per cent from residential families. A pilot survey of working children in Madras, Madurai and Coimbatore showed that 31.6 per cent of children worked 10 to 11 hours, 23 per cent for 12 to 13 hours, 12 per cent for 14 to 16 hours.

The tragic aspect of the situation is that the various statutory regulations and rules specifying minimum wages do not apply to small scale units which employ most of the children available as cheap and causal labour.

The 58th International Labour Conference held at Geneva, urged that—As long as child labour survives in any country, young people are being deprived of a proper education; in countries where the school leaving age is low, child labour is facilitated.

Introduction

Homer Folks (the Chairman of the United States National Child Labour Committee) defines child labour as, "...any work by children that interferes with their full physical development, their opportunities for a desirable minimum of education or their needed recreation."

Dr. V.V. Giri has distinguished the term child labour in two senses. First, as an economic practice and secondly, as a social evil. The first signifies employment of children in gainful occupation with a view to adding to the income of the family, and the second, a broad aspect which takes into account the dangers to which the children are exposed, which means the denial of opportunities of development.

Article 39 of the Constitution of India states, "The State shall in particular direct its policy towards securing that the health and strength of workers, men and women, and the tender age of children are not... forced by economic necessity to enter vocations unsuited to their age or strength and that children are protected against exploitation and against moral and material abandonment."

In sum, the child labour is economically unsound, psychologically disastrous and physically as well as morally dangerous and harmful.

Child-Labour and International Labour Organisation

The 58th International Labour Conference held at Geneva recommended that the minimum age at which young people should be allowed to work in industry, transport or commercial agriculture, should be 15, but it permitted the lowering of the limit to 14 in some of the developing countries which could not immediately comply with the overall minimum. In the case of work which might jeopardise the health, safety or morals of the young, it specified, the minimum age should be 18.

The ILO also urged that as soon as possible, the minimum age for employment should be raised to 16 and that, in any case, it should not be lower than the minimum age for compulsory education. Child labour and compulsory education are thus interrelated problems. As long as child labour survives in any country, young people are being deprived of a proper education; in countries where the school leaving age is low, child labour is facilitated.

The ILO since its inception in 1919, adopted the following Conventions and Recommendations relating to children and young person—

Conventions

(a) Minimum Age (Industry) Convention, 1919.
(b) Night Work of Young Persons (Industry) Convention, 1919.
(c) Minimum Age (Agriculture) Convention, 1921.
(d) Minimum Age (Trimmers and Stokers) Convention, 1921.
(e) Medical examination of Young Persons (Sea) Convention, 1932.
(f) Minimum Age (New Industrial employment) Convention, 1932.
(g) Minimum Age (Sea) Convention (revised) 1932.
(h) Minimum Age (Industry) Convention (revised), 1937.
(i) Minimum Age (Non-Industrial) Convention (revised), 1937.
(j) Medical Examination of Young Persons (Industry) Convention, 1946.
(k) Medical Examination of Young Persons (Non-Industrial Occupations) Convention, 1946.
(l) Night Work of Young Persons (Non-Industrial Occupations) Convention, 1946.
(m) Night Work of Young Persons (Industry) Convention (Revised), 1948.

Recommendations

(a) Night Work of Children and Young Persons (Agriculture) Recommendation, 1921.
(b) Minimum Age (Non-Industrial Employment) Recommendation, 1932.
(c) Minimum Age (Family undertakings) Recommendation, 1937.
(d) Medical Examination of Young Persons Recommendation, 1946.

In India, the first Factories Act was passed in 1881, which defined a child as "any person below 12 and prohibited the employment of children below 7." The hours of work of children between the age of 7 to 12 were fixed at 9 hours per day. Provision was also made for rest, intervals and holidays. The Act of 1891 raised the minimum age of employment of children to 9 and restricted the hours of work of children between 9 and 14 to a maximum of 7 hours a day. The minimum age of employment was raised to 12 in 1922.

Article 24 of the Constitution lays down that "no child below that age of 14 shall be employed to work in any factory or mine or engaged in any other hazardous employment.

Accordingly there are several Acts to the effect as follows:

Indian Merchant Shipping Act XXI of 1923; The Children Pledging of Labour Act II of 1933; The Employment of Children Act XXVI of 1938; The Indian Factories Act LXIII of 1948; The Plantation Labour Act LXIX of 1951; The Mines Act XXXV of 1952.

Social Aspects of Child Labour

Mainly the economic backwardness pushes the child to the world of child begging, juvenile delinquency, vagrancy, truancy, etc. Thus, they are thrown into a situation physically and morally polluted. The various causes may be summarised as follows:

(a) The emotional ties between children and their parents are disturbed.
(b) As a result of such interactional distortion, the children slip off from the family bondage and step into the world of disorganisation.
(c) The emotional affectionate relation between parent and child turns into commercial interaction.
(d) The parents who live below poverty line are compelled to sell the labour of their children, which results in exploitation of child, through demand of maximum turnover at minimum wages.
(e) Many of the problems created by working children are economic in nature. Child labour involves the use of labour at its point of lowest productivity and is, therefore, an inefficient utilisation of labour power. It frequently precludes the most productive adulthood by distributing child workers in blind alley occupations thereby causing economic loss to the country.
(f) Child workers are necessarily handicapped by limitations of physical strength and experience so that they are not so productive as the adults.

According to I.L.O. data, more than 52 million children are employed in a variety of occupations. Of this, 29 million are in South-East Asia and 9.1 million in East Asia. But the pride of place of putting children to work is taken by India with 10.7 million being forced to labour in different sectors of economy.

In India, of 10.7 million (constituting 6 per cent of the total population of workers), 8.5 million, that is, 79.4 per cent are agricultural labourers and cultivators; and a little less than 8 per cent engaged in live stock, forestry, fishing, hunting, plantations, orchards and allied activities. Six per cent is engaged in manufacturing and processing services and another 6 per cent in household and other industries. Trade, commerce, storage, communication, etc., engage about 2.4 per cent of the total workers. About 1.2 billion children are listed as workers in industries, mines and quarries.

The percentage of children working in rural sector is 93 and 7 in the urban sector. The percentage of male children in rural areas was 11.78 and only 4.21 per cent were from urban areas. For females, this percentage was 4.78 in rural areas and 1.28 in urban areas.

According to Rege Committee's Report on Labour Conditions, "In the glass industries it is almost impossible to describe sufficiently and accurately the wretched conditions in which labourers work. No wonder the children in the glass industry look emaciated, anaemic, myopic and gloomy and invariably suffer from rickets and eye-diseases."

As the ILO Report on the Protection of Children and Young Workers has so rightly emphasised, "the problem of prohibition of child labour is inextricably mixed up with the problem of the maintenance of the child and provision of a living wage for all employed persons adequate to maintain the family at an adequate standard."

According to the first Agricultural Labour Enquiry Committee, the percentage of child labour was 1.4 in North India; 3.6 in South and East India; 4.3 in West and North-West India, and 8.2 in Central India.

According to the 1981 census, Jammu and Kashmir had the highest number of child labourers that is 10.3 per cent. The figures for the other States are as follows:

Madhya Pradesh—7.9 per cent; Sikkim—6.8 per cent; Himachal Pradesh—5.8 per cent; Rajasthan—5.6 per cent; Bihar—3.7 per cent; Manipur—3.6 per cent; Tripura—3.0 per cent; West Bengal—2.8 per cent; Meghalaya—7.9 per cent; Karnataka—7.6 per cent; Maharashtra—6.4 per cent; Nagaland—5.6 per cent; Gujarat—4.7 per cent; Haryana—3.6 per cent; Punjab—3.6 per cent; Uttar Pradesh—3.0 per cent, Kerala—1.0 per cent. For some States the 1981 figures are not available and hence the finding of 1971 census; Andhra Pradesh—9.2 per cent; Assam—3.4 per cent; Orissa—5.3 per cent; Tamil Nadu—4.5 per cent.

The above figures clearly demonstrate that, the reasons for Kerala having the lowest figures for child labour is due to the fact that it has the highest school enrolement of 81 per cent in the 5-14 years age-groups, that too, about the same in both the sexes. However, the figure for school enrolement in similar age groups for Jammu and Kashmir is only 41 per cent while that for India is 44 per cent. The trend during the last decade (1971-1981) has been such that the work participation by boys of 0-14 years has decreased by 3.5 per cent while that for girls has increased by 3.2 per cent.

Thus, it can be inferred that compulsory and free schooling could help not only to curb, but also wipe out the problem.

TABLE 2.1

Child Population and its Percentage to the Total Population, by Five-Year Age Groups, 1901-1971

Year	*No. (000)*	*0.4 per cent*	*No. (000)*	*5-9 per cent*	*10-14 No (000)*	*per cent*	*0-14 No (000)*	*per cent*
1901	29,831	12.56	32,338	13.62	28,196	11.87	90,366	38.05
1911	34,116	13.58	33,861	13,48	27.068	10,78	95,045	37.84
1921	30,920	12.35	36,696	14.65	29,244	11.68	96,860	38.68
1931	36,660	13.18	38,914	13.40	31,469	11.32	107,043	38.50
1941	42,904	13.53	45,291	14.28	35,914	11.33	124,109	39.14
1951	48,085	13.48	45,437	12.74	43,542	12.20	137,064	38.42
1961	66,089	15.06	64,656	14.74	49,287	11.24	180,032	41.04
1971	79,560	14.51	82,007	14.96	68,768	12.55	230,335	42.02

TABLE 2.2

Decadal Change in the Child Population in India (1901-11 to 1961-71)

Decade	*Decadal Percentage change in the age group*			
	0-0	*5-9*	*10-14*	*0-14*
1901-11	14.36	4.71	4.00	5.18
1911-21	9.37	8.31	8.04	1.91
1921-31	18.56	6.04	7.61	10.51
1931-41	17.03	16.39	14.13	15.94
1941-51	12.08	0.32	21.24	10.44
1951-61	37.44	42.30	13.20	31.35
1961-71	20.03	26.80	39.52	27.94

TABLE 2.3

Selected Statistics on Population by State 1971-1981*

States/ Union Terri- tories	*Population in (000)*		*Inter Censal change (%)*		*Sex Ratio males per 1000 females*		*Literacy Rate*					
							Total		*Male*		*Female*	
	1971	*1981*	*1961-71*	*1971-81*	*1971*	*1981*	*1971*	*1981*	*1971*	*1981*	*1971*	*1981*
India	548,160	683,970	24.8	24.8	1,075	1,106	29.5	36.1	38.5	46.6	18.7	24.8
Orissa	21,945	26,272	25.1	19.7	1,013	1,018	26.2	34.1	38.3	46.9	13.9	21.1

* *Source:* Office of the Registrar General, *Sample Registration Bulletin*, Vol. XIV, No. 1 June 1980 and No. 2, Dec. 80.

TABLE 2.4

Birth and Death Rates: All India, Rural and Urban Areas (1970-1979)

Year	*Birth Rate (Per 1000 population)*			*Death Rate (Per 1000 population)*			*Rate of Natural Increase (Per 1000 population)*		
	Total	*Rural*	*Urban*	*Total*	*Rural*	*Urban*	*Total*	*Rural*	*Urban*
1970	6.8	38.9	29.7	15.7	17.3	10.2	2.1	2.0	2.0
1971	36.9	38.9	30.1	14.9	16.4	9.7	2.2	2.2	2.0
1972	36.6	38.4	30.5	16.9	18.9	10.3	2.0	2.0	2.0
1973	34.6	35.9	28.9	15.5	17.0	9.6	1.9	1.9	1.9
1974	34.5	35.9	28.4	14.5	15.9	9.2	2.0	2.0	1.9
1975	35.2	36.7	28.5	15.9	17.3	10.2	1.9	1.9	1.8
1976	34.4	35.8	28.4	15.0	16.3	9.5	1.9	2.0	1.9
1977	33.0	34.3	27.8	14.7	16.0	9.4	1.8	1.8	1.8
1978	33.3	34.7	27.8	14.2	15.3	9.4	1.9	1.9	1.8
1979	33.0	34.3	27.8	12.8	13.9	8.3	2.0	2.0	2.0
Average Annual Rate 1971-1978	34.8	—	—	15.2	—	—	2.0	—	—

TABLE 2.5

Age Specific Sex Ratio (No. of Males Per 100 Females) of Child Population, 1901-1971

Census	*Sex Ratio of Child in the Age Group*			
Year	*0-4*	*5-9*	*10-14*	*0-14*
1901	96.9	104.2	120.2	106.4
1911	96.8	104.4	121.2	106.0
1921	96.2	103.5	120.6	105.8
1931	96.4	105.3	118.1	105.7
1941	99.5	105.3	117.6	106.5
1951	100.8	103.3	110.0	104.5
1961	100.8	104.7	114.1	105.7
1971	102.2	106.1	113.1	106.7

Source: For All Tables:
From 1901 to 1961, based on S.B. Mukerjee, *The Age Distribution of Indian Population: A Reconstruction for the State and Territories*, 1881-1961, East-West Population Institute, Honolulu, 1976, pp. 65; and for 1961; Census of India, 1971, Social and Cultural Tables Series I Pt. II, New Delhi, 1976 pp. 199.

From the above Tables, it is evident that, the proportion of the total child population was more or less static till 1951, and thereafter it recorded a slight increase. The maximum decadal change in the population has been recorded for the age groups 0-4 and 5-9 and therefore, in the total child population in the age group 0-14 during the period 1951-61. Next in 1961-71, the change has been propounded for the child population.

The persistently high level of fertility in the past and the decline in mortality, particularly after 1951, has been responsible for the spurt in the child population.

The reasons for male predominance at birth, besides being a biological phenomenon, is also due to the higher age-specific death rates for females; and the improvement in mortality conditions has widened the gap between the age specific death rates for males and females, particularly in the younger age-group; and this has contributed to sex imbalance in the later ages of childhood.

So far as literacy rate is concerned, a large gap is found between the female and male children, and this difference is more pronounced in rural areas. In rural India, only 29.96 per cent of the female children are literate against 71.05 per cent in urban areas. Among the male children, the literacy percentage in the two areas are 54.64 in rural and 80.86 in urban areas.

Conclusion

The First Plan stated that "considering the numbers involved, the needs of children should receive much greater consideration than is commonly given to them. Therefore, during different Plans, increasing, outlay was provided for strengthening and expanding social welfare programmes."

In August 1974, a National Policy for Children was adopted, which recognised that the "for nations children are a supremely important asset." The identified Programme priorities in the Policy includes, "prevention and promotive aspects of child health; nutrition for infants, children in the pre-school age and nursing and pregnant women; maintenance, education and training of orphan and destitute, creches and other facilities for the care of children of working/ailing mothers, and care, education, training and rehabilitation of handicapped children."

The welfare of children is the welfare of the nation as a whole. In any future planning for the social and economic development, children should take the primary place, particularly in the programme of health and social planning, immunisation, health and nutrition, recreational and educational facilities etc.

The N.C.L. observes that "employment of children is most non-existent in organised industries. It, however, persists in varying degrees in the unorganised sector. Employment of children below the prescribed age is also reported to be continuing in far off places and in rural areas, where enforcement of statutory provisions is more difficult."

The I.L.O. Report on the Protection of Children and Young Workers, has rightly emphasised, "the problem of prohibition of child labour is inextricably mixed up with the problem of the maintenance of the child and the provisions of a living wage for all employed persons adequate to maintain the family at an adequate standard."

Suggestions/Measures

It may be conceptualised that in the face of poverty and starvation, child-labour cannot be eliminated. But one cannot deny that child labour is due to economic necessity and to some extent of class consciousness. If this is removed, then only the problem will be solved.

Paul Douglas has remarked, "The most effective way in which society protects children is in providing their parents with sufficient income so that they can be brought up properly. It is folly to expect wage earner with unduly low income to feed, clothe, and rear their children in any adequate fashion. Give a family of average intelligence sufficient money and it will not only be able to take care of its children, but it will gradually learn to do so. The most pressing obligation is for the industry to put its system of wage payment upon the adequate basis and until this is done, social reform will swing against the child."

The Gurupadaswamy Committee Report on child labour has rightly emphasised that "the major concern of the government should be in regard to evolving a meaningful policy for education of these children."

In this connection, the observations of the NCL need be noted. It says, "Quite often it is the feeling of sympathy rather than the desire to exploit which weighs with employers in employing child workers...... It is most cruel form of hypocrisy to pay insufficient wages to fathers of families and then to show sympathy by employing child workers and by contributing to child welfare agencies to feel that the duty has been done."

In view of the above, the following are to be stressed, if at all we are really serious about the problem posed.

(a) Compulsory and free education should be extended, not withstanding the difficulties of finance and language.

(b) While the economic difficulties are real, a way has to be found to give the child the necessary education in his more receptive years.

(c) Where the number of children is adequate, the employer with the assistance of the State Government, should make arrangements to combine work with education.

(d) The major emphasis should be on education and training, so that employment of children over the age of 14 helps in creating a skilled adult, a technician and a master craftsman.

(e) Problem children are the product of problematic, unhappy homes. So steps should be taken for the prevention of "child abuse", "Child battering" and "unwanted children".

(f) Thus, in matters of planning one's family, consideration of "quality of life" should dominate over the concern for quantity. At least in this case, the adage "more the merrier" is not true or correct. "Small is beautiful" is more apt both for one's family and the society at large.

REFERENCES

Report of the Labour Investigation Committee, 1946, p. 144-145.

National Institute of Public Co-operation and Child Development, Working Children in Bombay—A study, 1978.

Adarkar, B.P. (1946): *Report on Labour Conditions in the Iron Ore Industry*, p. 25.

Deshpande, S.R. (1946): *Report on an Enquiry into Conditions of Labour in the Coal Mining Industry.*

Indian Labour Year Book, 1970.

I.L.O. Regional Conference Report (1953): *Measures for the Protection of Young Workers in Asian Countries*, Tokyo, p. 13.

3

CHILD LABOUR: THE PROBLEM AND THE PROSPECTS

The International Year of the Child was celebrated in 1979 and since then working children and their problem shave been receiving the attention of researchers, voluntary organisations, activities and the media. This is reflected in the number of publications on child labour, seminars and workshops on child labour, and the coverage they received in the media in recent years. Government, however, has shown serious concern to this problem for a long time. The constitutional provisions and the several legislative measures resorted to by both the State and Central Governments, constitution of several enquiry commissions, committee to look into the problem and suggested measures to government to ameliorate the suffering of working children bear testimony to this. One estimate suggest that there were roughly about 300 legislations in India in 1982 that were concerned with children in general and many of them dealt with working of children.

Extent and Dimensions of Child Labour

Unfortunately, all the measures that the government has taken to reduce the incidence of child labour seem to have very little impact. The 1981 census report that there were 6.7 million male and 3.5 million female children working in India for major part of the year. In urban areas this number was 0.7 million respectively. If marginal workers are included this number would still increase. The National Sample Survey Organisation (NSSO), estimated that there were 16.6 million child workers in India in 1979 of which 10.4 million were boys and 6.2 million were girls. The study specially commissioned by the Labour Ministry and conducted by the Operation Research Group (ORG) of Baroda estimated that about 44 million children in India participate in work. These wide variations in the estimates demonstrate the problem of conceptualising, defining and measuring child work but confirm the fact that the number of working children in India is indeed very large. It is also difficult, under the circumstances, to assess whether incidence of child labour has increased or decreased over the years.

However, there is evidence to show that child labour has been virtually eliminated in the formal sector. The service statistics of the Labour Ministry show that the average daily employment of child workers in registered factories from 7.764 in 1950 to 3,592 in 1976. Children constituted only negligible proportion (0.07 per cent) of total employment in factories in 1976. Even though, these figures can be treated as gross underestimates it clearly indicates shifting of working children from organised sector to unorganised—semi-organised sectors and in small scale establishments. But hard data on pattern of child labour is difficult to obtain. Some pockets of concentration of young workers, however, are visible. For example the carpet weaving industry in Varanasi, Bhadohi, Mirzapur belt where about 90 per cent of looms exists and 80 per cent of production in the country originates it is estimated that about 1,00,000 children work. In Firozabad, the centre of glass and bangles production, as much as 25 per cent of all workers are children and are exposed to the risk of burns and other health hazards. Over 50,000 children aged 5-12 years are engaged in equally hazardous match-fire cracker manufacturing units in Sivakasi. Thousands of children work in diamond cutting and jem polishing industries in Gujarat. About 5 per cent of total labour force engaged in Bhivandi power looms comprises children aged between 5-15 years. Number of children working in handicrafts, bidi rolling, hotels and other small scale enterprises which are notorious for exploiting child labour are yet to be estimated.

Children working in the above mentioned occupations-industries suffer exploitation in the form of poor wages, long working hours and very poor working environments which can be said to be very hazardous to their health and physical development. Fortunately the proportion of working children there is small—about 20 per cent of total child workers. On the other hand a great majority of child labour exist in rural areas engaged in agriculture, animal husbandry and other household industries which has not received much attention from researchers and policy makers. Since it is carried out under the guidance of parents, many consider it as non-exploitative and perhaps, socialising process and only means of acquiring the necessary traditional skills required for survival in the given environment. Such work is believed to develop the confidence, self-respect and personalities of young workers and prepares them to take up the responsibility of family occupations from their elders as they grow.

The exploitative child labour existing in unorganised, semi-organised sector and child labour in rural agricultural sector represent two facets of the problem that need lasting solutions. The efforts of the government in bringing in several legislations to reduce child labour have not been successful because of several factors including the most important among them—lack of infrastructure required to implement these legislations. But the experience of many other developing countries is also not different in this respect. This has led to the government rethinking of the policies on the child labour. If child labour cannot be eradicated, efforts should be made to improve the working conditions of child labour. Keeping the commitment to totally eradicate it gradually in the years to come. The latest legislation on child labour (Prohibition and Regulation) Act of 1986 demonstrate the culmination of the thinking of the government on the problem of child labour. This act prohibits employment of children who have not completed 14 years of age in certain specified occupations and processes. Responsibility of policy formulation though lies mainly with the Ministry of Labour, the Central Government has constituted an Advisory Board on child labour which includes representatives from government, trade unions, voluntary organisations concerned with child labours and others. Similar advisory boards exist in several States of the country which indicate serious concern of both the State and Central Governments and better results may emerge gradually.

Research Priorities and Alternatives

Policy oriented research in the area of child labour is scarce and scattered. As stated, research concerning with child labour is increasingly concentrated on child labour intensive industries like match stick, carpet weaving, etc. and has been focused on highlighting the exploitation of child workers. In several other areas even the number of working children is not known. Census, NSS and other sources of data suffer from several deficiencies that include the concept of work. One of the ways of overcoming these deficiencies is to examine the time use of children in rural and urban areas and study how decisions regarding schooling and work of children are taken in a representating sample that should include wider geographical areas differing maximally in the incidence of child labour. It is also essential to know why children are employed in preference to adults when unemployment and under employment is so widely exist in the society. High and growing incidence of child labour can have serious consequences on the adult employment in the years to come. For this, study of employment markets is of great value. Such studies should focus on the demand and supply of child labour.

It is generally argued that poverty induces children to work and supplement the meagre family resources. It is also to be noted that employment opportunities, given the extent of unemployment and underemployment in the country, are essentially limited. Even if all children would like to work it is not possible to get work. Under the circumstances who are the children succeeding in getting employment and what are the conditions of such employment? Research in these areas in very inadequate.

If the constitutional provisions and legislations have not been able to curb child labour it is necessary to know what are the other alternatives?

Schooling is the obvious and the only best alternative to child labour, universalisation of primary schooling is the well recognised goal of the country and the Constitution of India in fact provides that the State shall endeavour to provide, within a period of the years from the commencement of this Constitution for free and compulsory education for all children until they complete the age of 14 years. With recent emphasis on human resource development and renewed commitment to reduce illiteracy before the turn of the century, primary schooling is going to be the best alternative to reduce child labour and totally eliminate it in the years to come. Large budgetary provisions, improved environment in schools and better trained teachers are certainly going to be effective steps in attracting more and more children to school and affect the child labour supply line adversely. The declining trend observed in the levels of fertility is certainly going to be an important contribution in this direction. In brief, better understanding of child labour—determinants, consequences and labour market, and renewed emphasis on primary education can lead to reach the professed goal of eradication of child labour and universalisation of primary schooling in the years to come.

CAUSES OF CHILD LABOUR

Child labour is a socio-economic problem. It is generally considered that illiteracy, ignorance, low wages, unemployment, low standard of living, and social life—all are roots of child labour. Mr. Madan, Deputy Director, Ministry of Labour, stated that "the children are required to seek employment either to augment the income of their families or to have a gainful occupation in the absence of availability of school going facilities at various places."[1]

It has been officially stated that "Child labour is no longer a medium of economic exploitation but is necessitated by economic necessity of the parents and in many cases that of the child himself."[2]

Thus, there are many causes of child labour but it is fruitful to study some of the principal causes in detail.

Poverty

The most important cause of child labour is widespread poverty. In India, which is a developing country, poverty forces the parents to send their children to seek employment. Diseases and other contingencies may need extra money and the employment of children is resorted to as an easily accessible method to bring in that money.

The Institute of Public Opinion conducted a survey in 1969, which showed that 41.2% of Indian population was under the poverty line. Half of these belonged to the scheduled castes and tribes. In villages a vast majority of agricultural labour belongs to these communities."[3]

A pilot study recently conducted in Madras, Madurai and Coimbatore, found that about three-fourth of the children were at work to supplement to their family income and 23% were doing labour because of the death of their father or guardian.

A seminar on the subject organised by National Institute of Public Co-operation and Child Development, New Delhi, on November 25-28, 1975, also came to the conclusion that millions of families were below the poverty line and they had to deploy their children in the labour market in order to eke out a bare subsistence.[4]

In big cities like, Bombay, Madras, Delhi, etc. a large number of migrants are seen. The employment of their children is a firm proof of economic helplessness and poverty. The report of Smt. M. Khandkar indicates that the migrant child labour in Greater

Bombay was 81% and residents 19%.[5] Following causes often compel children to join the labour force:

(i) Inadequate Income of Adult Bread Earners of the Family

The problem of child labour is inter-related to the problem of living wage of adult worker. This very inadequacy in wages of adults compels them to send their children to do some work in return of some wage and the employer also takes the benefit of this weakness by providing work to their children on low wages in spite of the various protective laws. The report of I.L.O. also indicates that this problem of child labour is not the problem of itself but it is the problem of the maintenance of child and the living wage of the adult wage earner so that they should maintain their family at adequate standard.[6]

It was observed in a seminar that parents force their children to take-up employment because their own earning power is low. If their incomes are enhanced, they are likely to desist from sending their children to work.[7]

(ii) Unemployment

Lumpkin and Louglas in "Child Workers in America" have rightly pointed out the fact by saying that two-fifth of the children seek their work because of their adult wage earners were unemployed and nearly two-third of children were at work because of their adult worker had no employment or had some part-time jobs and one-third children went to work due to the serious cuts in the pay of their adult.[8]

Padmini Sen Gupta says:[9]

> Labour is employed on the average for 189 days in agricultural pursuits, there are other rural employments which exist but the overall position would appear to be 100 days in the year of total unemployment. During the period of unemployment many women migrate to cities with families, and beg with babies in their arms. They are, therefore, employing their children from infancy for begging is an important employment, especially now, and children of the baby group are exploited while older children are pests in every part of the city including railway stations where begging is prohibited by law but where it thrives as officials turn a deaf ear to the wails of boys and girls.

Absence of Scheme for Family Allowance

Another cause of child labour, which is as causative as poverty, is the absence of schemes for family allowances. In our country there is no such allowance as can be given to the families so that people may have adequate standard and may not be forced to send their children to the labour market. Today, such type of allowance is given in a number of countries like Australia, New Zealand, The United Kingdom, France and the U.S.S.R.

The amount which is paid to widows as compensation or pensions is too insufficient to maintain their family without the help of their children's income.

Large Family

Large families with comparatively less income cannot have the happy notions in their mind. As a result, they cannot give sheltered-childhood to their children. If a family is limited and well planned there will be no question of sending their children to the labour market and the children can be carefully educated. But impoverished and illiterate parents think just contrary to this. They think if God has given you life, He will give you to eat, side by side they think that three or four children are better than one. For them, extra children mean extra income. But they forget:

वरमे को गुणी पुत्री, न च मूर्खशतान्यति।
एकश्चन्द्र स्तमो हन्ति, न च तारागणोऽपि च ।। 17।। हितोपदेश मित्र लाभ:

It means that only one qualified and intelligent son is better than hundred illiterate foolish. Sons, as millions of stars cannot remove gloom which can only be removed by one moon. Thus, if one has one child or two children, he can provide all facilities to their children which are necessary for their mental, physical and social growth. If he has more children he cannot provide all facilities which a person having one or two children can provide. On the one hand, where thieves, robbers, drunkards, prostitutes and beggars are a black spot on the society, there are on the other hand, wise, prudent high and healthy persons with higher qualification who are the creators of a prosperous society.

Child Labour is A Cheap Commodity

Mostly employers think that a lot of work can be done by the children in their establishment and this labour of children is very cheap labour in comparison to that of men. In fact, it ensures them more margin of profit over less investments. But some times enhanced demand of labour increases the demand of children e.g., in agricultural harvesting season when adult workers are not available to cope with the demand.

In this country children of very young age do domestic work because these children are very cheap. The middle class families which have lower income especially keep little boys and girls as domestic servants from 8 to 14 age group which is the age of eating and playing. They get little pocket money and food from their Masters. Jerome Davis stated that[10]

> "beside the compulsion of poverty within the family, is the stimulus of the manufacturer who desires to secure cheap labour and more profit. Child labour exists not because children are more able workers but because they can be had for less money. Children are employed by small concerns and large corporations."

Absence of Provision for Compulsory Education

Absence of any provision for compulsory education is another important cause of child labour. The provision of compulsory education up to a prescribed age could compel the children to attend the school so that there may arise no question of entering of children into the employment.

Mostly children finding non-availability of school going facilities at initial stage seek some job as an alternative.

This fact is indirectly admitted by National Commission on Labour 1969, when it states in its Report—"The gradual reduction in the employment of child labour since independence is due partly to the expansion of educational facilities by the State and also to relatively better enforcement of statutory provisions relating to child labour.[11]

The main obstacle in the way of making *education compulsory* to al children up to a prescribed age is rightly indicated by the above report in the following words:[12]

> An artisan cannot afford to educate his wards though education is free. For him an uneducated child is an asset; desire to be educated becomes a double liability because of (a) loss of earnings if the child does not work, and (b) expenditure on education, howsoever small.

A similar view was also expressed by Prof. Smt. N. Acharji, Xavier Labour Relation Institute, Jamshedpur[13] in the following words:

> Books and stationery are expensive. Will the parent choose between food and clothing, the primary needs or purchase books for the children? For scheduled castes and tribes even these may be available free of cost. But for all poor families the question posed is immediate supplementary income and to use the children as sources rather than postpone this prospect to an uncertain date, when he will pass his matric and may or may not get a job in an economy when millions are still unemployed. Thus psychologically the path of least resistence is adopted by them.

Illiteracy and Ignorance of Parents

In India, the lower socio-economic groups of population are illiterate. They only think about the present time which is their sole concern and worry. They never think of future. They are fully satisfied with what they gain by the earning of children. It is ignored by them that their children may participate even in educational opportunities, but child labour deprives the children of all the educational opportunities and minimises their chances for vocational training. It also affects their health and they are converted into labourers of low wages for all their lives.

A study made by student of Madras school of Social Work in Madras, Madurai and Coimbatore indicated that children coming in labour market were from low literary groups of society. About 44% are illiterate and another 33% parents of children are low literary group up to standard V only. Therefore, large majority of guardians are desirous of having money in place of intelligence.

A seminar on 'Employment of Children' held in November 1975 also indicated that 'Child labour is prevalent extensively in the lower socio-economic groups.... because of the lack of appreciation on their part of the role that education plays in improving life and living conditions of the people.'[14]

The gross ignorance on the part of parent in not sending their children to school is condemned by Addam. Addam predicted that "the child labourers today will be the paupers of tomorrow; they are the boys and girls who will grow up without either formal schooling or knowledge of a trade; sooner or later, their youthful energies exhausted, they will become dull, shiftless, driftless.[15]

Other Reasons

In addition to the above causes of child labour, there are also certain other significant reasons for child labour. Firstly, the process of protective labour legislation is slow which could not even cover the agriculture and small scale industries. Secondly, inspecting machinery which is provided by the State Government, is inadequate to check up the child labour. The Factories Act itself is also defective in various respects. Thus it does not apply to craftsmanship merely because it needed little strength and skill. The Labour Investigation Committee in 1946 and seminar on the subject in November 1975 reported that existing machinery is inadequate and ineffective.

NOTES

1. Madan, G.S., *Review of Legal Provisions relating to facilities for and working conditions of employed children—the impact on their health, education and development*, p. 9 (unpublished).
2. Government of India, *Child Labour in India*, 1954, p. 2.
3. Institute of Public Opinion, *Monthly Commentry on Indian Economic Condition*, December, 1973.
4. National Institute of Public Co-operation and Child Development—Seminar recommendations.
5. Smt. Khandekar M. Report on the situation of Children and Youth in Greater Bombay, 1970.
6. Report of I.L.O. quoted in the book *'Needs of Children'* published by UNICEF, p. 144.
7. Recommendations of Seminar on Employment of Children organised by NIPCCD, New Delhi held in Nov. 1975.
8. Lumpkin, K.D. and Douglas, D.W., *Child Workers in America* (1938), p. 7.
9. Smt. Gupta, Padmini Sen, *Child Labour as a Social Problem* (unpublished).
10. Davis, Jerome, *Workers Problems and Modern Industry*, p. 117.
11. Report of National Commission on Labour 1969, p. 386.
12. Report of National Commission on Labour 1969, p. 386.
13. Prof. Smt. Acharji, *Child Labour in India* (unpublished) read in seminar organised by NIPCCD in Nov., 1975.
14. Seminar recommendations issued by NIPCCD (unpublished).
15. Addam, Jane, *Child Labour and Pauperism* (1903), p. 117.

4

NATURE OF EMPLOYMENT AND TYPE OF WORK

It is the characteristic feature of employment in agriculture in this country that big landlords (*Kulaks*) generally do not work themselves and employ a labour force for their agricultural work. Motivated by their false notion of social prestige, most of the Caste Hindus also do not work on their agricultural land and employ labour for various types of agricultural work. Small farmers generally work on their own land and marginal farmers generally belonging to scheduled castes and scheduled tribes work on their own as well as on other's land due to very small size of their own land holdings which do not provide them sufficient opportunity to keep themselves busy throughout the year. There are different types of work performed by people engaged in agriculture. It is against this background that a detailed description of nature of employment and type of work of the child workers is being given in the ensuing paragraphs.

Nature of Employment

Children who work with their parents in their family occupations receive proper guidance and supervision, and love and affection in course of their work. They are engaged in work not injurious to their health and development, they are asked to work for a period of time in which they do not feel fatigued; they are generally not asked to do the work when the weather is inclement; they enjoy the freedom to break their work and take rest as and when they feel like doing so; and efforts are made to make proper arrangement to cater timely to their basic needs like food and water and their work is shared by other family members in such a manner that they do not feel the burden of their work as imposed upon them and as their sole and exclusive responsibility. Conversely, the wage-earning children in agriculture are given a harsh treatment, are inflicted upon with punishments, are forced to do work harmful for them, are compelled to work for long working hours without any break, let alone the rest-intervals with their convenience, are called upon to perform their work in all sorts of weather, and are not given the opportunity to satisfy timely even their basic needs; and the completion of work assinged to them remains their sole responsibility, any failure in which may make them a victim of the employer's fury which may assume different forms-the extreme being serve physical punishment coupled with termination of employment without payment of the wages earned by them in the past. Mendelievich (1979: 37) has rightly observed: "Normally, the child who works in the family undertaking, be it in agriculture, manufacturing, commerce or handicrafts, is exploited less than the wage-earning child. Indeed, the stress, fatigue and harmful effects to which he is exposed are partly compensated for by the personal attention and affection which his parents can give him during both work and rest periods.

Nature of Employment of the Child Workers by their Age

The information gathered from the child workers with regard to question as to weather they work on their own land, on land owned by others or on own as well as other's land and analysed in relation to their age on the assumption that nature of the employment of the child workers varies in accordance with their age, reveals that an overwhelming majority of the child workers in both the age-groups of 8-12 years (91.95%) and 13-18 years (80.63%) have been working on their own land. Similarly next has been the number of those who in both the age-groups of 8-12 years (7.38%) and 13-18 years (15.67%) have been working on their own as well as others land. The least has been the number of such child workers in both the age-groups of 8-12 years (0.67%) and 13-18 years (3.70%) as have been working exclusively on land owned by others. These facts lead to the conclusion that though work on own land is the characteristic of an overwhelming majority belonging to both the age groups yet work on land owned by others is the dominant feature of relatively older child workers aged between 13-18 years only.

Nature of Employment of Child Workers by their Sex

Data relating to nature of employment of the child workers analysed in relation to their sex on the assumption that there may be sex-wise variation in the incidence of working on own land, on land owned by others and on own as well as other's land, unravel that an overwhelming majority of the child workers in both the sex-categories of male (81-38%) and female (90.06%) have been working on their own land. Next to this have been working on own as well as others land. Least has been the number of those males (3.15%) and females (1.49%) who have been working exclusively on land owned by others. This indicates that the incidence of working on land owned by others has been relatively more in case of the male child workers as compared to their female counterparts.

Nature of Employment of the Child Workers by Their Education

Facts relating to nature of employment of the child workers anlysed in relation to their age on the assumption that the incidence of working on own land, on land owned by others and on own as well as other's land is considerably affected by education, particularly its continuity, show that majority of the child workers in all the three categories of education viz, no education ('84.27%) have been working on their own land. Next to this have been those who have been working on own as well as other's land (12.92%), in the category of 'no education', 2.67% in the category of continued education and 28.14% in the category of `discontinued education.' Work on land owned by others has been least prevalent and has been the characteristic feature of the categories of `no education' (2.81%) and `discontinued education' (9.28%) only. This leads to the conclusion that those child workers who have been continuing their education have not working exclusively on land owned by others.

Type of Work

Children working in agriculture do not work only in the fields but are also required to do different kinds of domestic work, particularly after their work in the field is over. In the field as also at their own as well employer's residence they perform different types of activities. It is noteworthy that the work done by children at their residence relieves other elder earning members of the family from taking up the burden of household chores and thus makes them more free to engage themselves in such pursuits as may be helpful in augmenting the economic resources of the family. Moreover, additional working hands will be required to be engaged to do the family work if the child workers do not participate in it. A detailed description of different types of work in agriculture as also at their homes is being given below.

Types of Agricultural Work Performed by the Child Workers by Their Age

The physical growth or decay takes place with an advancement in age on which depends the strength of the people to undertake any work. And this is the reason why people of different age-groups are assigned different types of work. In agriculture also, workers belonging to different age-groups are allotted different type of work keeping in view their age on which depends considerably their capacity to successfully perform it. It is against this background that an analysis of information collected from the child workers regarding different types of agricultural work performed by them in relation to their age has been attempted which reveals that an overwhelming majority of the child workers (72.40%) have been engaged in transplantation taking out seedlings from one field and planting them in another, followed by harvesting (70.20%), watching of crops (66.00%), weeding (59.00%), irrigation of field (51.80%), hoeing (41.80%), sowing (41.20%), threshing (40.40%), preparatory work (35.00%), storage (33.80%), ploughing (33.20%) and other miscellaneous activities (2.40%). In the age-group of 8-12 years, majority of the child workers (51.68%) have been engaged in transplantation followed by crop watching (44.29%), harvesting (30.07%), weeding (28.85%), irrigation (16.11%), threshing (14.77%), storage (12.75%), hoeing (10.07%), sowing (7.38%), ploughing (4.02%), preparatory work (2.68%) and other activities (1.34%). In the age-group of 13-18 years, an overwhelming majority (86.90%), of the child workers have been engaged in harvesting followed by transplantation (81.20%), crop watching (75.21%), weeding (71.80%), irrigating (66.95%), sowing (55.56%) hoeing (55.27%), threshing (51.28%), preparatory work (48.72%), ploughing (45.58%), storage (42.73%), and other activities (2.85%). This leads to the conclusion that in all the different categories of agricultural work, the percentage of older child workers engaged in work has been more as compared to that of their younger counterparts and that the most widely undertaken activity in the case of relatively younger child workers has been transplantation whereas in case of their comparatively older counterparts, harvesting has been such an activity. This difference should be understood in the light of capacity to undertake more difficult and hard work by adolescents as compared to children because of greater physical growth and more physical prowess of the former as compared to the latter.

Types of Agricultural Work performed by the Child Workers by their Sex

An analysis of information collected from child workers regarding different types of agricultural work performed by them in relation to their sex on the assumption that the type of agricultural work varies according to sex, reveals that in the category of males, the largest number of child workers (75.07%), have been engaged in crop watching followed by transplantation (73.93%), harvesting (73.35%), irrigating (61.90%), weeding (58.74%), hoeing (53.30%), threshing (49.86%), preparatory work and sowing (47.28% each), ploughing (46.70%), storage (27.51%) and other activities (2.58%), whereas in the category of females the largest number of child workers (63.87%) have been engaged in transplantation followed by harvesting (62.91%), weeding (59.60%), storage (48.38%), crop watching (45.03%), irrigating (28.48%), sowing 927.15%), threshing (18.54%), irrigating (28.48%), sowing (27.15%), threshing (18.54%), hoeing (15.23%), preparatory work (6.62%) and ploughing and other activities (1.99% each). This difference in the activities performed by the largest number of male and female child workers may be understood in the light of the fact that cropwatching is a work which is to be performed in the widely scattered and isolated fields located in distant areas where it is not safe to send girls alone for work and transplantation is a work which is relatively light and generally performed in a group with the result that it can be easily done by girls who are safe while performing the work. In a nutshell, child workers have generally been engaged in transplantation which has been more in vogue in the case of male child workers as compared to their female counterparts.

Types of Agricultural Work performed by Child Workers by Nature of Employment

A careful scrutiny of the data relating of type of agricultural work performed by child workers in relation to nature of employment on the assumption that the child workers working on their own land may be engaged in performing types of agricultural work which may be different from those done by their counterparts working on land owned by others or on own as well as others land, shows that the largest number of child workers working on own land have been engaged in transplantation (76.67%), followed by harvesting (74.76%), crop watching (66.67%), irrigating (59.9%), weeding (54.04%), hoeing (40.95%), irrigating (56.9%), weeding (54.04%), hoeing (40.95%), threshing (39.29%), sowing (38.09), storage (34.52%), preparatory work (80.95%), ploughing (28.18%), and other activities (1.67%). In the category of child workers working on land owned by others, the largest number (64.29%) has been engaged in transplantation, followed by sowing (57.14%) threshing, storage, crop-watching, and ploughing (35.71% each) preparatory work, irrigating, weeding and harvesting (28.57% each) and hoeing (21.43%).

In the category of those child workers who have been working on own as well as others land the largest number (66.67%) has been associated with cropwatching followed by preparatory work (62.12%), ploughing (61.61%), sowing (57.38%), weeding and hoeing (51.52% each), harvesting (50.00%), threshing (48.48%), transplantation (46.97%), storage (28.79%), irrigating (24.24%) and other activities (7.58%). An overall picture that emerges thus is that the incidence of work relating to transplantation has been maximum in case of the child workers belonging to all the three categories of nature of employment.

Suitability of Agricultural Work by Age

'Right man for the right job' has been a well established principal of personnel management. In case the work does not suit the person who undertakes it or the person who is assigned the work, many problems and difficulties crop up in course of performance of work. In case of children, this is more true because heavier and hazardous work adversely affects theirs growth and development. It was against this background that efforts were made to know the opinion of child workers regarding suitability of different types of work performed by them. An analysis of the collected information in relation to age on the assumption that the consideration of suitability may be different in case of people of different age-groups, makes it clear that storage (67.46%), transplantation (61.88%), irrigating (60.62%), sowing (57.77%), crop watching (54.24%), threshing (52.48%), have been considered suitable by the majority of child workers engaged in these activities. In the age-group of 8-12 years, storage (57.89%), crop-watching (54.55%) and weeding (53.49%) have been considered suitable by the majority of child workers where as in the age-group of 13-18 years, transplantation (67.72%), storage (66.89%), irrigating (62.13%), sowing (58.46%), weeding (56.35%), crop watching (54.17%), threshing (53.33%) and harvesting (50.82%) have been considered suitable by majority of child workers. This shows that the incidence of considering preparatory work, ploughing, harvesting, hoeing and threshing as suitable agricultural works has been more in the case of the child workers aged between 8-12 years than in the case of their counterparts aged between 13.18 years which may be understood in the light of the fact that being more arduous, taxing and demanding more physical labour, the pinch of these activities is felt more by relatively younger child workers because of their comparatively less developed physique.

Suitability of Agricultural Work by Sex

Further probe into data pertaining to the suitability of agricultural work attempted in relation to sex on the assumption that consideration of suitability of different types of agricultural works may be varied among male and female child workers, shows that in the category of male child workers, irrigating (63.43%), harvesting (62.10%), storage (60.42%), threshing (57.47%), other activities (55.56%), sowing (53.33%), and weeding (50.73%) have been the agricultural operations considered to be suitable by the majority whereas in the category of female child workers, transplantation (92.31%), crop-watching (77.94%), storage (76.71%), sowing (75.61%), and weeding (67.78%) have been the activities spelt out as suitable by the majority. This shows that transplantation has been considered as most suitable by female child workers and irrigating by their male counterparts. As for unsuitability, preparatory work, ploughing, harvesting, hoeing and threshing have been considered more unsuitable by female child workers than by their male opposite number which may be attributed to relatively weaker physical structure of the former. It is noteworthy that ploughing is the work which has not been considered suitable by any female child worker mainly because it requires very hard physical labour.

Conduciveness of Environmental Conditions Relating to Agricultural Work

Data gathered from the child workers regarding conduciveness of environmental conditions under which they work in agriculture unravels that majority of the child workers in all the categories of agricultural work-preparatory work (52.57%), ploughing (50.60%), sowing (68.45%), transplantation (93.10%), weeding (85.08%), irrigating (79.54%), harvesting (91.45%), hoeing (68.42%), threshing (64.85%), storage (60.35%) and crop-watching (92.72%), except in the category of other activities (33.33%), have expressed the view that different types of agricultural work undertaken by them have been conducive. However, the incidence of reporting the work as conducive has been maximum in the category of agricultural work known as transplantation.

Types of Domestic Work performed by the Child Workers by their Age

An analysis of information pertaining to domestic work performed by the child workers attempted in relation to their age on the assumption that domestic works performed by child workers of different age-groups are varied, unravels that the largest number of child workers (94.20%), have been engaged in the domestic work of bringing water followed by watching the house (79.20%), buying domestic things (62.40%), cattle grazing and feeding (54.20%), bringing firewood (38.00%), cleaning utensils (36.40%), looking after young ones (33.80%), cooking (27.20%), carrying food to the fields (23.20%), accompanying their employers (3.20%) and undertaking other activities (1.20%). In case of the child workers in the age-group of 8-12 years, the largest number (98.65%), has been engaged in bringing water followed by watching the house (72.48%), cattle grazing and feeding (57.72%), buying domestic things (49.66%), looking after young ones (42.28%), cleaning utensils (38.25%), carrying food to the fields (29.19%), bringing firewood (21.48%), cooking (17.45%), and accompanying employers and undertaking other activities (1.38% each). As for the child workers in the age group of 13-18 years, the largest number (92.31%) has again been engaged in bringing water followed by watching the house (82.05%), buying domestic things (67.81%), cattle grazing and feeding (52.71%), bringing firewood (45.01%) cleaning utensils (35.61%), cooking (31.34%), looking after young ones (30.20%), carrying food to the fields (21.08%), accompanying their employers (3.99%) and undertaking other activities (1.14%). This clearly indicates that an overwhelming majority of the child workers in both the age-groups have been engaged in work relating to bringing water followed by watching the house; and that bringing water, cleaning utensils, cattle grazing, looking after the young ones and carrying food to the field have been more pronounced in case of the child workers belonging to the younger age-group of 8-12 years as compared to their counterpart in the relatively more grown up age-group of 13-18 years as these activities are relatively more light and simple.

Types of Domestic Work performed by the Child Workers by their Sex

A probe into information gathered form the child workers in respect of the various types of domestic work performed by them attempted in relation to their sex on the assumption that male child workers perform different types of domestic work as compared to their female counterpart, reveals that an overwhelming majority of male (91.98%), as well as female (99.34%), child workers have been engaged in domestic work relating to bringing water. In the category of male child workers, various domestic activities undertaken have been: watching the house (77.36%), buying domestic things (68.77%), cattle grazing and feeding (59.02%), bringing firewood (38.97%), carrying food to the fields (22.92%), looking after the young ones (16.33%), cleaning utensils (15.19%), cooking (7.74%), accompanying their employers (4.66%) and undertaking other activities (1.15%). In the category of female child workers other works performed by them have been cleaning utensils (85.43%), watching the house (83.44%), looking after the young ones (74.17%), cooking (72.18%), buying domestic things (47.68%), cattle grazing to the fields (23.84%) and undertaking other activities (1.32%). This shows that cleaning utensils, cooking food, looking after the young ones and watching the house have been more the characteristic of the female child workers, cattle grazing and buying domestic things have been more marked in case of the male child workers; and that none of the female child workers has been performing the work of accompanying employer. Difference in the types of domestic work performed by child workers of the two sexes may be explained in the light of the fact that our culture prescribes that females should perform relatively lighter work, and that too inside the four walls of or near the house; and that works which are hard and are performed in distantly located and widely dispersed isolated places should be performed by males.

Types of Domestic Word Performed by the Child Workers by Place of Work

A close scrutiny of data collected from the child workers regarding various types of domestic work performed by the child workers in relation to their place of work done on the assumption that the types of domestic work vary in case of those who work at their residence, at employers' residence and at their own as well as employers' residence, shows that in case of the child workers working at their own residence, majority has been engaged in domestic work relating to bringing water (97.86%), watching the house (78.80%), buying domestic things (70.48%), and cattle grazing and feeding (51.42%). In case of the child workers who have been working exclusively at the employers' residence, domestic works undertaken by majority of them have been cattle grazing and feeding (64.29%), and accompanying employer (57.74%). As for the child workers who have been doing domestic work at their own as well as employers' residence, watching the house (89.29%), bringing water (84.85%), cattle grazing and feeding (69.70%), and bringing firewood (68.78%) have been the activities undertaken by majority of them. Thus, the incidence of bringing water has been at the top in case of the child working at their own residence, cattle grazing and feeding in case of those who have been exclusively working at employers' residence, and watching the house in case of those who have been working at their own as well as employers' residence.

Suitability of Different Types of Domestic Work by Age

An analysis of information relating to suitability of different types of domestic work performed by the child workers in relation to their age on the assumption that opinion regarding suitability may vary according to age, reveals that all the different types of domestic work except cattle grazing and feeding and bringing firewood have been considered suitable by majority of the child workers. In the age-group of 8-12 years, cleaning utensils, cooking, cattle grazing and feeding and bringing firewood have been considered unsuitable by a majority whereas in the age-group of 13-18 years only bringing fire-wood has not been considered suitable. This shows that the domestic work of bringing fire-wood has been considered unsuitable by majority of the child workers in general as also in both the age-groups; that the consideration of unsuitability of the work of bringing fire-wood has more pronounced in the age-grouped of 8-12 years; that larger number of domestic works have been considered to be unsuitable in the younger age-group of 8-12 years than in the relatively older age-group of 13-18 years, and that watching the house has been the only activity in which the percentage of younger child workers considering it to be suitable has been more than of their counterparts, may be because the younger child workers get an opportunity to play with their friends while remaining at home.

Suitability of Different Types of Domestic Work by Sex

A probe into the data relating to suitability of different types of domestic work attempted in relation to sex on the assumption that the opinion regarding suitability may vary according to sex shows that majority of the male child workers have considered the activities of carrying food to the field (86.25%), bringing water (84.42%), buying domestic things (83.74%), other activities (75.00%), looking after young ones (71.92%), watching the house (67.04%) and accompanying employer (64.29%), as suitable whereas majority of the female child workers have spelt out looking after young ones (78.57%), cooking (71.56%), cleaning utensils (61.24%) and watching the house (51.59%) as suitable. On the contrary, majority of the male child workers have considered the work of cleaning utensils, cooking, cattle grazing and feeding and bringing fire-wood as unsuitable where as majority of their female counterparts have considered the work of bringing water, cattle grazing and feeding, bringing fire wood, buying domestic things and carrying food to the fields as unsuitable. Such a difference in opinion may be attributed to difference in physical characteristic of males and females, cultural prescriptions, environmental conditions and physical safety and security.

Conduciveness of Environmental Conditions relating to Domestic Work

Data relating to conduciveness of environmental conditions in which domestic activities are undertaken by the child workers unravel that majority of them have considered the domestic work of bringing water (96.18%), buying domestic things (95.19%), cooking (89.70%) watching the house (80.30%), carrying food to the field (70.69%), cleaning utensils (68.68%), looking after young ones (68.64%) and bringing fire-wood (61.58%), as conducive. It has been in the categories of domestic work connected with cattle grazing and feeding, accompanying employer and other activities that majority has expressed the opinion in negative and pointed out that environmental conditions under which those works are performed have not been conducive.

Activities Other than Agricultural Domestic Work

The child workers, in addition to agricultural/domestic work, have been found to be engaged in helping parents in running their shops, planting on the forest land, wood cutting for commercial purposes, road construction on contract etc. In addition to these economic pursuits, they have been engaging them selves in study and play depending upon availability of time.

Working Conditions and Conditions of Work

Child workers in agriculture generally start working in their family occupations in which they are initiated by their parents to seek their assistance in order to reduce their burden of work. Those parents who do not have enough land in their possession or who work as landless labourers generally approach those big landlords with whom they have been working and request them to give employment to their children in order that the income of their families may be increased. Mendelievich (1979:35) has rightly remarked: "Usually the first employers to be approached is this way are those for whom the parents, relatives, friends or neighbors work themselves...parents...hand over their children at the age of 8 or 9 years, so that they may work as farm labourers...in return for which the parents usually receive a small loan or payment in cash or in kind."

Generally, it is out of sheer necessity that parents are forced to send their children to take up employment with employers who fish in the troubled water and considering that the children desirous of seeking employment cannot afford to remain without it, they dictate the terms and conditions in a most arbitrary and unilateral manner. Taking undue advantage of the helplessness of the working children, employers give a very rough treatment to them which may be of different kinds ranging form mild scolding, admonition and hurling of abuses to severe corporal punishment. The exploitation of children is done by adopting a number of ways which may involve not only punishment but also petty rewards which act as an incentive and motivate these young children to undertake arduous and hard work beyond their capacity for quite a long duration of time that adversely affect their health and development.

Own as well as others' land has been 0.69 km., 1.07 kms. and 0.81 km. respectively. This indicates that there has not been any significant difference in the distance between residence and work place in different categories of nature of employment, and that the distance between residence and work place in case of majority of the child workers has been walkable.

Mode of Conveyance and Distance between Residence and Work Place

An analysis of information gathered regarding mode of conveyance in relation to distance between residence and work place of the child workers reveals that all but 2.80% of them have been going to their work place on foot. In all the categories of distance excepting that of 4-5 kms. In which half of the child workers have been going to their work place on foot and the remaining half by bicycle, either majority or all of them have been going to work on foot.

Social Service Needs and Problems

In a country like ours where about half of the population lives below the poverty line, it is but natural that even the basic needs, let alone social service needs, of poverty-stricken people are not properly satisfied. The term social service needs in being used here to denote nutrition, clothing, housing, health, education and recreation needs. In addition to non-fulfillment of basic and social service needs, child workers are faced with a number of problems in their daily life and living. A detailed description of these needs and problems is being given in the ensuing paragraphs.

Needs on which the Child Workers Spend Money by Their Age

There may be a variety of needs—biological and social, on the fulfillment of which people spend money. Data gathered from the child workers regarding needs on the satisfaction of which they spend money and analysed in relation to their age on the assumption that the needs on which the money is spent may vary in case of child workers of different age-groups, unravels that the largest single group of child workers (45..07%) has been spending money on fulfillments of basic needs and entertainment needs followed by those who have been spending money to satisfy their basic needs (25.35%), basic needs and educational needs (16.90%), entertainment needs (5.63%), intoxicants (4.22%) and educational needs, and basic needs and intoxicants (1.40% each). In the age-group of 8-12 years, the largest single group has been spending money on fulfillments of basic needs, and basic needs and entertainment needs (42.11% each) followed by those who have been incurring expenditure on satisfaction of basic needs and educational needs (10.52%) and intoxicants (5.26%). In the age-group of 13-18 years. The largest single group (46.12%) has been spending money to satisfy basic needs an entertainment needs followed by those who have been incurring expenditure on fulfillments of basic needs, and basic needs and educational needs (99.23 each), entertainment needs (7.68%), intoxicants (3.84%), educational needs, and basic needs and intoxicants (1.92% each). This shows that the child workers have generally been spending money on the fulfillments of basic needs and entertainment needs, and that in the age-group of 8-12 years, the incidence of spending money on educational needs only has been missing.

Efforts made by Family Members to Satisfy Basic Needs of the Child Workers

Child workers contribute their mite towards augmenting the resources of their families by working hard in agriculture and thus share the family burden of their parents. This enjoins upon their parents and other elder family members to make their best efforts to satisfy at least the basic needs of these children. Information collected from the child workers regarding efforts, if any, made by family members to satisfy at least the basic needs, reveals that all the categories of elders-grand parents, parents and brothers/ sisters have been making their best efforts to satisfy the basic needs of the child workers relating to food (88.57%, 98.58% and 91.06% respectively), clothing (87.86%, 97.97% and 89.38% respectively) and shelter (87.86%, 98.18% and 89.94% respectively).

Nutrition

The word nutrition has been derived from 'nutricus' which means to suckle at the breast. Nutrition signifies a dynamic process in which the food that is consumed is utilized for nourshing the body. Park and Park (1977 : 100) have rightly observed: "Good nutrition is a basic component of health. It is of prime importance in the attainment of normal growth and development and in the maintenance of health throughout life." It is very important from the standpoint of health, especially of children whose growth is considerably affected by their food intake. Winston Churchill, in his country's gravest hour, had rightly insisted: "These is no finer investment for any community than putting milk into babies." Planning Commission, Government of India (Sixth Five Year Plan, 1980-85 : 379) have aptly maintained: "If children are not adequately nourished before they grow-up to enter the active labour force, they may remain physically and mentally so un-developed that their productivity when in employment will forever remain below the normal standards and there is a serious danger of long-term biological defects."

Malnutrition may be defined as "a pathological state resulting from a relative or absolute deficiency or excess of one or more essential nutrients" (Jelliffe, 1966). Malnutrition can make mild childhood diseases fatal. Prolonged poor nutrition can leave the child retarded or lacking in curiosity, energy and capacity of learning. Lack of calories, vitamins and minerals prevent the child from growing fully or cause dangers.

The problem of malnutrition is very acute in the present day world. UNICEF (1963: 45) has correctly depicted the entire situation in its observation that "from one-third to one-half of the worlds' population suffer from under-nourishment or malnutrition. This includes between 300 million and 500 million persons who, even in normal times, do not get enough food of any description, and as many as a billion more who do not receive an adequately balanced diet.....Mal-nutrition, unlike most of the communicable diseases, is often a slow, insidious process. Its manifestations are frequently masked by the more dramatic symptom of other disorders, to which it contributes by undermining the body's resistance.

In our country, the problem of mal-nutrition is very much prevalent, especially among children of weaker sections. Government of India (1979: 7) have reported: "Calorie-protein mal-nutrition has been identified as a crucial problem specially among younger children...at least 6% of all children between the ages one and six years suffer from nutritional anaemia and calorie-protein mal-nutrition in one from or another."

The recommended calorie intake for population in rural areas is 2400 calories per day. It has been demonstrated by some of the studies that the average energy intake is less than the recommended level in about 50 per cent of the population. The extent of mal-nutrition is to be reported in 15-30 per cent. According to 1971-72 National Sample Survey, about 57% people in the rural areas were below the prescribed calorific intake of 2400 calories recommended by the Indian Council of Medical Research in all expenditure classes, while 95% in lowest expenditure class belong to this category, about 19% in the highest expenditure class failed to receive the recommended intake (UNICEF, 1981: 32). People do not get minimum amount of cereals and pulses that are necessary to meet their normal requirements. (Planing Commission, Government of India, 1980-85: 377).

The effects of malnutrition are manifold—direct as well as indirect. In the words of Park and Park (1977: 100): "The direct effects are the occrrnence of frank nutritional deficiency, diseases such as kwashiorkor, marasmus, vitamin A deficiency, anaemias, beriberi, pellagra, goitre and rickets. The indirect effects are a lowered vitality of the people, arrested growth, high infant mortality, neonatal and still-birth rates, high incidence of low birth weight, high sickness rates and a lower expectation of life. Malnutrition predisposes to infections like tuberculosis."

Mal-nutrition not only leads to imbalanced development but also to hindrance in growth. Because of insufficient calories, body proteins are used for energy with the result that the protein available for tissue building is considerably reduced. Infections and parasites also affect the protein requirements to a marked extent. Marasmus and Kwashiorkor are the two main extreme forms of mal-nutrition out of which the former is more common in this country. The whole spectrum of conditions-including these two extremes and the intermediate "marasmic kwashiorkor", is known as protein—calorie malnutrition or as PCM. Marasmus is commonly seen in babies in whose case the breast milk remains inadequate and the mother tries to feed the baby on diluted milk obtained from goat, cow or buffalo, and due to poor hygiene there is frequent diarrhoea. It also results from the late introduction of semi-solid foods when breast milk is not enough to sustain growth. Kwashiorkor occurs when the child is displaced from the breast from another child. The main features are apathy, moonface, scanty lusterless hair and oedema. Skin changes such as pigmented or de-pigmented patches, peeling and even ulceration are frequently seen. (Ghosh, 1967 : 52-53).

The prescribed intake of nutrition food depends upon availability of food stuffs needed for balanced diet in sufficient quantity which varies from one age-group to another. Information gathered from the child workers regarding availability of food grains in sufficient quantity and analysed in relation to their age, makes it clear that an overwhelming majority of the child workers in general (82.20%), and in both the age-groups of 8-12 years (84.56%) and 13-18 years (81.20%) in particular, have been of the view that food grains in sufficient quantity have been available to them. This shows that there is no significant association between opinion of the child workers regarding availability of foodgrains to them in sufficient quantity and their age which is proved by the results of Chi-square test also [Chi-square (Cal.)=1.04, Chi-square (Tab.)=3.841, d.f.=1, p=.05]

Data pertaining to availability of foodgrains in sufficient quantity analysed in relation to state of education on the assumption that opinion of the child workers regarding availability varies in different categories of state of education, make it sufficiently clear that in all three categories of state of education namely, no education (82.02%), discontinued education (68.05%) and continued education (88.44%), and overwhelming majority of the child workers have spelt out that food-grains have been available to them in sufficient quantity. This shows that food grains in sufficient quantity have been available to the child workers irrespective of their state of education.

Consumption Pattern

In our country it is generally seen that poverty-stricken people remain semi-starved, especially during off-seasons when agricultural activities remain at a low ebb, and consume cereals which become readily available to them just after the harvesting of the crops. Facts gathered from the child workers regarding their consumption pattern clearly indicate that during summer, majority of the child workers have been consuming wheat (85.40%), gram (52.60%) and other foodgrains consisting of maize, barley, mandua, bajra etc. (66.60%). During winter, majority of them have been depending upon rice (84.20%), dal (53.80%) and other cereals comprising of maize, barley, mandua, bajra, etc. (71.40%). In rainy season, majority of the child workers have been subsisting on wheat (72.20%) and other cereals including maize, barley, mandua, bajra etc. This substantiates the contention made earlier that the child workers subsist on cereals which become readily available to them just after harvesting of the crop, and it is generally the coarse variety of cereals that is consumed by majority of the child workers in all the seasons.

Availability of Clothes

Clothes protect us from vagaries of weather and help in giving a decent look to a person. Clothes are essential for us because nudity is deprecated by society, and this is why it becomes obligatory on the part of every person to put on clothes on his body. These clothes may be used or purchased by the wearer. Production of clothes is confined to a particular section of population which knows how to weave and which is quite limited. Since none of the members in the families of the child workers has been found to have the knowledge of weaving, it becomes essential for them to purchase the needed clothes; and since majority of the child workers have been drawn from poverty-stricken families of the lower social strata, they are forced to remain semi-naked and to put on worn and torn clothes. Information gathered from the child workers regarding availability of sufficient clothes to them and analysed in relation to their age on the assumption that opinion regarding availability might have been influenced by age-composition, reveals that majority of the child workers in general (62.69%) and in both the age groups of 8-12 years (64.82%) and 13-18 years (61.82%) in particular, have averred that sufficient clothes have been available to them. This indicates that opinion of the child workers regarding sufficiency of clothes is not associated with their age which is also testified to by the results of Chi-square [Chi-square (Cal.)=0.37, Chi-square (Tab.)=3.84, d. f.=1, p=0.05].

An analysis of data pertaining to availability of sufficient clothes to the child workers in relation to their state of education on the assumption that opinion of child workers may vary according to their state of education, and availability of sufficient clothes may differ in different categories of state of education, reveals that in all the three categories of state of education namely, 'no education' (52.25%), 'discontinued education' (52.58%) and 'continued education' (70.67%), majority of child workers have averred that sufficient clothes have been available to them. It is noteworthy that the incidence of reporting the availability of sufficient clothes has been maximum in case of the child workers who in conjunction with their work have been going to school also and there by combining their work with education which may be explained in the light of the fact that their family members might have been giving greater attention towards maintenance and up keep of their clothes because of their realization that their school-going children should not suffer from any inferiority complex and also because of consciousness of their social status. This substantiates that opinion regarding sufficiency of clothes is associated with state of education which is proved by the results is Chi-square also [Chi-square (Cal.)=8.47, Chi-square (Tab.)=5.991, d.f.=2, p=.05].

Information gathered on the basis of field observations has shown that the largest single group of child workers (43.00%) has been ordinarily dressed followed by those who have been poorly dressed (37.60%) and well-dressed (19.40%). Majority of the child workers (69.20%) have been wearing cotton clothes followed by those who have been putting on synthetic clothes (17.40%) and woolen clothes (13.40%). As for the condition of clothes it has been observed that the clothes of majority of child workers have been intact (71.80%) and those of the remaining (28.20%) have been torn.

Housing Needs

Houses cater to the basic need of shelter. The quality of life, to a considerable extent, depends on the conditions that prevail in a house. The development of personality of children is considerably affected by the type of house in which they live. If the roof of a house is not in a proper condition in the sense that rain water leaks or comes down to the floor, or sun rays in summer or dew drops in winter directly come over people who reside in it, they adversely affect the health of the residents.

If the number of rooms available in a house is insufficient, children are likely to be subjected to the evil influence of the sex life of adults in the family and are bound not to get a separate study room. Similerly, if the house is constructed in accordance with the essential requirements of life in terms of inlet of light, sunshine, fresh air and arrangement for flush latrine, people living in the hosue will be healthy and cheerful. Likewise, if a house has electricity, it provides varied kinds of modern conveniences and comforts put in the service of mankind by electric revolution and varied kinds of activities including study of children may be undertaken during night according to convenience when the atmosphere is calm and quiet. If a house has tap water facility, a lot of time and effort which is wasted in pulling out water from a well or hand pump and bringing water from distant sources may be saved, and the time thus saved may be utilised for taking up economically gainful activities.

Unfortunately the housing condition of people in rural areas of our country is very bad inasmuch as human beings are compelled to share their living room with cattle and the same is used as drawing room, dining room, living room, store room and kitchen, and even a cattle shed. Houses having separate kitchen store, bathroom and latrine are exceptions. In a nutshell, the housing conditions of people in rural areas are deplorable and pitiable and exert myriad kinds of debilitating influences on the growth and development of children. Medelievich (1979:43) has rightly maintained, "In the less developed regions the living conditions of the child worker are generally appalling. Poverty and over-crowding are compounded by squalid housing with noisome sanitary installations, where these exist at all. The abysmal quality of the housing is a widespread social problem, above all in urban areas. Sometimes upto ten members of a family may be crammed to gether in the shacks and hovels in which they live-often in a single room, with little or no ventilation. Such conditions are typical of any developing country with a high rate of population growth." It has been admitted by Government of India (1980-85: 390) also that "housing conditions in the country are rather poor. A large number of people either live without any shelter whatsoever or in units below the lowest possible standards." Though concerted efforts have been made by the Government to tackle the problem of housing in rural areas under the Minimum Needs Programme by providing house-sites and assistance for construction of houses to the rural landless workers, yet the number of eligible families needing housing assistance has by now been around 15 million and the number of families in need of house sites 6.8 million.

Assuming that the housing problem in this country, particularly in rural areas, is very grave, information regarding sufficiency of residential accommodation was gathered from the child workers and its analysis in relation to their age on the assumption that opinion regarding sufficiency may differ in different age-groups, unravels that an overwhelming majority of the child workers in general (76.60%) and in the age-groups of 8-12 years (61.75%) and 13-18 years (82.91%) in particular have pointed out that sufficient residential accommodation has been available to them.

Data pertaining to sufficiency of residential accommodation interpreted in relation to state of education on the assumption that opinion of the child workers regarding sufficiency may vary in case of various categories of state of education, unravel tht majority of the child workers in general (76.60%) and in all the three categories of slate of education namely, 'no education (81.46%)', 'discontinued education' (69.07%) and continued education' (76,80%) in particular, have expressed the view that sufficient residential accommodation has been available to them. This shows that opinion regarding sufficiency of residential accommodation is not associated with state of education which is testified to by the results of Chi-square also [Chi-square (Cal.)=5.42, Chi-square (Tab.)=5.991, d.f.=2, p=0.05].

Information relating to housing conditions gathered on the basis of observation reveals that houses of 39.20% of the child workers have been centrally located followed by those whose houses have been sparsely located (34.60%) and peripherally located (26.20%).

It is notewarthy that in the localities in which the Scheduied Tribes have been living, houses have been constructed in a row with the result that some of the houses in which child workers live exist in the centre and some on periphery. It is also notable that due to scarcity of land fit for house construction, houses in hill areas are widely scattered and that is why quite a good number of houses have been sparsely located. The houses have generally been thatched (45.00%) some of them have been mud-walled (29.20) and brick-walled (21.00%). A few of the them have been plastered also (4.80). Generally the houes have been located in open surroundings (83.20%) with some of them having been situated in a closed atmosphere (16.80%).

Data based on observation furthur reveal that majority of the child workes (77.40%) have been making use of chimney (minilamp) as a source of light followed by those who have been few and far between (5.8%). The child workers have generally been using hand pumps-private (6.20%) and public (25.40%). Quite a sizeable number of them (26.80%) have been taking water form nullahs flowing in the adjoining areas. Artisan well has been found to be used by 19.40 of the child workers. Tap as a source of water has been least in use (6.00%) because it is quite difficult to lay down the pipe-line for tap water supply in hill areas. Drainage system in the case on an overwhelming majority of child workers (78.20%) has been open with the remaining 21.80% of the child workers living in areas having closed drainage-system. Just more than half of the child workers (51.60%) have beeen living in houses having separate kitchens. In all but 10.40% of houses of the child workers, bathroom facility has been missing. They have been taking bath in open which in the hill areas is quite troublesome. Latrine facility has been missing in all but 4.40% of the houses of the child workers. Flush and service latrines have been the characteristic feature of child workers living in the plains only. As for cattle shed, in case of just more than half of the child workers (52.60%), a separate cattle shed has been in existence followed by those in whose case either there has been an attached cattle shed (36.00%) or no cattle shed (11.40%). It is noteworthy that in hill areas, generally, there are two storeyed houses with one room in each storey. The room at the ground floor is generally used as a cattle shed though which, in few cases, of course, stair case of the room at the first floor passes.

Neighbourhood Environment

Neighbourhood enviornment plays a significant role in shapping the personality. If people in a neighbourhood provide healthy company, development of personality in the right direction takes place; and similarly if the atmosphere in terms of housing conditions, drainage-system, sanitary conditions, availability conditions, of healthy avenues of recreation is conducive, it becomes instrumental in proper personality growth and development. Data based on observation relating to neighbourhood environment reveal that in the case of an overwhelming majority of the child workers (68.40%), composition of the localilty has been homogenous in the sense that people of similar socio-economic and cultural background have been living to gether followed by those in whose case the locality has been mixed (24.40%) and heterogeneous (7.20). The homogeneity in the localities of child workers may be explained in the light of the fact that villages in hill areas are predominantly occupied by people of a particular caste or community. The neighbourhood has generally been clean (67.40%) and conducive (74.00%).

Health

The term health actually refers to a slate of complete physical, mental and social well-being. In common parlance, it denotes the physical condition of the body. Though health is wealth, yet its loss is socially recognised as much more severe than that of wealth. There is an old addage; when wealth is lost, nothing is lost; when health is lost. something is lost; when character is lost, everything is lost. Health is the basic means of attaining all varied is lost. Health is the basic means of attaining all the varied kinds of goals. There is a Sanskrit verse which says 'शरीरमाद्यम् खलु धर्म साधनम' (Body is the primary means of performance of the socially assigned duties).

Sustained efforts have been made in the direction of promoting health in this country. A network of health care services spread all over the country has brought about a significant improvement in the health status of the people which is evident from the fact that the life expectancy has risen to 52 years, infant mortality has been reduced to 123 (State Family Welfare Bureau, 1982:4) and health infrastructure has been multiplied many times and per-capita expenditure on health incurred by the state has gone upto about twelve rupees (Govt. of India, 1980-85:366). But still the health needs of quite a slzeable section of the Indian population, especially in rural areas, are not adequately met, despite, the adoption of a policy of 'Health for all by 2000 A.D. 'has been enunciated in Alma-Ata Declaration in 1977.

In rural areas, the health status of quite a big chunk of population is far from satisfactory mainly due to non-availability of not only nutrient diet owing to poverty but also wholesome drinking water; shortage of even curative medical facilities, let alone the preventive ones, ignorance of people about nutrition contents of different constituents of food and methods of preserving them, as also about the causes and symptoms of various diseases which can be easily cured provided they are detected at an early stage; belief of people in traditional ways like sorcery, witchcraft etc. of curing diseases, and the like. It was therefore, considered necessary to make observations regarding health of the child workers and information thus collected has shown that majority of the child workers (54.4%) have poor health followed by those whose health has been normal (28%) and robust (17.6%). This substantiates the allusion made above that health of people in rural areas including child workers is generally poor.

Availability of Medical Aid

The health of people depends considerably upon timely availability of required medical aid. Data gathered from the child workers regarding availability of required medical aid and analysed in relation to their age on the assumption that opinion regarding availability may vary in different age-groups not only because of different experiences but also due to different types and magnitude of problems faced by them, unravel that majority of the child workers in general (65.8%) and in both the age-groups of 8-12 years (52.35%) and 13-18 years (71.51%) in particular, have denied that required medical aid becomes available to them. However, the incidence of denial has been much more in the elder age-group than in the younger one. Results of Chi-square test show that opinion of the child workers regarding availability of required medical aid is significantly associated with their age composition [Chi-Square (Cal.)=19.80, Chi-sqaure (Tab.)=3.84, d.f.=1. p=.05].

Further analysis of data pertaining to availability of required medical aid in relation to state of education of the child workers on the assumption that responses regarding availability may vary in case of childworkers without any education, discontinued education and continued education, makes it sufficiently clear that in all three categories of education—'no education' (72.47%), 'discontinued education (66.01%) and continued education (66.00%) majority of the child workers have denied the availability of required medical aid. It is noteworthy that the incidence of denial has been most in the case of the child workers belonging to the category of 'no education' and least in case of their counterparts who have been fortunate enough to continue their education. This may be explained in the light of the fact that relatively greater attention is given by the parents/guardians to cater to the health needs of school-going children as also that some health services like immunization, health check-up, supply of medicines to children suffering from deficiency diseases etc. and welfare services like mid-day meals are made available in schools under the school health programmes. Results of Chi-square test also indicate that opinions of the child workers regarding availability is significantly associated with their state of education [Chi-square (Cal.)=6.97, Chi-square (Tab.)=5.99, d.f.=2, p=0.5].

Education

Education has come to be accepted today as one of the minimum needs of the people because of its essential nature from the point of view of proper personality development as also from the standpoint of understanding and adjusting with social reality. Despite the fact that we have been committed to achieve the goal of universal education to all children up to the age of fourteen years as enshrined in the Directive Principles of State Policy enunciated in our Constitution it has not been possible for us to realise it so far. With regard to the state of universal elementary education the Fourth All-India Educational

Survey (NCERT, 1980: 3-8) has revealed that in 1978 the total child population in the age-group of 6-10 years was 84016000 out of which the corresponding population in rural areas was 65556000. The child population in the age-group of 11-13 years was 47331000 including 35092000 in rural areas. For the country as a whole, the gross enrolment ratio for the age-groups 6-10 years and 11-13 years was 82.31 and 36.92 respectively. The overall age-specific enrolment ratio for the age-groups of 6-10 years and 11-13 years was 66.15 (for boys 76.95 and for girls 54.76) and 43.28 (for boys 54.44 and for girls 31.57) respectively. In classes I to V, girls constituted 38.64 per cent of the total enrolment. There were 474636 primary schools of which 431602 were located in rural areas. Enrolment in classes I to V was 69156038 including 26723133 (38.64%) girls. Enrolment in rural areas was 52534367 constituting 75.97% of the total enrolment in classes I to V. There were 19300231 girls in rural areas constituting 36.74% of total enrolment. There were 2940337 teachers working in educational institutions of whom 1287499 (43.79%) were working in primary schools. 23.37% of the teachers at the primary stage were women teachers. 86.27% of the teachers at the primary stage were trained. The pupil-teacher ratio at the primary stage at the national level was 41. Of the 474636 primary schools, 0.62% were without teachers, 34.75 were single-teacher schools, 27.27% two-teacher schools, 15.1% three-teacher schools, 8.16% four-teacher schools, 5.25% five-teacher schools and 8.85% more than five-teacher schools.

In order to fulfil the constitutional obligation of providing free and compulsory education to all children upto 14 years of age, spread of universal elementary education has been placed at point number 16 of the New 20-Point Programme which relates to the spread of universal elementary education for the age group of 6-14 years with special emphasis on girls. A number of steps have been taken for spread of universal elementary education. Important among which are as under:

Legislation for compulsory education has been enacted in 16 states including Uttar Pradesh and three Union Territories except in the State of Himanchal Pradesh where the Act covers the entire elementary stage (Class I-VIII) in all the remaining States and Union Territories, it covers only the primary stage (Class I to V). Now education in all schools-Government, Local Bodies and aided institutions, at the primary stage (Classes I-V) and at the middle stage (Classes VI to VII) is free in all States and Union Territories except for boys in classes VII-VIII in Uttar Pradesh. It is noteworthy that recently the education of girls upto class twelve has been made free. All the States and five Union Territories have non-formal education for out-of-school children including non-starters and drop-outs. The Centrally Sponsored Scheme of Non-Formal for elementary age-group children aims at providing the institutional infrastructure necessary both for coverage of non-enrolled and non-attending children, and for strenghtening the academic inputs of the entire system both under central and state's initiatives. The cost of the scheme is being shared equally by the Central and State Governments.

From 1983-84, the on-going scheme of non-formal education has been liberalised in order to increase enrolment of girls by providing financial assistance to the educationally backward States on 90:100 Centre-State sharing basis for establishment of Non-Formal Education Centres exclusively for girls.

During 1983-84, a centrally sponsored scheme of assistance on 80:20 Centre-State sharing basis for appointment of women teachers in primary school in the 9 educationally back-ward states was put into operation.

A scheme of awards/incentives was launched during 1983-84 in order to give recognition for excellence in performance for the spread of girls' education and thereby to give a further boost to the programme of universalisation of elementary education. Under the scheme, awards are given at different administrative levels viz. panchayats, C. D. blocks, tribal development blocks, districts and States/Union Territories.

Internatioal cooperation from Sweden in the form of paper assistance for facilitating Non-formal Education Programme for elementary age-group children, from United Kingdom in the form of help for construction of primary school buildings, and from the Federal Republic of Germany in the form of assistance for establishment of science workshops for the purpose of production of science kits for elementary schools has also been available.

Financial assistance is provided by the Central Government to voluntary organisations in the nine educationally backward state for running the Early Childhood Education Centres for children in rural as well as urban areas with a view to improving their communication (language) and cognitive (social, emotional, intellectual and personality development) skills as a preparation for entry into primary education.

Various curriculum reform projects are undertaken by the National Council of Educational Research and Training (NCERT) for introducing innovations in the existing curriculum with a view to bringing about qualitative improvement in pre-primary and elementary education.

Necessary play materials, picture books, graphic materials, audio-programmes, slide-tape programmes and video programmes have been developed under the project-Children's Media Laboratory (CML)—in order to provide inexpensive media of educational and entertainment value for children of pre-primary stages.

Assistance has been given by the Central Government to the States for setting up or strengthening Early Childhood Education (ECE) Centres, training teacher educators, orientation of supervisors and administrators to different aspects of early childhood education and development of basic learning and play materials for the use by pre-school children.

The NCERT has been implementing the UNICEF assisted project-Comprehensive Access to Primary Education (CAPE)-for development of target group oriented and decentralised programmes in respect of curriculum instructional/learning materials, methodology of instruction and evaluation.

In certain selected communities deprived of education, the UNICEF assisted project-Development Activities in Community Education and Participation (DACEP) -has been started with the object of developing and testing new types of educational activities for meeting the minimum educational needs of preschool and out of-school children, young children and women.

Work concerning renewal of education curricula and instructional materials to relate them to the needs of different groups of children from disadvantaged sections was undertaken under the UNICEF assisted project-Primary Education Curriculum Renewal (PECR)—in all States except Andhra and Union Territories.

Packages of instructional material on nutrition, health education and environmental sanitation for primary school children for teachers and for out-of-school girls and women have been developed under the project - Nutrition, Health Education and Environmental sanitation (NHEES).

The scheme of National Awards to teachers including those in primary schools has been in operation since 1958-59 with a view to raising the prestige to teachers and giving public recognition to the meritorious services of outstanding teachers. Each award carries with it a certificate of merit, a silver medal and a cash payment of Rs. 1500.

Despite the above mentioned series of measures undertaken to ensure universal elementary education and to improve quality of primary education for retaining those who get enrolled, quite a large number of children are still out of and drop out of schools and regularly do not attend to schools. Multiplicity of factors such as non-availability of schools within easy reach, absence of even essential facilities in schools, drab and dismal conditions in schools,. dire lack of committed and sincere teachers, expensive character of present education, inability of poverty-stricken parents / guardians to afford educational expenses, swelling number of educated unemployed, lack of any relationship between education and its ability to cater to varied kinds of demands of social reality etc. It's matter of common experience that on the one hand, there is paucity of educational facilities required for universalisation of elementary education, they are not being optimally utilised on the other. It has been against this background that information was gathered from the child workers regarding availability of sufficient opportunities for education, and its analysis in relation to age on the assumption that responses regarding availability may vary in case of different age-groups, unravels that majority of the child workers in general (63.8%) as also in the age-groups of 13-18 years (0.37%) in particular, have denied the availability of sufficient opportunities for education. However, just more than half of the child workers aged between 8-12 years (51.68%) have admitted the availability of sufficient opportunities for education. This age-specific difference in the responses may be understood in the light of the fact that parents of relatively younger child workers might have been giving greater attention to education of their young children and making their utmost efforts by providing the best possible facilities within their limits to ensure that education of their children does not get disrupted mainly because of ever-growing recognition and significance of education among people and also owing to realisation among them that these young children cannot be of much help to them due to their tender age. This shows that opinion of the child workers regarding availability of sufficient opportunities for education has been associated with age which is further testified to by the results of Chi-square also [Chi-square (Cal.)=21.90, Chi-square (Tab.)=3.841, d.f. 1, p=.05].

Further probe into the responses of child workers regarding availability of sufficient opportunities for education in relation to their state of education on the assumption that opinion regarding availability may vary in case of different categories of 'no education', 'discontinued education' and 'continued education, reveals that all the child workers who have never been to school and about 3/4 ths of their counterparts who have discontinued their education have been of the view that sufficient opportunities for education are not available to them. However, majority of the school-going child workers (72.00%) have held that sufficient opportunities for education are available to them which may be because of their own satisfactory personal experiences in respect of availability of opportunities for education. This leads to the conclusion that opinion of the child workers regarding availability of sufficient educational opportunities is associated with their state of education which is proved by the result of Chi-square test also [Chi-sqaure (Cal.)=234.17, Chi square (Tab.)=5.991, d.f.=2, p=.05].

Reasons for Not Joining Schools

There may be a number of reasons behind not joining school. Data gathered from the child workers regarding such reasons and put to analysis in relation to their age on the assumption that they may vary in case of different age-groups, clearly indicate that the largest single group of the child workers (38.2%) has expressed the view that poor economic condition has been the main reason behind not joining school followed by those who have averred lack of interest in studies (25.28%), distant location of school (19.10%) lack of interest in studies coupled with distant location of school (6.74%) lack of interest in studies together with lack of interest on the part of family members (6.19%), lack of interest on the part of family members (3.37%) and fear of punishment in school for not having done home work (1.12%).

In both the age-groups of 8-12 years (33.33%) and 13-18 years (39.71%) the largest single group has averred poor economic condition as the main reason followed by those who have pointed out lack of interest in studies and distant location of school. To conclude, poor economic condition has mainly been responsible for the child workers inability to join school.

Reasons for Leaving School by Age

There may be a multiplicity of reasons behind leaving school. Data collected from the child workers and analysed in relation to their age on the assumption that these reasons may vary from one age-group to another, point out that the largest single group in general (34.03%) has averred poor economic condition as the main reason for leaving school followed by those who have expressed need for supplementing family income (19.59%), poor economic condition coupled with need for additional working hands (15.46%), need for additional workers hands (10.31%), apathetic attitude towards studies together with failure in examination (7.22%), apathetic attitude towards studies (6.18%), maltreatment by teachers (5.15%) and failure in examination (2.06%) as reasons. In both the age-groups of 8-12 years (26.67%) and 13-18 years (35.36%), poor economic condition has been spelt out as the main reason. To conclude, it has been mainly because of their poor economic condition that the child workers, irrespective of their age composition, had to leave their school.

Willingness to Rejoin by Duration of Leaving School

Data pertaining to willingness to rejoin school analysed in relation to duration of leaving school on the assumption that those who have left school not long before are much more willing to rejoin school as compared to their counterparts who have left school long back and vice versa, unravel that majority of the child workers (62.89%) have been willing to rejoin school with remaining 37.11% having expressed their unwillingness to do so. The largest single group of the child workers (31.96%) has left the school less than a year back followed by those who have left school between 1-4 years (29.90%), 4-8 years (22.71%) and more than 8 years (4.43%). In the categories of duration of leaving school titled as less than one year (93.41%) and 1-4 years (72.41%) an overwhelming majority of the child workers have shown their inclination to rejoin school whereas majority of their counterparts in the categories of duration of leaving school need as 4-8 years (60.87%) and more that 8 years (85.71%) have expressed their willingness to rejoin school. This clearly establishes that shorter the duration of leaving school, more is the willingness to region school and vice-versa. Result of Chi-square test of significance [Chi-Square (Cal.)=34.01, Chi-square (Tab.)=7.815. d.f.=11, p=0.5] also establish that willingness to rejoin school and duration of leaving school are significantly associated with each other.

To conclude, duration of leaving school in case of the largest single group of child workers has been less than 1 year, majority of them have been wiling to join school again, and willingness to rejoin has been significantly associated with duration of leaving school.

Desire to Leave Work/School

Work load in excess of the desired quantity may adversely affect the health of child workers and develop a feeling among them to leave work. Information gathered from the child workers regarding their feeling towards workload being in excess and analysed in relation to their desire to leave work/school makes it clear that majority of them (65.33%) have expressed the view that their workload is in excess with remaining (34.67%) having averred that their work is not in excess. In both the categories of work-load being in excess (78.23%) and not being so (58.97%), majority of the child workers have expressed their desire to leave school. However, the desire to leave school has been more intense in the case of child workers who have the feeling of work load being in excess as compared to their opposite number who do not have such feeling. This leads to the conclusion that irrespective of the presence or absence of feeling of workload being in excess, majority of the child workers want to leave school may be because of inability of their parents to meet even their essential educational requirements due to their severe economic constraints. However, Chi-square test gives results to the contrary and shows that desire to leave work/school and feeling of workload being in excess are significantly associated with each other [Chi-Square (Cal.)=.66, Chi-Square (Tab.)=3.84, d.f.=1, p=0.05].

Recreational Needs

Derived from the Latin word *'recreatio'* the them recreation means to restore or represent an activity which restores the mind and body to a state of vigcur and alertness. It may be defined as a leisure time pursuit for pleasure or fun and resultant satisfaction. Recreation for children is as essential as the air they breathe in.

In a country like ours where about half on the population lives below the poverty line and is not in a position to adequately saefisfy even basic needs of food, clothing and shelter, recreation, especially a healthy one, is a far cry. In rural areas, the situation regarding availability of healthy recreation if still worse as there are no parks, cinema-house, theatres, circuses, T.V. sets, libraries, reading rooms etc. and the traditional indigenous means of recreation like folk-songs, folk-music, folk-dances nautanki etc. have been dwindling fast. The traditional games like gulli-danda, kabaddi, hide and seed, kho-kho, wrestling etc. are also fast waning. The most important means of recreation in rural areas today are playing cards and listening of transistors. It is pertinent to point out that playing cards are often used as a means of gambling, and have, therefore, lost their recreational value and have become a source of danger for many a family. Highly erotic songs broadcast on radio adversely affect the development of children in the sense that their impressionistic minds, instead of being geared towards serious involvement in educational and constructive pursuits, are diverted towards activities related to sex. Moreover, the materialistic and individualistic values advocated through radio programmes divorce our younger generation from traditional values of sacrifice and renunciation for social well-being which have been the distinguishing features of our culture. In a nutshell, there is a dire lack of healthy means of recreation in rural areas which are essential for children, not luxuries.

Data gathered from the child workers regarding availability of desired recreational facilities to them and analysed in relation to age on the assumption that the responses given by them with regard to availability may vary from one age-group to another, shows that majority of them in general (92.8%) as also in both the categories of 8-12 years (68.46%) and 13-18 years (88.89%) have denied the availability of desired recreational facilities to them. However, the extent of such denial has been more in the case of child workers in the age-group of 13-18 years, giving the impression that opinion of the child workers regarding such availability has been significantly associated with their age which is testified to by the results of Chi-square also [Chi-square (Cal.)=29.41, Chi-square (Tab.)=3.84, d.f.=1, p=.05]. It needs to be pointed out here that on the one hand, healthy avenues for recreation are scarce; on the other hand, child workers are too busy to spare any time for recreation because after working hard for the whole day, that too, at times in combination with studies, they become so terribly tired that they don't feel like involving them in any thing.

An analysis of information regarding availability of recreational facilities in relation to state of education on the assumption that opinion regarding availability may vary from one category of state of education to another, makes it sufficiently clear that in all the three categories of state of education namely, 'no education' (88.20%), 'discontinued education' (87.63%) and 'continued education' (76.45%), an overwhelming majority of the child workers have denied the availability of desired recreational facilities. However, the incidence of denial has been least in the category of continued education, may be because the child workers going to school might have been getting some opportunity for recreation in their schools. This indicates that responses regarding availability vary from one category of state of education to another which is proved by the result of Chi-square test also [Chi-square (Cal.)=12.8, Chi-square (Tab.)=5.99, d.f.=2, p=0.05]. To conclude, availability of desired recreational facilities to the child workers has been denied in all the three categories of state of education, more so to those who belong to the category of 'no-education' and 'discontinued education'.

Problems and Difficulties

Every person in this world comes across problems and difficulties of one kind or another depending upon his own personality structure and the milieu in which he is placed. A child workers in different walks of life faces a number of problems and difficulties which not only thwarts his efficiency but also mars his development prospects. A probe into these problems and difficulties in relation to the age of child workers on the assumption that such problems and difficulties may vary from one age-group to another, brings out that the largest single group of child workers (22.66%) has been faced with the problem of disturbance in studies coupled with excessive work-load (22.66%) followed by such child workers who have been confronted with problems and difficulties of disturbance in studies together with no time for playing (66.60%), no time for playing (15.79%), unsound physical development in combintion with no time for playing (10.53%), excessive workload (10.53%), stoppage of education (9.72%), disturbance in studies (8.50%), and unsound physical development (5.67%). In case of the child workers in the age-group of 8-18 years, the largest single group (21.06%) has been faced with the problem of disturbance in studies coupled with not time for playing whereas in case of these counterparts in the age-group of 13-18 years, the largest single group (26.32%) has been confronted with the problem of disturbance in studies together with excessive workload. The problems of no time for playing, stoppage of education, unsound physical development, excessive workload and disturbance in studies have been averred more by the child workers aged between 8-12 years as compared to their counterparts aged between 13-18 years which may be understood in the light of relatively greater tenderness among younger children.

An analysis of information relating to problems and difficulties of the child workers in relation to their state of education on the assumption that opinion regarding such problems and difficulties may vary from one category of educations to another, reveals that in the category of 'no education' the largest single group of child workers (34.15%) has reported no time for playing as the main problem. In the category of 'discontinued education', the largest number of child workers (31.03) has averred stoppage of education as the main problem. In the category of 'continued education', disturbance in studies coupled with excessive workload has been pointed out as the main problem by the largest single group of child workers (37.84). It is noteworthy that all the problems singly as well as in combination have been put forward by those child workers only who have been continuing their education. To conclude, problems and difficulties, especially these related to disturbance in studies coupled with excessive workload, have been more in case of the child workers who have been continuing their education in comparison to their opposite number who have never been to school or who have discontinued their education.

Man is the maker of his destiny. His future depends upon the soundness of the plans that he chalks out for is his future, and on the skilifulness with which he implements them. People, irrespective of the fact whether they are working or not, have certain future plans as long as they have any hope for survival. Those who are actively involved in work do chalk out their plan keeping in view the varied kinds of resources available to them for expansion and development of work they are engaged in. Some people are very clear about their plans, some are not. Some are meticulous, some are not. Some are clear about the means necessary for materialising these plans, some are not. Those who are clear and meticulous about their plans and means for implementing them, succeed in bringing about desired changes in their life in a planned manner; and conversely, those who suffer from ambiguity and carelessness and inability to mobilise necessary means, usher in change in a haphazard manner and generally do not succeed in achieving what they strive for. In the context of growing children their future plans assume a far greater importance because their entire future life depends upon them—if the future plans are realistic, there is likelihood of success in life and if they are ill—conceived and imaginary, they likely to create frustrations and conflicts making the life miserable. It is against this background that various aspects of the future plans of child workers are being discussed in the ensuing paragraphs.

Activities of Children in the Age-group of 8-12 Years considered Desirable by Age

These are certain activities considered desirable for people of different age-group. Information gathered from the child workers regarding the activities of children in the age-group of 8-12 years considered desirable and analysed in relation to their age on the assumption that responses in this regard may vary from one age-group to another, shows that majority of the child workers in general (77.57%) as also in the age-group of 8-12 years (79.78%) and 13-18 years (76.81%) in particular, have expressed the view that play and study are the desired activities for children in the age-group of 8-12 years followed by those who have pointed out play alone as the desired activity for this age-group. In a nutshell, play and study have been considered as desirable activities for children in the age-group of 8-12 years by majority of the child workers irrespective of their age-composition.

Activities of Children in the Age-group of 13-18 Years considered Desirable by Age

A perusal of data gathered from the child workers regarding activities of children in the age-group of 13-18 years considered desirable in relation to age on the assumption that opinion in this regard may vary form one age-group to another, brings out that the largest number of child workers in general (41.82%) as also in the age-groups of 8-12 years, (43.62%) and 13-18 years (41.22%) in particular, have reported that play together with study is the set of activities desirable for children in the age-group of 13-18 years followed by those who have expressed study coupled with work as the desirable set of activities for children in the age-group of 13-18 years. Emphasis on study as the describle activity may be a reflection of feeling of repentance among the child workers for discontinuing their studies and taking up work.

Possibility of Improvement in Working and Living Conditions

Good working and living conditions give rise to the feeling of job satisfaction and commitment to work and organisation among workers and consequently of higher productivity. Facts gathered from the child workers regarding possibility of improvement in working and living conditions analysed in relation to their age on the assumption that opinion in this regard may vary from one age-group to anather reveal that the largest single group of child workers (38.40%) has affirmed the possibility of improvement followed by those who have either not responded (33.00%) or negated any possibility of improvement (28.60%). In case of the child workers in the age-group of 8-12 years, the largest single group (39.60%) has expressed its inability to opine in this regard followed by those who have denied any possibility of improvement (32.88%) and those who have admitted that improvement can be brought about (27.52%). In the age-group of 13-18 years, the largest number of child workers have come out with the view that there is possibility of improvement followed by those who have either failed to give my response in this regard (30.20%) or have controverted (26.78%) such possibility. To conclude, the child workers in general and in the age-group of 13-18 years in particular have generally agreed to the possibility of improvement whereas the child workers in the age-group of 8-12 years have generally not been able to express any view in this regard which shows that opinion regarding possibility has varied from one age-group to another which is further testified to by the results of Chi-square test [Chi-square (Cal.)=12.72, Chi-sqaure (Tab.)=5.99, d.f.=2 , p=0.05].

Ways of Bringing About Improvement in Working and Living Conditions by Age

Data collected from the child workers regarding ways by adopting which improvements can be brought about in working and living conditions and put to analysis in relation to age on the assumption that opinion regarding such ways may vary from one age-group to another, unravel that the largest number of child workers in general (34.38%) have come out with the view that compulsory and free education can bring about improvement in working and living conditions followed by those who have suggested financial help (30.20%), legislation (12.50%), small scale industries (11.98%), suitable houses (5.73%) and other facilities and amenities (5.21%) as ways of improvement. In the age-group of 8-12 years, majority of the child workers (56.10%) have pointed out compulsory and free education followed by those who have averred financial help (21.95%), legislation (9.76%), small scale industries (9.75%) and suitable houses (2.44%) as ways of improvement in working and living conditions. In the age-group of 13-18 years, the largest number of child workers have advocated financial help (32.45%) followed by those who have suggested compulsory and free education (28.40%), legislation (13.25%), small scale industries (12.58%), suitable houses and other facilities and amenities (6.62% each) as ways of bringing about improvement. To conclude, compulsory and free education as a means of bringing about improvement in working and living conditions has been suggested by the child workers in general and younger child workers in particular, and financial help as a means has generally been advocated by the child workers aged between 13-18 years.

Ways of Bringing About Improvement in Working and Living Conditions by Educational Status

Further analysis of information relating to ways of bringing about improvement in working and living conditions in relation to educational status on the assumption that suggestions regarding such ways may vary from one category of educational status to another, indicates that compulsory and free education has been advocated as the way of bringing about improvement by the largest single group of child workers who have been illiterate (44.68%), educated upto primary level (38.81%) and educated upto intermediate level (39.13%). The largest number of child workers educated upto middle level (38.89%) have suggested financial help. Legislation as a measure of improvement has been put forward by the largest single group of child workers educated upto high school (47.37%). Other facilities and amenities have not been suggested by the child workers educated upto middle school and small scale industries and suitable houses have not been put forward by the child workers educated upto High School. Thus, the ways of improvement in working and living conditions suggested by the child workers do not appear to be associated with their educational status.

Impact of Work Stoppage on Family

Children working in agriculture also contribute to the income of their families. In case they stop working, their family earnings may be adversely affected. Data collected from the child workers regarding impact on their families in case they stop work and analysed in relation to their age on the assumption that responses in this regard may vary from one age-group to another, indicate that in the opinion of the largest single group of child workers in general (37.80%) as also in the age groups of 8-12 years (31.54%) and 13-18 years (40.45%), there will be significant impact on family if they stop working. It is noteworthy that the incidence of averring negligible impact and no impact on family has been more in case of younger child workers as compared to their elder counterparts which indicates some kinds of association between opinion of the child workers regarding impact on family if they stop work and their age, which is testified to by the results of Chi-square test of significance [Chi-square (Cal.)=15.14, Chi-square (Tab.)=7.82%, d.f.=3, p=0.05].

Hope to get rid of Work by Age

Facts gathered from the child workers regarding their hope to get rid of work put to analysis in relation to age on the assumption that views in the regard may vary from one age-group to another, unravel that majority of the child workers in general (57.40%) as also in the age-group of 8-12 years (69.13%) and 13-18 years (52.42%) in particular, do not have any hope of getting rid of the work they are currently engaged in. The sense of despair has been more prevalent among younger child workers as compared to their elder counterparts, indicating that hope to get rid of the present work varies in case of different age groups. Results of chi-square test of significance also prove that hope to get rid of and age are significantly associated with each other [Chi-square (Cal.)=13.94, Chi-square (Tab.)=3.84, d.f.=1, p=0.05].

Child Workers' Hope to get rid of Work by Educational Status

A perusal of data pertaining to the hope of child workers to get rid of work attempted in relation to their educational status brings out that majority of the child workers who have been illiterate (77.53%) and educated upto primary level do not have any hope of getting rid of their present work whereas majority of their counterparts who have been educated upto middle school (66.15%), high school (82.92%) and intermediate (79.49%) are hopeful of breaking the shackles of present work which shows that hope to get rid of present work is greater among relatively more educated child workers as compared to their counterparts who are either illiterate or not much educated. Chi-square test also shows that hope to get rid of the present work is significantly associated with educational status [Chi-square (Cal.)=260.88, Chi-square (Tab.)=7.82, d.f.=4, p=0.05].

In a nutshell, higher the educational status of child workers greater is their hope of getting rid of the present work and viceversa.

Assessment of Involvement in Work and Not in Study by Age

Child workers are those hapless ones who spend their time in earning their livelihood by involving themselves in different type of work which could have been utilised for getting education which is essential for proper personality development as also for getting more rewarding, respectful and convenient jobs in later life. Compelled by circumstances, these workers are left with no option but to work and after working for a long period they start accepting it as a way of life and even give up the idea of education. Data gathered form the child workers regarding their opinion towards involvement in work and not in study and analysed in relation to their age on the assumption that opinion may vary in different age-group, unravel that the largest single group (39.00%) has considered involvement in work and not in studies as a good step followed by those who have not been able to give any response (36.80%) because they were undecided or were unable to take decision on relative merits of work and study primarily due to their lack of understanding of things. In the younger age-group of 8-12 years, majority of the child workers (51.00%) have considered involvement in work and not in study as a bad step, may be because most of the children in their age-group in the village have been going to school. In the age-group of 13-18 years, the largest single group of child workers (43.87%) has considered the choice of work in place of study as a good step, may be because many adolescents in their age-group in the village have been engaged in similar types of work for many years and also because many educated youth are forced to do the similar kind of work due to their inability to find any suitable employment. This shows that involvement in work and not in study has generally been considered as a good step by child workers in general, especially by those aged between 13-18 years and that the child workers aged between 8-12 years have generally considered it as a bad step. This also indicates that opinion of child worker towards involvement in work and not in study has been associated with age which is proved by the results of Chi-square test also [Chi-sqaure (Cal.)=78.40, Chi-square (Tab.)=5.99, d.f.=2, p=0.05].

Assessment of Involvement in Work and Not in Study by Educational Status

A perusal of data relating to the opinion of child workers towards their involvement in work and not in study attempted in relation to their educational status on the assumption that such opinion may differ from one educational status to another brings out that the largest single group of child workers who have been illiterate (47.19%), and who have been educated up to primary (40.68%) and middle (40.00%) levels has considered involvement in work and not in study as a good step whereas majority of their counterparts educated upto High School (51.22%) and an overwhelming majority of their opposite numbers in the category of educational status titled as intermediate have expressed the involvement in work and not in study as a bad step. This shows that higher the educational status, greater has been the incidence of considering involvement in work and not in study as a bad step.

Desire Among the Child Workers to Educate Younger Children in their Families by Age

Information collected as a result of further discussion with those child workers in whose families there have been other children younger to them and analysed in relation to their age on the assumption that such desire may vary form one age-group to another reveals that an overwhelming majority of the child workers in general and in both the age-group of 8-12 years (73.79%) and 13-18 years (83.70%) in particular, have the desire to educate other younger children of their families. To conclude, the child workers, irrespective of their age composition, have to desire to educate other younger children of their families.

Desire among the Child Workers to Educate Younger Children in their Families by Educational Status

An analysis of data relating to desire among the child workers to educate other younger children in their families in relation to educational status on the assumption that such desire may vary from one category of educational status to another, indicates that in all the categories of educational status namely, illiterate (75.36%), primary (85.16%), middle (79.31%), High School (81.08%) and Intermediate (91.18%), an overwhelming majority of the child workers have desire to educate other younger children in their families which indicates that the desire for educating other younger children in their families has been significantly associated with educational status which is proved by the results of Chi-square test also [Chi-square (Cal.)=5.15, Chi-square (Tab.)=7.82, d.f.=3, p=0.05].

Child Workers' Opinion on Education by Age

Data gathered from the child workers regarding the type of education that should be given by educational institutions and analysed in relation to their age on the assumption that the opinion may vary from one age-group to another, unravel that the largest number of child workers in general (26.11%) as also in the age-group of 8-12 years (34.00%) and 13-18 years (23.00%) in particular, has been of the view that education should be compulsory and reality-oriented, followed by those who have advocated compulsory education (13.80%), reality oriented education (12.53%), academic education (9.15%), academic education coupled with manual labour (7.21%), education stressing manual labour (6.50%), compulsory education of boys only (6.58%), education of boys only (5.52%) and education of both boys and girls (3.82%). To conclude, the child workers, irrespective of difference in their age, have generally been in favour of compulsory and reality-oriented education.

Child Worker's Opinion on Education by Sex

A perusal data pertaining to child workers' opinion on education attempted in relation to their sex on the assumption that opinion of male and female child workers may be different, brings out that the largest single group of child workers in both the categories of male (29,72%) and female (31.88%) has been in favour of compulsory and reality-oriented education.

Child Workers' Opinion on Education by Educational Status

A further probe into material gathered from the child workers regarding their opinion on education attempted in relation to their educational status on the assumption that opinion of child workers may vary from one category of educational status to another, unravels that in case of the child workers who have either been illiterate (23.38%) or educated upto primary level (23.31%), the largest single group has been of the view that education should be compulsory and reality-oriented. In the category of child workers educated upto middle school, the largest single group (29.99%) has been in favour of reality-oriented education. Among those who have been educated upto High School, the largest number (29.95%) has advocated compulsory education. The child workers educated upto Intermediate have in largest number (33.33%) preferred compulsory and reality-oriented education. Thus, by and large, the child workers have advocated compulsory and reality-oriented education, irrespective of their educational status.

Satisfaction from Different Aspects of Working Conditions and Conditions of Work

Information collected from the child workers regarding their satisfaction from different aspects of working conditions and conditions of work has shown that majority of the child workers have been satisfied from nature of work (92.50%), behaviour of employer (88.75%), supervision of work (88.75%), wages (72.05%), rest-hours (80.00%) and status as compared to other workers (90.00%). It has been with facilities available at work place (66.25%) and leave with wages (100.00%) that the child workers expressed great dissatisfaction which is natural as there is hardly any facility which is made available to them at work place, and leave with wages are totally absent.

Suitability of Work

Children engaged in agriculture perform a wide variety of works ranging from light to heavy in their nature. Some of them are more harmful that other. Some of them can be performed by more grown up children only. Data gathered from the child workers regarding their opinion towards suitability of their work from different angles reveal that majority of them have considered their work as suitable from the point-of-view of sex only (59.20%). From the standpoint of age (51.80%), physical growth (54.20%) and mental development (52.60%), majority of the child workers have considered their work as unsuitable. From the point-of-view of education which is of utmost importance for their age-group, the largest number of child workers (42.60%) have again thought their work as unsuitable. It can, therefore, be maintained that either majority or the largest single group of child workers have considered their present work as unsuitable from all angles except sex.

5

CHILD LABOUR IN THE THIRD WORLD COUNTRIES

The first point of reference to any discussion on international action concerning child labour is the Declaration of the Rights of the Child proclaimed by the United Nations General Assembly on 20th November 1959 (Annexure 1). The following principles enunciated by the United Nations through this Declaration relate to child labour.

Principle 2

The child shall enjoy special protection, and shall be given opportunities and facilities to enable him to develop physically, mentally, morally, spiritually and socially in a healthy and normal manner and in conditions of freedom and digrtity.

Principle 4

The child shall enjoy the benefits of social security. He shall be entitled to grow and develop in health.... The child shall have the right to adequate nutrition, housing, recreation and medical services.

Principle 9

The child shall be protected against all forms of neglect, cruelty and exploitation. He shall not be the subject of traffic, in any form .... The child shall not be admitted to employment before an appropriate minimum age; he shall in no case be caused or permitted to engage in any occupation or employment which would prejudice his health or education, or interfere with his physical, mental or moral development.

International Labour Organisation (ILO) also has declared its commitment to protection of the child in the preamble to its constitution. Abolition of child labour has been one of its basic aims since its establishment. At the same time, it has pursued a systematic policy of protection of children at work from undesirable working conditions.

The activities of the ILO in this area fall under three main headings: (1) Prohibition and limitation of child labour in the framework of international instruments concerning minimum age of admission to employment. (2) Protection of children at work through regulation and supervision of working conditions. (3) Development of fitness for work through pre-vocational training. One of the principal ways of ILO has-been to adopt international labour standards. In addition ILO has also contributed to the cause through study and research as well as technical assistance.

The ILO has adopted several conventions and made special recommendations concerning minimum age, working conditions, and medical examination of child labour. There are several others relating to health and safety of workers also.

1) *Minimum Age*

The supplementary convention on the abolition of slavery and the Slave Trade (1956) prohibits the use of child labour as slaves. The convention, suggests that each state should take appropriate practicable and necessary legislative and other measures to bring about complete abolition of trading of children below the age of 18 years. The convention on Economics, Social and Cultural Rights imposes a general prohibition on such employment of children which leads to their economic and social exploitation. When their employment is harmful to their morals or health, or dangerous to life or likely to hamper their normal development, it should be punishable by law. States should also let age limits below which children should not be employed.

The first instrument setting a minimum age for admission to employment was in Convention 5 (Industry) adopted at the first session in 1919. This convention prohibited employment of children under 14 years of age in industry. ILO subsequently adopted several other conventions/recommendations fixing minimum age standards for admission to employment in various occupations such as on sea (1920), agriculture (1921), trimmers and Strokers (1932), non-industrial employment (1936 and 1953), coal mines (1953), fisherman (1959) and underground work (1965).

In 1973, the ILO adopted the Minimum Age Convention No. 138 with a view to achieving the total abolition of child labour and aimed at replacing the existing instruments applicable to limited sectors. This convention requires each state "to pursue a national policy designed to ensure the effective abolition of child labour and to raise progressively the minimum age for admission to employment or work to a level consistent with the fullest physical and mental development of young persons." The members are called upon to specify a minimum age for employment which should not be less then the age of completion of compulsory schooling, that is, 15 years and gradually not less than 18 years. The convention, provides that these age limits may be lowered where the economic and educational facilities are insufficiently developed, but such countries are required to report their gradual progress in the matter. The convention also provides that a country may allow employment in dangerous work from the age of 16 years if the health, safety and morals of the young persons are fully protected and that the young persons have received adequate training. This convention does not apply to work done by children in school as a part of education or training, and also allows for children's (13 to 15) years of age employment in light work which is not likely to arm their health and development, or their education. Though the convention allows for exceptions and relaxations to the countries where economic and administrative development is not adequate, it lays down that certain minimum categories of employment must be covered if a state government decides to ratify the conventions. These are mining and quarrying, manufacturing, construction, electricity, gas and water, sanitary services, transport, storage and communication, plantations and other agricultural undertaking producing for commercial purposes.

In 1973, the ILO also adopted the minimum age Recommendation No. 146, to supplement the Convention No. 138. This recommendation invites states to give high priority to planning for meeting the needs of children and youth in national development policies and programmes and recommends progressive raising of the minimum age to 16 years. The recommendation also requires that the types of employment or work should be reexamined periodically in the light of advancing scientific and technological knowledge to determine the types of employment or work to which the convention applies.

2) Working Conditions

The abolition of child labour is a long-term objective. In the meantime, it is necessary to protect child labour against abuse and exploitation. The ILO has therefore adopted a number of conventions and recommendations which regulate the working conditions of children when it is not possible to ban their employment altogether. These are: (a) conventions prohibiting night work by children and young persons in industry (1919; 1948), agriculture (1921), non-industrial occupations (1946), and on sea (1958) as well as corresponding recommendations; (b) conventions prohibiting the employment of children and young persons in certain categories of hazardous work such as, lead poisoning (1919), white lead painting (1921), radiation (1960), ground work (1965), maximum weight convention (1967), and benzene convention (1971), and, (c) instruments making provision for stricter standards for young workers with regard to hours of work, weekly rest, paid holidays and apprenticeship, such as, utilisation of spare time recommendation (1924), holidays with pay recommendation (1936, 1952 and 1954), apprenticeship recommendation (1939), weekly rest recommendation (1957), and reduction of hours of work recommendation (1962).

The convention concerning the night work of young persons industry defines the term night as the period of at least 12 consecutive hours including the interval between 10 p.m. and 6 a.m. for children under 16 years of age and the period including an interval of at least seven hours falling between 10 p.m. and 7 a.m. for children between 16 and 18 years of age. However, night work may be allowed by competement authorities for children between 16 and 18 years of age for purpose of apprenticeship or vocational training in specified industries or occupations which are required to be carried on continuously. The convention concerning night work in non-industrial occupations, lays down that children under 14 years of age who are still subject to full time compulsory school attendance shall not be employed for night work, and children between 14 and 18 years of age also shall not be employed for night work and non-industrial occupations.

3) Medical Examinations

Convention No. 77 concerning medical examinations of young persons industry (1946) lays down that young persons under 18 years of age shall not be admitted to employment unless they have been found fit through a medical examination. This fitness shall be subject to regular medical supervision. In occupations which involve high health risks, medical examination and re-examination for fitness for employment shall be required until at least the age of 21 years. The convention also requires that appropriate measures be taken for vocational guidance and physical and vocational rehabilitation of children who are found medically unsuited for certain jobs. There are similar provisions about medical examination in the convention for non-industrial occupations and the convention for underground work in mines. Recommendation No. 125 requires that young persons employed or to be employed underground in mines should be given practical and theoretical instructions: (1) in the health and safety hazards of the work, (2) in hygiene and first aid, and (3) in the precautions to be taken to safeguard health and safety. This recommendation also requires that young persons under 18 years of age working underground in mines should be entitled to an uninterrupted weekly rest which should be for at least 36 hours, and to an annual holiday of not less than 24 working days excluding public and customary holidays, and they should also be entitled to sick leave.

Recommendation No. 4 concerning the protection of women and children against lead poisoning requires that pregnant women and women under 18 years of age should be excluded from employment in certain specified processes. Convention No. 13 prohibits the employment of young persons under 18 years of age and all females in any painting work of an industrial character involving the use of white lead sulphate of lead or other products containing these pigments. Convention No. 115 requires that children under 16 years of age shall not be engaged in work involving radiation, and for other workers appropriate levels of radiation should be fixed. Convention No. 127 requires that no worker shall be permitted to engage in the manual transport of lead which is likely to jeopardise his health or safety. It also requires that the women and young persons shall be banned from manual transport of lead other than light lead. Convention No. 136 lays down that young persons under 18 years of age shall not work in processes dealing with benzene or products containing benzene. Recommendation No. 21 concerning utilisation of spare time requires institutions to be established for the physical development of children and for encouraging initiative and the spirit of emulation. Recommendation No. 47 concerning annual holidays with pay recommends holidays with pay for young workers under 18 years of age. Recommendation No. 103 concerning weekly rest (commerce and offices) requires that children under 13 years of age should be granted a weekly rest of two days. Recommendation No. 116 states that while reducing working hours priority should be given to industries and occupations which involve physical and mental strain and health risks for women and young persons.

In the international year of the child in 1979 the ILO adopted a recollection concerning the progressive elimination of child labour and transitional measures calling upon member states to strengthen their effort for the elimination of child labour and for the protection of children. It expresses deep concern that the working children work under conditions detrimental to their health and welfare. It recognises the need to ensure that the health and strength and the tender age of children are not abused and that children are not permitted to enter avocations unsuited to their age of strength. (Annexure 2)

Limitation of ILO Efforts

A study of these conventions and recommendations of the ILO shows that though a few of them are relating to agricultural and non-industrial occupations, they are mainly concerned with industrial employment. In other words they are more relevant to industrialised countries than to others. In a country like India where bulk of the work-force is in agriculture their relevance is very much limited. It may not be wrong to say that these conventions and recommendations have been framed and adopted with reference to the conditions prevalent in the industrialised countries and not much thought has been given to the needs of child labour in non-industrialised countries.

Adoption of these conventions and recommendations does not mean that these are enforced in all the member countries. These conventions can come into force only after their ratification by the concerned national governments. If a convention is not ratified its status is that of a recommendation which by its very nature is not mandatory. A state may enforce it fully or partly or may not enforce it at all. Table 1 shows the number of countries who have ratified the various conventions concerning child labour (as on 1-1-1986). Table 1 shows that out of the total of 162 member countries only a small number has ratified most of the conventions. The Committee of Experts on the application of conventions and recommendations has aptly noted the application of Convention No. 138 and Recommendation No. 146 that: "it is an inescapable fact that children work in most countries and in most regions, and that too many in violation of international standards and of national law .... of the total of 55 million child labour majority violate the international standards and national laws." It is also argued by experts that this figure of 55 million is a gross underestimation of the real size of the phenomenon. It seems that there is a great distance to be travelled before the objectives stated in Article 1 of Convention No. 138 are realised: "To ensure effective abolition of child labour and to raise progressively the minimum age for employment to a level consistent with the fullest physical and mental development of young persons.

Indeed, the Committee of Experts was struck by the fact that the goals laid down in Convention 138 are still very distant goals. In many cases the governments are simply unable to arrest child labour because of the extreme poverty of these countries. What measures can be taken to abolish child labour from these poor countries? It is apparent that there are certain sectors and areas where the incidence of child labour is high. These areas should be identified by investigations and specific efforts should be made, with the assistance of the ILO and other international agencies to undertake development programmes there. It will be necessary to conduct pilot programmes to determine what measurers are most effective. In addition, and equally important, national government should not delay the adoption of legislation, in accordance with international standards wherever possible, until they consider that the problem has already been resolved in practice. The ILO's experience demonstrates that the adoption of standards can in itself serve as an important impetus to the achievement of the objectives they represent. As economic development continues, and as labour administrations gradually are able to extend their effectiveness, these laws can be applied to wider areas and to more sectors of the national economy.

TABLE 35.1

Convention No.	*Name*	*No. of ratifications*
5.	Minimum age (industry)	50
6.	Night work of young persons.	48
7.	Minimum age (sea)	34
10.	Minimum age (agriculture)	32
15.	Minimum age (trimmers and stokers)	47
16.	Medical examination of young persons (SEA).	70
13.	Minimum age (non-industrial employment).	19
59.	Minimum age (industry revised).	20
60.	Minimum age (non-industrial employment).	1
77.	Medical examination (young persons) industry.	38
78.	Medical examination-young persons (non-industrial occupations).	34
79.	Night work of young persons (non-industrial employment).	16
90.	Night work of young persons (industry) (revised).	41
123.	Minimum age (undesired work).	32
138.	Minimum age.	33

The Committee has emphasised the crucial importance of consultations with the organisations of employers and workers in formulating measures to achieve the goals of these ILO instruments. Their involvement and acceptance of the aim of eliminating child labour will both lessen the burdens of government supervision and provide another example of the great potential in responsible tripartism. Voluntarism is no substitute for government responsibility; it may however be an effective supplement and spur to such action.

The fact that children are working, an are suffering because of it, is too important a problem to be set aside wholly until economic conditions can be improved to the point where it will no longer be necessary or profitable for children to work. However, as International Labour Conference felt, child labour cannot be abolished and controlled all at once and it must remain an objective for many countries for many years to come. But these countries should begin to take suitable measures at once so that the evil is eradicated in the long run. As it has often been said, "a nation's children are its future and they are the future of all mankind."

There has undoubtedly been a great deal of legislative activity with respect of child labour for which the ILO with the large number of conventions and recommendations on the subject has given a lead. But there is not enough information about the utility and effectiveness of the legislations. It has been recognised that applied research is urgently needed to determine whether or not these legislations had much impact on the extent and type of child work. It is said that an effective policy design in general requires an understanding of the roles of children within a broad social framework.[1] There have been few analyses of the economic role of children in the process of socio-economic transformation and economic development, that is, attempts to understand the causes, functions and consequences of child work as opposed to descriptions of its manifestations. The very failure of legislation to reduce child labour substantively in much of the world raises basic questions about the effectiveness of a purely legislative approach. It should therefore not be surprising if one is sceptical about the practical utility of these Conventions.

Categories of Child Labour

Child labour falls broadly under the following types[2]: (1) domestic work, (2) non-domestic, non-monetary work, (3) tied or bonded labour, (4) wage labour, (5) marginal semi-economic activities, and (6) others. The conventions and recommendations adopted by the ILO concern mainly wage labour although bulk of the children at work are employed in other types of activities. Some of the conventions also specifically exclude children's work in domestic occupations or in school as a part of the school curriculum. The scope of the conventions is therefore very limited.

It is said that child labour is exploited specially in carpet weaving, glass beading, diamond cutting etc. Unfortunately there is no convention or recommendation with respect to these industries. There is an obvious need for international standards for regulating working conditions in such industries.

The conventions and recommendations are concentrated mainly in the minimum age for employment and conditions of work for child labour. However, there is no instrument regarding social security for child labour. A child goes or is sent to work either because he or she has no one to look after him or her, or, because his or her parents or guardians are not able to look after the child. In the circumstances, the only consequence of abolition of child labour without providing an alternative means of livelihood and education would be starvation and death. While the "declaration of the rights of the child" requires that the child be protected against all forms of neglect, cruelty and exploitation, the measures adopted by the ILO, if strictly enforced without complimentary measures, are only likely to subject the child to greater neglect, cruelty and exploitation. It does not seem that such possible consequences of implementing the international standards in the developing countries have been given due consideration. It seems therefore necessary that before abolishing child labour the state should consider the need to provide an alternative means of livelihood to the children. One such means would be to establish orphanages, homes or hostels at state expense for the maintenance of the destitute and delinquent children and to provide them adequate nutrition, housing, recreation and medical facilities through such institutions. This is the basic function of social security. Regrettably the ILO has not thought of adopting an instrument on this subject.

Considering the magnitude of child labour in the developing countries it is a moot question whether they can be maintained at the state expenses. At the same time considering that a large proportion of the population in these countries live below the poverty line it should also be realised that the poor families find it necessary to send their children to work and to supplement their income. In the circumstances total abolition of child labour may not be a practical proposition in the third world and it is also not enough to protect child labour against unsatisfactory work conditions. It is necessary therefore to provide adults with employment and minimum living conditions. The programmes for the welfare of child labour should be dovetailed with those for adults as such.

Gerry Rodgers and Guy Standing have stated:[3] "Where child labour does have adverse effects - and in terms of personal development and social differentiation these are often serious - they can usually be traced to the socio-economic framework within which children work as much as to the work itself. Thus the suppression of child wage labour opportunities is unlikely to increase the welfare of the children concerned unless substitute income sources and alternative possibilities for personal development are developed at the same time. Action towards child work must be sympathetically oriented towards the need and perceptions of the children themselves. It must also be based on a thorough understanding of the motivations behind child work, its functions, and the individual gains from it, whether for the children themselves or for others who benefit from their work."

It seems to me that there has been a failure to develop substitute income sources and alternative possibilities for personal development in dealing with the child labour at the level of the UN or the ILO. Elias Sendelievich in his article on Child Labour[4] has made certain suggestions for improving the position of working children. He argues that child labour is only one of the unacceptable facets of a much broader socio-economic and cultural situation rooted in poverty, backwardness and the retrograde attitudes typical of underdevelopment. To combat it and at the same time to attack the circumstances that give rise to it, it will be necessary to take a number of concrete measures:

1) Within the framework of socio-economic development there is an urgent need to promote the programme of action for basic needs adopted in 1976 by ILO's World Employment Conference. The programme aims at ensuring adequate food, shelter and clothing for all, as well as basic services for the community at large. It also calls for prohibition of child labour and providing training and education for children.
2) Efforts to enforce legislation prohibiting child labour should be supplemented with measures of attacking poverty directly and compulsory primary education.
3) Provision should be made for the grant of allowances to low-income families who can prove that their children are not working and are attending school.
4) Measures to extend compulsory schooling to all should be strengthened. The content of education should be adopted to local needs and should comprise practical elements including vocational training and general cultural values.
5) In rural areas the school year should be organised with a view to the agriculture production cycle so that children can help their parents by doing light tasks for short periods without having to miss school.
6) The national economic policies should be aimed not merely at increasing GNP but bringing about equitable distribution of incomes.
7) Trade unions should take interest in the problems of child labour and should make efforts for the gradual elimination of the evil.
8) Tax deductions, subsidies and other inducements should be given to those employers who can show that they have improved the working conditions of their child employees.
9) Information campaigns should be organised to make people aware of the harmful effects of child labour and to explain then the possible alternatives. Governments should launch publicity campaigns using posters, leaflets, etc.
10) Research institutes should also undertake studies on the effects on the life and health of children of each of the occupations in which there is a preponderance of child labour.

It seems to me that the above suggestions are unexceptionable and that the existing policies and programme at the national as well as international levels need to be redesigned accordingly.

REFERENCES

1. Rodgers Gerry and Gay Standing, (eds.) *Child Work, Poverty and Underemployment.*
2. *Ibid.*
3. "Economic roles of Children Issues for Analysis. *In* Gerry Rodgers and Gay Standing (eds).*Child Work Poverty and Underdevelopment.*
4. Child Labour, *International Labour Review,* Sep.-Oct., 1979.

ANNEXURE-1

DECLARATION OF THE RIGHTS OF THE CHILD

Proclaimed by the United Nations General Assembly on 20 November 1959 (Resolution XIV)

Preamble

Whereas the people of the United Nations have, in the Charter, reaffirmed their faith in fundamental human rights and in the dignity and worth of the human person, and have determined to promote social progress and better standards of life in larger freedom.

Whereas the United Nations has, in the Universal Declaration of Humans Rights, proclaimed that everyone is entitled to all the rights and freedoms set forth therein, without distinction of any kind, such as race, colour, sex, language, religion, political or other opinion, national or social origin, property, birth or other status.

Whereas the child, by reason of his physical and mental immaturity, needs special safeguards and care, including appropriate legal protection, before as well as after birth.

Whereas the need for such special safeguards has been stated in the Geneva Declaration of the Rights of the child of 1924, and recognised in the Universal Declaration of Human Rights and in the statutes of specialised agencies and international organisations concerned with the welfare of children.

Whereas mankind owes to the child the best it has to give, Now therefore,

The General Assembly

Proclaims this Declaration of the Rights of the Child to the end that he may have a happy childhood and enjoy for his own good and for the good of society the rights end freedoms herein set forth, and calls upon parents, upon men and women as individuals, and upon voluntary organisations, local authorities and national governments to recognise these rights and strive for their observance by legislative and other measures progressively taken in accordance with the following principles:

PRINCIPLE 1

The child shall enjoy all the rights set forth in his Declaration. Every child, without any exception whatsoever, shall be entitled to these rights, distinction or discrimination on account or race, colour, sex, language, religion, political or other opinion, national or social origin, property, birth or other status, whether of himself or of his family.

PRINCIPLE 2

The child shall enjoy special protection, and shall be given opportunities and facilities, by law and by other means, to enable him to develop physically, mentally, morally, spiritually and socially in a healthy and normal manner and in conditions of freedom and dignity. In the enactment of laws for this purpose, the best interests of the child shall be the paramount consideration.

PRINCIPLE 3

The child shall be entitled from his birth to a name and a nationality.

PRINCIPLE 4

The child shall enjoy the benefits of social security. He shall be entitled to grow and develop in health ; to this end, special care and protection shall be provided both to him and to his mother, including adequate pre-natal and post-natal, care. The child shall have the right to adequate nutrition, housing, recreation and medical services.

PRINCIPLE 5

The child who is physically, mentally or socially handicapped shall be given the special treatment, education and care required by his particular condition.

PRINCIPLE 6

The child, for the full and harmonious development of his personality, needs love and understanding. He shall, wherever possible, grow up in the care and under the responsibility of his parents, and in any case, in an atmosphere of affection and of moral and material security a child of tender years shall not, save in exceptional circumstances be separated from his mother.

Society and the public authorities shall have the duty to extent particular care to children without a family and to those without adequate means of support. Payment of state and other assistance towards the maintenance of children of large families is desirable.

PRINCIPLE 7

The child is entitled to receive education, which shall be free and compulsory, at least in the elementary stages. He shall be given an education which will promote his general culture, and enable him on a basis of equal opportunity, to develop his abilities, his individual judgment, and his sense of moral and social responsibility, and to become a useful member of society.

The best interests of the child shall be the guiding principle of those responsible for his education and guidance ; that responsibility lies in the first place with his parents.

The child shall have full opportunity for play and recreation, which should be directed to the same purposes as education; society and the public authorities shall endeavour to promote the enjoyment of this right.

PRINCIPLE 8

The child shall in all circumstances be among the first to receive protection and relief.

PRINCIPLE 9

The child shall not be protected against all forms of neglect, cruelty and exploitation. He shall not be the subject of traffic, in any form.

The child shall not be admitted to employment before appropriate minimum age; he shall in no case be caused or permitted to engage in any occupation or employment which would prejudice his health or education, or interfere with his physical, mental or moral development.

PRINCIPLE 10

The child shall be protected from practices which may foster racial, religious and any other form of discrimination. He shall be brought up in a spirit of understanding, tolerance, friendship among people, peace and universal brotherhood, and in full consciousness that his energy and talents should be devoted to the service of his fellow men.

ANNEXURE-2

RESOLUTION CONCERNING THE INTERNATIONAL YEAR OF THE CHILD AND THE PROGRESS OF ELIMINATION OF CHILD LABOUR AND TRANSITIONAL MEASURES

The General Conference of the International Labour Organisation, Recalling resolution 31/169 adopted by the United National General Assembly, proclaiming 1979 as the International Year of the Child, with the general objectives of promoting the well-being of children, drawing attention to their special needs and encouraging national action on behalf of children particularly for the least privileged and those who are at work.

Noting the activities that were undertaken at the national, regional and international levels in preparation for the International year of the child and the Progress made since.

Convinced that the International Year of the Child provides for all members states an opportunity to review their economic and social policies concerning the child welfare and to formulate guidelines in this sphere.

Considering that a new and fair international economic order would greatly contribute towards genuine economic and social development, primarily of benefit to children.

Recalling the endorsement by the ILO of the aims of the International Year of the Child and its pledge to make every effort and lend all support to members states for their earliest possible fulfilment.

Recalling the United Nations Declaration of the Right of the Child, 1959 and particularly Principle 9, which, stipulates that the child should be protected against all forms of neglect, cruelty and exploitation; that he should not be admitted to employment before an appropriate minimum age ; and that he should in no case be caused or permitted to engage in any occupation or employment which would prejudice his health or education, or interfere with his physical, mental or moral development.

Concerning that since its foundation the International Labour Organisation has sought to eliminate child labour and to provide protection for children.

Noting with approval the Director General's Declaration on the International Year of the Child, deeply concerned that child labour still remains widespread in many parts of the world and that working children frequently work under conditions including those of exploitation detrimental to their health and welfare; recognising the need to ensure that the health and strength and the tender age of children are not abused and that children are not permitted to enter avocations unsuited to their age or strength, considering that the International Year of the Child should be an occasion to raffirm with practical measures and deeds the well-being of today's children, is the concern or all people everywhere.

Recalling the decision of the governing body of the International Labour Office, taken at its twentieth session (November 1978), to request the member states to supply a report in 1980 under article 19 of the Constitution on the extent to which effect has been given or is proposed to be given to the Minimum Age Convention (No. 138) and Recommendation (No. 146) of 1973:

1. Calls upon member states to strengthen their efforts for the elimination of child labour and for the protection of children, and in this context:

a) to implement the provisions of the Minimum Age Convention, 1973 (No. 138), and, where they have not already done so, to ratify this convention as early as practicable;

b) to ensure in particular full recognition of the principle that any work undertaken by children who have not completed their compulsory education shall not be such as would prejudice their education or development;

c) to apply the Minimum Age Recommendation, 1973 (No. 146), and the Minimum Age (Underground Work) Recommendation, 1965 (No. 124);

d) to report in detail in 1980 under the procedure of article 19 of the Constitution on the progress reached in the implementation of the Minimum Age Convention (No. 138) and Recommendation (No. 146), 1973;

e) pending the elimination of child labour, to take all necessary social and legislative action for the progressive elimination of child labour and during the transitional period until the elimination of child labour, to regulate and humanise it and to give particular attention to the implementation of special standards for children relating to medical examination, night work, underground work, working hours, weekly rest, paid annual leave and certain types of hazardous and dangerous work embodied in a number of ILO instruments;

f) to make every effort to extend the provisions of appropriate educational facilities, in order fully to apply compulsory education and to introduce it where it does not exist and where education is compulsory, to make it effective;

g) to ensure that appropriate protective labour legislation applies to all children at work in the sectors of activity in which they are employed;

h) to ensure that special attention is given to the provision of fair remuneration and to its protection for the benefit of the child;

i) to strengthen, where appropriate, labour inspection and to undertake all other measures conducive to the elimination of child labour;

j) (i) to identify the special needs of children, to strengthen efforts to improve the general economic and social well-being of the family, and to launch a national campaign aimed at creating awareness among the general public of the adverse effects of child labour on his/her development; and (ii) to develop international solidarity and cooperation with the developing countries and to activate efforts to establish a new and fair international economic order so as to respond more effectively to the basic measures undertaken by each state for better child protection.

2. Calls upon governments and employers and workers organisations to assess the situation of child work and to assist the competent bodies and the ILO to strengthen their action programme for children.

3. Invites the governing body of the International Labour Office to instruct the director-general to continue and reinforce the ILO's action through such means as factual surveys of national situations and practices for the elimination of child labour and for the protection of children at work, and to make the necessary preparations for the global revision of the relevant ILO instruments.

ANNEXURE-3

POLICY AND PROGRAMMES OF THE GOVERNMENT OF INDIA IN THE FIELD OF CHILD LABOUR

Background

The Government of India has been deeply concerned about the problem of child labour. Children are the most important asset of a society, and future of a nation depends upon how the children are educated and trained and how their physical and mental development is taken care of. It is indeed unfortunate that the energy of the growing children which should go into their physical and mental growth and development, is exploited by the owners of capital assets owing to unfavourable socio-economic setting in the country. The exploitation tells upon their health education, overall personality development and future career. Unless something is done to help them, they will not come out of a vicious cycle of drudgery and poverty, which has bene going on generation after generation.

The Nature and Magnitude of the Problem

According to 1971 Census, the number of child wage earners was 10.75 million representing 4.66 per cent of the total labour force. As per the estimates of the Planning Commission (on the basis of National Sample Survey) the number of child wage earners between the ages of five and 14 years was 17.36 million on 1st March 1983 and 17.58 million on 1st March, 1985. The proportion of child workers, either to the total child population, or to the total work-force, does not appear to have increased, over the last 15 years. As a matter of fact, according to the 1981 Census, based on a 5 per cent sample date, the number of child workers in the age group of 0 to 14 years was 4.24 per cent of the total child population. The comparable figures for other countries are much higher.

Also, according to the study entitled "Child Labour: A Threat to Health and Development" by Defence for Children International, Geneva, the ratio of working children to the total working population was 38 per cent for Turkey in 1975 (age group 12 to 14 years), 45 per cent for Mali in 1975 (age group 10 to 14 years), 44 per cent for Bhutan in 1975 (age group 10 to 14 years), 32 per cent for Bangladesh (age group 10 to 14 years) and 30 per cent for Tanzania (age group 10 to 14 years). The corresponding figure for India is 20 per cent for the same year. Thus, the incidence of child labour, judged by these percentages, does not appear to be alarmingly high in India in comparison with other developing countries.

The 1971 Census reveals that about 87 per cent of child labour is in agriculture and allied activities, and about 93.65 per cent is in the non-organised sector of employment. Only 6 per cent work in manufacturing, processing, serving, repairs, etc.

Causes of Child Labour and its Exploitation

One of the most important issues of child labour is poverty and unemployment. In addition to the visible unemployment, there is a substantial disguised unemployment particularly in the unorganised and rural areas which compells every member of the family, including children, to work to supplement the family income. Large family size also becomes a motivating factor for the parents to send their children to work. Moreover, lack of awareness and lack of educational facilities, also make the children work for want of anything better. Sometimes, when parents do not see a bright future even after education, they want their children to start early in life and get used to it. In addition, orphanhood, parental rejection, broken family, disabled parents and similar other situations in which the child has none to take care of are also the causes of child labour. And then employers generally prefer child labour, because of their sharp reflexes, greater efficiency in repetitive and fine operations, vigour and energy and because they can take advantage of their docile nature and physical weakness.

Strategy for Administrative Action

Government of India has formulated its strategy for administrative action keeping in mind the following aspects of the problem (a) The conditions of work are more exploitative in cases where children work on wage employment, rather than where they work along with their family members, in their own houses. (b) Looking at the socio-economic conditions at present it is not possible to eliminate child labour in all the sectors of employment, but it is imperative to do so in factories, mines and other employments which are hazardous for children. (c) Where it is not practicable to prohibit employment of children (the non-hazardous employments), efforts must be made to protect and regulate their conditions of work so that they get due protection of labour laws, and in particular, are assured of a reasonable wage, and minimum working hours. (d) It is also necessary to provide these children welfare inputs like non- formal education and vocational training for skill development and health care and supplementary nutrition for proper physical and mental development. (e) Even where child employment is prohibited under the law (for example, hazardous employments), it may be necessary to suitably rehabilitate the children removed from work; otherwise, their families may face hardship due to a fall in the family income or children may go back to work. (0 Efforts must be made to cover all the adults under the programmes ensuring income and employment generation, education, health and nutrition, and vocational training, in areas of concentration of child labour.

Legal Position

Article 24 of the Indian Constitution lays down that no child below the age of 14 years shall be employed in any factory or mine, or engaged in any other hazardous employment. Further, the Directive Principles of our Constitution urge that: (a) the government should see that health of workers including child workers and the tender age of children are not abused, and that citizens are not forced by economic necessity to enter a vocation unsuited to their age or strength; and (b) the childhood and youth is protected against exploitation and against moral and material abandonment.

Government of India has passed a number of legislations banning or regulating the working conditions of child labour (Appendix 1). The recent Act, namely, Child Labour (Prohibition and Regulation) Act, 1986 however is a comprehensive act which. prohibits employment of children under 14 years in specified occupations and processes, and regulates the conditions of work of children in employments where they are not prohibited from working. The Act also provides for a Child Labour Technical Advisory Committee to advise the government regarding banning child labour in different occupations and processes. The Committee is expected to examine all occupations and processes where children work and determine which are hazardous for children. After this exercise is over, child labour will be prohibited from all hazardous occupations. In the remaining occupations and processes, the working conditions will be regulated in a phased manner. The Act also provides for framing rules for the health and safety of the children employed in permitted employments and for severe penalties for their violation and for violation of the relevant portions of the Factories Act, 1948, the Mines Act, 1950, the Merchant and Shipping Act, 1951, and the Motor Transport Workers Act, 1950.

National Policy on Child Labour

Mere legislation, however, is not enough to cope with the problem. Therefore, a National Policy on Child Labour has been framed by the government to take care of the administrative and welfare aspects. The main features of the National Child Labour Policy are as follows:

1) It will be ensured that the legal provisions pertaining to prohibition of child labour in hazardous employments, regulation of their conditions of work in other employments, and provisions pertaining to health, safety, welfare amenities and other benefits are strictly implemented so that child labour does not live at the mercy of the employers under highly exploitative and inhuman conditions.

2) Ten specific projects will be undertaken in areas of concentration of child labour: (i) Ensuring that all the poor families from which child workers come, are covered by the income and employment generation programmes. This will enable them to cross the poverty line. In addition to the funds of the existing programmes additional funds will be spent in these areas, to cover all the families in three years. (ii) The programmes pertaining to education, vocational training, health and nutrition will be strengthened in the project areas. (iii) Special schools will be opened to rehabilitate the children removed from the prohibited (employments and to provide welfare inputs to the children working in the permitted employments. The schools for rehabilitation of child labour will provide non-formal education, supplementary nutrition and vocational training, along with a stipend so as to compensate the loss of income to their family. The schools for the working children however will be part-time running on holiday's or after hours, etc. and will not contain an element of stipend. The courses for non-formal

education and skill development programmes will have to be drawn up very carefully keeping in view the needs of the children, their aptitude and the local situation.

3. The programmes of education, health, medical care, supplementary nutrition as well as of income and employment generation for the parents of child labour are most relevant in the context of the problem of child labour. If these programmes are implemented well, the problem of child labour will be eliminated gradually.

Micro-projects Implemented by Voluntary Agencies

Under the Scheme, a number of voluntary agencies have taken up projects in different areas to provide welfare inputs to the working children, or to children removed from employment. The Central Government has launched a pilot project in the match industry area of Sivakasi, Tamil Nadu, which utilises inputs from various voluntary agencies. Another pilot project of a similar nature is about to be launched in the Varanasi District of Uttar Pradesh for the working children in the carpet weaving industry. These two pilot projects in major areas of concentration of child labour, and a number of isolated projects taken up by the voluntary agencies with the assistance of the Central Government are likely to provide useful guidance for further action. Government intends to cover all major centres of concentration of child labour gradually.

The problem of child labour is a very complex one. In addition to the legislative and administrative action of the government, involvement of voluntary organisations, social groups and trade unions is absolutely indispensable. Also, the society in general will have to be conscious against the social evil.

ANNEXURE-4

IMPORTANT RELEVANT PORTIONS OF THE INDIAN CONSTITUTION AND LEGISLATIONS PERTAINING TO CHILD LABOUR

Indian Constitution: Article 24 of the Indian Constitution lays down: No child below the age of 14 years shall be employed to work in any factory or mine or engaged in any other hazardous employment."

Article 39 (c) lays down that : "The health, strength of workers, man and woman and the tender age of children are not abused and that citizens are not forced by economic necessity to enter a vocation unsuited to their age or strength."

Article 39(f) proclaims: "That childhood and youth are protected against exploitation and against moral and material abandonment."

Legislations: With a view to eradicate the problems of child labour, the following two legislations have been enacted regulating the employment of children:

A. The children (Pledging of Labour) Act, 1933: The Act defines 'child' as a person who is under the age of 15 years. The act prohibits the making of agreements to pledge the labour of children and the employments of children whose labour has been pledged. The act also lays down that any agreements or contracts to pledge the labour of a child is void and imposes penalties on any such agreement or employment of a pledged child.

The Child Labour (Prohibition and Regulation) Act, 1986 which is reproduced as Annexure.

Several other legislations and acts have laid down special provisions and clauses pertaining to the employment of children.

I. The 'Child" is defined a follows in the different Acts:

1) *Beedi and Cigar Workers (Conditions of Employment)*
   Act, 1966:
   Section 2 (b): 'Child' means a person who has not completed 14 years of age.
2) *Factories Act, 1948,* and *Minimum Wages Act, 1948:*
   Section 2 (c) : 'Child' means a person who has not completed his 15 years.
3) *Mines Act, 1952:*
   Section 2(c) : 'Child' means a person who has not completed his 15 years.
4) Motor Transport Workers Act, 1961:
   Section 2 (c): 'Child' means a person who has not completed his 15 years,
5) *Plantations Labour Act, 1951:*
   Section 2(c): 'Child' means a persons who has not completed his 15 years.

II. The minimum age of employment is given in various acts as follows:

1) *Factories Act, 1948:*

   Section 67: No child who has not completed his fourteenth year shall be required or allowed to work in any factory.

2) *Mines Act, 1952:*

   Section 45: No person below 18 years of age shall be allowed to be present in any part of a mine above ground where any operation connected with or incidental to any mining operation is being carried on.

3) *Indian Merchant Shipping Act, 1958:*

   Section 109: No person under 15 years of age shall be engaged or carried to sea to work in any capacity in any ship, except —

- in a schoolship or trainingship, in accordance with the prescribed conditions; or,
- in a ship in which all persons employed are members of one family; or,
- in a home-made ship of less than 200 tons gross; or,
- where such person is to be employed on nominal wages and will be in the charge of his father or other near male adult relative.

4) *Motor Transport Workers Act, 1961:*

   Section 21: No child who has not completed his 15 years shall be required or allowed to work in any capacity.

5) *Beedi and Cigar Workers (Conditions of Employment)* Act, 1966:

   Section 24: No child who has not completed his 14 years shall be required or allowed to work in any industrial premises.

6) State Shops and Commercial Establishments Act:

   The minimum age of employment in shops and commercial establishments is 12 years in Bihar, Gujarat, Jammu and Kashmir, Madhya Pradesh, West Bengal, Goa, Daman and Diu and Manipur, and 14 years in Andhra Pradesh, Assam, Haryana, Himachal Pradesh, Kerala, Tamil Nadu, Punjab, Delhi, Chandigarh, Pondicherry and Meghalaya. The minimum age of employment is 15 years in Maharashtra. There are no separate shops and Commercial Establishments Acts in Andaman and Nicobar Islands, Arunachal Pradesh, Dadra and Nagar Haveli, Lakshadweep, Nagaland and Sikkin.

7) *Radiation Protection Rules, 1971:*

   Persons below 18 years of age cannot be employed under the Radiation Protection Rules, 1971.

8) *Apprentices Act, 1961:*

   Section 3 (a): A person shall not be qualified for being engaged as an apprentice to undergo apprenticeship training in any designated trade, unless he is not, less than 14 years of age.

9) *The Children (Pledging of Labour) Act, 1933:*
Section 3: An agreement to pledge the labour of child (below 15 years of age) shall be void.

III. Prohibition of allowing children (below the age of 14 years to 18 years) to work in hazardous occupations under the Factories Act, 1948, is given below:

1) *Factories Act, 1948*
Section 22 (2) : No young person shall be allowed to clean, lubricate or adjust any part of the prime mover or transmission machinery when in motion, or to clean, lubricate or adjust any part of machine, if the cleaning, lubrication or adjustment thereof would expose the young person to risk of injury from any moving part either of that machine or of any adjacent machinery.
Section 23 (1): No young person shall work at any machine to which this section applies unless he has been fully instructed as to the dangers arising in connection with the machine and the precautions to be observed and : (a) has received sufficient training at work on machines, or, (b) is under adequate supervision by a person who has a thorough knowledge and experience of the machine.
Section 23 (2): Sub-section (1) shall apply to such machines as may be prescribed by the (state) government, being machines which in its opinion are of such a dangerous character that young persons ought not to work at them unless the foregoing requirements are complied with.
Section 27: No child (that is, above the age of 14 years, but below the age of 15 years) shall be employed in any part of a factory for pressing cotton in which a cotton opener is at work. Provided that if the feed-end of a cotton opener is in a room separated from the delivery and by a partition extending to the roof or to such a height as the inspector may in any particular case specify in writing; children may be employed on the side of the partition where the feed-end is situated.
Section 34(2): The (state) government may make rules prescribing the maximum weights which may be lifted, carried or moved by children employed in factories or in any class or description of factories or in carrying on any specified process.

IV. The hours of work for children are regulated as follows:

1) *Factories Act, 1948:*
Section 21 (a): No child shall be employed or permitted to work in any factory for more than four and a half hours a day.

2) *Minimum Wages (Central) Rules, 1950:*
Section 24: The number of hours which shall constitute a normal working day shall be four and a half hours in case of children.

3) *Plantations Labour Act, 1951:*

   Section 19: No child shall be required or allowed to work on any plantation for more than 40 hours a week.

4) *State Shops and Commercial Establishments Acts:*

   The hours of work for young persons in shops and Commercial Establishments are seven per day in Andhra Pradesh, Bihar, Tamil Nadu, Tripura, Pondicherry and West Bengal; six per day in Gujarat, Maharashtra, Jammu and Kashmir, Uttar Pradesh and Delhi; five per day in Himachal Pradesh, Madhya Pradesh, Karnataka, Orissa and Punjab and three per day in Rajasthan.

5) *Apprentices Rules, 1962:*

   Section 8: The weekly hours of work of an apprentice while undergoing practical training shall be as follows:

- The total number of hours per week shall be 42 to 48 hours (including the time spent on related instructions).
- Apprentices undergoing basic training shall ordinarily work for 42 hours per week including the time spent on related instructions.
- Apprentices during the second year of apprentice- ship training shall work for 42 to 45 hours per week including the time spent on related instructions.
- Apprentices during the third and subsequent years of apprenticeship shall work for the same number of hours per week as the workers in trade in the establishments in which the apprentices are undergoing apprenticeship training, provided however, that short- term apprentices may be engaged to work up to a limit of 48 hours per week.

V. Children are prohibited from working at night according to the following acts:

1) *Factories Act, 1948: -*

   Section 71 (b): No child shall be employed or permitted to work in any factory during the night.

2) *Plantations Labour Act, 1951:*

   Section 25: Except with the permission of the state government, no child, worker shall be employed in any plantation otherwise than between the hours of 6 a.m. and 7 p.m.

3) *Beedi and Cigar Workers (Conditions of Employment)* Act,1966:

   Section 25: No young person shall be required or allowed to work in any industrial premises except between 6 a.m. and 7 p.m. (Young persons means a person who has completed 14 years of age but has not attained 18 years of age.)

4) *State Shops' and Commercial Establishment Acts*

Night work for children and young person is also prohibited under state laws relating to shops and commercial establishments. The children and young persons are allowed to work between 6 a.m. and 7 p.m. in Andhra Pradesh, Gujarat, Maharashtra, Tamil Nadu, Pondicherry ; 7 a.m. and 7 p.m. in Bihar, and Kerala; 7 a.m. and 9 p.m. in Jammu and Kashmir and Madhya Pradesh 6 a.m. and 8 p.m. in Karnataka; 6 a.m. and 10 p.m. in Orissa and Rajasthan, and 6. a.m. and 8 p.m. during winter and 7 a.m. and 9 p.m. during summer in Delhi. They cannot be employed after 8 p.m. in West Bengal and Tripura.

5. *Apprentices Rules, 1962*

Section 8(2): No apprentice, other than a short term apprentice, shall be engaged in such training between the hours of 10 p.m. and 6 a.m. except with the prior approval of the apprenticeship adviser who also shall give his approval if he is satisfied that it is in the interest of the training of the apprenctice or of the public interest.

6

CHILD LABOUR IN SOUTH ASIA

The problem of child labour in South Asian countries is indeed very acute, and it deserves urgent attention of policy makers, planners and others. This chapter discusses the nature of the problem and issues pertaining to polices/programmes in five countries of South Asia, namely Thailand, Philippines, Indonesia, Nepal and Sri Lanka.

THE CHILD LABOUR SITUATION IN THAILAND

During the past few decades more and more children between 11 to 14 years of age have been pushed into becoming labourers. They receive no welfare benefits and have no opportunities for recreation, protection or freedom. Their basic rights as human beings are threatened. Unfortunately few serious attempts have been made to help them. The Children's Rights prosecution centre (at the Foundation for Children) was set up to offer legal and social assistance to such children in accordance with the United Nation's Declaration of the Rights of Children and Youth. But not much has been achieved in concrete terms so far.

Definition of Child Labour

The ILO (International Labour Organisation) defined child labour to mean children below 15 who enter the labour market. Considering the crying social and economic conditions in different countries, the age has been fixed differently in different countries. What is important, however, is that children's work must not be dangerous to their health or development, and must not interfere with their education.

Why Thai Children Must Labour?

Poverty

The first and foremost cause of child labour is poverty. Thailand is an agricultural country, with 85 per cent of its people working in the agricultural sector. The average family earns a daily income of six baht (about US $ 0.23) per person. In the northeast the figure is 4.6 baht (US $ 0.17) per cent person per day (the minimum wage in Bangkok is 75 to 76 baht). This low income forces parents to send their children to work. It seems that the main causes of poverty are: depressed prices of agricultural goods and rising prices of consumer goods. Low and uncertain agriculture incomes due to limited irrigation and fluctuating rainfall and indebtedness of farmers.

Attitude of Employers in Industry and Commerce

Thai industrial growth has proceeded rapidly in the past two decades. There were about 135,000 factories in the country in 1987. Among these 5,000 factories employed less than 100 labourers. Employers prefer child labour because of their low wages, easy control, and high productivity. Also it is not necessary to pay for welfare benefits to child labour. Children are employed in the weaving, candle making, bead making, glass production and gum industries etc.

Inflow of Child Labour from Rural to Urban Areas

Rural people migrate to urban areas in search of jobs. Contractors and brokers help them and also exploit them in the process. It seems that there are three ways in which children from rural areas enter the city labour market: (1) through middlemen and brokers, or, through an employment agency; (2) on their own; and (3) through friends, relatives etc.

(1) *Through middlemen or brokers:* This was the original way of entering the Bangkok labour market. Under this system, a broker comes to the village to urge villagers to come with him to the city. There are two types of brokers who make a living by bringing child labour to Bangkok: free brokers, who know the employment agencies or factory employers who pay the children's train or bus fares and charge 300 to 400 Baht per child; and brokers under employment, who induce children who are looking for work to go with them, and get 50 to 100 Baht per child from the employment agencies. When there is a great demand for child labour, the agencies send these brokers out to the villages to find child labour.

(2) *At their own Initiative:* Sometimes children go to cities at their own initiative. In dry or unproductive years, villagers and their children go to Bangkok by themselves to seek work. These villagers frequently run into brokers at the railway station who take them to the agencies. Sometimes villagers go to the agencies themselves.

(3) *Through friends and relatives who have temporarily returned to the villages:* Children may be accompanied to Bangkok by friends or relatives who already work there but have returned to the village to present *Kathin* robes to local monks or for a *pa be* (cooperative fund-raising) ceremony. This method is safer than others, as it follows a direct route from a village to a Bangkok factory. In addition, there are no middlemen to pay in this case.

Working Conditions of Child Labourers in Thailand

Child workers invariably get less than the legal minimum wage. They receive about 200 to 400 Baht (US $ 7.50 to 15.00) per month and children under 12 do not earn more than 1,800 Baht (US $ 68) per year. Children also work fore more than 10 hours a day, without a day off. Their working conditions are usually unhealthy, work places are frequently hot, stuffy, and insufficiently lit. Children are forced to sit on cement floors for long periods, or stand up all day. Frequently, children have to lie on dirty floors and be bitten by mosquitoes, and when they get sick, they generally do not receive proper medical treatment. They are sometimes beaten up and abused also.

Our study has shown that 35 per cent of Bangkok child labour see their work as difficult, 63 per cent would like to return home because of home sickness, 37 per cent because of difficulty in the work, and 33 per cent because of trouble with employers. Some children do not want to return because the village is not a good place and there is no work for them if they go back.

However, those who stay back do not have a bright future to look forward to. Illness, handicaps (caused by accidents) and bad health are the factors contributing to the fate of most labourers. This situation has a profound effect on the bodies and minds of small children who living away from their families and struggle for existence by themselves. The working and living conditions of female child labourers in homes of the rich are even worse in may respects because such children have many bosses and have no set working schedule.

A study of by the Chulalongkorn University Social Research Institute on economic and social conditions in villages which send large numbers of children to work in Bangkok shows that child labour has some economic impact on rural villages—85 per cent of child labour are able to give some money to their families. Generally this amount is not more than 1,000 Baht per year. Most of this goes for family food and other daily expenses and for improving families' hosing. Some families receive no money at all from their children.

If children have obtained jobs through middlemen, the money that the family gets must be divided with the middlemen. And when children are beaten or when their health deteriorates, parents and guardians must spend their own money to locate and obtain treatment for them. All in all, child labour is able to solve its families' economic problems only to a very limited extent.

Attempts made at Protection of Child Labour in Thailand

A country's effort to protect the well-being of its child workers is a good yardstick of the level of concern on the part of adults towards the country's youth.

The ILO has laid down standards for member countries with respect to child labour. If we compare these standards with Thailand's, we find that Thailand's are much lower. For example, the ILO sets a lower age limit of 15 whereas in Thailand, it is 12. Also according to ILO standards, a child should work not more than six hours a day, while Thailand has no special limits for children (that is, eight hours as for adults). Thailand has passed only one child labour protection law, Revolutionary (Decree No. 103 of March 16, 1972. The essence of this law is: (1) Concerning the minimum age for child labour, employers are prohibited from hiring children under 12. (2) For hiring children between 12 and 15 prior permission from the Ministry of Labour must be taken, and these hired children can work only in commerce (except in liquor shops) in delivering newspapers, sports, packing, distributing, or delivering flowers, fruits dry foods etc. and in lifting or carrying loads which are less than 10 kg. Also, employers are prohibited from hiring children under 18 for work which endangers the health, such as, work with machinery, underground or under-water work, work with dangerous chemicals or poisonous explosives or inflammable materials and the work which involves handling radioactive substances. (3) Regulations concerning working hours say that children under 15 should work between 10 a.m. and 6 p.m. and they should have a weekly holiday. Employers violating these regulation will be imprisoned for not more than six months, or fined not more than 20,000 Baht, or both.

It seems that the protection of child labour in Thailand is not adequate. This is because: (1) the law is married by loopholes and other weaknesses (first of all, the law does not regulate wages); (2) the punishments provided for are light; (3) certain categories of child labour are not regulated at all, (for example, domestic servants or agricultural labourers). The implementation of the law is also not satisfactory because the number of government officials is too small compared to the huge number of factories to be inspected.

Towards a Solution to the Child Labour Problems in Thailand

It cannot be denied that Thailand, due to the failure of its domestic economic development plans, is facing serious economic problems. Poverty is one of the serious problems of the economy. For the time-being therefore, the elimination of child labour remains an impossibility. Nevertheless, child workers should be provided protection from exploitation. We would like to recommend the following in this context: (1) raise living standards of people; (2) improve the law through addition to clauses which are both appropriate to the Thai situation and are comparable with the ILO standards, and (3) the law should make provisions for its eventual elimination.

The law should therefore: (a) raise the lower age limit for child labours; (b) ensure better enforcement of the regulations on employers; (c) fix wages for children; (d) create an emergency fund for the welfare benefits, including education, upgrading of working conditions, rest facilities and health facilities for children; and (e) provide for more severe punishment to offenders. Attempts should also be made for educating parents and children about their rights under the law and for creating public awareness.

WORKING CHILDREN IN THE PHILIPPINES

Philippines is a beautiful and bountiful archipelago in Asia where about 20 million children are living in a state of crisis. Only in recent years hundreds have been helplessly killed by armed elements. To give an example, a 10 year old boy called Dodong Belmas was shot dead, along with others, when he was attending the funeral of a relative.

But this is not all. Millions of children are suffering, and some of them dying, due to the inhuman practice of child labour in the country. It has been estimated that about 50,000 street children are waging war against want in the metropolitan streets of the Philippines by using their small labour. They are collecting garbage, begging, washing cars, pick-pocketing, selling goods and selling themselves. Their plight becomes clear from the case of a child prostitute—Rose Baluyot. As she was the eldest of four children, she decided to sell chewing gum to U.S. servicemen in Olongapo city. Unfortunately, at the age of 10 she was raped by a pimp who introduced her to the prostitution business and two years later, she died after the doctors removed a broken vibrator that infected her uterus. The condition of the other 2000 prostitutes in Ermita area alone is no better. Our interviews with them reveal that customers beat them, hurt their bodies, or force them to take drugs. Troubled by these and by other problems like unwanted pregnancies and genital infections, they take drugs or drown themselves in a bottle of liquor. Their earnings are spent on the drugs or on expensive antibiotics. Consequently, they are addicted to both their job and the prohibited drugs.

Some children find food by foraging in the biggest dumpsites in Balut, Tondo. About 12,000 children residing at the Smoky Mountain work all day collecting refuse and eating whatever is thrown out as edibles. The majority of these children who do not even go to school, suffer from respiratory tract infection, worms, malnourishment and stunted growth. In fact, 13 million children in the Philippines cannot afford schooling. Instead, they work in the farms, in plantations, in garment factories, and even in the deep blue sea.

More than 6,000 children employed in the Muro-Ami Fishing Industry in Palawan know only the technique of driving the fish tot he big net. Three hundred of them jump into the sea, stay there for more than half an hour, and dive deep to drive the fish to the net. A child usually makes an average of 10 jumps per day and earns about 2,000 ($ 100) after 10 months of fishing in the sea. These children gradually lose colour of the hair, break ear drums and contact lung infection. Talampulan, the island near Palawan, where about 26 fishing vessels are harboured is also a graveyard of the young fishermen. Here the buried children are not identified by their names but by the name of the shipping vessels they stayed with.

Remedies

The short-term remedy of the problem is to sustain genuine organisations that work for the rights and welfare of our children and facilitate delivery of direct services to them. For example, our institutes for the protection of children, is one of them. There is also a federation of many such organisations, which is known as Salinlahi (a native word that means a generation to come).

In the long-term, however, we need to cure that ailing economy by consistently campaigning for the implementation of land reforms, and opening up of more industries by Philippino nationalists. Politically, we need a strong government that is not subservient to foreign interests in the country and is truly for the benefit of the majority of our people. And culturally, we have to learn new technology for self-management and self-determination. This needs education campaigns that will create awareness and bring about people's participation.

All these can be done if concerned groups in the Philippines are free to carry out their development activities and they continue to receive moral and technical support from other concerned people from progressive countries. For mutual development of our people and our children we should join hands so that we can reduce, if not totally eliminate, the problems of our working children.

CHILD LABOUR IN NEPAL: PROBLEMS AND PROSPECTS

Nepal is a tiny nation in the Himalaya situated between two big neighbours namely China and India. It is a country of multiracial, multi-ethnical, multi-linguistic and cultural diversifications with a population of around 17.5 million.

Nepal is regarded as one of the least developed nations and the second poorest country cf the world with more than 60 per cent people of Nepal living below the line of absolute poverty. Feudal socio-economic structure of the society coupled with under-developed conditions of the country has kept the nation's peasantry a poverty-stricken mass, inflicted with hunger, disease, malnutrition, malcustom and injustice. According to the World Bank Report, the average per capita income of the Nepali people has not gone above US $ 160, for many years—91 per cent of its population depend upon agriculture. However, 46 per cent of the land is occupied by 6.4 per cent landlords only, whereas 54 per cent of the land belongs to the rest of the 93.6 per cent people of Nepal. On the other hand, the industrial workers, although not a big number, also suffer from low wages and bad working conditions.

Child Labour in Nepal

The number of child workers in Nepal is estimated to be about 4.52 millions which comprise 60 per cent of the total child population. Although the existing law and order of the country put restrictions of the employment of children below 14 years, these restrictions have remained only on paper.

Child labour in Nepal can seen in farms, factories, road building, house building, brick factories, bakeries etc. The population census states that the working children of Nepal contribute about 6 per cent in the total income of the country. We think that this is an underestimation.

What compels children to work? Why do not they go to school? Unfortunately, the children do not know the answers to these questions. The only thing they know is that they have to work for their living and for their family's subsistence. It is obvious that the child labour system, originates from poverty as well as from illiteracy and ignorance of parents. The lack of adequate schooling facilities adds to this situation.

According to our study, children work mainly on farms, in cattle grazing, collecting firewood and plastics, loading and unloading goods in hotels and restaurants, shoe shining and motor car cleaning, weaving carpets, selling newspapers, cigarettes, fruits and flowers, working in *bidi* factories, match factories, bakeries, bricks kilns, printing press etc. and as domestic servants. Those who work in rural areas are in a slightly better condition than those who sleep on streets in urban areas. However, those who work in the landlords' houses are treated just like slaves. In urban areas employers pay nominal wages to children and provide them with no other facilities. Major problems of child labour can be listed as no chance of getting education, uncertain and long working hours, polluted working environment, cruel treatment by the masters, no medical support during sickness, low wages and no security of life in general.

Government Intervention

Government of Nepal has taken some actions for the protection of child labour. First of all, there is a law that prohibits employment of children under the age of 14 years in factories (under Civil rights Code 2012 and Factory Workers' Act.) In addition a separate body called Child Welfare Coordination Council has been set up as a part of the Social Service National Coordination Council. There are some programmes like Child Health Programme and Child Education Programme designed for children. However there is no comprehensive programme for these underprivileged and helpless children. The government has declared free and compulsory primary education, but in real practice, many children cannot afford to go to school. If the government sincerely wants to give them the education, they should first eradicate poverty of their parents.

A group of young social workers has set up Child Workers in Nepal: Concerned (CWIN) in January 1987 with the objective of helping working children. CWIN attempts to provide working children their rights, welfare and dignity. CWIN organises several programmes for child labour in Nepal: (1) Educational programmes, literacy programmes, consciousness building programmes, excursion and field trips and recreation programmes. (2) Publicity Programmes: newsletters, posters, pamphlets and stickers, and participation in organisations of seminars and symposiums on child workers. (3) Welfare and support programmes, such as distribution of educational materials, legal support and advice; formal education, contact with other welfare and charitable institutions and medical support.

CHILD LABOUR IN SRI LANKA

The situation in Sri Lanka with regard to child labour is not different from any other developing country in Asia. Of the 16 million people, ore than 40 per cent are children below the age of 17 years. In spite of the government providing free education with free text books and midday meals, around 800,000 children between the ages of six and twelve years did not attend school in 1985. This number could be considered as the potential child labour force in our country.

Child labour in Sri Lanka works mainly in four occupations, namely, domestic service, agriculture and plantation, small scale industries and small scale commercial ventures. The young persons and children Act No. 47 of 1956 strictly prohibited employing children under 12 years of age. However, the law permits children between the ages of 12 and 14 years in certain types of employment such as domestic service and family undertakings, technical colleges approved and supervised by public authority and agricultural occupations. Any employer who contravenes these provisions is liable to a fine not exceeding Rs. 50. This low penal provision has not changed in the last 30 years in spite of devaluation of the Sri Lankan currency.

The working and living conditions of child labour in various sectors are far from satisfactory:

1. *Domestic service:* According to a recent survey of the Development of Protection and Child Care, there are 200,000 children under 12 years engaged in domestic services. These illiterate and underfed children work long hours till late in the night chopping firewood, washing plates and polishing. The brokers get children from poor families and do a brisk business by supplying them to the rich and middle class families in the cities. Each month, the parents go and collect the salary from the employer.
2. *Agriculture and plantation:* Children are employed for weeding, plucking and tapping of latex in tea and rubber plantations. In coconut estates they climb trees to pluck nuts. They also help their parents with ploughing, cultivating, transplanting and harvesting as well as in tending cattle and goals.
3. *Small scale industries:* Child labour is common in small scale industries manufacturing coir ropes, brooms brushes, doormats, clay pots and pans, joss-sticks, wrapping of *beedis,* carving of wood objects, making bricks and tiles etc. and in the maintenance and repair works.
4. *Small scale trading:* Children are seen engaged in retailing and small trading in market places, terminals and pavements. They sell vegetables, toys, textiles, cigarettes, a sweets and many other things. They are also engaged in shoe shining, repairing and also begging. In the city of Colombo, over 1000 children work as private bus conductors, which is a very risky job.

Furthermore, children are forced to carry out certain illegal activities such as drug trafficking, smuggling of contrabands and transporting illicit liquor. Some children are also kidnapped and taken to fishing centres in the arid zones for processing dry fish. Hundreds of children are herded in unprotected sheds and are forced to work under very difficult conditions for which no wages are paid. Some children are also trained for "*sed* tourism".

According to the latest statistics, there are over 5,000 child prostitutes in the city of Colombo and in holiday resorts. They are looked after by the ring leaders who actually benefit by this trade and are sent away when they become old. These discarded children start living on payments or in slums and get involved in all sorts of notorious activities.

As the main reason for child labour in our country is poverty (the per capita income in Sri Lanka is less than US $ 350.) laws alone will not eradicate the evil. Government will have to take stern steps to combat poverty. As long as poor families have to depend on the earnings of their minor children, child labour cannot be abolished.

CHILD LABOUR IN INDONESIA: PROFILES OF SOME SHOESHINE BOYS IN YOGYAKARTA

Yogyakarta is not a big city as Jakarta, Surabaya or Bandung. Its population is less than 400,000 people. But a lot of people consider Yogyakarta as one of few important cities in Indonesia as it is the centre of Javanese culture and the second tourist spot in Indonesia after Bali. It is also known as the educational city because of a large number of schools and universities located there.

Malioboro is a main shopping centre in Yogyakarta. In this 2.5 km of the busiest street in town you can buy everything. As soon as the shops close at 9 p.m., food stalls start which work till around 5 a.m. Malioboro supports child labour in various petty form of work, such as, shoe shining, petty selling, helping in hotels and restaurants. In this paper we have described a few case studies of shoeshine boys which show as to how a rich and fashionable shopping centre can accommodate poor children from deprived families.

In Malioboro we met some 16 shoeshine boys between the ages of nine and 17 years. Most of them do not know where they are born. Eleven of them operate during the day and five operate till late at night. The daytime workers are studying in school, but the night workers are not. Sugeng is a 10 year old boy who starts work after his school is over and after he has taken his lunch at home. He has an older sister who is 13 years old and a younger brother seven years old. His father is a rickshaw puller and mother washes clothes of their neighbour. Both his parents can earn around rupiah 3,000 or about US $ 2 a day. With this income they are able to have three simple meals a day, which consist of a portion of rice with a piece of *tahu* (crushed soya) or *tempe* (fermented soya) and vegetables. Once in a week they eat a piece of meat or fish. Once in a year, his parents buy shrimp, a pair of clothes but not shoes. Sugeng started shoeshining at the age of nine because he needed a pair of shoes. His father gave him some money to buy two cans of shoe polish and his friend taught him how to polish shoes.

Sugeng earns much more money than others but it fluctuates very widely. He wants to finish his elementary education and continue his study to secondary school. He works to fulfil this ambition because he knows that only through higher education his life will change.

Harso is another shoeshine boy of 14 years of age. His parents live in a village called

Gunungkidul, about 35 km. away from Yogyakarta. His father is a farmer, with a very small piece of land, and his sisters are working as housemaids with two families in the same city. After the long dry season in 1985, his parents rented their land to a neighbour, and they are now working as landless labourers. Harso left school, though it was free, when he was only 12 years old and became a domestic servant with a family in Yogyakarta. He was fired from service as he had a physical fight with two children of the family and he started this new job as a shoeshine boy with the help of his sisters. Though his income was very small initially, he earns more money now as he works at night also. He is now used to the night life. At 13 years of age he has experienced sex. A part of his income he sets aside for his sex life. He knows that there is no brighter future waiting for him.

Kasidi is another shoeshine boy of 13 years. His father was fired five years ago from his job in a *batik* factory. His mother is therefore the breadwinner who works as a cleaning woman in a hospital and earns a small income. The drunkard father demands money from his wife which invariably results in a quarrel. Two of his brothers are working as construction workers in Jakarta and his elder sister works as a junior cleaning woman at the same hospital where her mother is working. His father forced Kasidi to become a shoeshine boy. Though he does not earn much, his father demands most of the money. He now does not go home regularly. He goes to school, but he thinks that he will not pass his final examination.

The above case studies show that poverty of parents in rural as well as in urban areas drives children to work. These children do not seem to be having any bright future either. As the extent of poverty is not showing any sign of decline, the phenomenon of child labour will continue in the future also.

7

CHILD LABOUR IN INDIA: DIMENSIONS, ISSUES AND POLICIES

On the basis of historical experiences, one can say that the origin of the problem of child labour lies in the process of industrial revolution. Industrialisation process leads to migration of labour, including child labour, from rural to urban areas to employers of factories, mines etc. who exploit child labour to minimise their costs and maximise profits.

Over the years, however, global consciousness about the seriousness of the problem has been created. The Constitution of India also is committed to the protection and promotion of the interests of the child. This has established the superiority of the welfare considerations over the economic ones. It was not surprising, therefore, that a series of committees and commissions have been appointed by the Government of India either specifically on the question of child labour or on labour conditions in general, which give us insights into the problem and give suggestions to alleviate this problem. The Royal Commission on Labour in 1929, the Labour Investigation Committee in 1944, The National Commission on Labour in 1966, Gurupadswamy Committee on Child Labour in 1979 and Sanat Mehta Committee in 1986 are the major committees which deserve special attention.

While the social concern is genuine and widespread, the wide cleavage between intentions and reality calls for a deep understanding of the interrelated processes of economic development, social and political development and population. Children's activities are after all determined and often a consequence of these realities. This paper attempts to understand children's activities, so that their determinants and implications are placed in a proper perspective for conceptualisation of the issues involved in the child work. Such an understanding would also lead to a better appreciation of legislations on the subject, which may help in formulating an integrated approach for child welfare. Rogers and Standing have developed a very thorough typology of child work across the countries which may prove useful in this context.

Rogers and Standing divide children's activities into different categories: (1) Domestic non-monetary work is usually within the family. It is self-employment and is generally 'time intensive'. (Examples, cleaning, cooking, washing, child care etc.). (2) Non-monetary and non-domestic work which is usually found in the poor agrarian/rural economies. This is self-employment, which is a part of family activity and includes activities like tending of livestock, protecting crops from birds and animals, hunting, gathering and weeding. This work is also time intensive and is often intermixed with domestic work. (3) Children also work in the non-agrarian environment, such as artisan production, small scale production and in the informal sector activities in trade, manufacturing and services, (such as, running errands, looking after goods for short periods and marketing of domestic produce). Although there is a low level equilibrium in many such activities, it represents an efficient allocation of the available family time and to that extent the activities of the children and the activities of the adults become complementary. (4) The fourth type is the work where children work as bonded labourers and are pledged by their parents in lieu of debt. Although bonded labour is abolished by law the prevalence of the practice is noted in a number of studies.

While the above types represent unpaid work mainly within the family and is self-employment, as Rogers and Standing point out child labourers are also employed on wages. A child wage labourer is sometimes a part of the family labour force wherein the entire family works on wages and children become a part of the group. These practices are noted in agricultural field labour, brick making, carpet making, domestic service, digging operations etc. The other part of the child wage labour is where children are independently employed as wage earners either on fields or in factories in the service sector. Children are also engaged in economic activities, partly economic but mainly illegal or antisocial.

Almost all of these activities of children either directly deprive the child from opportunities for full physical and mental development of or indirectly cause low level equilibrium in terms of a life-times chance. In fact, sometimes children's work is such where they work under such conditions that it would lead to physical handicaps and even cause death. Even when alive, they end up as a family and social burden. It is these consequences which are at the back of one's mind when one looks at the social concern for the children which is voiced all over the world.

Estimated Number of Child Workers in India

Data regarding the extent of child labour are inadequate in India. One major source, namely, the Census of Population does not permit a study over time due to the changes in definitions etc. National Sample Survey (NSS) data are usually regarded more reliable. In addition, the extent of child labour was indicated in the first and the second agricultural labour enquiry reports and in periodic surveys f the labour bureau.

Table 7.1 shows that the number of child labourers has gone up from 16.33 million in 1972-73 to 17.36 million in 1983, although as the percentage of the child labour to the total labour force, it shows a decrease. NSS figures too are disputed as underestimates. Unofficial figures of child labour are in the range of 44 to 100 million. Roughly 91 per cent of the child labour in accordance with the Census of Population are in the rural areas as per the 1981 Census. About 86 per cent of child labour is in agriculture and allied activities (43 per cent agricultural labourers, 36 per cent cultivators and 8 per cent livestock) and broadly 44 per cent self employed in non-domestic and non-monetary activities mainly in rural areas. Outside agriculture, manufacturing, processing and repairs accounted for 6 per cent, other services 4 per cent, and trade and commerce 2 per cent. There is a reduction in the percentage of child workers in 'cultivators', partly attributable to definitional change, and partly to the generally accepted phenomenon of growing marginalisation and inability of marginal holdings to sustain more labour. An increasing proportion of children opting for wage labour in agriculture is, therefore, in conformity with the same process which is observed for small and marginal landholdings. (See Appendix).

TABLE 7.1

Estimated Number of Child Workers in India

Agricultural labour enquiry reports	*Percentage of child labour (Below 15 yrs. of age)*
1. First (1950-51)	4.8
2. Second (1956057)	7.7
3. Population Census, 1961 (14.50m)	8
4. Population Census, 1971 (10.74m)	6
5. Population Census, 1981 (11.17m)	

National Sample Survey Rounds: (Million)

Round	*Year*	*Rural*	*Urban*	*Total*
27th	1972-73	15.04	1.29	16.33
32nd	1977-78	14.68	1.57	16.25
38th	1983	15.57	1.79	17.36

Activity Breakup of Child Workers

Table 7.2 gives the percentage breakup of activities of child workers. It shows the percentages of child workers in different activities.

Child Workers in Factories

The percentage of child workers to the total average daily employed workers in factories submitting returns under the Factories Act has been 0.14 per cent in 1972, 0.10 per cent in 1973, 0.07) per cent in 1976 and 0.1 per cent in 1977 (Appendix -3). It is worth noting that there were only 4,178 child workers in the factory sector in India in 1977. Though there is likely to be some underestimation in this, it is generally accepted, that the incidence of child labour in factories has decreased over the years and the number has now become insignificant. Within the factory sector however, food and food products, textile products, and hosiery and chemicals, employ more child labour. In general, child labour is seen most concentrated in organised manufacturing activities and in plantations (see Table 7.3).

TABLE 7.2

The Percentage Distribution of 10.7 Million Child Workers Reported in the Census of 1971, According to Their Main Occupations

Activity	*Percentage*
1	2
1. Cultivators	36.10
2. Agricultural labourers	42.70
3. Livestock, forestry, fishing, hunting and orchards etc.	08.10
4. Mining and quarrying	00.20
5. Manufacturing, processing, servicing and repairs.	06.10
6. Construction	00.60
7. Trade and commerce	02.00
8. Transport, storage, communications	00.40
9. Other services	03.80
Total	100.00

Committees and Commissions on Child Labour in India

We may briefly look at some of the observations and the findings of various Committees and commissions which have investigated the conditions of labour in general and of child labour in India from time to time.

The Royal Commission on Labour (1929), which was set up in 1929, observed that there was considerable incidence of child labour in *bidi* making and plantations as well as in carpet weaving in Mirzapur district (United Province) and in tanneries in Amritsar district (Punjab). The Commission referred at length to the child labour on plantations where children, accompanied by parents, lived on tea gardens. Chances of education of these children were almost nil and hence the Commission recommended that the owners of the tea plantations should contribute towards the establishment of facilities for ensuring their minimum education. The employers, however were interested in the steady supply of labour and employed children of four to six years and nine to eleven years. (One of the employers mentioned that children begin to work as soon as they can walk.) The Commission recommended legal prohibition for children to work below the age of 10, and to have any entry of the names of all working children in the wage book. The commission observed that in many cities a large number of young boys were employed in *bidi* making, who worked for long hours and under strict discipline. As regards the children working in ports and on loading of coal on ships, the 1922 Act made it obligatory for the local governments to frame rules under the Indian Ports Act 1908 which prohibited employment of children under the age of 12 years in handling goods at piers, jetties, docks, warehouses and ships. The commission wanted that this minimum age for employment should be raised to 14 years.

TABLE 7.3

Incidence of Child Labour in Indian Industries

	% of child Labour
1	2
A. Organised Sector (Industry)	*% of child labour*
1. Tea factories	11.5
2. Cashew processing and *gur* making	9.4
3. Manufacture of food and food products	26.7
4. Manufacture of textile products	12.0
5. Hosiery industry	34.0
6. Manufacture of chemicals and chemical products	14.0
Match and fire works	(97% of child workers are casual and unskilled)
7. Non-metallic mineral products	6.0
8. Tea, coffee plantations	9.0
B. Unorganised Sector	
Handloom Industry	
Kerala	9.0
Chinalapathi, Kanchipurak } Tamil Nadu	10.0
Beedi industry	
1. Tiruchirapalli	33.0
2. Tichurcenture	26.0
3. Tirunvelle	low
Glass Bangles	
1. Glass factories and potteries;	66.0
including bangle making/joining.	30.0
2. Bangle cutting	9.0
3. Carpet weaving	24.5
4. Shops and commercial establishment	24.5
5. Coir	16.25
6. Fishing—Quilon	60.0
Kanyakumari	10.17

Source: *Report of Child Labour in Indian Industries*, Labour Bureau, Simla, Ministry of Labour, Government of India.

The Commission's efforts to prohibit and regulate the work of children below the minimum age was faced with contrasting issues such as dislocation and hardship of parents of these children. The Commission recommended that children should not be allowed to work overtime or take work home and prohibited the pledging of children, observing the economic realities of the time and of child labour. It observed that "child's right to childhood and even to such education as may be available should make no appeal comparable to its earning capacity."

On the whole the Commission adopted a conciliatory approach and recommended cooperation between the government, the local authorities and the employers to develop child welfare centres and clinics for children.

Labour Investigation Committee 1944: The Labour Investigation Committee, popularly known as Rege Committee, observed that child labour declined from the peak of 74,620 (5.3 per cent of total employment) in 1923 to 9,403 (0.5 per cent in 1939, but showed a slight increase during war time. As the data were thought to be unreliable, the committee concluded that "the employment of children (between 12 and 15 years as well as below 12 years) has gone down considerably since the beginning of the century." The child labour aspect was predominant in *bidi* making, carpet weaving, glass and other small scale industries. The report specially referred its prevalence in the match industry in South India, in cement industry in Rajasthan, in the spinning industry in Cochin, and in carpet weaving in Kashmir. The Committee recommended that it is not enough to prohibit the employment of children, but it is also essential to adopt simultaneously positive measures to wean them away from industrial employment.

National Commission on Labour, 1966: The National Commission on Labour observed that the employment of children is indeed more of an economic problem than anything else. However, denial of opportunity to children for their proper physical development and education was considered a serious issue keeping in view the larger interest of the society. The Commission recommended fixing of the minimum age for children, fixing working hours of child labour and making arrangements for work with education for them.

Gurupadswamy Committee, 1979: The Gurupadswamy Committee on Child Labourer set up in 1979 was further evidence of the nation's resolve to initiate concrete policy measures for the protection of working children. The report, which was both analytical and comprehensive, dealt at length with the questions, such as, the dimensions of child labour, status of legislation and its implementation, and welfare and training schemes for child labour. The report also carried out some enquiries for ascertaining the points of views of workers, employers and the government on aspects such as what is child labour, what compels children to work, what are the occupations in which children are employed, why child labour is preferred etc. (Appendix-2).

Some of the observations and the recommendations of the committee are: (1) A multiple policy approach is necessary in dealing with the problems of working children. (2) Child labour is not a homogeneous group and therefore should be divided among the categories of wage earners, family workers, apprentices in traditional crafts and children who are both working and going to school. (3) The minimum age for entry into employment should be 15 years. (4) The existing law relating to prohibition and regulation of employment of children should be consolidated into a simple comprehensive one. (5) There should be a minimum educational qualifications say the eighth standard, for entry into any regulated employment. (6) The government should initiate dialogue with the trade unions for developing institutional framework for collective bargaining in respect of the needs of the working children. (7) The Planning Commission should work out the feasibility of removing children below 15 years from the labour market in order to find out employment for the unemployed and able-bodied persons. (8) The educational policy should have an appropriate curriculum and suitable schedules of vacations and holidays to suit the rural environment. Non-formal educational facilities should be arranged in the areas, where there are more working children. (9) Creches/child-care centres should be established at the school premises or at community centres in rural areas so as to encourage girls who have to take care of young siblings in the family to attend school. (10) Periodical medical check-up should be arranged for child labour and rules should be made to ensure a hygienic working environment. (11) The Apprenticeship Act should be enforced effective. (12) Systematic efforts should be made to identify hazardous jobs for children and their occupational diseases and treatment.

The Sanat Mehta Committee reiterated the concerns which have been voiced both in the report of National Commission of Labour and in the Gurupadswamy Committee. The Committee emphasised the need for a uniform age for children for entry into employment and wanted to combine work with education.

The Child Labour Act, 1986: The latest act called the Child Labour (Prohibition and Regulation) Act of 1986, prohibits engagement of children in certain employments and regulates the condition of work of children in certain other employments. When viewed in the context of the earlier reports on the problems of child labour, the present act represents the concerted effort of the nation to realistically meet the aspirations expressed from time to time. The act has identified some hazardous industries and 11 hazardous industrial processes in which employment of children under 14 is prohibited. The act also provides for the inclusion of more processes in the banned category with the appointment of a committee. In the rest of the sectors, the approach is regulation of the employment of child labour through various measures.

Education of Child Labour

All children who are not at work are not necessarily in schools. Even if they are enrolled in schools, the droupout is a major problem particularly among the children of the weaker sections. Out of 100 children enrolled in class I, about 25 to 30 reach standard V and those who complete the middle level education are even less. The reasons for this seem to be academic failure, lack of availability of middle school, parents' low incomes and so on. Restructuring of content of education, different schedules for vacations, timing for schools etc. have been suggested by Gurupadswamy Committee for longer retention of more and more children in schools.

It may be argued that when the poor see widespread unemployment around them, they prefer early entry into 'informal sector' work. However, this does not allow them to complete middle school education, which may not be an entry into the job market, but may be a base for the further learning process.

How do we expect an agricultural labour household to dispense with child's work which is supplementing the family income? What can be done when the family cannot afford to send the child to school even when free schooling is available? It can be said that an assurance of the legal minimum wages to adults may motivate them to send their children to school. Fixing up minimum wages for child labour is, however, likely to be counter-productive. It will be desirable if the concerned industries (some of which are expanding and are export oriented) bear a financial burden for hostel for working children which can also provide subsidised food, recreation and education-cum-training.

The entry into white collar jobs needs 12 to 15 years of schooling, and these requirements often go up as more and more candidates with higher degrees come to the labour market. Given the low probability for employment, it sometimes seems rational that the poor parents want their wards to opt out of school. Can we promise these children an appropriate job say after 12 to 15 years of schooling? The lifetime earnings curve rising slowly and tapering off fast is often the arguments which are advanced but hardly convince the poor parents even if they take a medium term view.

The economic activity and schooling are sometimes combined. For example, in the manufacture of incense—sticks, which is a home-based industry, majority of the child workers attend schools and also work at home for three to four hours a day. This flexible production system is seen in the manufacture of ready made garments, *bidi* etc. It is however, often the parents who force long hours of work on their own children.

It is argued that the abolition of child labour would increase the employment for adults and relieve the unemployment problem. The child workers, particularly the wage paid in the total labour force is hardly 3 per cent. The removal of child workers therefore, cannot ease the unemployment problems although in a few specified activities, more adults could find jobs. It is however not sure that these adults come from the families of children who are removed from work.

It may be concluded that, prohibition of child labour in selected works and the provision expanding this list, as it is laid down in the latest act in India, is a realistic approach at this stage of socio-economic development. The strategy to progressively retain more and more children in schools for longer period would need action on: (1) poverty alleviation programmes, (2) creation of more avenues for production employment, (3) educating parents through functional literacy programmes about the role of education, (4) establishment of working children's hostels to take care of foods, and (5) education-cum-training and recreation programmes for children in major cities of India.

REFERENCES

Rodger, Gerry and Guy Standing. *"Child Work, Poverty and Underdevelopment"*, International Labour Office, Geneva, 1981.

Enid Schildkrout, "The employment of Children in Kano (Nigeria)" in *Child Work, Poverty and Underdevelopment*, International Labor Office, Geneva, 1981.

S. Marla. "Bonded Labour in Medak District (Andhra Pradesh)" In *National Labour Institute Bulletin* (New Delhi), Vol. 3 No. 10 Oct. 1977.

Marla, S. and R.N. Maharaj. National Survey on the Incidence of Bonded Labour (Preliminary Report), (New Delhi, Gandhi Peace Foundation and National Labour Institute) 1978.

Mead, Cain and A.B.M. Khorshed. "Labour Market Structure and Reproductive Behaviour in Rural South "Asia" in *Child Work, Poverty and Underdevelopment*, International Labour Office, Geneva, 1981.

Patel, B.B. *Work, Working Conditions and Earnings: Agarbathi Workers in Ahmedabad*, Gandhi Labour Institute, Ahmedabad, India, 1986.

Patel, B.B. *Slums in Ahmedabad: A study of Migration, Employment and Housing* (Mimeo), Sardar Patel Institute of Economic and Social Research, Ahmedabad, India, 1980.

Patel, B.B. *Status Report on the Problem of Child Labour with a Focus on Diamond Cutting and Polishing Industry in Gujarat* (Carried out at the instance of Ministry of Labour, Government of India), Gandhi Labour Institute, Ahmedabad, India, 1987.

Report of the Royal Commission on Labour in India, Government of India, Central Publication Branch, 1931.

Report of the Labour Investigation Committee, Government of India, Delhi, 1958.

Report of the Labour Investigation Committee, Government of India, Ministry of Labour and Employment and Rehabilitation, 1969.

Report of the Committee on Child Labour, Ministry of Labour, Government of India, December, 1979.

Sanat Mehta Committee Report on Child Labour, Ministry of Labour, Government of India, 1984.

APPENDIX-1

ESTIMATES OF CHILD LABOUR IN INDIA

Source	*Age group (years)*	*Rural male*	*Rural female*	*Rural*	*Urban male*	*Urban female*	*Urban*	*Grand total*	*Remarks*
1	*2*	*3*	*4*	*5*	*6*	*7*	*8*	*9*	*10*
Census, 1961	0-14	8.16	5.56	13.72	0.58	0.23	0.81	14.53	
	5-9*	0.80	0.52	1.32	0.03	0.01	0.04	1.36	
	10-14*	7.36	5.04	12.40	0.55	0.22	0.77	13.77	
	5-14	8.16	5.56	13.72	0.58	0.23	0.81	14.53	
NSS (1972-73)	5-9	0.88	0.63	1.51	0.05	0.03	0.08	1.59	
(27th round).	10-14	7.78	5.75	13.53	0.80	0.41	1.21	14.74	
(usual status)	5-14	8.66	6.38	15.04	0.85	0.44	1.29	16.33	
NSS (1977-78)	5-9	0.88	0.63	1.51	0.05	0.05	0.10	1.62	
1st March, 1978**	10-14	7.96	5.21	13.77	0.94	0.53	1.47	14.62	
	5-14	8.84	5.84	14.68	0.99	0.58	1.57	16.25	
1st March, 1983	5-9	0.90	0.64	1.54	0.06	0.06	0.12	1.66	
	10-14	8.44	5.59	14.03	1.07	0.60	1.67	15.70	
	5-14	9.34	6.23	15.57	1.13	0.66	1.79	17.36	

* Estimate for the quinquennial age group are based on a special study vide Appendix V of the Report of the Export Committee on Estimates on Employment, Planning Commission, 1970.

** Projection for 1978 and 1983 are based on usual status rates of NSS 2nd round (1977-78).

Source: The Report of the Planning Commission, Government of India, New Delhi.

APPENDIX-2

CHILDREN EMPLOYED IN DIFFERENT OCCUPATIONS AT TWO-DIGIT LEVEL ON THE BASIS OF 1 PER CENT SAMPLES FROM 1971 CENSUS FIGURES IN INDIA

Sr. No.	*Activity*	*Rural*	*Urban*
1	2	3	4
	Cultivation	37732	450
	Agriculture	43934	1149
00	Agro production	38	5
01	Plantation	408	24
02	Livestock production	7628	220
03	Agro. service	94	15
04	Hunting, trapping and game propagation	4	1
05	Forestry and logging	92	8
06	Fishing	181	39
07	Coal mining	22	10
08	Crude petroleum and natural gas	20	—
09	Metal ore mining	109	2
10	Other mining	130	28
11	Mfr. of food products	98	45
12	Mfr. of beverages, tobacco and tobacco products	41	338
13	Cotton textile mfr.	433	443
14	Mfr. wool silk and synthetic textiles	57	68
15	Mfr. of jute, hemp and mesta textiles	18	15
16	Manufacture of textile products (including wearing apparel other than footwear)	457	339
17	Manufacture of wood and wood products, furniture and fixtures	4	166
18	Manufacture of paper and paper products and printing, publishing and allied industries	11	77
19	Manufacture of leather, leather and fur products (except repair)	75	47
20	Manufacture of rubber, plastic, petroleum and coal products	8	19
21	Manufacture of non-metallic mineral products	471	140
22	Manufacture of chemicals and chemical products (Except products of petroleum and coal)	104	85
23	Basic metal and alloys industries	9	26
24	Manufacture of metal products and parts, except machinery and transport equipment	120	119

1	*2*	*3*	*4*
25	Manufacture of machinery, machine tools and parts except electrical machinery	20	49
26	Mfr. of elect, machinery, apparatus, appliances and supplies and parts	2	9
27	Mfr. of transport equipment and parts	4	21
28	Other Mfr. industries	211	167
29	Repairs	78	265
30	Electricity	6	2
31	Gas and steam	—	—
32	Water works and supply	2	—
33	Construction	297	186
34	Activities allied to construction	19	7
35	Wholesale trade in food, textiles, live animals, beverages and intoxicants	17	12
36	Wholesale trade in fuel, light chemicals perfumery ceramics, glass	—	1
37	Wholesale trade in wood, paper, other fabrics hides and skin and inedible oils	6	4
38	Wholesale trade in all types of machinery equipment including transport and electrical equipment	—	1
39	Wholesale trade in food and miscellaneous manufacturing	6	6
40	Retail trade in food and food articles, beverages, tobacco and intoxicants	391	405
41	Retail trade in textiles	18	60
42	Retail trade in fuel and other household utilities and durables	75	89
43	Retail trade in others	58	148
44	Restaurants and hotels	213	429
45	Land transport	80	160
46	Water transport	6	9
47	Air transport	2	—
48	Service incidental to transport	1	2
49	Storage and warehousing	—	2
50	Communication	6	2
51	Banking and similar type of financial institutions	2	6
52	Provident funds and insurance	—	1
53	Real estate and business services	7	35
54	Legal services	1	1
55	Public admn. and defence services	44	51

1	2	3	4
56	Sanitary services	24	12
57	Education scientific and research services	36	32
58	Medical and health services	10	17
59	Community services	18	249
60	Recreational, culture services	34	24
61	Personal services	496	1099
62	International and other extra territorial bodies services	1	1
63	Services not elsewhere classified	637	420
64	Personnel without any affiliation to any particular industry (including fresh entrants to labour force)	—	—
65	Activities not adequately defined (other than in 65)	—	—
	Total workers	97706	7839

APPENDIX-3

EMPLOYMENT OF CHILDREN IN FACTORIES

Year	*Average daily no. of children employed.*	*Total average Daily employment in factories.*	*Percentage of Children to total employment.*
1	2	3	4
1892	18,888	3,16,816	5.96
1948	11,444	21,76,724	0.48
1950	4,764	25,04,516	0.31
1955	4,975	26,90,403	0.18
1960	3,220	33,67,803	0.10
1965	2,264	41,17,692	0.05
1970	2,427	42,63,988	0.06
1971	3,702	42,08,343	0.09
1972	0.094	44,93,730	0.14
1973	4,457	45,70,751	0.10
1974	4,310	46,33,200	0.09
1975(P)	4,310	47,64,532	0.09
1976(P)	3,592	59,78,414	0.07

Source: *Labour Bureau*, Simla.

8

WHY CHILD LABOUR?

Conventionally labour force consists of persons in the age group 15 to 59 years. However, there are about 52 million child workers in the world. More than 50 million working children are from under-developed countries, where Asia alone accounts for 38 million, with concentration in South and South East Asia of 29 million. The child labour is a symptom of poverty, unemployment and illiteracy. The child labour is normally found in unorganised sectors where he is highly vulnerable to exploitation.

India has the largest number of the world's working children. According to the Census of Population estimates, in 1961, 14.47 million children out of the total child population of 180 million (8.04 per cent) were working, in 1971, 10.73 million out of 230 million of child population (4.66 per cent) were working, while in 1981, 13.59 million out of 263.06 million child population (5.1 per cent) were working, in the country. The census estimates of child labour however seem to be underestimates. As per the National Sample Survey (NSS) data, there were 16.33 million child labour in 1972-73, 16.25 million in 1977-78, 17.36 million in March 1983, and 17.58 million in 1985, (on the basis of NSS 32nd Round 1977-78). These estimates exclude subsidiary workers.

In the estimates of child labour amongst 27.10 million subsidiary workers in 1985, the ratio of marginal to main workers amongst child labour in 1981 Census could be used. Children in the age group of zero to 14 years constituted 19.33 per cent of male marginal workers and 9.38 per cent of the female marginal workers in 1981. In other words, there were about 3 million child workers among subsidiary workers; and therefore 20.5 million total child workers in the country in 1985. Though these data are not strictly comparable over time, broadly it can be said that the magnitude of child labour has increased in India during 1961 to 1985 from 14.5 to 20.5 million.

Another factor which should be taken into consideration for estimating the magnitude of child labour is enrolment of children in the school in the age groups of five to nine and 10 to 14 years. With development, school enrolment of children increases. If a child is enrolled in a school, it can be presumed that he is not a part of the child labour. In the Indian situation, if the child is not in the education stream, he would normally be working even for a pittance, which may not have been captured by Census and NSS. The child population in the age group of five to 14 years should be normally in school in India where primary education for all children below 14 years in free. However, the total number of children attending school in the age groups five to nine and 10 to 14 years are 36 million (38.45 per cent) and 43.22 million (5.45 per cent) respectively. The higher percentage of children attending school in the age group of 10 to 14 years seems to be untenable because middle school capacity is lower than the capacity of primary school in the country. However, as per the Ministry of Human Resource Development, Government of India, the enrolment in the age groups of six to 11 years and 11 to 14 years is 77 million and 22 million, respectively. This seems to be the correct picture since it matches with educational facilities available for these age groups in the country. Of the 179.31 million children in the age group of five to 14 years, 13.59 million are workers and 99 million in the education stream. Thus about 66.72 million are idlers.

TABLE 8.1

Estimates of Child Labour in India, 1961-2000

Source	*Age group (years)*	*Rural male*	*Rural female*	*Rural*	*Urban male*	*Urban female*	*Urban*	*Grand total*	*Remarks*
1	2	3	4	5	6	7	8	9	10
Census, 1961	—	0-14	8.16	5.56	13.72	0.58	0.23	0.81	14.53
		5-9*	0.80	0.52	1.32	0.03	0.01	0.04	1.36
		10-14*	7.36	5.04	12.40	0.55	0.22	0.77	13.77
		5-14	8.16	5.56	13.72	0.58	0.23	0.81	14.53
NSS (1972-73)	—	5-9	0.88	0.63	1.51	0.05	0.03	0.08	1.59
(27th round)	—	10-14	7.78	5.75	13.53	0.80	0.41	1.21	14.74
(usual status)	—	5-14	8.66	6.38	15.04	0.85	0.44	1.29	16.33
NSS (1977-78)	—	5-9	0.88	0.63	1.51	0.05	0.05	0.10	1.62
1st March, 1978**	—	10-14	7.96	5.21	13.77	0.94	0.53	1.47	14.62
		5-14	8.84	5.84	14.68	0.99	0.58	1.57	16.25
Census 1981	—	0-14	7.34	5.21	12.55	0.76	0.29	1.05	13.59
1st March, 1983	—	5-9	0.90	0.64	1.54	0.06	0.06	0.12	1.66
		10-14	8.44	5.59	14.03	1.07	0.60	1.67	15.70
		5-14	9.34	6.23	15.57	1.13	0.66	1.79	17.36
1985**	—	5-14	—	—	—	—	—	—	17.58
1990*	—	5-14	—	—	—	—	—	—	18.17
2000**	—	5-14	—	—	—	—	—	—	20.25

Source: Planning Commission, Census 1961, 1971 and 1981.

* Estimates for the quinquennial age-group are based on a special study vide Appendix V of the Reports of the Export Committee on Estimates of unemployment, Planning Commission, 1970.

** Projections for 1978 and 1983, 1985, 1990, 2000 are based on usual status rates of NSS 2nd round (1977-78).

Though it may be difficult estimate how many out of 66.72 million idlers in the age group of five to 14 years are working it will be quite safe to assume that many of them must be working particularly in the age group of 10 to 14 years due to economic reasons and non-availability of schooling facility. It may be quite useful to find out about these idlers and the reasons behind idling particularly if it is due to non-availability of schooling facility. Child labour and idlers both lead to deprivation and both are a matter of concern which needs to be looked into.

As per the projections of the Planning Commission, the magnitude of child labour is likely to be 20.25 million in the year 2000, (excluding the subsidiary workers). The increase and persistence of child labour is the negation of our basic principle of social justice laid in the Constitution and of the development plans which aim at universal, free and compulsory primary education for children in the age group of six to 14 and health for all by 2000.

Article 45 of Indian Constitution provides for free and compulsory education to all children below 14 years by 1960. Article 24 says, "No child below the age of 14 years shall be employed to work in any factory or mine or engaged in any other hazardous employment." Article 39 (e) says: "The health and strength of workers, men and women, and children shall not be abused and children shall not be forced by economic necessity to enter avocations unsuited to their age or strength." Articles 39 states: "Childhood and youth are protected against exploitation and against moral and material abandonment." In addition, there are about a dozen legislations on child labour which have been enacted for the benefit of children engaged in certain specific occupations and industries. The provisions of these acts prescribe the minimum age, minimum wage and working conditions of child labour in various employments, such as, factories, mines, transport, construction and plantations.

Where do Children Work?

Rural areas have 91.2 per cent of child labour, while 9 per cent is in urban areas. About 90 per cent of child labour is between the age of 10 and 14 years and about 10 per cent is between five and nine years of age. This is true for both male and female labour in rural as well as urban areas.

Amongst rural child labour, 91 per cent is engaged in primary sector, 6.19 per cent in secondary and less than 3 per cent in tertiary sector. In urban areas, however, the percentages are 23.4, 42.4 and 34.2 respectively. Factories registered under the Factories Act (1948) employ only 2,327 children. This means that the employment of children is mainly in the informal sector.

Table 8.2 gives state-wise information about child labour (1981). It shows that in all the states 90 per cent of child labour is in rural areas. It also shows that seven states, namely, Andhra Pradesh, Madhya Pradesh, Maharashtra, Uttar Pradesh, Karnataka, Bihar and Tamil Nadu together have more than a million child labour each and they account for 70 per cent of the child labour in the country. In the states of Orissa,

Rajasthan, Gujarat and West Bengal their strength is from 0.5 million to 1 million each. In other words 92 per cent of child labour is concentrated in these 11 states.

TABLE 8.2

Statewise Child Labour Distribution (1981)

(Figures in Millions)

		Rural			*Urban*		*Grand*
		Male	*Female*	*Total*	*Male*	*Female*	*Total*	*Total*
1.	Andhra Pradesh	0.97	0.83	1.80	0.92	0.45	0.15	1.95
2.	Assam	—	—	—	—	—	—	—
3.	Bihar	0.69	0.34	1.03	0.36	0.0085	0.044	1.07
4.	Gujarat	0.31	0.25	0.56	0.04	0.0095	0.05	0.61
5.	Jammu and Kashmir	0.12	0.13	0.25	0.012	0.0051	0.017	0.27
6.	Kerala	0.04	0.038	0.078	0.0069	0.0062	0.0131	0.092
7.	Madhya Pradesh	0.87	0.76	1.63	0.045	0.022	0.067	1.70
8.	Tamil Nadu	0.43	0.40	0.83	0.095	0.056	0.151	0.98
9.	Maharashtra	0.69	0.76	1.45	0.075	0.034	0.11	1.56
10.	Karnataka	0.56	0.45	1.01	0.084	0.039	0.124	1.13
11.	Orissa	0.42	0.26	0.68	0.02	0.009	0.029	0.71
12.	Punjab							
13.	Rajasthan	0.42	0.35	0.77	0.031	0.01	0.041	0.81
14.	Uttar Pradesh	1.00	0.30	1.30	0.11	0.01	0.125	0.142
15.	West Bengal	0.41	0.11	0.52	0.047	0.027	0.074	0.59
16.	Himachal Pradesh	0.039	0.058	0.097	0.0008	0.00044	0.0012	0.098
17.	Andaman Nicobar Islands	—	—	0.0011	—	—	—	—
18.	Delhi	—	—	—	—	—	—	—
19.	Lakshadweep	—	—	0.000025	—	—	0.000021	0.00004
20.	Manipur	—	—	0.018	—	—	0.002	0.020
21.	Tripura	—	—	0.024	—	—	0.001	0.025
22.	Dadar and Nagar Haveli	—	—	—	—	—	—	—
23.	Goa, Daman and Diu	—	—	0.0071	—	—	0.0022	0.0093
24.	Pondicherry	0.0011	0.00088	0.00198	0.0016	0.00036	0.002	0.00398
25.	Chandigarh	—	—	—	—	—	—	—
26.	Nagaland	—	—	0.015	—	—	0.0006	0.0156
27.	Sikkim	—	—	0.0079	—	—	0.00054	0.00844
28.	Haryana	—	—	—	—	—	—	—
29.	Arunachal Pradesh	—	—	0.018	—	—	0.0003	0.0183
30.	All India	7.34	5.21	12.55	0.76	0.29	1.05	13.59

Source: Various State Reports and Tables Based on 5 per cent Sample Data (Census of India 1981).

Rural economy which is characterised by a relatively higher level of poverty, unemployment and illiteracy compared to urban economy (per capita rural incomes as well as the percentage of the population below the poverty line are significantly lower than the same in urban areas) supports 90 per cent of the total child labour in the country. The aggregate unemployment in rural areas (on daily status basis) also is 14.22 million as compared to 4.95 million in urban areas (1977-78), and the literacy rates also are much lower (34.06 per cent compared to 64.89 per cent in urban areas). We tried to find out a relationship between the phenomenon of child labour, with the incidence of poverty, unemployment and illiteracy at disaggregated level. The Table 8.3 shows the number of child labour, the number of people below the poverty line and the unemployed persons in the millions on daily status basis in the rural and urban areas of different states in 1981.

We find a highly significant positive correlation (+0.78) between the number of child labour and the number of people below the poverty line in 1981. The correlation between the number of child labour and the number of unemployed on a daily status basis is also found to be significant and positive (+.50). This indicates that child labour is a symptom of poverty and unemployment. As the problem of poverty and unemployment persists, the problem of child labour will also remain. The legislations alone will not be able to solve the problem of child labour.

The incidence of child labour is also associated with the overall literacy, the correlation (excluding the zero to four years age group) being significant and negative. The correlation coefficient is estimated to be (0-0.75), (-0.71), and (-0.71) in 1981, 1971 and 1961 respectively. Thus, raising the level of literacy among the population is one of the very effective methods for bringing down the incidence of child labour in India.

The agricultural labourers as well as Scheduled Castes and Scheduled Tribes are poor. These overlapping groups together cover around two-thirds of all the rural poor. We found that the incidence of child labour and the percentage of agricultural labourers in the total population in a state are significantly and positively correlated (+0.68). This is a further vindication of our earlier hypothesis that child labour exists because of the poverty and unemployment.

Unfortunately, the major instrument used to deal with the problem of child labour in India has been legislative action. These have not had the desired effect. One major instrument which could solve the problem of child labour is the free and compulsory education to all children in the age group of five to fourteen years. To start with, the government should prohibit the employment of children in the age group of five to nine years and to provide schooling to this entire group. The child labour in this age may not affect the family incomes adversely. Poverty alleviation programmes should also give a very high priority to those families who are compelled to send children to work in this age group. In the second stage schooling facility should be extended to all of 50 million children in the age group of 10 to 14 years. At present, parents send their children to

TABLE 8.3

Number of Child Labour, Number of Poor and Number of Unemployed on Daily Status Basis by States

		Rural			*Urban*		
	Name of states	*Child labour 1981*	*No. of poor persons 1981*	*Unemployed persons 1981*	*Child labour 1981*	*No. of poor persons 1981*	*Unemployed persons 1981*
1.	Andhra Pradesh	1.80	183.02	1.83	0.14	4.46	0.38
2.	Assam	—	9.40	0.10	—	0.77	0.04
3.	Bihar	1.03	36.00	1.54	0.044	4.02	0.19
4.	Gujarat	0.56	10.15	0.46	0.05	3.08	0.33
5.	Jammu and Kashmir	0.25	1.54	0.18	0.017	0.50	0.026
6.	Kerala	0.078	9.51	1.66	0.013	2.45	0.32
7.	Madhya Pradesh	1.63	24.88	0.39	0.067	5.09	0.21
8.	Madras (T. Nadu)	0.83	18.07	2.85	0.15	7.17	1.02
9.	Maharashtra	1.45	22.78	1.15	0.11	6.95	0.56
10.	Karnataka	1.01	13.17	0.89	0.124	4.72	0.52
11.	Orissa	0.68	16.04	0.79	0.029	1.31	0.13
12.	Punjab	—	1.44	0.19	—	1.15	0.11
13.	Rajasthan	0.77	9.13	0.47	0.041	2.44	0.14
14.	Uttar Pradesh	1.30	45.69	1.07	0.125	9.80	0.40
15.	West Bengal	0.52	23.65	2.16	0.074	5.02	0.68
16.	Himachal Pradesh	0.097	1.11	0.024	0.0012	0.05	0.006
17.	Andaman Nicobar	0.0011	—	—	0.0003	—	—
18.	Delhi	—	—	0.015	—	—	0.028
19.	Lakshadweep	0.00025	—	—	0.00002	—	—
20.	Manipur	0.018	0.32	0.001	0.002	0.096	0.0006
21.	Tripura	0.024	1.18	0.025	0.001	0.06	0.007
22.	Dadra and Nagar Haveli	—	—	—	—	—	—
23.	Goa, Daman and Div	0.0071	—	—	0.0022	—	—
24.	Pondicherry	0.00198	—	—	0.002	—	—
25.	Chandigarh	—	—	—	—	—	—
26.	Nagaland	0.0150	—	—	0.0006	0.004	—
27.	Sikkim	0.00790	—	—	0.00054	—	—
28.	Haryana	—	2.34	0.15	—	0.90	0.65
29.	Arunachal Pradesh	0.0180	—	—	0.0003	—	—
30.	Meghalaya	—	0.59	—	—	0.04	—
	All India	12.55	267.04	9.21	1.05	61.00	5.22

Source: Planning Commission, *Sarvekshana*, April, 1986.

work after the fourth standard partly because further schooling facilities are not available. However, with the expansion of this facility parents may send their children to school, and this may take care of a substantial proportion of child labour. Improvement in the overall literacy is an important instrument to deal with the child labour problem.

So far major indicators of poverty are in the caloric norm. However, the incidence of child labour is another very important parameter of the poverty which is non-caloric in nature. If the poverty removal programme fails to make any impact on the incidence of child labour, then obviously the child labour problem would persist.

TABLE 8.4

Percentage of Child Labour and Literacy by States, 1981

States	*Rural*		*Urban*	
	Percentage of child labour to child population	*Literacy rate excluding (0-4) age group*	*Percentage of child labour to child population*	*Literacy rate excluding (0-4) age group*
1. Andhra Pradesh	16.59	26.5	4.7	58.9
2. Bihar	5.95	26.0	1.9	59.4
3. Gujarat	8.75	41.5	1.9	68.3
4. Karnataka	13.83	35.6	4.6	69.4
5. Kerala	1.5	77.6	1.2	84.5
6. Madhya Pradesh	13.9	24.6	2.4	61.7
7. Maharashtra	12.9	43.5	2.1	72.2
8. Orissa	10.5	35.7	3.6	62.3
9. Rajasthan	9.9	21.0	2.2	55.6
10. Tamil Nadu	10.8	43.6	4.0	70.9
11. Uttar Pradesh	5.1	26.7	2.3	52.6
12. West Bengal	4.6	37.8	2.2	68.7

Source: Census 1981.

9

CHILD LABOUR IN THE 18TH AND 19TH CENTURIES

1. Child Labour in Germany Between 1750-1850

Historically, child labour[1] has been prevalent in Germany in:

1. Workshops as well as factories of the Proto-industrial and Early Industrial Phases between 1750-1850.
2. Factories during the peak phase industrialisation.

Even as early as in the 16th and 17th centuries, child labour was practiced in orphanages and work houses. In 1667, for instance, children worked together with convicts at the loom in the orphanage of Basel, in order to turn out products of sale.

"One of the first to criticise the cruel exploitation of children in workshops, particularly in the workshops run for orphans, was Christian Gotthilf Salzmann, a representative of the Enlightenment Movement. His criticism is voiced in his novel "Carl von Carlsberg or on Human Misery" which appeared in 1783. The portrayal of the scene wherein five children are "tortured" in a workshop for orphans because they had not "spun up all the wool and cotton given to them," though ficticious, probably does bear some degree of authenticity since surrogate parents at the orphanages were often discharged because they were torturing the children too much during work or because the mortality rate in the orphanages had risen too high as a result of child labour."[2]

To a large extent, the entrepreneurs who ran workshops employing orphans had a free hand where their access to child labour was concerned. However the attempts to develop workshops for orphans into independent enterprises failed due to inadequate profits. *A system of "renting out" cheap child labour* developed next, with the entrepreneurs working in conjunction with feudal political authorities (kings") here. As a result of this, the spheres of life and work of the children were duly separated from each other.

The cottage industry had gradually broken away from the agricultural sector in the 16th and 17th centuries and itself grown into an independent sector. Textile workers constituted the largest section of those carrying on a cottage industry. Besides, they could also be found in areas with iron industries. In the second half of the 18th century, middle-men, putting out work to cottage industry began gaining an increasingly stronger hold over these cottage industry workers, resulting in negative economic consequences for the latter. The cottage industry manufacturers then *began to rent out their children* to other manufacturers in the cotton industry, or to manufacturers of silk, lace, thread, needles cotton and chains. A report of the factory commissioner Eversmann dating back to 1797 corroborates, by way of example, this *link between the subsistence crisis of manufacturers of thread who worked at home and child labour*. With this, the separation of the spheres of life and production took place here as well.

In the 18th century, orphans and beggar children (of whom there was an abundance after the 7 Years War) played a significant role as a cheap wage factor in mercantilist-economits policy.

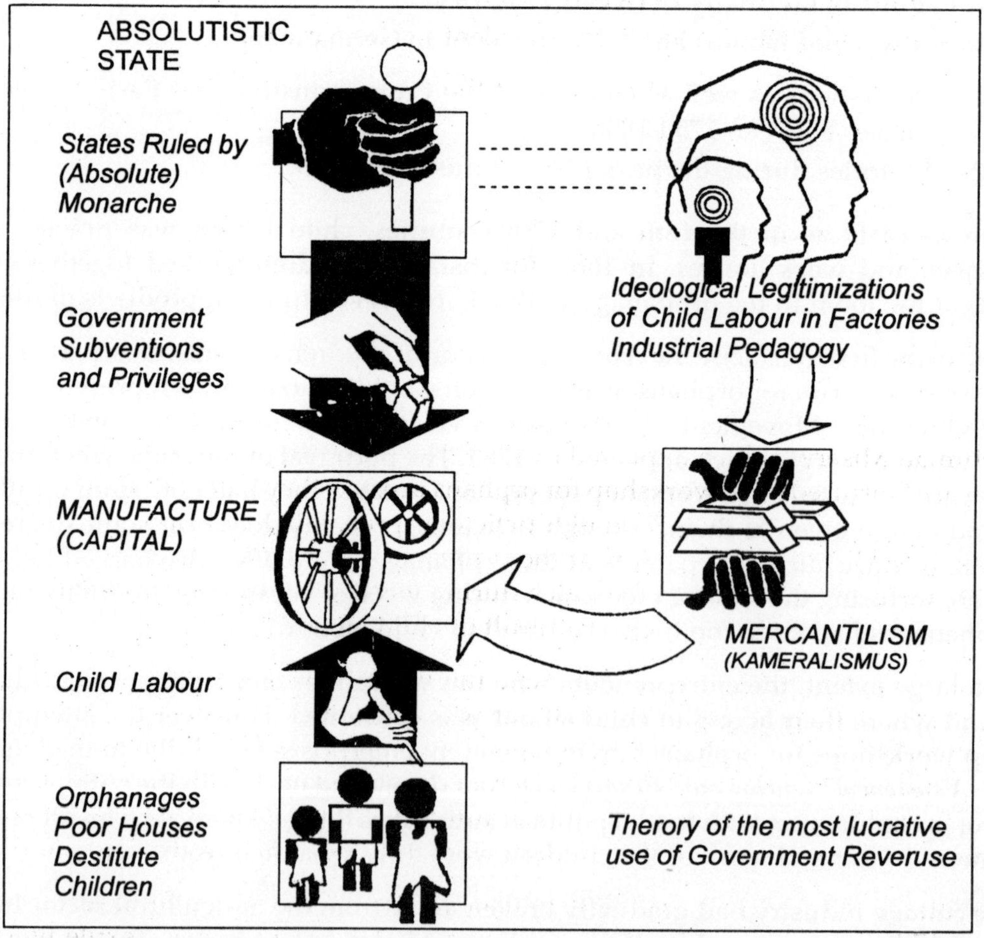

Fig. 9.1 Structural System of Child Labour is in Manufacture and Proto Factories.

The setting up of production centres offered itself as a possibility of overcoming mass poverty. The establishment of production centres was regarded as a most effective way of eradicating pauperism. The establishment of government-run poor houses especially served this cause. But the state, of course, preferred to be relieved of this task by having entrepreneurs erect workshops, followed by proto-factories.

Governmental entrepreneurial and pedagogic interest converged at the expense of (beggar) children. Even so-called 'enlightened' economic theorists and pedagogues justified child labour. Requests of manufacturers for state privileges—whether it was for the granting of a monopoly status for subsidies for a workshop or for sustaining a whole branch of industry—therefore never failed to refer to the "benevolence" of the workshop concerned in getting children off the streets.

The Napoleonic system had led to the liberalisation of the economies in the Western territories. Prussia followed suit by promulgating the Hardenberg Legislation in 1810. There remained only a few small territories in which efforts were being made to restore the economic system of the Ancient Regime. The change-over to the liberal system triggered off an economic crisis which was especially marked in the textile sector which found itself competing with the more advanced sectors in Great Britain.

The idea of balancing out production costs with low labour costs and of achieving this primarily by engaging child workers, suggested itself. As during the Ancien Regime, pointing to *child workers as providing a cheap source of labour grew to be the favourite line of argumentation of entrepreneurs in the liberal phase as well.* The gradual intesification of the development of proto-factories made work in workshops appear to be mere *"child's play."* The reference to the subsistence level of the lower classes being assured as a result of this, provided yet another reason for politicians and the general public alike to view child labour in factories as a completely natural phenomenon.

A description of the region of Wuppertal drawn up in 1809 by an official of the Napoleonic Age states yet the consequences which child labour brought in its wake:

"The great majority of the inhabitants of the Arrondissement of Elbersfeld are in an extremely wretched condition. This state of degeneration can probably be ascribed to the practice of sending children to work in factories too early in life which is characteristic of this region. Herded together in great numbers in the factories and confined to a sedentary occupation which requires them to sit in a bent position for long spells at a time, these children cannot but remain physically underdeveloped."[3]

2. Efforts Towards Child Protection in 19th Century Germany

A point of interest is the fact that the Protective Labour Legislation enacted in the wake of the industrialisation of Europe was the outcome of efforts to protect child labour. The first measures towards child protection were initiated in England in 1802, sparking off a controversy in Germany about the pedagogic value of child labour, its deleterious effects on health and its economic benefits. The protective clauses for labour embodied in the statutes of guilds dating back to the Middle Ages were either no longer in keeping with changes in reality or were forgotten. It was not altruistic but rather socio-political considerations which led to Legislation for Child Protection. Here, the statement made by General von Horn in 1828 that as a result of child employment for night work in factories the army was being deprived of sufficient stand-by recruits, induced suitable legislation.

Individual entrepreneurs—as for e.g. the manufacturer Schuchart from Barmen—, the English Laws and warnings from teachers induced the Rhineland Diet, in the face of the miserable plight of children, to petition for official factory inspectors. The Law of 16.5.1953 stipulated that factory inspectors be engaged for the well-being of young labourers—the objective being to lay down afresh conditions of work at factories requisite for the protection of health and the prevention of accidents, and to regulate anew the hours of work and night work for children. As in several developing countries, factory inspectors had often to fight opposition from manufacturers, political authorities and even from politically unconscious parents. According to the statement made by the future Chancellor of the German Reich, Bismarck, in the Reichstag (Imperial Diet) in 1869, the law remained a 'dead letter' in those branches of industry in which there were no factory inspectors: It was only with the new social and economic policies pursued by the State that opposition from liberal industrialists and conservative landed gentry could gradually be overcome.

However, Chancellor Bismarck dismissed the idea of protective labour legislation and, above all, the regulation of the hours of work as well as the restriction of women and child labour which had long since formed the base and core of social legislation in England.

On the other hand, the laws initiated by Bismarck—the Sickness Insurance Act (1884) and the Old Age and Disablement Insurance Act (1889)—helped Germany attain the world lead in social reform by a generation.

3. The Failure of Industrial Pedagogics

Industrial pedagogics proceeded on the assumption that the disciplining of child factory workers could be combined with the development of creative skills. However, no specific line of teaching was developed for this purpose. Today, against the background of prevailing standards, here the polytechnique approaches could be a possibility or even a "political line of teaching" for working children. Equally it is necessary to raise the awareness of their parents through means of adult education.

In the "Communist Manifesto," Marx and Engels already defend the parents of working children against these accusations. But they seized on a realisation which was to surface later when they formulated the following question addressed to the bourgeoisie: "Are you accusing us of wanting to put an end to this exploitation of children by the parents?", to which they replied: "We admit to this crime." Marx lashed out at the "pharisaicalness" behind these accusations in 1863 in his "Das Kapital."

Education in the workshop—that is, if individual lessons were conducted regularly at all-was secondary to the entrepreneurs' interest in profit-making.[4]

In 1872, the world renowned "bourgeois" pedagogue F.A.W. Diesterweg criticised the utilitarian standpoint of industrial pedagogics for the very first time in his study "On the Utilisation of Children as Factory Workers—A View from the Pedagogic Angle." However, he did not at the same time question the phenomenon of "capitalist exploitation." (Arno Herzig, p. 350). In Diesterweg's opinion, children under 10 should not be allowed to enter a factory and should only work for a maximum of 4 to 6 hours there. He pleads for socially corrective state intervention in economic life through the education system.

4. Social Democrats Speak Out Against Exploitation of Children in the State Parliament of Saxony

With the emergence of the Proletarian Movement in the "Fraternity of Workers" (`Arbeiterverbruederung') official protests against child labour were articulated for the very first time by the workers themselves. Accordingly, the Congress of Workers which convened in Berlin between 23.8.1948 and 3.9.1348 resolved that no child should be engaged in industrial work of any sort which prevents regular and full attendance of school before completing 14 years of age; however, the recruitment of children in factories and for peddling is not permitted on any grounds whatsoever before the child completes 14 years of age."

In opposition to the representatives of the bourgeois parties the Social Democratic members of Parliament attacked child labour during the last quarter of the 19th century and questioned their ideological justification that child labour "has educational value." They also voiced strong criticism on "the transformation of immature human beings into mere machines" (Karl Marx) and pointed out the harm this was causing to the mental, physical and moral development of these. Child labour—"social assassination" as Engels termed it—was an expression of the prevalent bougeois form of society. Despite legislation against child labour, the number of children working in factories doubled between 1880—1886. According to a census on working children in Germany in the year 1898, 532.238 children were registered as being employed. This figure corresponds to 6.5% of all children of school going age. In the kingdom of Saxony, however, 137.831 children of school going age were counted who were working against wages of factories and other enterprises, a figure which corresponds to 22.8%.

Due to a shifting of child labour into the areas of cottage industry and agriculture after 1890, the Social Democrats demanded a safety and health control which the representatives of the "bourgeois" parties denounced as an interference into "holy family life."

The rejection of exploitative child labour did however not imply that Social Democrats did not realise that children and juveniles had to be instructed and educated through productive work. Children were to be inducted gradually into different practical activities such as horticulture, fruit-growing and apiculture, as well as farming, factory work and processes of production. They were guided by the observations of their party chairman of many years, August Bebel, made in 1879 in his most important book: "*Women and Socialism*" ("Die Frau under Sozialismus"):

"Child labour today is the most infamous form of exploitation which in Socialist society should only be allowed as a means of education commensurate with the strength and capability of the individual and in course of time should be reduced to a point where it can only be beneficial and not detrimental to health and well being."

The Social Democratic education movement of the "Friends of Children" (`Kinderfreunde'), since 1908 in Austria and 1923 in Germany became the largest non-professional paedagogical and child movement of its time. Co-educational, a religious child education and self-managed children's groups formed an alternative to bourgeois and clerical institutions of education and followed the thoughts of August Bebel.

5. Some Consideration and Questions

In which historical period of time ("historische Zeit") did child labour prevail in Europe and when was it finally abolished? To what extent can this "veritable" historic period of time spanning several decades, even centuries, be realistically curtailed under changed socio-economic conditions and through the partial integration of the public/private sector of a national economy into the world market?

Germany serves an interesting case in point to observe how acute social problems, like child labour, for instance, were handled by the rulers under specific conditions of rule and finally "resolved" ("the Social Question").

The suppression by the State (the Anti-Socialist Law of 1878) of the proletariat emerging under social democracy, with its Marxian Eisenach Programme, was simultaneously or soon after supplemented by the positive role played by the State through Social Legislation in moulding social conditions.

Is child labour necessarily an integral part of certain early stages of development of the capitalist mode of production or was it to a considerable extent dependent on socio-cultural and religion-based values as well?

It is necessary to clearly define the role played by child labour with its low wage costs in the overall economic process or the process of industrial accumulation.

Child labour served to assure the lower classes their means of subsistence—and was a means of depressing wages—, a role not confined to Germany alone.

A retrospective glance at European or German history in the light of the problem of "child labour" throws open the possibility of gaining a clearer perspective of the stage of social and economic evolution attained in countries with developing societies despite the many socio-cultural differences between the developed and developing world.

The study of the subject of child labour constitutes one of the key instruments to a sound, value-based social analysis of any nation-state.

What do the tremendous proportions assumed by child labour reveal about the inner fabric of a society and to what extent does it—alongside social malconditions and contradictions—threaten even the international credibility of expressions of legitimation articulated by political, economic and trade union elites?

To what extent would the contention of entrepreneurs that child labour with its low wage costs is inevitable on account of prevailing conditions of competition in the world market, stand the test of a sound analysis?

Transnational corporations are the basic acting units in the International Economic System, challenging or at least-relativising the very existence of newly independent nation-states in the historical perspective. To what extent does their role in national economies impair the independent development of these economies and release uncontrolled entrepreneurial forces which, amongst other things, for reasons of a competition increasingly exploit the factor of labour, and with that child labour as well, thereby indirectly initiating the very practice of child labour?

Other than historical examples illustrating the overcoming of child labour in developed industrialised countries, are there known examples of success in the drastic reduction or elimination of child labour in the various countries of Asia, Africa or Latin America?

Though the possibility cannot completely be ruled out, Europeans as generations born in the wake of the Industrial Revolution are not exactly preeminently legitimised to point an accusing finger at conditions prevailing in developing countries, on account of their own history of child labour. How could European trade union fedrations, industrial unions or non-governmental organisations contribute in a non-interventionist manner within the framework of the efforts made, for instance, by Indian trade unions or voluntary agencies to protect children.

To what extent could commissions for child protection formed by women of the Social Democratic Party of Germany or the trade unions at the beginning of the 20th century serve as stimulating precedents if not as standing examples to similar groups in developing countries?

Of what relevance are experiences with industrial pedagogics in the late 18th and 19th centuries for efforts to educate child labour in developing countries today?

What form should pedagogics, specially devised for child labour, take?

The subject of child labour can be dealt with in didactic texts at various levels of schooling, or explicitly made a subject of education for unionised labour, with examples, even historical references to child labour and its abolition during the Industrial Revolution in Europe, to serve as illustration.

6. Chronology of Child Labour, Child Protection Measures/Laws and Workers' Resistance Against Child Labour in Germany

16th/ 17th century onward	Child labour introduced in orphanages to ensure economic survival. It existed in commercially oriented workshops for orphans.
From approx. 1750	"Lending out" of orphan children as cheap labour to entrepreneurs from outside, as a result of which the spheres of work and daily life of children are separated.
1988	The Poor disposition of Hamburg with financial incentive (the so-called "Sitzgeld" or "attendance allowance") for attending Poor School.
1821	Evening school for child factory workers in Iserlohn.
1827	The celebrated bourgeois pedagogue F.A.W. Diesterweg questions the permissibility of child labour and the utilitarian standpoint of industrial pedagogues in his study "On the Use of Children for Factory work—an Observation from the Pedagogic Angle."
1827	The Government of Arnsberg promulgates school regulations for children employed in factories. Factory schools, however, only remained episodic.
1827	General Heinrich Wilhelm von Horn complains of the inability of the industrial areas to adequately complement the ranks of the Army.
1828	The King of Prussia prohibits night work for children in an Order on Council.
1839	Regulation on Child Labour in Factories, the first Supervisory Law for the textile industry; — Prohibition of Child labour in the case of children below 9 years of age. — Proof of three years school attendance. — Maximum hours of work fixed at 10 hours, with a two hour break at noon. — Prohibition of work on Sundays, holidays and at night.
1840	First Labour Protection Ordinance of favour of children promulgated in the Kingdom of Bavaria.
1840	First Child Protection Ordinance in Baden.
1842	Prohibition of female labour and the employment of children below 10 in mines.

1848	The Congress of Workers in Berlin denounces the employment of children below 14.
1849	State inspection of steam boiler plant in the Kingdom of Saxony.
1853	Law on the engagement of factory inspectors for the well-being of young workers.
1853	The Prussian Government prohibits factory work for children below 12.
	Factory control by industrial inspectors. Child labour continues in agriculture and the cottage industry for decades on end.
1961	Legislative protection for child labour in factories in Saxony.
1862	First statutory regulation (Factory Act) for child labour in Wuerttemberg.
1866	The First International condemns child labour and calls for solidarity on this issue.
1870	Introduction of honorary factory inspection in Baden.
1978	Compulsory factory inspection with obligatory annual submission of reports introduced by a majority of the "Reichstag" (Imperial Diet) against the will of the government.
1891	Amendment of the Industrial Regulation of 1878: Prohibition of factory work for children of school-going age.
	Lower age limit for child workers in factories raised from 12 to 13 years.
1895	According to Kaete Dunker's interpretation of the results of the enumeration of the employed, about 2 million, i.e. 25% of the children of school-going age, were engaged primarily in agriculture and as domestic servants.
1903/04	Child Protection Law: Prohibition of child labour in those branches of industry having pernicious effects on health and in smaller industrial establishments; agriculture and as domestic help, however, being excluded here.
1904	1.7 million children employed in the agricultural sector.
1904/05	The formation of social democratic Child Protection Commissions by women in order to enforce existing laws and improve protective legislation.
1908	Extension of protective Legislation to cover cottage industrial units with a minimum of 10 workers.
1911	Extension of the Cottage Industry Legislation to cover even workshops in which only members of the family worked.
1910	The Child Protection Commission of the Social Democratic Party (SPD) and the Trade Union Commission of Berlin call for a ban on children of school-going age being recruited for any kind of wage employment.
1913	The Social Democratic Faction in the Reichstag calls for an improvement in the Child Protection Law.

4.8.1914 Beginning of the First World War: Almost all Laws for the Protection of working children were annulled. The ban on recruitment of children below 13 years is repealed. Children under 14 may once again work more than 6 hours.

7. Selected Documents

7.1 The Path to Protective Legislation for Child Workers in Factories

In order to comprehend the inordinate delay in the development of Protective Legislation for children and the slow tediousness of the path leading to the promulgation of the first law—the regulation of 1839—, one has to be clear on the reasons for industrial child labour being taken for granted at that time. The most important reasons are stated in the following:

2.1 Reasons for Industrial Child Labour Being Regarded a Natural Phenomenon

1. Firstly, child labour was not invented by the Industrial Age but had always existed, for instance in agriculture or in the cottage industry. "The child grew up by the spooling wheel." According to Robert Alt, there were many workers in the factories who "as a result of their own habitual practices during adolescence or their former occupation, found the induction of children as wage labour most natural...." —in other words, to utilise children as factory labour. It can, therefore, be said that the second phase of child labour started with industrialisation.
2. In the 19th century child labour was not only prevalent in England and Prussia but all over the world. "The over-exploitation of children as labour is not peculiar to individual kingdoms, provinces or regions. It can be found in varying degrees in all countries of Europe: from the tobacco plantations of Bessarabia to the sulphur pits of Southern Italy, in the industrial and agricultural sectors of Germany, England, Austria, France, Belgium, Spain and Switzerland."
   Ellen Key draws attention to the magnesium mines of Spain employing children between 6 and 8 years of age, to the bast-mat weaving centres of Russia, with three year olds and the sulphur pits of Sicily where even children between 12 and 14 were rendered unfit for work.
3. The laws already in existence were considered adequate to protect children from exploitation; particularly the Provisions of the Universal Law of the Land of 1794, the codification of all laws in force in Prussia:
   (a) Parents who could not prove that their child was receiving the necessary level of education at home could be compelled, by the use of coercive means and threat to punishment, to send their child to school after completion of 5 years.
   (b) Regular schooling was to be continued as long as the pastor was satisfied that the child had procured sufficient knowledge to assume his growing into a rational being.

(c) A child could be exempted from attending school over a longer period only with the permission of the authorities and clerical members of the school governing body.

4. The emergence of mass poverty (pauperism) as a transient, if not even permanent state of affairs resulting from industrial development, made even child labour appear natural. The "commonly portrayed picture" of early industrialisation is characterised by long hours of work, female and child labours, low remuneration, insufficient security, lack of safeguards at the place of work and miserable living conditions.

   Robert Alt draws attention to the vicious circle inherent in this situation, namely that the parents on the one hand needed the additional income accruing from children's wages and on the other contributed to depressed ages and increased unemployment amongst themselves by accepting child labour.

5. The new machinery employed initially permitted the engagement of workers with low muscle power. "To the extent to which machinery makes physical strength dispensable, it becomes the means of employing workers without muscular strength or of immature physical growth, albeit with greater suppleness of limb. Female and child labour was thus the primary outcome of the capitalist employment machinery."

6. The nascent industry was faced with severe competition and needed cheap labour. This is found in industrial child labour. This motive has, time and again, been brought to attention during conflicts between industry and law enforcement authorities and even in the struggle to enforce overtime for adolescent workers.

7. Industrial child labour was at the time considered to be a pedagogic value—a view which the industrial schools helped create. The educational value of industrial labour was considered to lie in its training the children to acquire the qualities of diligence, perseverance, self-discipline, conscientiousness and dexterity. Keller, Privy Councillor to the Administration made precise observations on the educative value of child labour during his journey across the Rhineland in 1834.

   He was particularly impressed by the educative effect of production with division of labour in a needle factory in Aachen. The work allotted to the children employed there, who numbered about 100, was, in his opinion, indeed exhausting and not exactly free of danger, but at least it was not too difficult and the "deftness, agility and dexterity displayed by the children while executing all these tasks is astonishing. The tools and machines they handle are ingenious; the children themselves sitting side by side in a row while working, at times bending forward and at times back-ward, all synchronising almost perfectly in the rhythm of their movements, remind the observer of machines. But they are strong, healthy, cheerful and bright and even mischievous and lively.... There is certainly some truth in the assumption that the educative value of industrial work was only recognised for child workers in factories at the time and not for pupils of the "Gymnasium."*

8. The so-called social question did not exist at all during the early phase of industrialisation. There were, at the time, still no social reformist movements which could have balanced out the social and techno-economic demands against each other. The top priority and objective of the state at that time was to assure itself power and privileges so much so it did not interfere in economic life. The reluctance of the state to concern itself with social issues, and with that the emergence of industrial child labour as well, can be attributed to this. It is also true that the rapidly developing industrial sector held the fascination of entrepreneurs and statesmen to such an extent that the latter were initially blind to accompanying social problems.

Except from Report Compiled by a Privy Councillor, 1834:

"Children are made to work every day from 5 o'clock in the morning till noon, and then from 1 o'clock in the morning till noon, till late in the evening; in winter naturally as long as there is light. These children have never known the benefits of schooling, neither in their younger days nor during the time when they are employed. They have never even attended Sunday school which is practically unknown in Bonn.

Those who did work in factories, therefore, were still considered the most well behaved and decent. The others perished from begging, from being exposed to the rigours of the weather or due to the vagaries of the lives they led. However, although children working in factories have to put in 12 to 15 hours of work per day, it is only through this that they regularly earn their daily bread and are treated to that indispensable disciplining. The urchins who crouched by roadside ditches all day in the hope of pitifully whining their way to a few pennies from the next traveller through pretence and false-hoods, and who interspersed this with thefts in fields and gardens are in my opinion too hardened for and unaccustomed to any form of disciplining. They will probably only die in the open of poverty and want or put an end to their lives in the provincial penitentiaries and workhouses near Werden or Brauweiler."

7.3 Accident of a Child Worker

"I wish to give yet another example. I have a brother who is 8 years old. My mother was persuaded by a spinner into sending him to work in a factory where he earned 10 Reichsgroschen every week as a piecer operating a new mill spinning machine. One day he was asked to clean the machine which is generally done while the machine is still running. This meant that one had to be very careful for the piecer has to crawl in quickly during the run-out of the carriage, do some cleaning and again crawl out quickly before the run-in. A delay of a few seconds could result in death, as was the case in 1862 in the joint-stock spinning factory at Chemnitz where a live child was reduced to a corpse in just two minutes."[5]

7.4 Child Workers During Famine Years

The following account of a worker in the cotton spinning factory of Himmelmuehle in Saxony provides vivid depiction of the situation of child workers in factories during the famine years of 1846/47:

"It was simply frightful in the scarce years of 1846/47 when the poor young workers at the tender age of 9, 10 to 14 and 15, had to brave the fiercest of storms and blizzards early in the morning and late in the evening to set out for work; often lean and hungry, heart broken when their weekly wages were consumed for buying dry bread right in the beginning of the week, for the cold, metallic air from the power driven machines sapped one of all energy and made one hungry. The spinner could give them nothing; he himself had to go hungry during those years, with just dry bread to eat, while continuing to work all the time in this state. His heart bled as he watched his piecers make their way hurriedly during the lunch break in the last few days of their week, over the hill to the farmers in villages lying a good half hour away, to beg for a few pieces of bread, for they had to be back at the stroke of 1. A factory owner could frown down despotically upon this with characteristic lack of empathy when told—upon asking where the children hurried off to every afternoon towards the end of the week, whilst they always stayed behind in the dining hall during the first few days of the week—that these children had gone to beg for a few pieces of bread.

The workers lived within the narrow confines of their lodgings, crowded together. The rooms were hardly aired out for fear of losing any heart. Generally the living quarters were far off from the factories so that apart from working for 14 hours at a stretch, the workers also had to spend a great deal of time walking to and fro.

In winter this meant wading through slush and snow without adequate clothing. Most of the time the children arrived at the factories completely drenched, whereby their chest and lung ailments, which they had developed due to the unhealthy air in the factories, were only further aggravated. The children could hardly resist as they were "dragged away crying and protesting to such a prison by their mothers, early in the morning at 5 o'clock, even in cold or wet weather." Everyone stood against them: the authorities, the manufacturers, the parents and even the workers with whom they worked in the factories. The right of disciplining the children wielded by the overseer formed part of the control system in proto-factories. The worst cases of child abuse" by overseers were recorded in 1824 by the Provincial Administrative Counsellor of Iserlohn. The factory workers of the cotton spinning factory of Himmel-muehle also confirmed that the chief overseer, Schuessler, administered slaps to the "poor hungry children for the slightest mistake they committed" and dug his fist into their sides and ribs. The "fraternisation" (Verbruederung") recorded similar instances in 1849: Children were kept awake and attentive at work by being beaten with whips, lashes and canes. Their helplessness, especially that of the female child workers, before the overseers were revealed in a recent on the conditions in Elbersfeld, presented in the Rhineland Provincial Diet of 1843. Here, it was revealed that an overseer had passed on syphilis to the young girls working in the factory, causing great misery and hardship to their families.[6]

Except from Friedrich Engels "The Condition of the Working Class in England, From Personal Observation and Authentic Sources[7]

"In the coal and iron mines which are worked in pretty much the same way, children of four, five, and seven years are employed. They are set to transporting the ore or coal loosened by the miner from its place to the horse-path or the main shaft, and to opening and shutting the doors (which separate the divisions of the mine and regulate its ventilation) for the passage of workers and material. For watching the doors the smallest children are usually employed, who thus pass twelve hours daily, in the dark, alone, sitting usually in damp passages without even having work enough to save them from the stupefying, brutalising tedium of doing nothing. The transport of coal and iron-stone, on the other hand, is very hard labour, the stuff being shoved in large tubs, without wheels, over the uneven floor of the mine; often over moist clay, or through water, and frequently up steep inclines and through paths so low-roofed that the workers are forced to creep on hands and knees. For this more wearing labour, therefore, older children and half-grown girls are employed. One man or two boys per tub are employed, according to circumstances; and, if two boys, one pushes and the other pulls. The loosening of the ore or coal, which is done by men or strong youths of sixteen years or more, is also very weary work. The usual working day is eleven to twelve hours, often longer; in Scotland it reaches fourteen hours, and double time is frequent, when all the employees are at work below ground twenty-four, and even thirty-six hours at a stretch. Set times for meals are almost unknown, so that these people eat when hunger and time permit.

The children and young people who are employed in transporting coal and iron-stone all complain of being over-tried.

It is constantly happening that children throw themselves down on the stone hearth or the floor as soon as the reach home, fall asleep at once without being able to take one bite of food, and have to be washed and put to bed while asleep; it even happens that they lie down on the way home, and are found by their parents late at night asleep on the road. It seems to be a universal practice among these children to spend Sunday in bed to recover in some degree from the over-exertion of the week. Church and school are visited by but few, and even of these the teachers complain of their great sleepiness and the want of all eagerness to learn."

BIBLIOGRAPHY

Adolphs, Lotte, Erziehung und Bildung im 19. Jahrhundert. Kinderarbeit, Lehrenrverhalten, Schulrevision.

(Child Rearing and Education in the 19th century. Child Labour, teacher's attitudes, school revision). Disburg, 1979.

Dahrendorf, Ralph: Gesellschaft und Demokratie in Deutschland (Society and Democracy in Germany). Muenchen 1967.

Ebeling, Hans/Birkenfeld, Wolfgang: Die Reise in die Vergangenheir. Ein geschichtliches Arbeitsbuch. Band 3, Das Werden der modernen Welt. Lehrerausgabe. Braunschweig 1972.

(The journey into the past. A historical workbook. Vol. 3, the development of the modern world. Teacher's edition).

Engels, Friedrich: The condition of the working class in England, From personal observation and authentic sources. Moscow 1973.

Gebhardt, Bruno: Handbuch der deutschen Geschichte. Band 3: Von der Franzoesischen Revolution bis zum Ersten Weltkrieg. (Handbook of German history. Vol. 3: From the French revolution to world war I). Stuttgart 1965.

Herzfeld, Hans: Die Moderne Welt, 1989-1945. Teil I: Die Epoche der buergerlichen Nationalstaaten. (The modern world, 1789-1945. Part I: The era of the bourgeois nation states). Braunschweig 1961.

Herzig, Arno: Kinderarbeit in Deutschland in Manufacture und Proto-Fabrik (1950—1850), S. 311-375, in: "Archiv fuer Sozialgeschichte," herausgegeben von der Friedrich-Ebert-Stiftung in Verbindung mit dem Institut fuer Sozialgeschichte. Braunschweig—Bonn. XXIII, Band 1, Bonn 1983.

(Child Labour in Germany in manufacture and in protofactories (1750—1850), pp. 311-375 in "Archives of Social History," published by Friedrich Ebert Foundation in collaboration with "Institut fuer Sozialgeschichte." *Braun-schweig-Bonn.* XXIII, Vol. I, Bonn 1983.

Hug, Wolfgang: Unsere Geschichte. Band 2: Vom Beginn der Neuzeit bis zum ende des 19. Jahrhunderts. (Our history. Vol. 2 : From the beginning of modern times to the end of the 19th century.) Frankfurt/Main, Berlin, Muenchen 1985.

Jenss, Harro: Jugendarbeitsschutz. Von den Anfaengen der Industrialisierung bis zur Gegenwart. (Legislation on Juvenile labour. From the beginning of industrialisation to the present. Frankfurt/New York 1980.

Lesanovsky, Werner: Die Bemuehungen der Sozialdemokratischen Abgeordneten im Saechsischen Landtag um die Verbesserung der proletarischen Familienerziehung und der Kampf gegen die kapitalistische Kinderausbeutung (1877-1900). In : "Saechsische Heimatblatter," 28. Jahrgg., Heft 3/1982.

(Efforts of the social democratic members in the state parliament of Saxony for the improvement of proletarian family education and fight against child exploitation (1877-1900). Published in: "Saechsische Heimatblaetter," XXVII, no. 3, 1982.

Meyer, Thomas/Klaer, Karl-Heinz/Miller, Susanne/Nory, Klaus/Timmermann, Heinz: Lexikon des Sozialismus. (An Encyclopaedia of Socialism). Koeln 1986.

Quandt, Siegfried: Kinderarbeit und Kinderschutz in Deutschland, 1783-1976. Quellen und Anmerkungen. (Child labour and legislation in Germany, 1783-1976. Sources and Notes). Paderborn 1978.

Stark von der Haar, Elike and Heinrich: Kinderarbeit in der Bundesrepublik und im Deutschen Reich. Eine Bestandsaufnahme ueber Ausmass und Folgen der Beschaeftigung von Kindern und ueber den gesetzlichen Kinderschutz. Mit zahlreichen Dokumenten und einer Unterrichtseinheit.

(Child labour in the Federal Rebublic and in the German Reich. A Reassessment of extent and effects of employment of children and child labour legislation. With numerous documents and teaching instructions). Goettingen 1980.

NOTES

1. The continuous occupational employment of children below 14 years for the entire duration of the working day.

   Child labour is a particularly unscrupulous form of human exploitation leading to serious physical and moral injuries. Already widely prevalent in workshops, child labour assumed mass proportions with the introduction of mechanised production at the end of the 18th century. Often unpaid for work in the cottage industry, child labourers were paid minimal wages in factories as a lever to enforce lower wages for adult workers.

2. Arno Herzig, p. 327.
3. Arno Herzig, p. 331.
4. Arno Herzig, p. 359. "Out of 7415 children of school going age in Aachen, 2600 hail from wealthy families and 4815 from the poorer classes or those social sections which cannot afford to pay school fees for their children. A school with two certified teachers has been created for these impoverished classes in which approximately 250 pupils are given lessons."
5. Arno Herzig, pp. 342, 343.
6. Arno Herzig, pp. 344/45.
7. Friedrich Engels, pp. 281 and 282.

10

CHILD LABOUR: A HARSH REALITY

Child labour has existed from times immemorial. Children in every society have assisted in the activities characteristic of their social group. They have helped their parents in household chores, in family run businesses and also outside in factories and an assortment of big and small commercial establishments. Children worked along with their parents in the fields, in family crafts, in domestic and non-domestic work.

Some Historical Aspects of Child Labour in India

In Ancient India, it was the duty of the King to educate every girl and boy and parents could be punished for not sending their childrens to school called Ashrams, which were really residential schools under a Guru (a learned sage). Child labour existed only in the form of child slaves. Children, sometimes even less than 8 years of age, were purchased to do so-called 'low and dishonourable' work. Kautilya (4th century B.C.), considered it degrading to make children work on such jobs and hence prohibited the purchase and sale of slave children below 8 years.

Children, however, helped their parents a household activities and family crafts. They learnt the skills by observing and participating in such activities. A predominantly rural society is inevitably characterised by small and marginal economic units. India, through its medieval period, was no exception. Increasing pressure on land led to fragmentation of holdings. Growing families had to look beyond personal cultivation for subsistence. A class of landless labourers came into existence, often bonded to the large landowners. These labourers used their children to help in their economic activities.

The rural artisan rarely worked alone. In fact, the entire family was a work unit with the 'pater familia' being the master craftsman. Occupations were determined largely on the basis of heredity, and children were introduced to their traditional craft at a young age.

In the late 17th Century the most significant change was the growth of organisations involving the employment of large numbers of artisans. The Dutch silk factory at Kasimbazar in Bengal, employed 700-800 weavers. But the characteristic unit of production was still the small unit. "The persistent dominance of family based work units indicates that any disciplined organisation of an industrial society was not in sight."[1]

In the middle of the 19th Century there was an enormous growth of European industry in India especially during 1860-70 as seen by the growth of the tea, coffee, indigo and jute industry. At this time, the factory industry began taking the place of handicrafts. It was in the fifties that the cotton and jute industry and coal mining were started in an organised way. However, even in 1880 the number of people employed in these industries was rather small even though people were quickly being driven out from their old crafts.

It was after the Industrial Revolution in the early 19th Century that a change started taking place. Factory type units started springing up. Agriculture became more mechanised and small land holdings were no longer economically viable. Small land owners left their lands and started working as farm labourers on bigger farms. Factories required cheap and plentiful labour. Children started being employed both on farms and in factories because they provided a cheap, uncomplaining labour force as against adults who could be more demanding and hence more difficult to handle. In the course of the 19th and early 20th Century, people, especially in the European countries, became conscious of the evils of this exploitation of children and the International Labour Organisation (ILO) was set up in 1919 to formulate guidelines to improve the working conditions of children and ban their employment before the age of fourteen. In the Preamble to the Constitution of the ILO, it is stated that in many regions the conditions of labour are such as to result in untold misery which disturbs the peace and harmony of the world. Children and young persons especially must be protected. At the very first session of the International Labour Conference, a convention was adopted fixing the minimum age as 14 years for children in industrial employment. Between 1919 and 1965, there were 10 conventions on the minimum age. Finally in 1973, the convention concerning Minimum Age for Admission to Employment (No. 138) and the Recommendation (No. 146) were adopted and these replaced all the previous conventions. However, much needs to be done through national legislation in the various countries where exploitation of children still exists. Today child labour is almost non existent in the developed countries of the world. However, it still persists in alarming proportions in the developing countries. According to the ILO, the number of working children the world over increased from 43 million to 52 million between 1970 and 1979. Of these approximately 29 million were from South East Asia, 10 million from Africa, 9 million from East Africa, 3 million from South America and about 1 million from the developed countries.

According to the 1981 Census in India there are 13.59 million working children. Unofficial figures are of course much higher; National Sample Survey (1983) estimates 17.36 million; Operations Research Group, Baroda (1983) says 44 million; CWC, (Concerned for Working Children) Bangalore (1985) says 100 million!

No. of working children less than 15 years old

Area	*Total (Million)*	*Unpaid family workers**	
		Million	*Percentage of total*
World	52.0	41.2	80
South East Asia	29.0	23.2	80
East Asia	9.1	6.4	70
Africa	9.7	9.2	95
Latin America	3.1	2.0	65
Europe	0.7	0.4	50
USSR	—	—	—
North America	0.3	—	10
Oceania	0.1	0.1	85

*Includes a very small number of persons working on their own account.
Source : ILO Bureau of Statistics and Special Studies.

The reason for employing children has been two-fold. First, to supplement the family income when it has not been sufficient to meet the requirements of the family. This is the main reason for child labour in India today, where more than 37% of people live below the poverty line. Any addition to the family income helps to case the burden of a very tedious existence. "Child labour exists in inverse relation to the degree of economic advancement of a society, country or region."[2] In most developing countries having more children is considered a great advantage because every child means two extra hands to work, which means more income for the family. Children are not sent to school mainly because preparing them for a brighter future is unimportant when the immediate present is so bleak. The child by working is able to reduce to a great extent the poverty in which he lives and hence satisfies some of his basic needs. Even the smallest payments in cash or kind are welcome in his poor home and he shares in the maintenance of his family.

The second reason is that children were taught a traditional craft at a very early age to make them proficient in a job which would then be a source of income to them on gaining adulthood. It is a recognised fact that in childhood the body is more flexible and pliable and can hence bend, twist, stretch more easily to acquire postures required for particular jobs. It is both a physical and mental adjustment which is required in the learning process. Even musicians and dancers start to train their children at the early age of 5 or 6. It is for the same reason that craftsmen train their children in their hereditary crafts because the nimble fingers and keen eyesight of early childhood are an asset in the learning process. Carpet weaving, pottery, skill and cotton weaving, wood carving, etc. are some of the traditional crafts taught to young children within their homes. In the villages, the boys at a young age are made to handle a plough, reap the harvest, cut and bring fuel from the forest, catch fish from the village ponds, graze the cattle, guard the crops against birds and monkeys, etc. while the girls help in weeding the fields, looking after younger siblings, sweeping the house, etc. These may not be viewed as 'gainful' activities. However, they do free the mother or older siblings for working in the fields or in other wage earning activities.

Children from an integral part of the household economy. They are trained while still young and gradually start contributing individually to the family's income. There is no obvious oppression and they learn mainly through observation, imitation and assistance to elders. Soon parents find that children cannot only assist in the household activities but can even be made to work for others in return for wages in cash or kind. In family run businesses the children who are made to work outside their homes are far more exploited by having to work long hours in arduous and often hazardous tasks, at low wages, and often in unhygienic work sites with hardly any facilities. Most of these jobs are "monotonous, strenuous, harmful or unduly prolonged", and "the very many children who are engaged on them grow up prematurely and sadly, instead of leading a carefree existence with their friends during what could be the happiest days of their lives."[3]

The family is not the only one to blame, it is society as a whole that is at fault. Besides the parents, it is the employers who are responsible for perpetuating this terrible practice. Even in family run units, where the child is generally better looked after by his parents and may not suffer from any physical hardship, be goes through mental strain because of problems and anxieties regarding the undertaking which he shares with his parents.

Child Labour in General

A child labourer is differentiated from an adult worker on the basis of age. Usually a child worker is someone below the age of 14 or 15 years who is involved in any productive activity whether paid or unpaid, with the family or outside. Children are involved in all types of work. They work in agricultural activities, looking after cattle and sheep, scaring away birds from the fields, helping at the time of sowing and harvesting. In their homes, they look after the younger siblings, collect fire wood and water, and participate in other domestic and non-domestic work as in a cottage industry. In the urban sector, they work in a wide variety of activities from organised factories to roadside cafes, motor repairing workshops, street vending, shoe shining, selling of newspapers, fruits and peanuts, domestic help in homes and even in organised beggary. Parents put their children to work at a very early age, sometimes when they are only 6-7 years old. As the child grows older, he gains more expertise in the tasks he has been performing since early childhood.

A large percentage of children start working because of being orphaned, rejected by parents or because of broken families and other domestic problems. These children go into the streets totally abundoned with no one to care for them. They have no option but to take to work for their bare survival. It is in these unfortunate circumstances that young girls are drawn into prostitution and young boys and girls have been forced into organised beggary, even being maimed in the process.

In the case of agricultural labour, it has been seen that when the family head moves from one area to another depending on the agricultural cycle, his wife and young children will either move with him or stay back to look after the small family plot in his absence. In both cases, it is a traumatic experience for the young children. Moving around constantly, they feel insecure and insettled and being without their father for long periods often makes them indisciplined and irresponsible.

In the urban areas, the case is similar. When whole families move from their village to the cities, they face the traumas of lack of shelter, hunger, joblessness, etc. Staying back in the village alone for long periods is gain not a happy situation. In the cities, young children start to work by helping their father in petty jobs on the streets, usually without payment. Later they start to work on their own or for somebody else. The type of jobs they do are cleaning cars, polishing shoes, selling magazines and newspapers, selling fruit and peanuts, guarding parked cars, carrying messages, etc. In the bigger cities, children have been caught selling drugs. It is a common sight to see them begging. In Delhi, on a cold water evening or in the hot summer afternoon, one sees these children braving the weather in their scanty clothes. One often reads of the police catching gags which deliberately main young children for the purpose of begging. In the cities again, children work as domestic help with no set hours of work. They provide various kinds of services in workships, dhabas (roadside cafes), petrol pumps, etc. Their hours of work are irregular and often they do not even go home—if they have a home at all—and sleep in the place of work itself. Their day starts early in the morning and goes on till late at night. In the organised sector, there are various manufacturing units and processes where children are preferred, such as the glass and bangle industry, matchbox and fireworks manufacture, carpet weaving, etc. The reason given by the entrepreneurs is that they have soft, nimble fingers and are hence able to do the job better than adults. But this has been found to be only partially true. The same work can easily be done by women and even men. It is convenient to have children because they constitute a cheap, silent, uncomplaining workforce.

Working Conditions

Children begin work in family undertaking from an early age alongside their parents. Later parents, relatives or friends take them to their future employers. The treatment meted out to the working child depends entirely on the temperament of the employer. Some children may be illitreated and humiliated, even beaten; while others are looked after with parental care. Most of the work they do is monotonous, repetitive and dull and is often not suited to their physical and mental capabilities. The child continues to work in appalling conditions because he expects very little from his job, knowing that at least he is employed and can earn some money.

Normally, the child who works in a family undertaking, whether in agriculture, manufacturing, commerce or handicrafts, is exploited less than the wage-earning child. Certainly, "the stress, fatigue and harmful effects to which he is exposed are partly compensated for by the personal attention and affection which his parents can give him during both work and rest periods."[4]

The number of hours spent in working varies considerably from 6 to 8 hours per day to even 12 or 14 hours, much more than their young bodies can stand. Often they have no fixed hours at all as in roadside cafes, workshops or domestic work. To this one should add the time spent in travelling to and from home.

Children's wages also vary considerably. In agricultural work, they may get no payment in cash but may get paid in kind by receiving small portions of grain. If they work as a family unit then the head of the family will receive the payment while the child may get no share of it separately. Often the children do odd jobs in the homes of big landowners. For this they rarely get any payment at all except a free meal every day. In family undertakings, the child earns nothing separately, whatever is earned by the family is kept by the head of the family. In the unorganised urban sector, the wages of the child depend entirely on the importance of the work done by him. In any case, the child is paid much less than what an adult earns for the same work. Employers will explain this discrimination by stating that the children are in experienced, the quality and quantity of work produced by them is not the same as adults, they have to be trained and a lot of time and effort is involved in this. The truth of the matter is that children provide cheap, uncomplaining labour, and the employers take full advantage of this. Even in the organised sector, children are hardly ever paid the legal minimum wage. They are supposed to be on training for long periods of time during which they are not paid at all even though they have gained expertise and are really working while being trained. The child may have secured his job through a labour contractor as in the case of carpet weaving. Here the contractor will take his commission, often as much as 25%, on the wages earned by the child. Where the children are paid on a piece-rate, they are again at a disadvantage. Being illiterate, they are unable to calculate how much work they produce in a month and hence have no way to check what payment is due to them. Parents of working children often take large advances and loans from their employers. These advances are slowly deducted from the child's wages, which means that his monthly takings get reduced. It takes years to repay these loans by which time the family needs a fresh loan and this cycle goes on. The children in this way get 'bonded' to work. There is no getting away for them. There have been a few cases where children are pledged to work while still in the mother's womb and advances taken against this pledge!

Whatever the occupation, the element of risk is always there as far as a child concerned. Some occupations like firework and match making, glass and bangle manufacture, and carpet weaving are extremely hazardous and yet children continue to be employed in them. Because their bodies are young, they get tired easily and fatigue sets in. They work in unhygienic conditions, with little or no ventilation and bad light. Their bodies are often in uncomfortable positions for long periods of time and they have to concentrate on minute, detailed work. In carpet weaving, they sit in a crouched position for eight hours a day because of which their legs and joints become stiff and their growth gets retarded. The intense concentration on the loom all the time leads to eye strain and fatigue. Inhaling wool fluff constantly gives them breathing problems. In the match and fireworks industry, the children inhale lungfulls of toxic fumes from the chemicals, suffer intense heat, run the risk of being badly injured and suffer intense strain from lifting heavy frames. Working in the glass and bangle factories, the workers are affected by the silica dust which causes silicosis, a killing disease of the lungs; the intense heat near the furnaces affects the body cells and the blazing glass can result in accidental burns and other injuries. Accidents often occur at the worksites and there are usually no first aid facilities available. The employer does not even bother to take them to a doctor, and the children learn to look after one another. Social security and accident insurance schemes hardly exist. The machinery, tools etc. are designed for adults and not for children. Some of the chemicals can be extremely dangerous. In agricultural work, contact with pesticides and fertilizers leads to skin problems and poisoning. Agricultural work is, in any case, strenuous and puts a great strain on the young body of a child. Self-employed children working in street trades have no health security at all. They are exposed to extreme weather conditions, traffic hazards, besides becoming victims of unhealthy habits like smoking, drinking, etc. They continue to work even when they are ill because the daily earnings are so important to meet their basic needs in life.

Home Environment

The living conditions of working children are appalling. Families, though extremely poor, are large in size. Family planning has not been very successful with the illiterate working classes. In any case, the general opinion is that many children mean many more hands to work and earn. Their homes are congested and overcrowded with hardly any ventilation or sanitary facilities. The entire "Basti", (living area with a cluster of houses or huts) is unhygeinic with water logging, dirt, insects and flies. This in itself results in illnesses of all types like typhoid, malaria, hepatitis, etc. The presence of life is so intense that the adult males spend their evenings drinking and have no time or inclination to look after or supervise the children. The children roam the streets unattended and uncared for. Working children have very little contact with their parents because they spend a greater part of the day at work away from home and come back only late at night. Children who leave their village home and come away to the cities to work face acute housing problems. Most of them either sleep on the pavements, in corridors or market places or in a corner in the `dhaba' or the workshop where they work. Their diet is frugal, comprising of dal, chapati or rice, often just dry chapati, sliced onion and salt. They suffer from malnutirtion and hunger. They continue to work even when they are ill and hence weaken their bodies further. Vitamin deficiency, anaemia, bronchitis and tuberculosis are common diseases which working children suffer from.

The mental and physical development of working children suffers. The child has no time to play or take part in any healthy exercise which is so important for the proper physical development of his body. He has no time to go to school because the hours clash with his time at work and hence his mental faculties are not developed. Since he starts working at such an early age, he remains illiterate and unskilled for the rest of his life and this hinders any progress or advancement in his life, and "he spend his whole life at the bottom of the social ladder, performing routine, unskilled jobs, when he is not out of job altogether."[5]

Education

Working children can be divided broadly into three categories, education wise. First those who do not go and have never been to school. Second, those who have spent a few years in school and heave left school to start working. Third, those who work and still spend a few hours in school everyday. The greatest percentage of working children in India come from the first category. The reason for this is that parents feel that educating the child will not help to feed them whereas a working child brings money into the home to take care of certain basic needs. Secondly, our curriculum does not take into consideration their actual requirements in daily life. It is rigid and examination-oriented. If it was non-formal, with more emphasis on vocational training, then it would be of far greater use to the child. Thirdly, in the agriculture sector children are needed when there is pressure of work during sowing and harvesting. At this time, it is impossible to spare them for school. "What comes through loud and clearly is that children are working in almost every sphere of economic life; they are exploited both by their parents and by the employer, and above all that the child is deprived. This deprivation is of two types; one related to the impact on its health. . ., the second concerns its educational status. . . ., (they are) unable to go to school."[6]

Some Statistics on Child Labour in India

The problem of child labour in India is of immense magnitude when one considers the number of children involved. According to the 1971 Census, there were 10.74 million child workers, representing 4.66% of the total child population and 5.95% of the total labour force. According to the 1981 Census, workers in the age group below 14 years of age (excluding Assam) were 13.59 million. On the basis of the National Sample Survey (32nd round), the number of child workers as on 1st March, 1983 was 17.36 million. The working children mainly belong to the age group 5-14 years. Nearly 93% of the total child labour force works in the rural areas and the rest in urban areas. A great majority of these children work in agriculture and the unorganised sector like small commercial establishments and shops, or quasi-family undertakings. Seventy-nine per cent are employed as cultivators or agricultural labourers, 8% in livestock, forestry, plantations, etc., 6% in household and other services, the rest in trade, commerce and transport.

	1971	*1981*
Cultivators and Agricultural Labourers	8458	8786
Livestock Fisheries Hunting, Plantation etc.	885	704
Minings Quarrying and Construction	83	1056
Manufacturing processing Servicing and Repairs	654	964
Trade Commerce, Transport, Storage and Communications	253	278
Other Services	406	326

Fig. 10.1 Distribution of Child Workers in Various Activities
(Figures in thousands)

Source: Census of India 1971 and 1981, Registrar General and Census Commissioner, India New Delhi.

According to a report prepared by the Indian Social Institute on Child Labour, 80% of all child labourers belong to the Scheduled Castes and Tribes that have been exploited and marginalised in India for centuries. A major consequence of this "is the deprival of the possibility of education and the consequent upward mobility. Thus child labour has become a mode of perpetuating an unjust social system and of ensuring the continued availability of subservient, unskilled, illiterate labourers who do not have the bargaining power to question the system that marginalises them and deprives them of their right to be human."[7]

REFERENCES

1. Raychaudhuri, "Japan; Habib, Irfan (Eds.), *The Cambridges Economic History of India*, Vol. I, 1981. Orient Longman, Hyderabad, p. 287.
2. Mendelievich, Elias (Ed.) *Children at Work ILO*, Geneva 1979, p.4.
3. *Ibid*, p. 3 and 4.
4. *Ibid*, p. 37.
5. *Ibid*, p. 46
6. Burra, Neera; Child Labour in India; Poverty, exploitation and vested interest, Social Action Vol. 36, July-Sept. 1986, p. 251.
7. Fernandes, Water; Burra, Neera; Anand, T.S., *Child Labour in India, A Summary of a report* prepared by Indian Social Institute 1986, p. 2 and 3.

11

HYPOTHESISED CAUSES AND CONSEQUENCE OF CHILDREN'S PARTICIPATION IN ECONOMIC ACTIVITIES

Several factors are expected to be the causes of the participation of children in economic activities. These are poverty, caste, tradition, size of the family, labour scarcity, wage rates, illiteracy, schooling facilities, neighbourhood effect, etc. These factors are interlinked and exert their influence directly and/or indirectly on the work participation of children. The hypothesized influences of these factors on child work participation is diagrammatically represented in Fig. 3.1. Fig 3.2 shows the possible consequences of child work participation on the child, on the family and on the society. This chapter presents a logical elaboration on the various causes and consequences of children's participation in economic activities.

Causes

Poverty: Poverty is common feature of developing countries. In these countries, a considerable proportion of the population lives below the poverty line. The term poverty line refers to a line "drawn in the light of the socially expected minimum standard of living" (Sen, 1974: 67-68). All those persons whose standard of living is below this minimum are called `absolute poor.' In developing countries a large proportion of the poor if found in the rural areas. They are mostly concentrated in the agricultural sector. In India, for example, 70 per cent of the population is engaged in agriculture. A bulk of this agricultural population lives below poverty line with a very low standard of living. This accounts for about 60 per cent of the rural population (Bardhan, 1970: 135), most of them being found among rural labour households and small land owners or cultivators (Minhas, 1970: 107). This is reflected through the inequitous distribution of land in India. Occupation-wise poorest among the poor are found in agricultural labour class compared to cultivators and non-agricultural workers (Bhatty, 1974:302). These labourers are at the mercy of the land-owners for employment, for, they themselves do not have any land for cultivation. On the other hand, land-owners who employ the workers

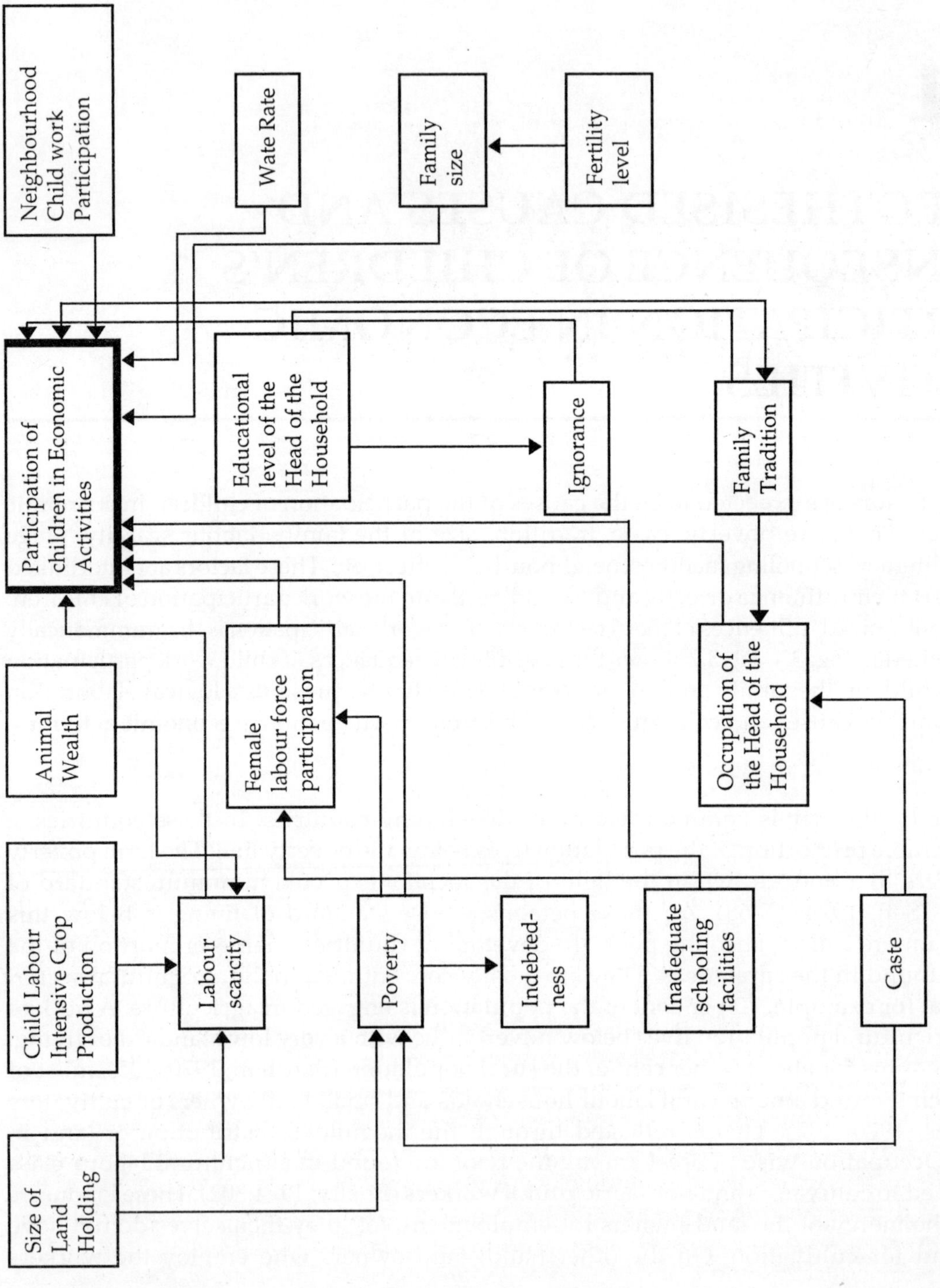

Fig. 11.1: Causes of Child Work Participation: A Schematic Representation.

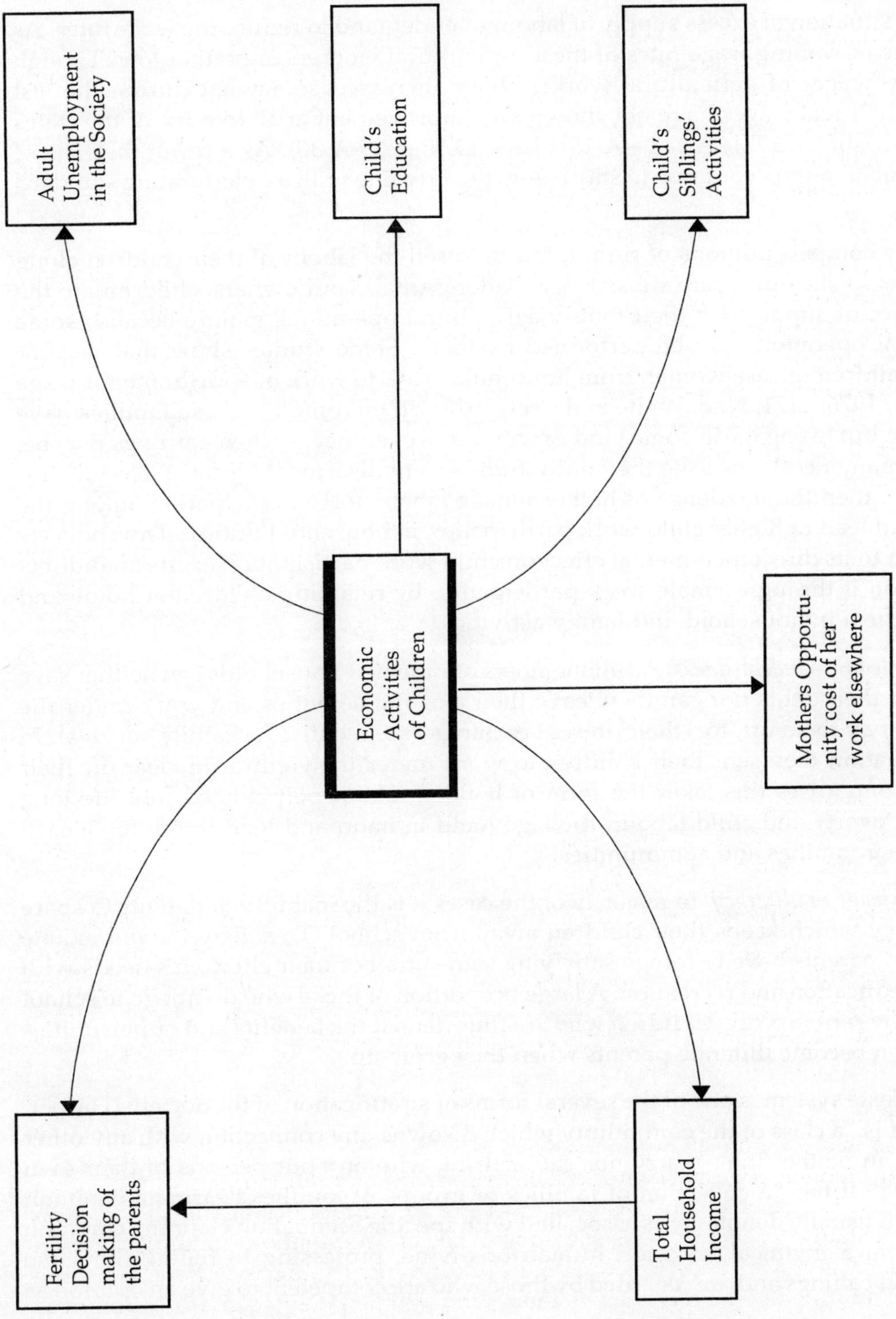

Fig. 11.2: Consequences of Child Work Participation: A Schematic Representation

utilise the situation of excess supply of labour over demand to reduce the wage rates. As a result the prevailing wage rates of these agricultural workers are rather low. Though the money wages of agricultural workers have increased somewhat during the last decades, their real wages have not shown any improvement at all in most of the states of India (Krishnaji, 1971: A 148—A 151; Jose, 1974: A 25-A 30). As a result millions of agricultural labourers continue to stay below poverty line with a deteriorating standard of living.

Poverty compels millions of rural families to sell the labour of their children along with adults to eke out a bare subsistence. Among small land owners, children are the main source of support for their family agricultural operations mainly because some agricultural operations can be performed by them. Some studies show that in poor families children release women from household work to work outside home for wage (Nadkarni, 1976: 1171; Nag, White and Peet, 1978: 297). Women in these families have no other go but to engage in some kind of work, however meagre their earnings may be, which in many occasions save the family from severe disaster (Myrdal, 1968: 1073). If this is true, then the incidence of higher female labour force participation among the poor should lead to higher child work participation in household duties., Thus poverty in addition to its direct incremental effect on child work participation exerts an indirect influence on it through female work participation by retaining children at home and engaging them in household and family activities.

Poverty leads to indebtedness. Adult members of indebted households can neither save to clear off their debts nor can they leave their existing activities and work under the creditor to pay them off, for, their present earnings are essential for family survival. In such a situation they sent their children to work under the creditor to clear off their debts. In some cases this takes the form of bonded labour perpetuated into life long bondage. Poverty and child labour, thus, go hand in hand and tend to reinforce each other in poor families and communities.

Poverty leads to illiteracy. In majority of the cases it is the inability of parents to spare some money which keeps their children away from school. To satisfy the immediate vital needs, parents have to forego satisfying some or all of their children's needs with respect to education and recreation. A large proportion of those who do not go to school are generally sent to work. Children who are thus denied the benefits and opportunities of education become illiterate parents when they grow up.

Caste: Caste system is one of the several forms of stratification of the Society (Harper, 1970: 51). It is "a class of the community which disowns any connection with any other class and can neither inter-marry nor eat or drink with any but persons of their own community." It has "a collection of families or groups of families bearing a common name which usually denotes or is associated with specific occupation claiming common descent from a mythical ancestor, human or divine, professing to follow the same professional callings and are regarded by those who are competent to give an opinion as forming a single homogeneous community" (Ketkar, 1979:4). It membership is limited only to those who are born within the group (Ketkar, 1979: 15). In recent years, however, inter-caste marriage and inter-occupational mobility are more common, but still exceptions rather than rule.

The economic structure of the society is influenced by the caste factor. The rural rich is usually found among the upper castes and the poor among the lower castes. A study conducted by the Institute for Public Opinion in 1969 shows that 41 per cent of the population in India is below the poverty line, out of which about one-half belongs to the Scheduled Castes and Scheduled Tribes (as cited by Kulshrestha, 1978 : 13). In villages a vast majority of agricultural labourers belong to these communities and hence a majority of child labour must also be found among them.

It is generally found that women work participation rates are high among those sections of the people who rank low in the caste hierarchy (Articles, 1971: 29-64; Myrdal, 1968: 1073). So there seems to be a close relationship between women work participation and the caste factor. The influence of caste on women work participation can be explained in two ways, First, there is a social status consciousness attached to the women of upper castes which makes them reluctant to participate in work activities outside home. But the lower caste women do not have any such social status consciousness and hence take up jobs when need arises. Moreover, activities generally taken up by the lower castes do not require any formal education or training and therefore are easier for them to perform (Radhadevi, 1978: 32).

The influence of women work participation on the work participation of children has already been discussed. We concluded that child work participation is high in those families where women labour force participation is high, for, children are retained at home to perform household and other allied activities to free the women to participate in work force.

Tradition: It has been observed that even in situations where there is no compelling necessity, a child is traditionally expected to contribute to the family income (Mendelvich, 1979: 560). This is because parents traditionally perceive certain advantages in child work participation. They believe that the child will be disciplined by entering labour force, it is prestigious to the family if the child terminates its dependency at the earliest age, child is protected against delinquent culture by taking up a job, it provides their parents moments of privacy, in cases of parental incapacitation early in life they can depend on children if they start working early in life and so on. "Children too, in many cases, have the fear of being discarded by their parents if they dò not earn and prove they are useful to the family" (Government of India, 1979: 11).

In India, tradition does not favour sending girls to school. This may be one of the reasons why duration of schooling is briefer for girls compared to boys. Girls are traditionally expected to learn and perform domestic chores because these are essential training for future house-wives and education is regarded as irrelevant for that task.

Even if girls enter primary schools, ".... after the first year of school, custom and the need to keep girls at home to help in the house work, and look after the younger children and in some areas early marriage, resulted in considerable wastage among girl pupils" (Myrdal, 1968: 1726).

Family Size: Fertility performance of a woman depends upon many factors like age at marriage, infant mortality, sex composition of surviving children, economic status of the family, religion and so on. Given the infant mortality a high fertility leads to a large family size. The relationship between family size and child work participation is assumed to be direct among poor families. In large families of the lower strata of the society parents are forced to send some of their children to work, for, the available resources do not allow them to send all their children to school. Only a few children (generally male) of these families attend school and others work either to support the expenses of their school going siblings or to keep away from idleness.

Labour Scarcity: Agricultural activities are characterised by two seasons, viz. busy season and off season. During busy season, there is labour scarcity in the agricultural labour market because the demand for labour is more than its supply. During off season, the extra labour is thrown out of production (Myrdal, 1968: 1075-1076) Thus, seasonality in agriculture causes seasonal disequilibrium between demand for and supply of labour in the agricultural labour market. The equilibrium is restored by the introduction and withdrawal of children and women in the labour market (Mellor, 1976: 95). Accordingly, seasonal variations in child labour are the result of labour scarcity during busy season. During these seasons certain time consuming, less productive but important activities like weeding, guarding crops, etc. are created for which the supply of adult labour is scarce. In such a situation the employer entertains children to work and the poor households, in an effort to restore the economic balance of the family, send their children to work for small pittance. As in agriculture, seasonal variations in employment are found in certain non-agricultural activities also. The same mechanism operates in the introduction and withdrawn of children in the non-agricultural activities as well.

The cultivators, sometimes, have a hire-in labour for cultivation. A large cultivator, generally a rich cultivator, can afford to do so. Small and marginal cultivators who are cultivating for their subsistence and in several cases highly indebted, have no other go but to send their children to work on their family farm or to retain them at home to release women to work on the farm.

In agriculture, the incidence of child work participation varies with the cropping pattern. If the cropping pattern is such that a large proportion of crops grown are child labour intensive, obviously the incidence of child work participation in that area is high. Raising of crops which involves more time-consuming and unskilled activities provide more opportunities for children to enter into labour force. Crops grown like jowar, cotton, groundnut, etc. require less skill during harvesting and they involve time consuming activities such as picking, sorting and cleaning. Crops like paddy, wheat, ragi, etc. on the other hand, require more skilled work and hence are not child labour intensive.

When irrigational facilities are available to the cultivator throughout the year, the seasonality in agriculture is minimised by increasing the number of busy seasons and reducing the span of slack seasons. As a result, there will be a persisting demand for child labour due to the creation of child labour intensive activities which may lead to higher child work participation rates in those areas (Myrdal, 1968: 1077-1078).

The possession of live-stock such as cattle, sheep, etc. by a family also demands children to work. The work involved in caring for and tending these animals are so time consuming that children's services are often sought. The elder members of the family engage in other more productive activities which fetch them direct returns and for which hard labour is necessary.

Wage Rates: The relation between wage rate and economic activities of children is direct. An increase in wage rate for children normally increases the child work participation rates in the initial stages. When the demand for labour is in excess of the supply, the wage rate is increased. Given the full employment of the available child labour in a given-area, the creation of additional activities for which only children are preferred or adult labour is scarce leads to an increase in child wage rates to attract more children from school to work and to pirate more workers from other employers.

Schooling Facilities: In developing countries, a significant proportion of children are denied of their education due to the inadequacy and the inaccessibility of schooling facilities. By the standards of Western countries, in these nations the conventional minimum age of entry into the potential labour force is low because of the absence of comprehensive, compulsory and adequate-accessible educational facilities. In India, for example, out of about 548,000 villages as many as 50,000 villages were without schools and more than 160,000 rural schools were functioning with only one teacher a piece. "In most places, the school presents a drab and dismal picture and holds little attraction for the child" (Government of India, 1979: 12).

Absence of educational facilities in a village deprives children of their opportunities of education. Children have to travel long distance to neighbouring villages for attending schools, if schooling facilities are not available in their home villages. Parents who are willing to send their children to schools find schooling of children more expensive when it involves travelling expenses. Some of them feel it risky to send their children to neighbouring villages for attending school (particularly female children) as children have to leave home early in the morning and can come back only late in the evening. As a result, many parents are reluctant to enrol their children in schools. Even if they are enrolled, the inconveniences experienced by children make them dropout early from schools. Thus children who do not go to school have two alternatives—they either remain idle without doing any work or participate in economic activities. As parents of these children would like them to do some kind of work instead of remaining, idle, they are thus compelled to engage in economic activities.

Neighbourhood Effect: "The neighbourhood is ordinarily viewed as a smaller version of a local community" [Sills (ed.)], 1972: 121]. It is ".... a group of people experiencing social interaction within a localised area with one or two social Institutions as the focal point or means by which the area can be identified physically." [Bertrand (ed.) 1958: 77].

Neighbourhood households have some social ties. They participate in one another's family rituals, help one another by lending utensils, food or by exchanging labour and more than all, they discuss on family maters like family health, occupation, children's education, etc. on a common platform. Men gather in verandhas or workshops during leisure time whereas women make us of their trips to those places where women of neighbouring households meet (Mandelbaun, 1972: 341). This type of get-together of neighbours are of great importance as their attitudes and behaviour influence the attitudes and behaviour of a family. If neighbouring households send their children to work, that might positively influence the attitudes of the parents towards child labour. On the contrary if the neighbouring households send their children to schools. That might induce a parent to send his children also to school. This is termed as neighbourhood effect.

A locality is usually determined by the factors like caste and income. Neighbours of an upper caste household are normally found to be belonging to upper caste and that of a lower caste household belonging to lower caste. Admittedly, the attitudes of these groups towards engaging children in work is predetermined by other factors. However, by neighbourhood effect we mean the influence of neighbourhood households alone on the economic activities of children of a family within the group.

Consequences

The first and foremost consequence of the participation of children in economic activities is on their own health and education. The work participation of children adversely affects their health and education, partially or fully, depending upon the degree of their participation in work. There are two categories of child workers—one which consists of those who do not go to school at all and the other category consists of those who work as well as go to school. Children of the first category remain illiterate in their life. Children who are in the second category could hardly attend classes regularly due to their involvement in work activities and as a result they dropout gradually due to repetitions and slow progress. Consequently these children fail to reap the fruits of education fully even though they are literate by definition. "The lack of literacy is equivalent to the lack of nutrition in early child development which causes fatal damage or retardation in brain development and physical growth" (Correa, 1979: 77). Early participation in hazardous activities shortens their length of life and their future earnings. As Woodward puts it (Kulshrestha, 1978: 10) for every dollar, earned by a child under fourteen years of age ten fold will be taken from its earning capacity in later years."

Child work participation contributes to the household income directly and/or indirectly. Children's work at home, on the family farm and in the family business are their intangible contributions to the household income, whereas when they work outside the family enterprise, for returns in cash and/or kind they could supplement their family income in real terms.

Children help their family also by reducing the opportunity cost of their mothers' work outside home. The opportunity cost of mothers' work outside home is nothing but the activities and income mothers sacrifice at home to perform their work outside home. It has already been mentioned that children free women (especially mothers) from household chores to enable them to participate in labour force. The extent to which they free women refers to the consequence of their work activities.

Economic activities of children add to their economic value to parents in rural societies. They regard them as productive agents and hence as assets to the family. The more the number of children family has got, the stronger it becomes financially is the norm they stick on to. A rural family therefore, would prefer to have many children, expecting each one of them to work and add to the family income. High fertility, hence, is one of the consequences of the economic activities of children.

Employers view the employment of children as advantageous. As child labour is paid less than adult labour, it emerges as a source of cheap labour for the employer. Besides, children have less developed ego and status consciousness and are less afflicted by feelings of guilt and shame. A consequence of the employment of children on the community is that it reduces adult wages. All the more it displaces adults from the labour market and adds to the unemployment problem. It has been estimated that atleast fifteen million vacancies can be created for the adult unemployed by siphoning off the existing child labour in India (as cited in Kulshrestha, 1978: 9).

Finally, the work participation of children encourages their siblings also to participate in labour force. Many a time children imitate their elder brothers and sisters which eventually lead them on to engage themselves in work activities. When elder siblings move into heavier and more productive work as they grow up, younger siblings generally take up the activities which the elder ones were performing earlier.

12

ECONOMIC ACTIVITIES OF CHILDREN

Available data on child labour from secondary sources have been gathered and analysed in this chapter. The main focus here is on some of the dimensions and determinants of the economic activities of children in rural areas with special reference to India. Evidence is presented with regard to the magnitude, intensity and the nature of activities performed by children. Information regarding wages earned is also given. Selected socio-economic indicators are used to analyse the possible causes of child work participation.

Data Sources

Data on economic activities of children are rather scarce. Data on the size of child population, dependency ratios and those children who wee reported as engaged in any gainful activity is obtained from the decennial censuses of India. Nevertheless, problems arise while comparing these data for different census years because of the definitional changes particularly on work. Problems are also encounted with respect to the reporting of age, occupational classification of children, etc. Labour Enquiry Survey Reports, National Sample Survey Tabulations and Publications of the Bureau of Economic and Statistics are the other major sources of data. A few micro level studies also have been conducted in the country, but they are all area specific and the scope of these enquiries varies from one to the other. Besides, information is also extracted from some of the micro-level studies conducted in other developing areas of the world.

Empirical Evidence

About 40 per cent of the population in India comprises of children in the age group 0-14. This young age structure is a consequence of relatively higher levels of fertility and declining mortality. The dependency burden is thus higher especially in the rural areas. The census classification to categorise a person as worker or non-worker does not prescribe any minimum age limit. However, it may be safe to assume that no child under age five is entered as working. Among the child population in rural India nearly one-third are dependents as they belong to the age group of 0-4. Another third of the child population or about half of those aged 5-14 are entered as dependents as shown in Table 12.1. These are the persons who have no activity of their own, but are dependents on other members of the family for their living. Remaining children either go to school or work. It is rather difficult to estimate those who combine schooling and work. The conditions in rural areas are conducive for school-going children to work either by withdrawing from school for a couple of days or intermittently or after school hours. During the last several years the number of children entering school has increased, and as a consequence, the percentage of children working has declined. However, we are not sure whether the proportion of children combining work with schooling has changed over years. One estimate places the percentage of student workers to total child workers at 51 per cent in the case of male and 36 per cent in the case of females in 1961 (Premi, 1973: 72).

The 1971 Census data show that 11.5 per cent of males and 4.6 per cent of females of 5-14 years were full-time workers in rural areas. Considering children performing household duties as those who were engaged in useful activities, the child work participation rate in rural India is estimated to be 13.3 per cent and 22.4 per cent for males and females, respectively. Child work participation rate for girls was thus higher than that for boys. Reciprocally, proportion of full-time school attending girls in the female child population (5-14) is lower than the proportion of full-time school attending boys in the male child population (5-14). This information is presented in Table 12.1 Data presented in the Table show that the ratio of school-going children to the non-school going children is higher for male than for females in both 1961 and 1971 Census.

The 1961 and 1971 Census data on students, dependents and os on presented in Table 12.1 are not strictly comparable due to definitional differences. It is more so with regard to data on work. The 1961 Census data includes marginal workers in the work force whereas the 1971 census data is based on main activity only. Assuming no substantial change in the actual work participation rate of children over 1961-71, the marginal child workers can be estimated to be roughly about 5 per cent for males and 7 per cent for females. Looking at the statistics given for students, children performing household duties, dependents and others in both the censuses, one gets the impression that a bulk of the female marginal workers were children performing household duties and the male marginal workers were students and dependents in 1971 Census. The dependent children (5-14) of 1961 Census refer to those who neither work nor go to school. They perform no other economic activity and are not seeking any work either. The dependent children of 1971 Census on the other hand may be consisting of some marginal workers. However, according to both the censuses 47 per cent of male children and nearly 60 per cent of female children are reported as dependents (see Table 12.1). But we are not sure whether children who neither work nor go to school are absolutely idle. It is possible that a substantial proportion of these children are performing activities which do not come under the purview of the census definition of work or household duty. It is also possible that non-school going marginal workers are under-reported and are counted as dependents. In bot the cases certain activities performed by children are concealed.

TABLE 12.1

Size and Distribution of Child Population in Rural India

Sex		*Child population (0-14) in thousands*	*Per cent of child population to total population*	*Per cent of children (0-4) to the total child population (0-14)*	*Per cent distribution of children (5-14) as*					
					Child workers	*Students*	*Children performing household duties*	*Dependents**	*Other***	*Total*
1971	Males	96,867	43.0	65.9	11.4	36.6	2.0	49.4	0.6	100.0
Census	Females	90,884	42.5	64.3	4.6	19.0	17.8	58.3	0.3	100.0
1961	Males	76,585	41.8	63.9	16.6	35.4	0.3	47.5	0.2	100.0
Census	Females	72,719	41.2	62.1	12.3	14.7	13.2	59.8	0.1	100.0

* Dependents include all non-workers, even if able bodies, who have no other activity coming under any of the above classification and who are not seeking any work, but are purely dependent.

** Persons who are not engaged in any activity but are seeking work and those who are with independent means, beggars, vagrants, etc. inmates of penal, mental and charitable institutions are categorised as 'others.'

Source:
1. Census of India, 1971, *Series 1, India, Part II—B(i), General Economic Tables*, Controller of Publications, Delhi, 1977:18-21.
2. Census of India 1971, *Series 1, India, Part II-B(ii), General Economic Tables*, Controller of Publications, Delhi, 1978: 417-423.
3. Census of India 1971, *Series 1, India, Part II—C(ii), Social and Cultural Tables*, Controller of Publications, Delhi, 1977: 106.
4. Census of India 1961, *Volume 1, India, Part II—B(i), General Economic Tables*, Manager of Publications, Delhi, 1965: 86-87.
5. Census of India 1961, *Volume 1, India, Part II—B(iii), General Economic Tables*, Manager of Publications, Delhi, 1965: 590-593.
6. Census of India 1961, *Volume 1, India, Part II—C(i), Social and Cultural Tables*, Manager of Publications, Delhi, 1965: 408.

A meaningful indicator of the incidence of child labour is the child work participation rate. It indicates the magnitude of child labour in relation to the child population. The age-specific child work participation rate (child workers to the population 5-14 years of age, with the assumption that children blow five years are not working) shows that according to 1971 Census, the highest participation rate is found in Sikkim (30.7 per cent). Among the major states Andhra Pradesh stands first (16.3 per cent) followed by Karnataka (11.5 per cent), Madhya Pradesh (11.1 per cent), Maharashtra (9.3 per cent), Rajasthan (9.1 per cent), Tamil Nadu (8.6 per cent), Orissa (8.4 per cent), Jammu and Kashmir (6.0 per cent) and so on. Among all the major states child work participation of male children is found to be higher than that of female children.

TABLE 12.2

Industrial Classification of the Child Workers in Rural India, 1971 Census

Industrial classification		*Number of child workers*		*Per cent of child workers to the total workers in each category*	
		M	F	M	F
1.	Cultivators	3,092,973	748,455	4.6	8.2
2.	Agricultural labourers	2,928,901	1,544,584	9.7	10.2
3.	Livestock, Forestry, Fishing, hunting, Plantations, orchard and allied activities	716,424	138,245	23.5	19.3
4.	Mining and quarrying	12,133	7,436	2.4	7.7
5.	Household industry	150,520	108,919	4.0	10.9
6.	Other than household industry	92,704	48,442	3.1	11.0
7.	Construction	24,453	11,172	2.4	10.2
8.	Trade and Commerce	73,459	8,906	2.9	3.2
9.	Transport, storage and communications	10,534	2,481	0.9	5.1
10.	Other services	182,560	74,154	2.7	7.8

Source: Census of India, 1971, *Series I, India, Part II-B (ii) General Economic Tables*, Controller of Publications Delhi, 1978, 417-423.

The sectors engaging children in various economic activities vary from country to country, but child labour is most common in agriculture followed by services and industry. Agricultural child labour constitutes nearly 10 per cent of the total agricultural labour force in the country. In livestock, forestry, fishing, hunting and plantations, they constitute nearly 21 per cent of the total labour force. Children work in all sectors of the economy. In rural areas, about 91.9 per cent of the child labour is found in agricultural sector. Secondary sector makes up 4.6 per cent and service sector 3.5 per cent of the total child workers. Industry-wise classification of child workers is given in Table 12.2.

On the basis of 1971 Census data, fourteen groups of occupations are identified in rural areas as child labour concentrated occupations. Occupations in which more than 25,000 children are engaged-in and which have a child worker-adult worker ratio of more than 3 per cent are considered as child labour concentrated occupation. These data are presented for All India and for Karnataka and Kerala States separately (see Table 12.3).

As was seen in the case of sectoral concentration of child workers, the occupational concentration of child workers also shows the child worker-adult worker ratio, generally, in favour of girls than of boys. This is true for All India as well as for Karnataka and Kerala states. The pattern of occupational concentration of child labour of Karnataka is almost similar to that of All India pattern for both the sexes. For Kerala, however, higher concentrations is found only in four groups of occupations, viz., other farm workers, maids and other house-keeping service workers, cooks, waiters, bar-tenders and related workers and tobacco prepares and tobacco product makers (see Table 12.3). Thus, unlike All India and Karnataka patterns, the highest concentration of child workers of Kerala is found in service sector.

Generally, wage employment and schooling are competitive for children both in agriculture and non-agricultural occupations. In the case of self-employment or working at home to help other members of the household, schooling and work can be combined. In beedi rolling, for example, working and schooling can be combined as beedi rolling work is usually carried out in the household itself and there are no rigid working hours or working norms that have to be met. Similar is the case in occupations such as spinning, weaving, dress making, etc.

A major concentration of working children in rural areas is in livestock rearing. Though not proportionate, generally in areas where relatively larger number of livestock are raised the child work participation is found to be high. In states like Rajasthan, Karnataka, Madhya Pradesh, Andhra Pradesh, Orissa, and Jammu and Kashmir, both the number of livestock raised and the number of children working per household are much higher compared to Kerala, Tamil Nadu, Uttar Pradesh, West Bengal, Assam and Tripura.

The Report of the Rural Labour Enquiry Survey (Government of India, 1965) conducted during 1963-65 provides information for the number of days worked per annum by

TABLE 12.3

Ratio of Child Workers to adult Workers in Child Labour Concentrated Occupations* in Rural Areas—1971 Census

Occupational groups (as given in census of India)	*Occupation*	*Per cent child workers (0-14) to adult workers (15+)*					
		India		*Karnataka*		*Kerala*	
		M	*F*	*M*	*F*	*M*	*F*
52	Cook, waiters bar tenders and related workers (Domestic and Institutional)	10.8	25.8	10.5	13.7	11.0	33.1
53	Maids and other housekeeping service workers	25.7	21.5	20.8	22.6	30.8	28.4
55	Launders, dry cleaners and pressers	7.1	10.0	5.8	8.1	1.6	1.3
62	Farmers other than cultivators	75.2	123.6	98.4	135.8	1.7	2.0
64	Plantation labourers and related workers	3.0	5.0	6.7	13.4	1.1	2.7
65	Other farms workers	57.3	102.6	101.8	142.8	35.3	26.7
75	Spinners, weavers, knitters, dyers and related workers	4.4	10.0	5.5	12.3	2.3	6.3
77	Food and beverage processors	3.0	5.0	3.8	4.5	1.6	3.1
78	Tobacco prepares and tobacco product makers	10.7	28.4	23.0	41.4	6.4	41.2
79	Tailors, dress makers, sewers, upholderers and related workers	3.9	6.8	4.7	6.7	1.6	2.1
89	Glass formers, potters and related workers	4.1	8.5	4.6	6.0	2.0	5.1
94	Production and related workers without specific classification	5.6	8.8	7.4	11.3	2.3	4.2
	Cultivators	4.7	8.9	5.7	8.9	0.4	0.8
	Agricultural Labourers	10.7	11.3	14.3	13.9	1.5	2.0

* Occupations in which more than 25,000 children are engaged and which has a child worker-adult worker ratio of more than 3 per cent of All India are considered as child labour concentrated occupations.

Sources:
1. Census of India, 1971, *Series, I, India, Part II-B(v), General Economic Tables*, Controller of Publications, Delhi, 1978: 393-692.
2. Census of India, 1971, *Series, 14, Mysore, Part II-B (iii), Economic Tables*, Controller of Publications, Delhi, 1979: 425-610.
3. Census of India, 1971, *Series, 9, Kerala, Part II-B (ii), Economic Tables*, Controller of Publications, Delhi, 1977: 262-367.

children in the agricultural labour households and all rural labour households. When the major portion of the household income was derived from the wage paid manual labour they were categorised as rural labour households. According to this report children in rural labour households were working on an average for 267 days per year out of which 187 days were accounted for by wage employment. In agricultural labour households separately, the corresponding figures were 280 days and 202 days. Non-agricultural child labourers were found to be working more number of days than the agricultural child labourers and self-employed and salaried children. These data separately for agricultural labour households and rural labour households are presented in Table 12.4.

TABLE 12.4

Employment and Unemployment of Usually Occupied* Children in Terms of Estimated Number of Full Days, in 1964-65

	Average number of days worked in.					*Average number of days not worked*			
Usual occupation	*Wage employment basis*	*Employment on salary basis*	*Self employ ment*	*Un-classified*	*Total*	*Due to sickness, bad weather, etc.*	*Due to want of work*	*Unclassified*	*Total*
Agricultural Households									
Agricultural labourers	224	N	22	14	260	11	62	19	92
Non-agricultural labourers	190	N	66	57	313	3	23	12	38
Other Occupations**	25	7	255	2	289	10	4	8	22
All Occupations	202	1	62	15	280	10	51	17	78
All Rural Labour Household									
Agricultural labourers	223	N	22	14	259	11	63	18	92
Non-agricultural labourers	212	N	51	34	297	13	30	10	53
Other Occupations**	26	8	247	1	282	14	9	8	31
All Occupations	187	2	64	14	267	11	50	17	78

Notes: The total number of days of columns 6 and 10 falls short of 365 days due to the fact that the days of partial activities have not been taken into account.

N = Nil

** = Includes self employed and salaried persons.

* = The usual occupation of a child was the gainful occupation which he/she usually pursued.

Source: Government of India, Ministry of Labour, *Rural Labour Enquiry, 1963-65*, Final Report, Simla. 1965: 154.

The Survey Report provides state-wise statistics for the intensity of child work. Data show state-wise variation in the intensity of work performed by children in terms of number of days employed per annum. In West Bengal agricultural and non-agricultural child labourers of both agricultural labour and all rural labour households worked for about 320 days in a year. In Gujarat, Punjab-Haryana and Jammu and Kashmir, children who were working as agricultural labourers worked for about three-fourth of a year. Karnataka, Kerala, Punjab-Haryana and West Bengal are bracketed for the highest number of days worked by non-agricultural child labourers among agricultural labour households and Assam, Bihar Punjab-Haryana, Kerala and West Bengal among all rural labour households.

With respect to educational variables that affect participation of children in different kinds of work we have to consider literacy and educational levels of population, schooling of children, school drop-outs and wastage and availability of schooling facilities. The Literacy levels of adult population is a good indicator of the levels of enrolment of children in schools. Illiteracy among the population particularly among females acts as a major deterrent to school enrolment of children. When schooling is denied they are usually forced to work.

Data for Karnataka State have been presented in Table 12.5 to show the negative relationship between literacy among general population and schooling of children. For both sexes this relationship was found highly significant. Higher illiteracy in the general population of Karnataka State showed higher child work participation for males (r =.728*) whereas with respect to females the general illiteracy increased the participation of girls in household duties (r = .831*) rather than in the directly productive activities. The direct relationship between illiteracy and child work participation was found at micro level as well. A study conducted in rural Uttar Pradesh of India showed absolute illiteracy among the parents of more than 80 per cent of children engaged in work (Sawhney, 1979: 208).

Since Independence school enrolment of children has been improving for both sexes in the country. School enrolment ratio which stood at 65 per cent for boys in 1953 -54 rose to 76 per cent in 1958-59, further to 96 per cent in 1968-69, and 100 per cent in 1975-76. The corresponding figures for girls were 28, 38, 59 and 66 per cent respectively (Government of India, 1962: 300; Government of India, 1980:20-22). However, school enrolment may not be uniform among all sections of the population. School enrolment of children among weaker sections in the rural areas are definitely on the lower side. The difference between the school enrolment ratios of scheduled population and general population widened from primary school to high school (Rayappa and Grover, 1980: 27-28). Enrolment ratios of male and female children are also not the same.

Even though school enrolment ratios may be high, school retention rates may not be

---

*Significant at 1 per cent level.

TABLE 12.5

Educational Levels of the General Population, School Enrolment of Children, Educational Wastage and Child Work Participation in Karnataka

District	*Per cent illiterate to the total population 1971*		*Per cent schooling going children the total chld population (5-14) 1971*		*Educational wastages to among children in classes I-VIII (1964-75)*		*No. of high schools per 10,000 children (5-14)*	*Per cent children (5-14) performing household duties, 1971*		*Child work participation rate (5-14), 1971*	
	M	*F*	*M*	*F*	*M*	*F*		*M*	*F*	*M*	*F*
1	*2*	*3*	*4*	*5*	*6*	*7*	*8*	*9*	*10*	*11*	*12*
Bangalore	48.7	66.7	52.0	39.7	53	63	3.0	1.2	15.8	10.1	2.9
Belgaum	57.5	81.7	45.4	25.6	81	91	2.3	1.5	25.3	15.5	5.6
Bellary	64.7	85.4	34.7	19.0	81	91	2.1	3.4	20.8	16.5	8.7
Bidar	69.1	91.3	35.1	11.9	84	95	2.3	6.2	31.5	13.9	3.1
Bijapur	59.7	85.7	46.9	21.4	83	94	1.9	1.5	25.1	16.7	6.5
Chickmagalur	56.1	74.6	45.1	29.5	75	87	2.5	3.4	18.0	10.7	4.6
Chitradurga	58.0	79.8	40.5	23.2	80	90	2.5	7.3	22.1	16.4	8.3
Coorg	49.8	62.2	51.5	44.7	67	70	4.2	1.8	7.9	10.5	7.9
Dharwar	48.7	75.0	49.3	31.4	83	91	2.4	1.6	22.1	15.9	7.0
Gulbarga	71.3	91.4	30.4	12.3	88	96	1.8	4.3	28.1	17.0	4.6
Hassan	58.9	80.3	40.4	30.5	80	91	2.4	3.1	22.9	13.8	3.6
Kolar	63.4	82.9	41.6	24.0	78	89	2.0	1.8	20.5	15.3	7.1
Mandya	68.4	86.9	34.2	18.2	80	90	2.1	1.3	26.0	16.3	3.4
Mysore	66.8	82.4	34.7	22.4	78	88	2.1	2.2	21.6	14.7	3.0

Uttara Kannada	50.4	68.7	54.3	39.6	77	83	4.7	2.5	16.0	9.2	3.2
Raichur	69.1	90.7	30.1	11.9	88	96	1.6	8.8	32.2	18.7	8.1
Shimoga	54.4	73.1	46.5	32.2	75	86	2.3	2.6	19.9	11.3	3.7
Dakshina Kannada	47.7	65.0	58.1	43.1	71	73	2.9	1.5	8.7	8.1	10.9
Tumkur	60.1	81.7	43.7	26.2	74	87	2.7	2.0	22.3	14.6	4.2

Source:
1. Census of India, 1971, Mysore, *Series 14, Part I—A, Volume II, General Report*, Controller of Publications, Delhi, 1975: 588.
2. Census of India, 1971, Mysore *Series, 14, Part II—B (i) Economic Tables*, Controller of Publications, Delhi, 1974: 105-569.
3. Census of India, 1971, Mysore *Series, 14, Part II—B (ii) Economic Tables*, Controller of Publications, Delhi, 1980: 423-441.
4. Census of India, 1971, Mysore *Series, 14, Part II—C (ii) Social and Cultural Tables* and Fertility Tables, Delhi, 1980: 82-115.
5. Rajeshwari Chandrashekaran, *A Critical Study in Depth of the Various Measures Taken by the Government of Karnataka (Mysore) in the field of Primary Education during the Period, 1947-1972*, Unpublished Doctoral Thesis, Institute for Social and Economic Change, Bangalore, 1978: 103.
6. Government of Karnataka, Bureau of Economics and Statistics, *Statistical Abstract of Karnataka: 1973-74*, Bangalore, 1975: 150.0.

so. This has been amply demonstrated by the amount of wastage in school education particularly in rural areas. The wastage rate which was as high as 60 per cent for primary state in the country in 1958-59 (Government of India, 1962:301) has not shown any improvement even after more than ten years. In fact, it has worsened to 66.9 per cent in 1970-71 (Government of India, 1977: 20). The higher the school wastage, the higher the chance of children participating in economic activities. The data presented in Table 12.5 for the district of Karnataka brings out a high positive correlation between these two variables for both boys and girls.*

* For boys, the correlation co-efficient between wastage rate and work participation rate was found to be .726. In the case of girls the relation between wastage and participation rate in household duties was found very significant (r-.840). In both the cases the correlation coefficient is statistically significant at 1 per cent level.

13

CAUSES AND CONSEQUENCES OF CHILD WORK PARTICIPATION: FINDINGS FROM THE PRIMARY INVESTIGATION

This chapter presents the descriptive analysis of the relationship between the socio-economic and demographic variables and child work participation and discusses some of the consequences of child work participation on the family. The descriptive analysis of the causes of child work participation shows the magnitude and intensity of child work participation-cross-classified by background variables. Chi-square test is used to show the significance and the strength of the relationship between the background variables and the child work participation.

Causes

In this section the observed variation in the magnitude and intensity of child work participation by household income, land ownership, caste and religion, highest educational level of any member of the household, family size and availability of schooling facility are described. Variations in the magnitude of child work participation by socio-economic groups is studied in terms of the variations in the composition of children of each socio-economic group in the four identified work-school status categories. Proportion of children of each socio-economic group in the above said four categories are taken and the variations in each category by socio-economic groups are looked into. Variations in the intensity of work are studied in terms of the average number of man days worked per annum and the average number of hours worked per day by children in each socio-economic group. The number of man days worked per annum takes care of not only the number of hours worked per day, but also the number of days worked per annum. Hence it appears to be a better index of work intensity.

Household Income and Child Work Participation

As hypothesized, household income and chld work participation should show a negative relationship. In other words the highest the income, the lower the child work

TABLE 13.1

Percentage Distribution of Children in Each Work-School Status Category by Background Variables

Background variable	*Work-School Status of Children (6-15)*											
	Children who were attending school but not working		*Children who were attending school and also working*		*Children who were working but not attending School*		*Children who were neither working nor attending school*		*Total*		*Chi-square value between work-school status of children and the background variable*	
	M	*F*	*M*	*F*	*M*	*F*	*M*	*F*	*M*	*F*	*M*	*F*
	1	*2*	*3*	*4*	*5*	*6*	*7*	*8*	*9*	*10*	*11*	*12*
Annual Household Income (Rs.)												
Less than 2500	38.9 (28)	29.0 (20)	19.4 (14)	7.3 (5)	12.6 (9)	26.1 (18)	29.2 (21)	37.7 (26)	100.0 (72)	100.0 (69)		
2501—4000	33.0 (30)	28.3 (26)	29.7 (27)	25.0 (23)	14.3 (13)	18.3 (17)	23.1 (21)	28.3 (26)	100.0 (91)	100.0 (92)	11.69 d.f., 6 not	19.40 d.f., 6 sig. at
4001 and above	41.7 (50)	41.7 (48)	27.5 (33)	15.7 (18)	19.2 (23)	25.2 (29)	11.7 (14)	17.4 (20)	100.0 (120)	100.0 (115)	sig. at p. 0.05	p. 0.05
Total	38.2 (108)	34.1 (94)	26.2 (74)	16.7 (46)	15.9 (45)	23.2 (64)	19.8 (56)	26.1 (72)	100.0 (283)	100.0 (276)		
Operational Land Holding Size												
Landless	39.1 (66)	21.6 (35)	20.1 (34)	12.4 (20)	16.6 (28)	29.6 (48)	24.3 (41)	36.4 (59)	100.0 (169)	100.0 (162)		
1-2.99 acres	39.0 (23)	50.3 (31)	38.8 (17)	24.6 (15)	17.0 (10)	11.5 (7)	15.3 (9)	13.1 (8)	100.0 (59)	100.0 (61)	12.86 d.f. 6	48.02 d.f. 6
3 acres and	34.6	52.8	41.8	20.8	12.7	17.0	10.9	9.4	100.0	100.0	sig. at	sig at

above	(19)	(28)	(23)	(11)	(7)	(9)	(6)	(5)	(55)	(53)	p. 0.05	p. 0.05
Total	38.3 (108)	34.1 (94)	26.2 (74)	16.7 (46)	15.9 (45)	23.2 (64)	19.8 (56)	26.1 (72)	100.0 (283)	100.0* (276)		
Number of Siblings (6-15)*												
0-1 sibling	35.3 (59)		18.6 (31)		16.8 (28)		29.3 (49)		100.0 (167)			
2 siblings	34.0 (67)		22.8 (45)		19.8 (39)		23.4 (46)		100.0 (197)		8.80 d.f. sig. at p.	6 not 0.05
3 and more siblings	39.0 (76)		22.6 (45)		21.5 (42)		16.9 (33)		100.0 (195)			
Total	36.1 (202)		21.5 (120)		19.5 (109)		22.9 (128)		100.0 (559)			
Highest Educational Level of any Adult Member of the Household												
No education	24.8 (26)	22.6 (23)	24.8 (26)	6.9 (7)	18.1 (19)	27.5 (28)	33.0 (34)	43.1 (44)	100.0 (105)	100.0 (102)		
I-IV std.	44.2 (19)	28.6 (12)	11.6 (5)	21.4 (9)	23.3 (10)	19.1 (8)	20.9 (9)	31.0 (13)	100.0 (43)	100.0 (42)	31.78 d.f. 6	42.14 d.f. 6
V Std. and above	46.7. (63)	44.7 (59)	31.9 (43)	22.7 (30)	11.9 (16)	21.2 (28)	9.6 (13)	11.4 (15)	100.0 (135)	100.0 (132)	sig. at p. 0.05	sig. at p. 0.05
Total	38.2 (108)	34.1 (94)	26.2 (74)	16.7 (46)	15.9 (45)	23.2 (64)	19.8 (56)	26.1 (72)	100.0 (283)	100.0 (276)		
Caste/Religion												
Muslims	39.5 (45)	14.5 (14)	18.4 (21)	10.3 (10)	15.8 (18)	32.0 (31)	26.3 (30)	43.3 (42)	100.0 (114)	100.0 (97)		

	1	2	3	4	5	6	7	8	9	10	11	12
Scheduled Castes and Tribes	27.1 (16)	22.2 (10)	27.1 (16)	8.9 (4)	15.8 (9)	35.6 (16)	30.5 (18)	33.3 (15)	100.0 (59)	100.0 (45)	23.40 d.f. 7	70.07 d.f. 7
Middle Castes	43.9 (25)	52.4 (33)	29.8 (17)	23.8 (15)	15.8 (9)	11.1 (7)	10.5 (6)	12.7 (8)	100.0 (57)	100.0 (63)	sig. at p. 0.05	sig. at p. 0.05
Upper castes	41.5 (22)	52.1 (37)	37.7 (20)	23.9 (17)	17.0 (9)	14.1 (10)	3.8 (2)	9.9 (7)	100.0 (53)	100.0 (71)		
Total	38.2 (108)	34.1 (94)	26.2 (74)	16.7 (46)	15.9 (45)	23.2 (64)	19.8 (56)	26.1 (72)	100.0 (283)	100.0 (276)		

Note: Figures in the parentheses refer to the number of observations.

*Data are not presented separately by sex.

participation and the lower the income, the higher the child work participation. We have seen in the review of literature and secondary data analysis that the relationship between poverty indicator and child work participation need not be inverse up to some threshold level. Of course, it is not all that easy to figure-out the break-even point and indicate the level from where the inverse relationship between poverty indicator and child work participation starts operating. Moreover, the threshold level may not be the same everywhere and it may vary over a period of time (Rao, *et. al.*, 1983: 198).

In our anlaysis household are divided into three groups according to their annual income. Those with an income of less than Rs. 2,500 per annum constitute the lowest class, Rs. 2,501 to Rs. 4,000 the middle class and those with an income of more than Rs. 4,000 per annum constitute the upper class. Children belonging to each income receipt class are then classified by work-school status for comparison. Annual household income and the work-school status of children are associated and that association is found to be statistically significant for girls as shown in Table 13.1 (first panel).

Looking at the data presented in Table 13.1, one could see that there is no clear pattern in the relationship between household income and children's participation in school and/or work in Dakshina Kannada. However, the negative relationship between the household income and the idleness rate is well pronounced and is as anticipated for both the sexes. An increase in household income brings down the idleness rate among the children. The drop of idleness rate by 6 per cent points from the lowest class to middle class and by 11 per cent points from middle class to upper class in the case of male children and by 9 per cent points from lower class to middle class and by 11 per cent points from middle class to upper class in the case of female children are apparent in Table 13.1. The pattern becomes clearer for the other three categories of children when we consider only two income receipt classes, *viz.* those with less than Rs. 4,000 and those above Rs. 4,000 per annum. An increase in income boosts up the proportion of full-time school attending children. The percentage of children attending school and not working increases from about 36 per cent in the case of males and 29 per cent in the case of female in the lower income group to 42 per cent for both the sexes in the higher income group. Richer families can easily afford school expenses—direct and indirect—which result in a larger proportion of full-time school going children. Altogether about 69 per cent male and 57 per cent female children in the sample attend school in the higher income receipt class as against 60 per cent male and 46 per cent female children in the lower income receipt class.

The observed relationship between child work participation and the household income is not inverse. The work participation rate tends to increase with an increase in income as can be seen from Table 13.1. The proportion of boys who work but do not go to school increases remarkably with an increase in income. While about 20 per cent of boys among the households with an annual income of Rs. 4,000 and above participate in full-time work without attending school, the participation rate of boys among households with an annual income of less than Rs. 4,000 is around 14 per cent. In the case of female children the difference is marginal, (*i.e.* about 22 per cent in the lower income group and 25 per cent in the higher income group). Among those who combine schooling and work similar trend is found only in the case of male children.

In the light of the positive relationship between household income and child work participation rate, it can be said that the break-even point for the operation of the inverse relationship-between these two variables has not been reached or has been observed due to lack of some more data on the work participation of children among higher income brackets. Below the break-even point, perhaps the inverse relationship between these two variables is disturbed by other factors like asset ownership, number of adult workers in the family, the number of wage-earning children, etc. Possession of assets like land and live-stock by the 'richer among the poor,' provides additional opportunities and encourages participation of their children in work. More number of adult workers in the family in activities like beedi rolling, etc. in spite of improving the household financial condition seek family child labour as helpers. This appears to be the case particularly in Dakshina Kannada district.

There is thus a reciprocal causation between household income and child work participation below the break-even point. To begin with, lower household income induces the households to hire out their children's labour for direct monetary benefits. Thus, lower household income acts as the cause and the child work participation the effect. In many cases children's participation in wage employment improves the financial status of the households and consequently results in asset ownership which in turn encourages further participation of children in work. Ultimately, where it lands up is in a situation with higher income and higher child work participation. In this case, child work participation is the cause and higher household income is the effect. Thus what initially might be an inverse relationship between household income and child work participation ends up in a direct relationship up to a certain level of income. This can be stated as the Paradox of Child work Participation. Briefly, the paradox of child work participation at household level is presented as follows:

Low Y —> CWP in Wage Employment —> Enhancement in Total Y —> + ve Net Income over Expenditure (savings) —> Purchase of Assets (land, live-stock etc.) —> Increased Opportunities for CWP —> Increase in CWP rate.

The above argument gets empirical support from our sample. It has been found that about 80 per cent of the wage earning children belong to the higher income groups and about 75 per cent of the cultivating land owners have an income of more than Rs. 2,500 per annum.

Households belonging to lower income groups, generally do not own any assets; this limits the work participation of children within the family. Those who work within the family work by helping the adult members in their tasks. Not all the children in the households with lower income work for wages. Some do not find wage employment and have no family assets to engage in. Those who can manage schooling do so and others remain idle. Even among those who work for wages, some work as casual labourers. Eventually, some of the households belonging to lower income groups remain where they were and the employment of children do not significantly improve their financial conditions.

The nature of the relationship between child work participation rate and the household income can be graphically illustrated. This has been done in Fig. 13.1 which depicts the Backward Bending nature of the child work participation rate curve.

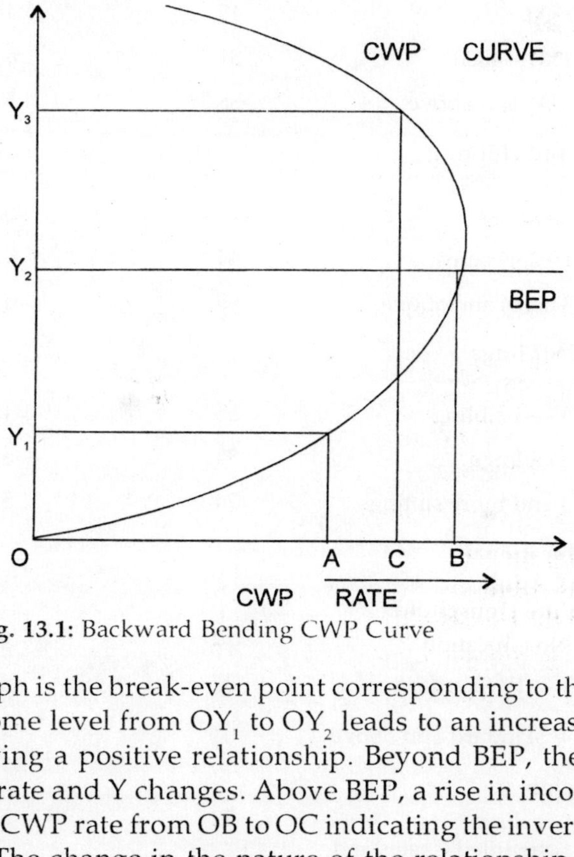

Fig. 13.1: Backward Bending CWP Curve

The point BEP in the graph is the break-even point corresponding to the income level of OY_z. The increase in income level from OY_1 to OY_2 leads to an increase in OWP rate from OA to OB, thus showing a positive relationship. Beyond BEP, the nature of the relationship between CWP rate and Y changes. Above BEP, a rise in income level (from OY_2 to OY_3) bring down the CWP rate from OB to OC indicating the inverse relationship between CWP rate and Y. The change in the nature of the relationship between CWP rate and Y beyond BEP may be due to the status consciousness among the members of the households belonging to higher income groups, effective demand for hired labour, etc.

Now, coming to the intensity of child work participation we have followed the same income groupings for the analysis. Here, working children numbering 214 are classified by their household income and their average annual and daily time input to work is analysed. Table 13.2 (first panel) presents this information.

TABLE 13.2

Intensity of Child Work Participation by Background Variables

Background Variable	N	*Average number of hours worked per day*	*Average number of man-days worked per annum*
Annual Household Income (Rs.)			
2500	45	4.5	104
2501—4000	81	5.1	125
4001 and above	88	5.5	170
Operated Land Holding Size			
Landless	121	5.9	174
1 - 2.99 acres	44	4.3	107
3 acres and above	49	3.9	87
Number of Siblings			
(6—15) 0 — 1 sibling	56	4.9	145
2 siblings	34	5.0	132
3 and more siblings	74	5.3	148
Highest Educational Level of any Adult Member of the Household			
No education	77	5.8	147
I — IV Standard	36	6.0 } 4.7	192 } 138
V standard and above	101	4.3	118
Caste/Religion			
Muslims	72	5.5	179
Scheduled Castes and Scheduled Tribes	476	6.0	129
Middle Castes	46	4.3	132
Upper Castes	50	3.9	104

As in the case of the magnitude of child work participation, Table 13.2 shows a positive association between the household income and the intensity of child work participation both in terms of the average number of man days worked per annum and the average number, of hours worked per day. Once again, this relationship is confined to the area below the break-even point in the graph. Hence the explanation rendered for such a relationship between these two variables follows from the one given for the relationship between the magnitude of child work participation and household income in the earlier paragraphs. What one can understand in the earlier discussion is that working children who belong to the households which remain in the lower income groups are mainly marginal workers in the sense that they either work as helpers to the adult workers in the family or as casual wage labourers. On the other hand, households, with higher income have full-time wage-earning child workers. As a result, the average duration of work by children in higher income brackets is found to be higher than that of those in the lower income groups.

Land Ownership and Child Work Participation

Size of operated land holding has been taken as an indicator of the income status of the household. But the question whether it provides a true indication of economic status leads us to suspect the validity of the indicator, especially in the present study under different reasoning. First, in the sample, about 50 per cent of the households are landless and hence definitely are deriving the major portion of their household income from non-farm activities and wage labour. A large proportion of those who own land are marginal land owners. Rest are small and medium land owners. Secondly though the households derive some income from farm, it is reasonable to think that the major portion of their income need not come from agriculture. Moreover agricultural yield depends upon the quality of land, irrigation and variety of other factors. Therefore it appears that land ownership is 'not' a good indicator of the economic status or the disposable income of the household. However, we have made an attempt to analyse the variations in chld work participation by operated land holding size.

For purpose of analysis, three land ownership categories are made, *viz.*, landless, marginal and owners (1 to 2.99 acres) and small (3 to 4.99 acres) and medium land owners (5 to 9.99 acres). Large land owners (10 acres and above) in our sample, are totally absent. One-half of children aged 6-15 years in the sample belong to landless households. The rest belong to the marginal, small and medium land ownership class. The classification of work-school status of children by operated land ownership class are provided in Table 13.1 (second panel). The association between these two variables is found to be statistically significant for both boys and girls.

In Table 13.1, idleness rate of children is found to be the highest among the landless households (24 per cent among boys and 36 per cent among girls) and it drops sharply as the household possess more and more cultivable land. Thus land ownership seems to encourage child work participation and/or schooling. Table 13.1 shows that, within landowning classes, possession of more land improves the schooling rate and increases the work participation rate of boys where as it does not exercise significant influence on

---

*The work intensity of those children who combine schooling and work is comparatively lower.

the participation (both school and work) of girls. The schooling rate of boys improves from 68 per cent among marginal land owning class to 76 per cent among small and medium land owners. The increase in work participation rate is from 46 per cent to 55 per cent.

When we compare the participation rates of children of the landless and the land-owning class, a clear pattern emerges in the schooling and work participation rate for both the sexes. The schooling rate shows an improvement from 59 per cent to 72 per cent for boys and from just 34 per cent to above 70 per cent of girls. This supports the common belief that the better off families can well afford and their attitudes are inclined to send their children to school. Also, our data support the argument that land ownership taps potential family labour and encourages children to participate in labour force very early in their life. Though the rate of participation of girls in work does not increase by possession of land, that of boys shows a steep rise from about 37 per cent among the landless to 50 per cent among the land owning class. Thus, the possession of land facilitates children to combine schooling and work. The proportion of those who combine schooling and work shows a definite increase with the possession of land. The proportion of boys combining schooling and work rises from about 20 per cent among landless to 35 per cent among the land owning class. The corresponding increase for girls in this category is from about 12 per cent to 22 per cent. It should be noted that possession of land draws more boys to work than girls and on the other hand, the improvement in the economic status of the household as indicated by the land-ownership has a better impact on the schooling rate of girls than that of boys.

This finding is similar to that of Vlassoff's observation in rural Maharashtra as far as the impact of land acquisition on child work participation (Vlassoff, 1979: 424) is concerned. But the difference to be noted between Vlassoff's and this study is that when we study the variations in the actual child work participation rates by land ownership class, he constructed a work index for children where parents were asked to say whether the economic activities children performed were of much help, some help or no help. Inherently the answers would be subjective. Moreover, Vlassoff did not classify the households by landownership. Instead his conclusion is based on the variations observed by standard of living where land was one of the elements of standard of living index. However, Nadkarni's (Nadkarni, 1976: 1165) analysis based on data from Maharashtra is similar to the one carried out in this study. Of course, the findings of this study contradicts Nadkarni's observation in Maharashtra. But no comparison of the findings of the two studies is ventured in this regard, especially, because the mode of classification of the land-holdings is entirely different.

Through land ownership results in higher child work participation rates, the intensity of child work participation need not be very high. In fact, the average number of hours worked per day and the man days worked per annum by children cross-classified by land ownership (Table 13.2, second panel) shows a negative relationship between these two variables in rural Dakshina Kannada. Before explaining the observed nature of the relationship, it should be remembered that the working children of landless households are not engaged in farm activities within the family and hence are either engaged in non-farm activities carried out by the family (beedi rolling, etc.) or in wage labour. The difference in the proportion of full-time workers by the acquisition of more land, on the other hand, is not all that significant and hence the intensity of work by children slackens with the possession or more land.*

Sibling Number and Child Work Participation

We assume that, given the limited resources, the higher the number of children in the family, the lower is the average time-input to work. But Nag et al., (Nag et al., 1978: 297), in their study observed the contrary. They observed that the children with more number of siblings put-in more time to work (including household duties) than the children with less number of siblings or no siblings at all. One of the reasons suspected by them suggest that children in large families are encouraged by the presence of elder siblings to participate in work and to begin work at an early age. If this is true, the work participation rate among children with more number of siblings should be higher than the rate among the children with less number of siblings or no siblings at all., Even our hypothesis shows a direct relationship between these two variables although our reasoning is different. We hypothesised that, given the financial constraints, parents are forced to send some of their children to work to keep them away from idleness, for, the available resources do not allow them to send all their children to school. In the light of the data presented in Table 13.1 (third panel). Nag et al's., argument seems to be more acceptable and more reasonable. However, they did not explicitly distinguish between magnitude and intensity of child work participation. Though their argument appears to be applicable to the direct relationship between the number of siblings and the child work participation rate, the information provided by them show the direct relationship between the number of siblings and the intensity of child work participation. Moreover, their argument is based on the work-input of children in all the activities (including household work). In the present analysis, the effect of number of siblings on the magnitude and intensity of child work participation are studied separately.

Table 13.1 (third panel) presents the schooling, work participation and the idleness rates of children by sibling (6-15 years) number. The rates are computed for three groups of children, viz. those with one sibling or none, with two siblings and with three or more siblings. Results show that the highest work participation rate is among those who have three or more siblings (45 per cent) followed by those with two siblings (43 per cent) and with one sibling or none (35 per cent). Schooling rate also shows a similar pattern. The highest schooling rate is found among those with three or more siblings (62 per cent), next highest among those within two siblings (57 per cent) and the lowest rate is among those with one sibling or none. It appears that the reason suspected by Nag et al., for the pattern of higher work participation of children in larger families and the lower work participation of children in smaller families holds good with regard to schooling rate as well. If the above pattern to work participation and schooling rates are due to 'encouragement' factor, then the idleness rate in larger families should be much lower than what it is in smaller families. Data in Table 13.1 however, show the assumed pattern of the idleness rate. The highest idleness rate is detected among those children with one or no sibling (29 per cent), than among those with two siblings (23 per cent), and the lowest idleness rate is found among those with three or more siblings (17 per cent). Based on this information one would accept Nag et al's, hypothesis that participation of elder siblings encourages the younger siblings to follow suit. Nevertheless, the Chi-square value obtained shows that the association between the work-school status of children and the number of siblings they have got is not significant in statistical terms.

Work intensity of children and number of siblings seem to have a positive association in rural Dakshina Karnataka (Table 13.2, third panel). With due note that, in the present analysis the components of work intensity excludes the time spent for household duties, the similarity of the results obtained in the present investigation with that of Nag et. al., study in Java and Nepal is worth-mentioning. Again, it may be the 'encouragement' factor which is operating. On the other hand, there is no significant direct variation in the proportion of subsidiary child workers with the number of siblings. Full-time workers include those who are working on their own farm, at home, and for wages. Comparatively they put-in more time to work than the subsidiary workers. Thus, more time input to work by children with larger number of siblings compared to those with smaller number of siblings is self-explanatory.

Educational Level and Child Work Participation

As hypothesized, the educational level of the members of the family affect the child work participation. The nature of this relationship is expected to be negative. The highest educational level of any adult member of the family is the proxy used in this analysis to study the influence of the educational achievement of the decision-maker on child work participation.

It has been assumed here that educated adult members in the family will be having a say over the decision of the head of the household regarding children's schooling or work. The main reason for not taking straight-away the educational level of the head of the household (decision-maker) as the indicator is due to the fact that a large proportion of them are illiterate. Rest of them are semi-literate or just literate with a couple of years of schooling. Percentage of the heads of households with educational level of more than primary school is negligible. It has been anticipated that variations in child work participation will not be distinguishable between households with illiterate, semi-literate or just literate heads of households.

There educational groupings are made for the present study, *viz.* households whose highest educational level of any member is (i) no education, (ii) primary schooling (I-IV standard, and (iii) middle schooling and above (V and above). Out of 559 children in our analysis 37 per cent belong to households with no literate adult member. Another 15 per cent children belong to those households whose highest educational level of any adult member is primary level. Remaining 48 per cent children have in their family at least an adult member with an educational level of Standard V and above. The observed difference in the work-school status of children by these educational groups is statistically significant for both boys and girls.

The association of he highest educational level of any adult member of the household with the rate of exclusive participation of children in school *vis-a-vis* the idleness rate is well marked for both the sexes. The relationship with the former is direct and with the latter it is inverse. The overall schooling rates of boys and girls also give positive relationship with the educational variable of the household. But the variation in the child work participation by the variation in the independent variable under consideration is not apparent. This information is presented in Table 13.1 (forth panel).

One anticipates higher child work participation rate with illiteracy prevailing among the adult members in the households and lower child work participation with highest levels of education among the adult members. But data presented in Table 13.1 do not reveal a clear picture of the anticipated nature of the relationship. Even when we consider separately those child workers who combine schooling with work and those who do not, the expected nature of the relationship does not emerge with clarity. However, when we consider only two groups of households in the sample, viz. one consisting of those who do not have any educated adult person and the other consisting of those households having atleast one educated adult member, the deterring impact of educational level on child work participation rate becomes obvious in the case of male children. The work participation rate of boys comes down from about 43 per cent in the illiterate group to 41 per cent in the literate groups. Though the fall in the work participation rate is not significant, the declining trend is noted. In the case of female child workers the expected trend is still not observed.

From the above analysis, one can argue that the educational level of the adult members of the household has a better impact on the schooling rate of children than on the child work participation rate. Besides it exerts a tremendous downward influence on the idleness rate. Higher schooling rate by the presence of educated persons in the household draws children away as much from the work force as it is from the idle group. While there is a 29 per cent point improvement in the schooling rate of boys and a 38 per cent point improvement in that of girls from the lowest educational group to the highest educational group, a large percentage of this increase (80 per cent for boys and 84 per cent for girls) is seemingly explained by the decline in the idleness rate.

Though not the work participation rate, the educational level of the adult members in the household may significantly influence the duration of work of children. Table 13.2 (fourth panel) provides data on the work intensity of children by educational level of the adult members in the household. The Table shows a clear trend with high work intensity of children among the illiterate group and low work intensity among the literate group. Thus one can infer that educational levels of adult members in the household starts exercising its influence on the child work participation by reducing the duration of work performed by children.

Caste Religion and Child Work Participation

Caste is assumed to be an important factor influencing child work participation in India. It determines the economic status of the family, family size and the educational status of the household. In the present sample, out of 285 households 188 belong to Hindus (66 per cent) and the remaining 97 (34 per cent) belong to Muslims. Since Muslims constitute a significant proportion in the sample, a comparison of child work participation between Muslims and Hindus is possible in this analysis. Among Hindu households, 33 per cent belong to Scheduled Castes and Scheduled Tribes, another 33 per cent belong to Middle caste group and the remaining 34 per cent households belong to upper castes. The upper caste Hindus include. Brahmins and Bunts whereas middle caste group comprises of Pujaris, Acharis, Devadigas, Moilies, etc. The observed' association between caste/religion and the work-school status of children is statistically significant for both the sexes.

Caste/religion influences child work participation not directly but through intervening variables which are economic, demographic and educational. This necessitates a knowledge of economic demographic and educational characteristics of the households belonging to various caste/religion groups. There are given in Table 13.3 As per the Table upper caste Hindus are economically the most advantage section in the society both in terms of annual income and in terms of land ownership. This has a reflection on their educational status About 91 per cent of the household belonging to the upper castes has atleast one literate adult member in the family. The corresponding figures for middle castes, scheduled groups and Muslims are 74 per cent, 27 per cent and 57 per cent respectively. In terms of annual income, middle caste households stand as second highest in the sample followed by Muslims and Scheduled Castes and Tribes. The land ownership pattern shows that Muslims are generally landless. The major source of their income is from non-farm activities such as trading, business, beedi rolling, etc. The average size of land-holding of the middle castes and the Scheduled Castes and Tribes do not vary much in the sample. A better land ownership position of the Scheduled Castes and Tribes could be due, to the recent land redistribution policies of the government.

Data presented in the Table show that the social groups have distinct demographic characteristics. The size of the household is found to be the largest among Muslims and Brahmins among Hindus. Scheduled Caste and Tribe households in the sample are characterised by the smaller size of their household. Large household size among Muslims may be due to the high fertility prevailing among them whereas among upper caste Hindus the still existing joint-family system may be the major reason. Information collected from the field reveal that Scheduled Castes and Scheduled Tribes prefer nuclear family in view of the benefits they receive from the government. This may be the reason for the smaller size of households among the Scheduled groups.

TABLE 13.3

Economic, Demographic and Educational Characteristics of Households by Caste/Religion

Caste/Religion	*Average annual income per house-hold (Rs.)*	*Average size of land holding acres)*	*Average size of the household*	*Per cent household with at least a literate member*
Muslims	3978	0.70	8.4	56.7
Scheduled Castes and Scheduled Tribes	2768	2.19	5.8	27.4
Middle Caste	4498	1.85	6.3	73.8
Upper Caste	5013	3.22	7.5	90.8

Based on our analyses presented in the previous sections of this chapter one can envisage higher schooling rate, higher work participation rate and a very low idleness rate among the children of the upper caste mainly because of the fact that they are the land-owning group in the society. According to the data presented in Table 13.1 (fifth panel) it is so with respect to schooling rate and idleness rate and partially so with respect to work participation rate. The schooling rate is the highest among the upper caste group for both the sexes. The schooling rate of boys among them is 79 per cent whereas among middle castes, Scheduled Castes and Scheduled Tribes and Muslims, it is 74 per cent, 54 per cent and 58 per cent respectively. The schooling rate for girls is 76 per cent among upper caste and middle caste, 31 per cent among Scheduled Castes and Scheduled Tribes and 25 per cent among Muslims. Low schooling rates of both the sexes among the unprivileged castes (Scheduled Castes and Scheduled Tribes) can be clearly noticed from the data. The schooling rate of boys is the lowest among the Muslims. The religious prejudices against sending girls to school prevalent among the Muslims could be the cause for the lowest schooling rate of girls among them. Between Hindus and Muslims, the former have higher schooling rate than the latter for both the sexes. It has been observed that a large number of Muslims children attend religious classes to learn Koran and Arabic at the cost of formal schooling.

The overall work participation rats by caste/religion show different patterns for boys and girls. The highest work participation rate for boys is found among Hindus (47 per cent) than among Muslims (34 per cent). Within Hindus, it is the participation rate of boys belonging to the upper castes which is higher compared to those belonging to the lower castes. With regard to female children, higher work participation rate is found among Muslims (42 per cent) than among Hindu (39 per cent) and within Hindus,

*The work participation rates of boys who do not attend school are almost the same by caste/religion.

among Scheduled Castes and Tribes (44 per cent) than among upper castes. (37 per cent). Probably, the work participation rates are determined more by economic factors than by sociological or educational factors. It could be noticed that higher work participation rates of boys are among those caste/religion groups whose land-ownership position is relatively better. It is the work participation rates of those boys who attend school which makes all the difference in the overall work participation rates by caste/religion.* On the basis of these two observations, we conclude that it is the land ownership pattern which resulted in higher work participation rates of boys among upper castes compared to lower castes and among Hindus compared to Muslims. With regard to female children, however, the expected higher work participation rate among Scheduled Castes and Scheduled Tribes was observed. But comparatively higher participation of girls in work among Muslims than among Hindus was not anticipated. This may be because of the low schooling rate among them and the predominance of beedi-rolling industry in the Muslim dominated area of the study. Beedi-rolling activity does not compel them to go out of their houses and hence they need not break their religious sanction by participating in work. Otherwise, possibly the work participation rate of Muslim girls would have been very low. In fact, more than 90 per cent of Muslim girls participating in work are beedi rollers. When we consider the participation of children in wage employment, the highest percentage of boys is found among Scheduled Castes and Scheduled Tribes (58 per cent) and among Muslims (36 per cent). The percentage of girls in wage employment is found to be the highest among Scheduled Castes and Scheduled Tribes (69 per cent) followed by middle castes (24 per cent).

Idleness rate has a clear pattern by caste/religion in rural Dakshina Kannada. One can expect more number of idle children among Muslims and Scheduled Castes and Scheduled Tribes whose schooling rates are comparatively lower. The expected pattern emerges for both the sexes with very high idleness rates among Muslims (26 per cent for boys and 43 per cent for girls) and Scheduled Castes and Scheduled Tribes (31 per cent for boys and 33 per cent of girls) and low rates among upper castes (4 per cent for boys and 10 per cent for girls) and middle castes (11 per cent for boys and 13 per cent for girls).

So far we were discussing about the association between caste/religion and child work participation rate. Now to analyse the caste influence on the intensity of child work participation, we shall turn our attention to Table 13.2 (fifth panel). The Table indicates that Muslim Children put in more time to work than Hindu children. Among the Hindus, it is the Scheduled Caste and Scheduled Tribes children and the middle caste children who spend more time for work than the upper caste children. In terms of the average number of hours worked per day, Scheduled Caste and Scheduled Tribe children worked for a longer time than the Muslim children or children belonging to the middle or upper caste. While Scheduled Caste and Scheduled Tribe children worked for about six hours on normal days, Muslim children worked for 5.5 hours, middle caste children for just above four hours and upper caste children for less than four hours.

Higher work-input per day by Scheduled Caste and Scheduled Tribe children and Muslim children may be due to their higher participation in wage employment.

Schooling Facility and Child Work Participation

The association between schooling facility and child work participation, in this study, is not analysed at the household level but at the village level. The three villages selected for the study, *viz.* Ajjavara, Munnur and Neriya are listed in that order on the basis of schooling facilities available. As mentioned in other Chapter, the presence of and/or the distance to the high school has been taken as the criterion to classify them by schooling facilities. To repeat what we have said in Chapter, Ajjavara has got a high school in the village, Munnur though does not have a high school has the nearest high school not very far from the village, with frequent bus transport convenience and in Neriya children are deprived of a high school, the nearest high school being secluded from the village by about 14 kilometres without proper transport facility.

Child work participation rate was expected to be high in Neriya where children are forced to drop-out from school once they complete their primary schooling due to the absence of a high school facility in the village. High cost (direct, indirect and opportunity cost) of high school education make schooling beyond primary education possible only for the better off families. When asked about the reasons for the school drop-out in spite of successful completing primary education, a significant proportion of the respondents expressed their inability to finance the children's stay outside the village so as to provide them high school education. In Munnur and Ajjavara this problem is not encountered due to the proximity to the high school.

Children who drop-out from schools may join the work force. If it is true, then the work participation rate in the village without a high school may be higher than the work participation rate in the village with a high school. However, the observed work participation rates for boys show the highest participation rate in Neriya (61) per cent) and the lowest in Ajjavara (21 per cent). In Munnur about 44 per cent work participation is observed among boys. The village-wise pattern of work participation rates among boys thus observed may be partially due to the varying distance to the nearest high school. A similar pattern of village-wise work participation rates would have been observed for female children also but for the highest work participation rate for girls in Munnur (54 per cent). It has to be borne in mind that Munnur is a Muslim dominated village and hence the proximity to the school may not have much impact on the participation of girls. However, the participation rate of girls in work is found to be higher in Neriya (41 per cent) than in Ajjavara (18 per cent).

Consequences of Child Work Participation

In this section some of the consequences of child work participation are presented. First, the consequences of child work participation on the child are elaborated and this is followed by a description of the impact of child work participation mainly on the family.

Child work participation may adversely affect child's attendance or performance in school and its physical or psychological development. Thought it was not possible to collect data on school attendance and performance for children in the sample (working and non-working) due to identification problem, school level information pertaining to the attendance of children at different points of time in a year and the general performance of children in school examinations were collected. This has been compared villagewise. It was expected that in Neriya and Munnur where the proportion of children combining schooling and work is relatively higher, the attendance in the school will be lower which may result in the poor performance of children in examinations. In Ajjavara both school attendance and performance were expected to be better since their proportion is lower. The expected variation was, however, not observed with regard to attendance. School attendance in Neriya and Munnur was more or less similar to that found n Ajjavara in all the classes. The impact of child work participation on school attendance is, thus, not explained by the data collected. However, difference in the overall school performance of children belonging to the three villages is noticed. The performance of children studying in schools located in Munnur is recorded to be poorer (less than 60 per cent promotion in all the classes) than of those studying in schools located in Neriya or Ajjavara (more than 70 per cent promotion in all the classes) than of those studying in schools located in Neriya or Ajjavara (more than 70 per cent promotion in all the classes). If the difference in school performance of children belonging to Munnur and Ajjavara is partially due to work participation of school-going children, then the school performance of children belonging to Neriya also should have been poorer compared to those belonging to Ajjavara. But that is not so. This may be attributed to the difference in the mode of compatibility of schooling and work observed in these two villages. Children combining schooling and work in Munnur are mostly employed in beedi-rolling activities whereas in Neriya, they are largely engaged in agricultural activities. In Neriya, children who combine schooling and work, do so during school vacations whereas in Munnur beedi rolling children besides working during school vacations engage in that activity after school hours. This may be directly hindering their studies to result in poor performance in the school. While collecting data from the school, headmasters were asked to give an account of the attendance and performance of children in general. In Munnur, headmasters of both the Government Higher/Primary schools reported that children who fared very badly in the examinations were those who rolled beedies at home. They were reported to be regular to school but were often late. Frequency of late arrivals of students to the schools located in Ajjavara and Neriya is reported to be very less.

It is not possible, in this study, to provide evidence for answering how the work participation of children retards their physical and psychological development. In fact, no attempt was made to collect information on this aspect because that itself becomes a separate research theme. However, during the stay in the village beedi-rolling children were found to be less socialised and lacking recreation. Also, poor performance in the school by these children indicates the slow development.

Child work participation may result in additional income to the household. This is particularly so when there are wage-earning children in the family Child's contribution to the household income may be direct in terms of cash/kind or may be indirect in terms of production. Those children who work for wages, most of the time, give their earnings wholly or partially to their parents (head of the household), thus contributing directly to the family income. Other category of children who work on the family farm, in family business or in household industry add to the total production in the household economy and hence indirectly contribute to the household income.

TABLE 13.4

Annual Contribution of Wage Earning Children to Their Family Income

Annual contribution (cash) in terms of percentage to the household income	*N*	*Percentage distribution*
Less than 10%	17	44.7
10%-25%	9	23.7
25% and above	12	31.6
Total	38	100.0

Table 13.4 shows that more than 55 per cent of the wage-earning children in the sample contribute very significantly to their household income in terms of cash. While about 32 per cent of them contribute more than 25 per cent of their annual household income, remaining 24 per cent children's contribution accounts for 10 to 25 per cent. The point to be highlighted here is the excess dependence of the families to which these children belong upon the earnings of children. Then, is it not the economic reasons which forced these families to let their children enter the labour market for an economic contribution? It appears to be so. Probably, when we ask this question directly to the members of these families they may admit it. But, there is a large proportion of households wherein children's contribution to the household income is indirect. Those who benefit from their work contribution do not realise it especially due to the nature of the activities they perform. In Munnur, children who help the adults by tying the rolled beedies, or by cutting the leaves for beedi-making in a way are adding to the total beedi production of the household, thereby contributing to the household income. By working on the family farm, they may be sharing the work-input of the adults which otherwise would have reduced their leisure time. At home definitely they are useful to the adult females for looking after younger ones and for performing other time-consuming activities as it was observed especially in the Scheduled Caste households in Ajjavara. Incidentally, the women's work participation among these households is also found to be comparatively higher,. One may, therefore, conclude that children who perform household chores and other menial time-consuming activities free adults, especially women, from these activities to perform more productive and important tasks.

Children working for wages in Dakshina Kannada put in almost as much time (daily input) to work as by the adults. On the family farm a full-time child workers' time-input to work makes up one-third to two thirds of an adult member's duration of work. In the beedi-rolling industry a full-time beedi-rolling child, like an adult rolls beedies for about eight hours a day. Those who combine schooling and work put in around one-third of an adult member's time input to work both for family farm activities and for beedi-rolling activities. Thus, the information regarding the time-input to work also chimes that the child work-input is significant to the household production.

Assuming the low cost of bearing and rearing children in rural areas, it has been argued that a large family with more number of children is preferred to a small family with less number of children due to the significant economic contribution of children in terms of money or work. This leads us to presume that given all other determinants of fertility, higher economic contribution of children to the family in a particular area should, for this area, show higher fertility rate and the lower economic contribution of children should show a lower fertility rate. To test this hypothesis we do not have any data to indicate fertility levels. However, from the available data we have used the child-woman ratio as the fertility indicator.

The unit of analysis to show the consequence of the economic contribution of children on the fertility levels is the village. Neriya and Munnur where the child work participation of children is higher are expected to have higher child-woman ratios compared to Ajjavara. Data show that it is so with the highest child-woman ratio of 898 in Munnur, followed by 605 in Neriya and 566 in Ajjavara. High child-woman ratio in Munnur may also be due to the concentration of Muslims in that village. Absence of household level analysis, in this study, to understand the impact of economic contribution of children on the parents' desire for children make us reluctant to draw any conclusion on this aspect. All that we can show is the indication of higher levels of fertility in the areas with higher child work participation.

Finally, the impact of child work participation on the adult employment situation in the society and on the overall wage rate are untouched aspects in this study. Yet, it should be noted that adults found it difficult in Neriya to get into the estate work (especially during coffee seeds plucking seasons) due to the preference shown for children to adults for that job. It has been reported that children are paid only Rs. 4 per day, whereas adults doing the same quantum of work have to be paid Rs. 7.

14

CHILD LABOUR IN PRACTICE

SOME DATA ON POPULATION

The inevitable result of the population explosion that occurred in most countries, especially those of the Third World, during the 1950s and 1960s was a considerable increase in the number of young people. Figures dating from 1975 show that, out of a total world population of 3,968 million souls, 1,428 million, or 36 per cent, were less than 15 years old. The proportion in the developed regions was 25 per cent (1,132 million and 283 million respectively), as against 40.4 per cent in the developing regions (2,836 million and 1,145) million respectively (see table 14.1). In many developing countries children less than 15 years of age make up between 40 and 50 per cent of the total population, although in a few the proportion is nearer that which is commonly found in Europe, as for example in Argentina where it is about 29 per cent.[1] If, however, we leave aside these few developing countries where the lower percentages are found; it is apparent everywhere in the Third World that the presence of such a large number of young people causes tremendous social and labour problems. What is to be done, for instance, about their upkeep, their employment, their wages?

Statistics on Child Workers

We have already seen that in the developing countries there is a traditional tendency to place children in jobs that could well be done by adults. This pressure by young people on the adult labour market is increased by the very fact that there are so many of them. The figures given in table 14.1 are revealing in this respect.

The ILO estimates that at the time of writing, in the world as a whole, 52 million children aged less than 15 years are working. By far the majority of these are unpaid family workers, as table 14.2 shows. Moreover, this figure of 52 million may well be an underestimate, since in some countries young workers less than 15 years old are not included in the labour force statistics. In others young people who both work and go to school are rarely considered as being part of the labour force. Again, the statistics cover only those youngster who have a fixed job, and thus exclude the majority of those who work only occasionally. In short, it is impossible to make an accurate estimate of the numbers employed, for the simple reason that, since in most countries child labour is clandestine, it is in the interest of all the parties concerned to conceal it.

TABLE 14.1

Total and Economically Active Population by Sex and Age-group (Mid-year 1975) (Thousands)

Area and age-group	*Males*			*Females*			*Total*		
	Total population	*Economically active population*		*Total population*	*Economically active population*		*Total population*	*Economically active population*	
		Number	*Per cent*		*Number*	*Per cent*		*Number*	*Per cent*
1	2	3	4	5	6	7	8	9	10
World									
-15	727 757	32 630	4.5	700 428	22 086	3.2	1 428 185	54 717	3.8
15-19	199 893	111 018	55.5	192 389	70 953	36.9	392 282	181 972	46.4
20-24	176 661	152 268	86.2	171 322	87 800	51.3	347 983	240 069	69.0
25-44	497 162	479 573	96.5	484 253	246 286	50.9	981 415	725 859	74.0
45-54	173 396	163 753	94.4	177 004	91 330	51.6	350 400	255 083	72.8
55 64	114 679	92 868	81.0	126 084	42 031	33.3	240 764	134 899	56.0
65 +	97 600	37 759	38.7	129 425	15 218	11.8	227 026	52 977	23.3
Total	1 987 149	10 69 870	53.8	1 980 905	575 705	29.1	3968 054	1 645 575	41.5
More developed regions									
-15	144 468	972	0.7	138 563	577	0.4	283 031	1 549	0.5
15-19	50 377	22 603	44.9	48 466	18 374	37.9	98 843	40 976	41.5
20-24	47 775	40 206	84.2	46 337	30 721	66.3	94 111	70 927	75.4
25-44	152 301	147 394	96.8	152 148	90 870	59.7	304 449	238 264	78.3
45-54	63 039	59 140	93.8	71 449	43 147	60.4	134 488	102 287	76.1
55-64	43 082	32 425	75.3	55 188	15 759	31.8	98 271	50 003	50.9
65 +	46 295	10 627	22.9	72 196	5 449	7.5	118 491	16 076	13.6
Total	547 337	313 366	57.3	584 348	206 715	35.4	1 131 684	520 082	46.0
Less developed regions									
-15	583 289	31 658	5.4	561 865	21 509	3.8	1 145 153	53 168	4.6
15-19	149 516	88 416	59.1	143 923	52 580	36.5	293 439	140 995	48.0
20-24	128 886	112 062	86.9	124 985	57 080	45.7	253 872	169 142	66.6
25-44	344 861	332 179	96.3	332 105	155 416	46.8	676 966	487 595	72.0
45-54	110 357	104 613	94.8	105 555	48 183	45.6	215 912	152 796	70.8
55-64	70 597	60 443	84.4	70 896	24 453	34.5	142 493	84 896	59.6
65 +	51 305	27 132	52.9	57 229	9 769	17.1	108 535	36 901	34.0
Total	1 439 812	756 504	52.5	1 396 558	368 989	26.4	2 836 370	1 125 493	39.7

1	*2*	*3*	*4*	*5*	*6*	*7*	*8*	*9*	*10*
Africa									
— 15	88 965	6 087	6.8	88 354	3 555	4.0	177 319	9 641	5.4
15-19	20 865	13 748	65.9	20 655	7 335	35.5	41 519	21 083	50.8
20-24	17 373	15 589	89.7	17 438	7 262	41.6	34 811	22 852	65.6
25-44	45 406	44 199	97.3	46 975	20 425	43.5	92 381	64 624	69.9
45-54	13 005	12 539	96.4	13 623	6 179	45.4	26 628	18 718	70.3
55-64	8 089	7 262	89.8	8 795	3 316	37.7	16 884	10 579	62.7
65 +	5 428	3 353	61.8	6 534	1 292	19.8	11 962	4 645	38.8
Total	199 130	102 777	51.6	202 374	49 366	24.4	401 504	152 142	37.9
Latin America									
— 15	69 016	2 447	3.5	67 215	831	1.2	136 231	3 278	2.4
15-19	17 337	9 690	55.9	17 017	3 947	23.2	34 354	13 637	39.7
20-24	14 543	12 699	87.3	14 428	4 617	32.0	28 971	17 316	59.8
25-44	36 526	35 109	96.1	36 814	9 182	24.9	73 340	44 282	60.4
45-54	11 566	10 745	92.9	11 764	2 507	21.3	23 329	13 252	56.8
55-64	7 509	5 963	79.4	7 905	1 194	15.1	15 415	7 157	46.4
65 +	5 722	2 615	45 7	6 730	475	7.1	12 452	3 090	24.8
Total	162 220	79 269	48.9	161 872	22 753	14.1	324 092	102 022	31.5
Northern America									
— 15	30 794	253	0.8	29 572	125	0.4	60 366	378	0.6
15-19	11 831	5 308	44.9	11 419	3 982	34.9	23 251	9 290	40.0
20-24	10 874	9 128	83.9	10 639	6 207	58.3	21 513	15 335	71.3
25-44	29 667	28 299	95.4	30 202	14 812	49.0	59 870	43 111	72.0
45-54	12 545	11 655	92.9	13 472	7 720	57.3	26 017	19 375	74.5
55-64	10 203	8 207	80.4	11 540	4 946	42.9	21 742	13 153	60.5
65 +	9 919	2 375	23.9	14 165	1 218	8.6	24 084	3 593	14.9
Total	115 832	65 224	56.3	121 010	39 010	32.2	236 841	104 234	44.0
Asia									
— 15	444 234	23 281	5.2	424 490	17 171	4.0	868 724	40 453	4.7
15-19	116 936	67 186	57.5	111 690	43 002	38.5	228 626	110 187	48.2
20-24	103 008	88 780	86.2	99 065	49 085	49.5	202 073	137 864	68.2
25-44	285 532	275 011	96.3	271 059	137 259	50.6	556 591	412 269	74.1
45-54	93 892	89 127	94.9	88 910	44 425	50.0	182 801	133 552	73.1
55-64	61 307	51 634	84.2	60 549	22 577	37.3	121 857	74 211	60.9
65 +	45 169	23 376	51.8	50 332	8 947	17.8	95 501	32 324	33.8
Total	1 150 079	618 394	53.8	1 106 094	322 466	29.1	2 256 173	940 859	41.7

1	2	3	4	5	6	7	8	9	10
Europe									
-15	57 831	477	0.8	55 261	341	0.6	113 093	817	0.7
15-19	19 174	9 607	50.1	18 375	8 036	43.7	37 549	17 643	47.0
20-24	18 555	15 717	84.7	17 896	11 185	62.5	36 451	26 902	73.8
25-44	63 819	61 803	96.8	62 201	31 479	50.6	126 020	93 282	74.0
45-54	27 899	26 264	94.1	30 194	14 929	49.4	58 093	41 193	70.9
55-54	19 801	15 204	76.8	23 779	7 502	31.5	43 581	22 706	52.1
65 +	23 548	5 109	21.7	34 764	2 652	7.6	58 313	7 761	13.3
Total	230 628	134 181	58.2	242 470	76 124	31.4	473 098	210 305	44.4
Oceania									
-15	3 431	86	2.5	3 272	64	1.9	6 703	149	2.2
15-19	1 029	591	57.4	973	501	51.5	2 002	1 092	54.5
20-24	946	860	90.9	885	514	58.0	1 832	1 374	75.0
25-44	2 780	2 691	96.8	2 590	1 141	44.1	5 370	3 832	71.4
45-54	1 114	1 060	95.1	1 055	453	42.9	2 170	1 513	69.7
55-64	817	683	83.7	838	211	25.2	1 655	894	54.0
65 +	694	176	25.4	882	46	5.2	1 576	222	14.1
Total	10 812	6 147	56.8	10 496	2 929	27.9	21 308	9 076	42.6
USSR									
— 15	33 846	—	0.0	32 263	—	0.0	65 749	—	0.0
15-19	12 720	4 888	38.4	12 261	4 150	33.8	24 981	9 039	36.2
20-24	11 362	9 495	83.6	10 971	8 930	81.4	22 333	18 426	82.5
25-44	33 431	32 462	97.1	34 413	31 987	92.9	67 844	64 449	95.0
45-54	13 376	12 363	92.4	17 987	15 118	84.0	31 362	27 481	87.6
55-64	6 953	3 915	56.3	12 677	2 284	18.0	19 630	6 199	31.6
65 +	7 120	755	10.6	16 018	588	3.7	23 138	1 343	5.8
Total	118 448	63 878	53.9	136 589	63 058	46.2	255 038	126 935	49.8

Source: ILO: *Year Book of Labour Statistics 1978* (Geneva, 1978), pp. 16-47.

We can therefore see why estimates of the extent of child labour should vary so widely in different countries. In Italy, for example, the most favourable estimates put the figure at a maximum of some 100,000, on the grounds that there is a marked decline in child labour throughout southern Europe. The ILO *Year Book of Labour Statistics* for 1978 gives a figure of 114,000. Yet some estimates that have appeared in the press recently maintain that the figure is nearer to half a million, and maybe much higher. In Spain it has been suggested in various periodicals that there could be some 200,000 children at work, whereas the *Year Book* gives 142,000 only.

TABLE 14.2

Number of Working Children Less Than 15 Years Old

Area	*Total (millions)*	*Unpaid family workers*[1]	
		Millions	*Percentage of total*
World	52.0	41.2	80
South-east Asia	29.0	23.2	80
East Asia	9.1	6.4	70
Africa	9.7	9.2	95
Latin America	3.1	2.0	65
Europe	0.7	0.4	50
USSR	—	—	—
North America	0.3	—	10
Oceania	0.1	0.1	85

1. Includes a very small number of persons working on their own account.

Source: ILO: *Bureau of Statistics and Special Studies.*

In the developed countries generally, thanks to legislation, compulsory schooling, tradition and the economic situation, the number of working children is very low. The only exceptions here are children who work in agriculture, a certain number of street traders and delivery boys (especially of newspapers) and those who work in family undertakings.

USUAL AGE AT WHICH WORK IS BEGUN

The age at which children usually begin work depends on tradition, the size of the undertaking and whether or not it is a family concern.

In some countries parents set their children to work on household chores, in the fields or on other family tasks when they are still at a very early stage of physical development. Again, children may be apprenticed to a craft when they are very young indeed—sometimes no more than 6 or 7 years old. Of course, the higher the age-group, the greater the proportion of children in that age-group who go out to work; thus, most working children are between 13 and 15 years of age. In general, the intensity and the duration of the work they perform also increases as the years go by, not only because the children gradually become stronger and more skilful but also because they spend less time playing games and going to school (if they do so in the first place). The age at which domestic servants are hired ("adopted" is perhaps the more exact word, as we shall see later) usually varies between 9 and 10 years.

In some countries a child may be illegally declared to be older than he really is, so that on the face of it his employment situation seems to be in order.

In many cities in all regions of the world a large number of children aged between 11 and 13 begin their working life delivering newspapers, doing their round every morning before going to school.

An inquiry[2] carried out among some child workers in India revealed the following points: 24.7 per cent of the children had begun work between the age of 6 and 9 years; 48.4 per cent between 10 and 12 years; and 26.9 per cent between 13 and 15 years. The results of another inquiry,[3] carried out a few years ago in Portugal by the Portuguese Industrial Association among 19,040 adult workers in 230 mechanical engineering undertakings, showed that 3.6 per cent of the women had begun their working life between the ages of 5 and 7 years, that 10.3 per cent of them had done so between the ages of 8 and 10 and that the proportion for those who had begun to work between the ages of 11 and 13 was 41.1 per cent. In other words, 55 per cent of the women in this survey had started work before they had reached the legal minimum age for admission to employment.

SELF-EMPLOYMENT AND DIFFERENT TYPES OF EMPLOYMENT RELATIONSHIP

Many young people work for themselves, usually by providing street services or by peddling goods for sale. However, a good proportion of the children engaged in these activities are not self-employed but work for third parties (who may or may not be members of their own family), either for a fixed payment or for a percentage of the monies they earn or receive from sales. These two types of payment are also found in the more stable jobs: for example, when the child is a genuine wage earner; when he is apprenticed to a craft but has no contract; and when he collaborates with an adult worker from outside his family (in agriculture, a factory or a home industry) and has no direct relationship with the adult worker's employer. When the child works within the family circle (generally without payment) he may be a member of a small handicrafts undertaking, a group of peasant small-holders, a landless farming family working for a third party or a family group working at home for a third party. The children who work in some shops and stores have no contact, either direct or indirect, with the owners, who simply agree to their presence as packers or errand boys, and it is the customers themselves who tip the children for their services.

SECTORS IN WHICH CHILDREN WORK

In which sectors of economic activity are children usually employed when they go to work? Several factors have a bearing on this question—economic needs, tradition, the relative speed of modernisation, the rate of population increase, rural-rural and rural-urban migration (seasonal or more or less permanent), whether the country or region is predominantly rural or urban and/or industrialised, whether the society in which the child lives is a tribal one, and so forth.

Developed Countries

In the more developed countries the overwhelming majority of children who work do so in agriculture, in family or non-family undertakings, during the school holidays and outside school hours, but above all at harvest and sowing time, on a wide range of jobs which may at times be heavy and dangerous. The minority who work in urban centres are employed in the sales or distribution sector (delivering papers, milk, etc.), in hotels and restaurants,[4] especially in holiday resorts and during the school holidays, and in some light and occasional jobs such as baby-sitting.

Developing Countries

In the developing countries child labour is most common in agriculture,[5] in services (provided for the most part on the street) and, as a last resort, in industry. Those who are wage earners generally work in the informal sector, usually in small undertakings that are often not registered as such and that hence do not observe the legal requirements as regards taxes, social security, safety and health, and so on. The larger, registered undertakings in the modern sector, which comply with all legal and other requirements, obviously do not usually employ children—rather than run the unnecessary risk of falling foul of the labour inspectorate, they prefer to have recourse to the large reserves of non-qualified or semi-qualified adult manpower.

In agriculture children are accustomed from an early age to working with their parents, either on the family plot or for a third party. When they work on the family holding they begin by carrying out light tasks such as looking after animals, collecting firewood and fodder and drawing water; later they learn to sow and to reap. In commercial agriculture in very many developing countries children commonly form part of the work team composed of the whole family; they are kept busy on jobs such as weeding, spreading fertiliser and tending plants, but often they share in the heavy work done by the adults—ploughing, sowing and reaping. In southern Europe they are frequently employed individually as labourers on large farms. In particular, it has been reported that in almost all regions of the world the plucking of the coffee bean is a job largely done by women workers helped by their children.[6]

In many developing countries entire families will move from one farming area to another, following the cycle of agricultural work; however, when the head of the family goes off alone to work for a few seasons as a day labourer on someone else's estate, the wife and children of these small farmers look after the family plot in his absence.

Following the rapid urbanisation of the past few decades, child labour in the cities has greatly increased. The child who arrives in the city on this own accepts the first job that he is offered, in order to survive. In reality the job opportunities in the disadvantaged urban zones are fewer than back home in the countryside, and only a few of the young migrants manage to earn a little money. In the big cities there are more opportunities for children to little money. In the big cities there are more opportunities for children to work in the services and handicrafts sectors than in small towns and, especially, rural areas.

Many of those who work on the streets begin by helping their father (usually without payment). Subsequently they might strike out on their own or continue to work for their father or for a third party. The jobs they do are very varied: cleaning shoes, guarding parked cars, loading and unloading goods, carrying messages, selling magazines, food, sweets, flowers, lottery tickets and so on, collecting junk and other goods, and so forth. In certain specified areas in both developed and developing countries young people are involved in drug-running or prostitution, in which may of the girls exploited by adult organisations begin their economic activity at the age of 12. Finally, on the streets in the less developed countries one can see many children begging on their own account or exploited and it has been reported that they are sometimes deliberately maimed by their own parents.

Many children provide various kinds of service in small workshops and commercial establishments, acting as assistants, messengers, packers, car-washers, mechanics, panel beaters, cleaners, petrol-pump attendants, waiters, bellboys, chambermaids, barbers, and so on. A large number of children are also employed in domestic service.

In manufacturing and handicrafts undertakings in the developing countries children are, relatively speaking, fewer in number. They are nevertheless very active, both in family and in non-family undertakings or doing jobs on their own account in their own homes. In many factories they do not participate directly in production operations but carry out tasks such as packing, glueing and labelling. In other undertakings they are in fact engaged in production jobs—for example, in bakeries, in matchworks, in the food industries, in the textile industry (winding, carding, spinning, weaving, etc.), in the tailoring and leather industries (cutting, sewing, embroidering), in metal, leather and woodwork shops, in pottery shops (fring, modelling, painting), in undertakings making shoes, toys, fireworks, and so forth. In cigarette factories, especially in south and south-east Asia, children clean and cut the tobacco and roll the cigarettes. In many countries, over a vast area stretching from north-west Africa to south Asia, children are an important source of labour for the traditional carpet-manufacturing industry. In south and south-east Asia they are also employed in glassworks. In some countries they work in the building industry, especially in the informal sector: usually (though not always) they carry out light tasks such as carrying materials or cleaning up. In some countries children of 10 or 11 years old can be found in almost all industries performing the same jobs as adults.[7]

SECTORS RESERVED FOR BOYS OR FOR GIRLS

In many regions and social groups tradition dictates which jobs should be done by boys and which by girls. It often happens that boys are preferred because they are stronger, because they produce more and because they are less exposed to the dangers of the street and other workplaces. For example, in agriculture, in those regions where tradition allows the employment of both sexes, the heavier tasks (ploughing, weeding, sowing and reaping) are generally reserved for boys, while the girls busy themselves in milking, cooking, sewing, looking after their younger brothers and sisters, and so on.

As regards work on the public highway, the situation can vary greatly, depending on local tradition: either the boys alone provide services or engage tin selling, so that the girls are not exposed to the hazards of the street; or the boys perform certain services and sell certain goods, with others being performed or sold by the girls. For example, boys can often be seen selling newspapers and cleaning shoes whilst the girls sell food.

In general, family undertakings employ children of both sexes, depending on the nature of the jobs to be done and the type of business.

In some countries or regions certain jobs are not thought worthy to be done by children of one or the other sex. In others a combination of tradition and conservatism ensures that boys are employed much more than girls, especially within certain social classes, or when there is a desire to emulate the standards of those classes. In some circles it is not considered "honourable" that a girl or a woman should contribute economically to the running of the household and the practice of sending girls to work outside the home is frowned upon. For women not to have to work outside the home is a sign of a higher social status. In various countries regions, and social and cultural milieux, marriage is the sole or principal purpose in life for the woman, and to this end the girl needs only a learn how to do domestic tasks. This tradition is, however, changing more or less rapidly, depending on the region, and the proportion of girls who work seems generally to be on the increase. Where there exists a marked sexual discrimination regarding the jobs that girls can do, it is justified by arguments such as: girls are only interested in and capable of jobs that are traditionally or typically women's jobs and that are compatible with their future life as housewives; girls should not, and in any case have no desire to, work in industry and services because these sectors call for skills and knowledge that are more masculine in nature; boys should show interest only in jobs that call for strength, skill, greater knowledge, etc. These beliefs go back many centuries, during which the economic roles of the sexes were based on their degree of physical strength, and a major cause of the present trend towards a levelling of the differences seems to be the reduced importance of this physical strength and the increased importance of skill, intelligence and the use of tools.

If there is a strong resistance to female child labour in some regions and social milieux, in others the fact that the boys are looked upon as being the more important members of the family means that a greater effort is made to send them to school, whereas the lot of the girls—who "have no need of book learning"—is to work. This practice is usually more widespread in rural than in urban areas: the girls work on the family farm or do paid seasonal work. This is why in schools in these areas there may be many more boy pupils than girl pupils.

Finally, in some countries and sectors differences of sex have no influence on the jobs undertaken: thus, in some handicrafts workshops in some countries (for female, Thailand, boys and girls are employed on the sole criterion of personal ability.

NOTES

1. See Chapter 8.
2. M. Singh, V.D. Kaura and S.A. Khan, *Working children in Bombay: A study* (New Delhi, National Institute of Public Co-operation and Child Development, 1978), p. 90.
3. "O trabalho dos menores", in *Infancia e Juventude* (Lisbon), Jan.-March, 1973, p. 17.
4. "Work out of school: The Emrys Davies Report", in *Education* (London), 10 Nov. 1972.
5. See, for example, Chapters 8 and 15; and Mostafa H. Nagi: "Child labour in rural Egypt", in *Rural Sociology* (Urbana, Ill.), Dec. 1972, pp. 623-627.
6. ILO, *Conditions of Work of Women and Young Workers on Plantations*, Report III, Committee on Work on Plantations, Sixth Session, Geneva, 1970, p. 24.
7. For further information concerning the sectors in which children work, see ILO: *Minimum age for admission to employment*, op. cit., Ch. III.

15

WORKING CONDITIONS AND ENVIRONMENT

GENERAL CONSIDERATIONS

In the developing countries the children in families which have their own undertakings are introduced to work gradually by their parents. However, other parents, together with relatives or family friends, often get in touch with possible future employers in order to "place" a child in a job at a later date. Usually the first employers to be approached in this way are those for whom the parents, relatives, friends of neighbours work themselves. When a child takes up a job on the street, here too it is often the parents or relatives who first push him into it. In some countries employers who need a child to work as an unqualified assistant (for example, in a pastry shop or a dairy) look for and engage one in a small rural town. Female domestic servants usually come from rural areas: often they get in touch themselves with the families for whom they are going to work, but in other cases their parents hand them over to their future employers so that they çan be "adopted" as a subordinate member of the household.[1] This is virtually tantamount to selling the child or giving her away. In parts of Africa, Latin America, Asia and southern Europe it is not unknown for parents to hand over their children at the age of 8 or 9 years, so that they may work as farm labourers or shepherd boys, in return for which the parents usually receive a small loan or payment in cash or in kind. (Needless to say, this practice is a flagrant breach of the law.) In this way many needy parents forgo the custody of their children and the exercise of parental authority. There have been reports that in south and south-east Asia some employers take possession of a number of children, against their will, and exploit them ruthlessly. The newspapers in the countries concerned sometimes bring to light cases of the exploitation of young people—inhuman conditions of work in factories, shepherd boys being sold, children being given away, and so on.

In these regions, when a child is depending on the employer in this way, it is the employer himself who, in the vast majority of cases, fixes the child's general conditions of work, arbitrarily and unilaterally. As a result the treatment that the employer metes out to his dependent young workers varies widely and depends on his character, on the mood he is in and on local customs. Thus the working child may find that he is greatly imposed upon and severely treated, with neither respect or consideration. Ill-treatment may include corporal punishment, abuses of all kinds, humiliation and frustration. The possibilities for exploitation are, in practice, unlimited. Other employers may be paternalistic, protective and generous. Between these two extremes the general tendency is for the child to be treated rather badly since, as we have been, he has no way of defending himself.

If children were allowed to work in the formal sector, their general conditions of work would be much better; but because they are legally prohibited from doing so (and in the formal sector this prohibition seems to be respected), instead of not working at all they are generally thrown back on to the informal sector, where general conditions of work are usually appalling and where welfare facilities are conspicuous by their absence.

Many children who are claimed by the employers to be apprentices do in fact learn very little about the job in which they are supposed to be qualifying; more often than not they are kept busy running errands on carrying out disagreeable or difficult tasks which often have little connection with the job to which in theory they are apprenticed, or are treated as servants and receive little or no remuneration. The lucky ones, however, do serve some sort of apprenticeship, despite the poor conditions under which they work.

Notwithstanding these manifestly bad working conditions, many child workers seem to be satisfied with the pay and benefits they receive, with their hours of work, with their working environment and with the attitude of their employer and older fellow-workers, as well as with the treatment they receive. The reasons behind this feeling of job satisfaction probably lie in the low level of their job expectations and in the fact that they are receiving some small income and are not unemployed.

The tasks on which they are engaged are generally monotonous and repetitive in nature; occasionally, they are light but often they are ill suited to the child's physical and mental capabilities.

There is no doubt but that it is a urban areas that child workers are treated the worst, exploited the most and undergo the greatest privations, especially in manufacturing industry. Very frequently they have to work under difficult conditions, as for example in stifling heat in a restricted space or, if in the open air, without being able to shelter from the rain or keep out of the sun. They may be forced to work in an awkward position in badly lit, badly ventilated, noisy or unhealthy premises, in damp and unhygienic surroundings, in an atmosphere contaminated with dust or gases, inhaling tobacco dust, crammed together with other workers, without adequate means of security, without special resting areas, without medical facilities, without water for washing, without adequate toilet facilities, and so on and so forth. It is not unusual for them to have to lift and carry heavy loads, in violation of the principles laid down in the relevant ILO standards.

Although the number of women in domestic service is tending to decrease in most countries, it is common knowledge that in many cases domestic servants are exploited with no consideration being shown to them, and sometimes are even ill treated. In most of the countries where domestic service is widespread, the difference in social status between the employer and the employee is such that the former may adopt a somewhat contemptuous attitude towards the latter, even when he is paternistically inclined towards her.

Although many self-employed workers work in their own homes, others have to travel varying distances, on foot, by bus or by train, to reach their workplace, just as many wage earners do. Children who are more or less self-employed, and child street traders generally, feel that they are freer than children who work in other sectors. Some are exploited only a little, others not at all, and some enjoy the protection of their parents. Many of them, however, despite their relative freedom, are exploited by their parents or relatives as well as by adults outside the family circle. When carrying out their activities they are hardly ever protected from the vagaries of the weather; if they do not operate from a fixed location they are molested by the police or by groups of youths or adults, and if they do have a fixed location this does not usually met even the most elementary conditions of hygiene nor does it have toilet facilities.

Normally, the child who works in a family undertaking, be it in agriculture, manufacturing, commerce or handicrafts, is exploited less than the wage-earning child. Indeed, the stress, fatigue and harmful effects to which he is exposed are partly compensated for by the personal attention and affection which his parents can give him, during both work and rest periods.

A recent study observes that in one country the children of farm workers who migrate to another part of the country work in conditions that recall the exploitation to which in earlier times the children of the Western world were exposed in the factories and mines. Their plight is aggravated by the educational problems they have to face.[2]

HOURS OF WORK

In the developing regions there seems to be more employment instability among working children than among adults. This reflects the general instability that is characteristic of those in the younger age-groups, of whom it many be said that the more they are under the control of their parents or employers, the less they are likely to change jobs; but when the initiative lies in their own hands, the poor working conditions, low wages and ill-treatment which are their lot give them ample reasons for doing so.

The length of time that wage-earning children work each day and over the year varies considerably according to their availability for work (i.e. whether they go to school or not and/or whether they have other jobs as well), the parents' wish to keep them at work more or less continuously, how long the employer needs them, and so on.

The child who is self-employed can vary his working hours according to his own capabilities and needs, although, if he is to ensure that his activities are to be profitable as possible, he must take account of the times when his potential customers are at their most numerous and adjust his working hours accordingly: for example, a child selling newspapers or food must be at his site very early in the morning when the newspapers are published, and again during the rush hour, when the cinemas empty, during market hours, and so on. Even so, it is not unusual to find 8-or 9-year-old children outside the big hotels of a Third World metropolis at 11.30 at night, still trying to sell the morning edition of the daily newspaper.

Many youngsters work only during the school holidays, at weekends, early in the morning or late at night. Temporary jobs are common in the construction industry (usually in the informal sector) and in public works: here the youngsters work for as long as the job for which they were taken on lasts, or for that part of the job for which child labour was foreseen. Seasonal work in the tourist industry, especially in the services sector, is also often undertaken bv children; agricultural work too needs many young people and children for seasonal tasks such as sowing and harvesting.

The number of hours worked by children each day varied considerably. They may be at their jobs every working day but for part of the day only, or they may work eight hours a day for six days a week, and so on. Since, as we have seen, the general conditions of work are generally fixed by the employer alone, all kinds of abuses are encountered: working days of 10, 12 or 14 hours for six or sometimes seven days a week, that is to say far beyond what the child can tolerate both physically and mentally.[3] Sometimes children do not work strict hours at all—they merely stay on in the shop or cafe where they work until the last customer has left.

To gain an idea of the length of time that many child workers spend away from home, one must of course add to the number of hours worked the time for work breaks and for travelling to and from home.

As has already been mentioned, in some countries girls work longer hours than boys, because boys spend more time at school. Two studies carried out in Indonesia (Java) and Nepal recently produced the details shown in table 15.1 on the daily hours of work for children of both sexes.

For both, self-employed and wage-earning children the working week seems generally to be excessively long, with six or even seven days per week being worked in various sectors of activity. It is common knowledge that girls in domestic service usually work very long hours, since they must be available at virtually and time to carry out their employer's bidding.

At certain times of the year in specific localities in the developed countries there is a great and urgent need for child labour. At sowing and harvest times and in the high summer season many children work an excessive number of hours per day on seasonal jobs. In these countries the number of hours worked by the minority of children who do some part-time job during the school term is usually not related to the socio-economic status of their families.[4]

TABLE 15.1

Indonesia (Java) and Nepal: Daily Hours Worked by Children

Country and age-group	*Hours worked per day*	
	Boys	*Girls*
Indonesia (Java)		
6-8	3.6	3.5
9-11	3.3	5.4
12-14	4.8	8.7
Nepal		
6-8	3.7	4.9
9-11	6.5	8.4
12-14	7.5	9.9

Source: M. Nag, R.C. Peet and B. White, "Economic value of children in two peasant societies", in International Union for the Scientific Study of Population: *International Population Conference, Mexico, 1977* (Liege, 1978), Vol. 1, tables 1-4.

Some wage-earning children are permitted to take work breaks at fixed intervals during the working day. Others are not allowed to do so, however—despite the fact that a child needs a break more often than an adult, if he is to recharge his physical and mental batteries. It will be readily understood that, in the case of a girl in domestic service, her work breaks (and indeed her conditions of employment generally) depend purely on her employer's wishes: she may have the right to rest after lunch, or again she may not; and it can happen that she has to work for six, seven or even more hours at a stretch.

The period of daily rest is often insufficient, especially in agricultural work, industry, some service industries and domestic service.

The weekly rest is sometimes granted and paid, sometimes granted but not paid and sometimes not allowed at all—that is, the working week is a seven-day week.

In many countries and undertakings young wage earners do not enjoy the annual paid holidays that are laid down by law for adult workers carrying out the same job. Nor do young people working at home enjoy annual paid holidays.

REMUNERATION

In the less developed regions especially, children who work in the family undertaking usually receive no payment for their work, since the family income is considered to be one indivisible whole. This is equally true when the family carries out agricultural work for a third party: the children take part in the work and the head of the family receives the total sum earned.

When the child is a wage earner, his wages are usually derisory in relation to the value of the work he produces, and are in any case much lower than those received by an adult doing the same job—perhaps only a half or a third (or even less) of what the adult worker earns, according to the criterion applied by the employer. To justify this criterion the employer put forward various reasons, depending on the case: the child worker has not had enough experience, and so his work cannot be well done; he has no family responsibilities; training him costs the employer money, which he has to recover by paying the child less....

In previous chapters there is a very typical example of this: the workers suggested to the employers that, as in this particular case the children were clearly doing the same work as the adults, the children should be paid the same wage as the older workers. This suggestion was not accepted.

A still more flagrant example is that of the supposed apprentices who are in fact working rather than learning, and are not being paid for it. Such a state of affairs may sometimes last for years. Even in countries where the legal age for admission to employment is 12 years, young people of that age are often not paid the legal minimum salary. When they work overtime they generally paid at the normal rate (which is already unfairly reduced). When the child does not work directly for the employer but with an adult worker, the latter usually pays the child a share of what he has earned.

With regard to payment for piece-work, the child is at a clear disadvantage here as compared with adult workers, since, for obvious reasons, the usually produces less than they (or is more tired, or both).

Some child workers are aid a fixed wage plus tips. Others live by tips alone, and under such a system there can of course be no regular source of income. Takings can very greatly, according to circumstances, and offer no guarantee of a basic minimum wage.

In general, the income of child street traders is irregular, for many reasons: location of their pitch, time of the month, times when the streets are crowded, nature of the goods offered for sale in relation to the taste and purchasing power of the potential buyers, percentage of the takings the child retains if he is working for a third party, and so on.

In commercial agricultural undertakings there are children whose wages are extremely modest (when in fact they are not merely housed and fed). In some kinds of commercial and industrial undertakings it is customary for part of the wages to be paid in cash and part in kind. For many parents the fact that a child is housed and fed outside the home, even though he contributes nothing to the family budget, at !east takes part of the pressure off it.

OCCUPATIONAL RISKS

To a greater or lesser extent, the risk of occupational accidents or diseases is present in every employment sector. The risk that child workers run in this respect is heightened in that their bodies are not so strong as those of adult workers. During his day's work, and depending on the job he is doing, a child experiences fatigue, faces one or more potential accident situations, adopts uncomfortable positions which give him aches and pains, and often works in dirty conditions, with all the dangers of infection that this implies.

The self-employed child who has an accident or contracts a disease of occupational origin obviously benefits from no form of social protection. If the child is a wage earner he is not usually protected either, since in the vast majority of cases he is working illegally, as we have seen. If he is the victim of an occupational accident or disease, he and his parents must be prepared for fearful and irreversible consequences. For obvious reasons, the official statistics reveal only a very small proportion of the occupational accidents and diseases that affect young people.

Agriculture is one of the most hazardous sectors for the physical safety and health of workers, for several reasons: the prevalence of dangerous modern machinery; prolonged exposure to heat, sunlight, dust, wind and insects; the almost constant physical effort that agricultural work demands; contact with various chemical products, such as fertilisers and pesticides, whose long-term effects on man may be completely unknown and for the majority, of which, in cases of poisoning, specific antidotes exist. Children are particularly at risk from endemic and parasitic diseases, diseases of the respiratory tract, dermatosis and fatal accidents.

In industry the unhealthy conditions have a greater impact on the safety and health of child workers than on that of adults, because of their want of experience in handling tools, because of that lack of concentration which is quite normal for their age and because of a shortage of security and prevention equipment such as masks and special gloves. For example, in glass-works children suffer greatly from the suffocating heat and run the risk, amongst others, of sustaining cuts and burns. Children employed in carpet manufacturing breathe wool dust throughout the working day, and this penetrates deep into their lungs.

It should also be borne in mind that, as machinery, tools and workplaces in general are designed for use by adults rather than by children, they are a further potential source of more or less serious accidents, and call for increased effort by the child as well as causing numerous problems of adaptation.

Of the countless occupational hazards which can befall children especially, we may mention that in several countries if has been discovered that, after several months of use, a certain glue used in the leather industry can produce paralysis, which affects in particular at the more delicate organisms— that is, those of children. In general, solvents (for descaling metal, for example) and glues (in carpentry and the leather industry) are particularly harmful to children because of the toxic vapours that such products give off.

In the construction and public works sectors, even though here children usually carry out light tasks only, they are none the less exposed to a wide variety of potential accidents and other hazards—fails, injuries, consequences of inclement weather, and so on—because on the one hand these are sectors in which accidents are common and on the other hand the immaturity and lack of concentration of children make them more liable to accidents than adults.

Young street traders are exposed, at times until late at night, to the vagaries of the weather, to dirt of all kinds, to traffic hazards, to detention by the police on grounds of vagrancy and to everything that is most sordid in city life. Reflecting on the large numbers of child workers among juvenile delinquents, the authors of an inquiry carried out in the United Sates in the early years of the present century found that the mere fact of going to work on the streets, rather than bad home influences or lack of schooling, was the major cause of juvenile delinquency.[5]

The problems and dangers inherent in work in commerce, the service industries in general and domestic service are less serious. However, the risks to children of such accidents as falls, injuries and cuts, and the consequences of carrying loads that are too heavy for them, especially in domestic service, need to be borne very much in mind.

NOTES

1. See ILO, *Minimum Age for Admission to Employment,* op. cit., p. 27.
2. Costin, op. cit., pp. 77-78.
3. In Bombay it was found that children employed in hotels and restaurants were working an average of 11.61 hours a day (Singh, Kaura and Khan, *op. cit.,* table 67). See also Chapters 12 and 13.
4. *Work Out of School: The Emrys Davies Report,* op. cit.
5. Edward N. Clopper: *Child Labour in City Streets* (New York, Macmillan, 1912; reprinted by Garrett Press, New York, 1970), pp. 159 ff.

16

LIVING CONDITIONS

HUMAN ENVIRONMENT, HOUSING AND HEALTH

In the less developed regions the living conditions of the child worker are generally appalling. Poverty and over-crowding are compounded by squalid housing with noisome sanitary installations, where these exist at all. The abysmal quality of the housing is a widespread social problem, above all in urban areas. Sometimes up to ten members of a family may be crammed together in the shacks and hovels in which they live—often in a single room, with little or no ventilation. Such conditions are typical of any developing country with a high rate of population growth.[1]

Human relationships under such conditions are frequently not good, and the child does not receive as much affection as he ought. The father is frequently an alcoholic. Inevitably, the child's welfare is affected by living under such conditions. Not enough attention is paid to the young members of the family, nor are they adequately supervised; consequently, many of them lead a semi-independent life from an early age. The combined incomes of all members of the family rarely make it possible to improve their conditions and quality of life.

In some developing countries with warm climates children who have either been abandoned or who have made their own way from rural areas can be seen wandering about the city streets. As they usually have nowhere to go, they sleep on the pavement. Other who have a job but no home sleep in market stalls or in a corner of the workshop where they work (which can be damp, dirty, unhealthy, full of vermin, and generally unpleasant). Others sleep in the kitchen of the cafe or bar where they are employed, others again do so surrounded by the scrap metal and junk they have collected during the day, and so on.

Children who work or are looking for work are usually badly clothed and undernourished, especially in urban areas. They generally do not have enough calories, protein, calcium and vitamins. Their diet is usually very poor and unbalanced: in Mexico City, for example, they basically live on *tortillas* (maize cakes), coffee and beans.

The number of children in these regions who suffer from poor health is enormous. Working children are even worse off in this respect. The great majority of them work even when they are ill. Vitamin and protein deficiency, anaemia, bronchitis and tuberculosis are widespread. The onset of tuberculosis, although this is not a typical occupational disease (unlike the others) but one caused by grim living conditions, is encouraged when the child begins to work at a tender age and works long and tiring hours in a harmful work environment.

The child who works on the streets can quickly be led astray into begging, delinquency and other social evils. In an attempt to counteract this trend, homes and centres have been established in some countries for those children who do not want to go back to their own homes, from which they may have run away and where the social atmosphere may be demoralising.

Housing, sanitary conditions and the nutrition and physical development of working children in southern Europe are showing a general improvement over those that obtained in the past.

PERSONAL PROBLEMS OF WORKING CHILDREN

In the less developed regions children who do not work in the family undertaking do not have enough contact with their parents, because they spend the greater part of the day away from home and often come back late in the evening. This is yet another factor contributing to the disorganisation of family life.

When a child begins to earn some money, he has the feeling that he is more important than he was before, even though his earnings may be very low. He may also enjoy greater esteem within the family because he is bringing in a little money and thus contributing to its upkeep. He looks upon himself as more grown up than other children of his age because, as well as working and mixing with adults and being paid a little money for what he does, he can to some extent decide himself how he is going to spend the part of this wages that this parents give back to him to cover his expenses. All this gives him a feeling of importance and greater independence, as some Italian writers have shown.[2] To increase this feeling of independence he often falls into the trap of trying to compensate for his small physical size, his poverty and his lack of basic needs by incurring extravagant expenses and indulging in bad habits (smoking, gambling, etc.).

However, the seemingly positively aspects of child labour are quickly and fully countered by the immediate problems they bring in their train. First, the working child has no time for playing, or at least for playing enough, not for taking healthy exercise—and this at a time of life when these activities are so important for his future development. Second, hours of work and school hours generally clash, and in many cases the need to work puts any idea of attendance at school out of the question; in other cases, the child's tiredness and lack of concentration are reflected in his repeated failure and lack of progress at school. Third, because he does not have the time or the energy to learn, the working child cannot develop his mental faculties. Fourth, as a result of his lack of development and early entry into unskilled working life, his aspirations quickly become fixed at a very low level.

The child worker's extreme fatigue is due to the fact that his powers of resistance and his muscular strength are below those of adults; when he is obliged to exert himself as much as they do, at the same speed and without any extra work breaks, it is only to be expected that he should feel more tired than they.[3]

In industrial and commercial milieux the child's normal sensitivity, coupled with his poor conditions of work, increase the difficulties he has in adapting himself to a new and complex pattern of human relationships. But these difficulties may not only be subjective: he may also not be made welcome, unkind jokes may be played on him, he may be ill treated and may be left out of the adult workers' conversation during breaks.

Work in the streets is generally less difficult for a child. However, problems do arise (apart from occupational problems), for example when the child has to compete with more experienced adults, when he is threatened by groups of youths or adults who demand a percentage of his taking or when he falls into bad company and drifts into vagrancy, begging, drug addiction and drug-running, delinquency, sexual deviance, prostitution, and so on. Interestingly enough, as long ago as 1912 Edward Clopper listed the effects that street work could have on child, under three headings: material, physical and moral deterioration.[4] Under "material deterioration" three effects are suggested: that the child may acquire a distaste for regular employment; that he has small chance of acquiring a trade; and that he may drift into a large class of casual workers. The effects due to "physical deterioration" are given as: night work; excessive fatigue; exposure to bad weather; irregularity of sleep and meals; use of stimulants (cigarettes, coffee, alcohol); and disease through contact with vice. The following effects are listed under "moral deterioration": the child may be encouraged to play truant; he may show independence and defiance of parental control; he may develop weaknesses cultivated by the formation of bad habits; he may form a liking for "petty excitements of the street"; opportunities may arise for him to drift into delinquency; and street work furnishes a large percentage of the recruits to the criminal population.

In addition to occupational risks as such, the various jobs that a child does expose his frail body to a wide range of complaints, ranging from headaches, coughs and colds, hearing disorders and visual fatigue to fever and advanced lung diseases.

The younger the child is, the more serious most of these problems become, because he is less strong (and hence more vulnerable) and because he is more easily influenced. Further, the lack of concern shown by some parents, coupled with the lack of healthy exercise and physical recreation, non-attendance at school, the fatigue caused by work, the unhappy experiences of, in particular, children who work on the streets (which can mark them for the rest of their lives), the illnesses that their weakened bodies may contract, and the occupational accidents to which they are exposed because of their lack of self-discipline, makes the risk of their material, physical and moral deterioration greater still.

Since it is the normal thing for these underprivileged children to work, or at least to look for work, it would be a contradiction to say that the fact that they do work sets them apart from other people in some way. However, there is no doubt but that child workers, irrespective of their actual numbers and the percentage of the total population that they represent, are on the fringe of society, when society is construed of being composed of groups of persons more skilled than they are and having greater social influence. This results from their narrow outlook, which itself is a result of their lack of education and vocational training and their own increasing awareness of the gap that separates them from other social and occupational groups.

REPERCUSSIONS OF CHILD LABOUR

Social and Labour Repercussions

How will the child worker of today fare, from the social and labour view—point, in the years to come? This will depend very much on the character of the child in question, the kind of job he is doing, the circumstances in which he is doing it, and his personal hopes for the future. Although often these hopes are inevitably far from high, working children to sometimes manage to set up as employers themselves or succeed in graduating to more skilled work. As a general rule, however, when a child performs stultifying, precarious and insignificant work from an early age, this prevents (or at least considerably hinders) his acquiring any genuine qualifications for more skilled work. This, together with the lack of inclination to learn that stems from his immaturity, effectively puts an end to his chances of better employment, higher pay and social advancement. It is therefore very likely that a man who has been at work from an early age will spend his whole life at the bottom of the social ladder, performing routine, unskilled jobs, when he is not out of work altogether.

Physical Repercussions

Many of the jobs that children do are harmful for their physical development. Their growing bodies suffer continually from the effects of fatigue, over-exertion, lack of hygiene and all the other problems with which they are confronted. For example, excessive heat, work in bad weather and continuous contact with dust cause morbid conditions that are more or less chronic and are difficult to cure: skin troubles, bronchitis, tuberculosis, and so on.

Many jobs done by children are the cause of physical deformities and various illnesses, or else they aggravate defects or maladies such as heart disease, affections of the throat, flat feet, and so on.

An interesting experiment was carried out recently in Japan on young workers and students.[5] It was found that until they reached the age of 12 there was no difference in height between children in the two groups; however, those who began to work before they were 14 years old were subsequently found, on average, to be 4 cm shorter than the students who had not entered working life until after they were 18 years old.

Heavy loads and awkward body positions in particular can affect physical growth—especially the growth of the bones, which are still soft in children. When a child is regularly bent double under a heavy burden or is obliged to stay in an unnatural position for long periods, deformation of the spinal column, pelvis and/or thorax may be the result. This is because before puberty the strength, powers of resistance and physical defences of children of both sexes are proportionally lower the younger they are. During the years leading up to and during puberty the immature organism is constantly growing; it undergoes regular endocranial and vegetative changes which are adversely affected by certain types of fatigue—especially continuous and excessive fatigue—and by unhealthy and dangerous conditions.[6]

In the less developed regions the malnutrition of the majority of working children, the fatigue, lack of proteins and amino-acids, and the anaemia and other affections from which they often suffer, can seriously damage the central nervous system.

It is thus clear, and has been scientifically proved, that, in the conditions in which it is usually carried out, the employment of children (not to mention the frequent risks of occupational accidents and diseases as such) is both directly and indirectly harmful for the child, and its results will be carried over into adult life.

Mental Repercussions

When a young child begins to work, and especially when he leaves the family circle to do so, the parents must be doubly vigilant, since the age at which he usually starts to work coincides more or less with a period of profound mental change in the child. Clearly, if to the working child's unfavourable intellectual status is added an ill directed mental development, there will be undesirable consequences and behaviour problems, caused by the child's inadequate comprehension of the adult world and by his imitating, distorting and exaggerating what he wrongly believes to be the essence of that world. These failings, linked with his lack of adequate general education and vocational training, restrict his ability to make a significant contribution to the social milieu in which he lives.

The normal needs and tendencies of puberty and adolescence, which instead of being satisfied are converted into a premature "pseudo"—maturity, have a permanent limiting and disturbing effect on the psychological life of the adult. Again, the feeling of injustice and frustration, stemming fro their inability to do what others do and be on the same intellectual level as others, can have a permanent effect on personal relationships and even lead to aberrations of behaviour and personality.

THE EXPLOITATION OF CHILDREN AN UNNATURAL SITUATION[7]

In a child who starts to work full time, or for whom work becomes the most important element in his life, and under conditions of exploitation, a set of reflexes and physical changes is triggered off which marks an abrupt and unnatural transformation from childhood to premature adulthood. By forcing him to work, the social milieu which envelops him virtually compels him to leave his childhood behind—that is, to abandon the motivations, problems and interests that are characteristic of childhood.

One of the most obvious activities of childhood is "play"—a spontaneous, free, uncontrolled, non-productive outburst of energy. The child worker cannot give free rein to this entirely natural urge, which consequently withers away for lack of use. Sometimes these children pastimes are replaced by others that more resemble adult games, in which the "play" element nevertheless emerges but in an attenuated form in order not to appear too childish. Thus the games in which children play at being "grown-ups" suddenly stop, because the child workers is in fact playing a adult role in earnest.

Young children usually have vivid imaginations and may live in a fantasy world. There is no place for these in the world of work, so they fade away in the working child's mind, to be promptly replaced by the practical realities that mark the world of production and services. The child's creativeness and ability to transcend reality are thus blunted, and his whole mental world is thus impoverished.

The indecision and changeability that are so characteristic of childhood give way to a rapid and precocious crystallisation of the sudden need to adopt adult attitudes.

The irresponsible elements in a child's nature must also be curtailed or eliminated altogether when a he begins to work, since he is obliged to carry out specific tasks in a set way, so as not to cause accidents, spoil material or reduce quality or productivity, and so that he may earn enough to live on and not be dismissed. The responsibilities that bear on him also lead to premature economic worries that are unhealthy for the present and future well-being of himself and his family.

When all the elements that are characteristic of childhood are combined, the result is recreational play—something typical of childhood that the working child cannot enjoy. Indeed, if he does not behave in a way that is contrary to his natural inclinations, if he does not bring all his concentration to bear on the job that has been assigned to him, inter alia the risk of accidents is increased.

It is only to be expected that such constant pressure on him to abandon his childhood has a powerful effect on his nervous system. And if, by chance, the childish elements in the child worker's personality manage to elude the repression or distortion to which they are subjected and to blossom out into the behaviour, attitudes or expressions of childhood, or if these elements obstruct the smooth running of the production operations, his employer and his adult fellow-workers disapprove of his conduct, and this can have a strong effect at the emotional level. The child immediately takes the criticism to heart, without understanding its true social function—that is, to ensure the smooth running of material operations carried on for profit.

NOTES

1. For further information on the implications of rapid population growth for the training, employment and welfare of workers and on the ILO's activities in population matters, see ILO: *Population and labour* (Geneva, 1973).
2. Piccione, op. cit., pp. 47-48; Rosa Miragliotta: "I minori del 'Borgo vecchio' a Palermo", in *Esperienze Sociali* (Palermo), July 1977; *Libro biancho sul lavoro minorile* (Rome, Edizioni ACLI, 1967).
3. H. Desoille: *La medecine du travail*, Collection "Que sais-je? (Paris, Presses Universitaires de France, 1967), p. 76.
4. Clopper, *op. cit.*, pp. 128-129.
5. Desoille, *op. cit.*, pp. 76-77.
6. *La medicina sociale per i fanciulli ed i giovani*, Proceedings of a seminar held in Bari, 24-25 May 1971 (Rome, Istituto Italiano di Medicina Social, 1971), p. 9.
7. This section draws heavily on Mauro Quinzi: "Aspetti psicopedagogici del lavoro minorile", Part 2, in *Problemi Minorili* (Rome), Nov.-Dec. 1969.

17

CONVENTION CONCERNING MINIMUM AGE FOR EMPLOYMENT*

The General Conference of the International Labour Organistion,

Having been convened at Geneva by the Governing Body of the International Labour Office, and having met in its Fifty-eighth Session on 6 June 1973, and

Having a decided upon the adoption of certain proposals with regard to minimum age for admission to employment, which is the fourth item on the agenda of the session, and

Noting the terms of the Minimum Age (Industry) Convention, 1919, the Minimum Age (Sea) Convention, 1920, the Minimum Age (Agriculture) Convention, 1921, the Minimum Age (Trimmers and Stockers) Convention, 1921, the Minimum Age (Non-Industrial Employment) Convention, 1932, the Minimum Age (Sea) Convention (Revised), 1936, the Minimum Age (Industry) Convention (Revised), 1937, the Minimum Age (Non-Industrial Employment) Convention (Revised, 1937, the Minimum age (Fishermen) Convention, 1959, and the Minimum Age (Underground Work) Convention, 1965, and

Considering that the time has come to establish a general instrument on the subject, which would gradually replace the existing ones applicable to limited economic sectors, with a view to achieving the total abolition of child labour, and

Having determined that this instrument shall take the form of an international Convention,

adopts this twenty-sixth day of June of the year one thousand nine hundred and seventy-three the following Convention, which may be cited as the *Minimum Age Convention, 1973*:

Article 1

Each Member for which this Convention is in force undertakes to pursue a national policy designed to ensure the effective abolition of child labour and to raise progressively the minimum age for admission to employment or work to a level consistent with the fullest physical and mental development of young persons.

* Convention No. 138.

Article 2

1. Each Member which ratifies this Convention shall specify, in a declaration appended to its ratification, a minimum age for admission to employment or work within its territory and on means of transport registered in its territory; subject to Articles 4 to 8 of this Convention, no one under that age shall be admitted to employment or work in any occupation.

2. Each Member which has ratified this Convention may subsequently notify the Director-General of the International Labour Office, by further declarations, that it specifies a minimum age higher than that previously specified.

3. The minimum age specified in pursuance of paragraph 1 of this Article shall not be less than the age of completion of compulsory schooling and, in any case, shall not be less than 15 years.

4. Notwithstanding the provisions of paragraph 3 of this Article, a Member whose economy and educational facilities are insufficiently developed may, after consultation with the organisations of employers and workers concerned, where such exist, initially specify a minimum age of 14 years.

5. Each Member which has specified a minimum age of 14 years in pursuance of the provisions of the preceding paragraph shall include in its reports on the application of this Convention submitted under article 22 of the Constitution of the International Labour Organisation a statement—

(a) that its reason for doing so subsists; or

(b) that it renounces its right to avail of the provisions in question as from a stated date.

Article 3

1. The minimum age for admission to any type of employment or work which by its nature or the circumstances in which it is carried out is likely to jeopardise the health, safety or morals of young persons shall not be less than 18 years.

2. The types of employment or work to which paragraph 1 of this Article applies shall be determined by national laws or regulations or by the competent authority, after consultation with the organisations of employers and workers concerned, where such exist.

3. Notwithstanding the provisions of paragraph 1 of this Article, national laws or regulations or the competent authority may, after consultation with the organisations of employers and workers concerned, where such exist, authorities employment or work as from the age of 16 years on condition that the health safety and morals of the young persons concerned are fully protected and that the young persons have received adequate specific instruction or vocational training in the relevant branch of activity.

Article 4

1. In so far as necessary, the competent authority, after consultation with the organisations of employers and workers concerned, where such exist, may exclude from the application of this Convention limited categories of employment or work in respect of which special and substantial problems of application arise.

2. Each Member which ratifies this Convention shall list in its first report on the application of the Convention submitted under article 22 of the Constitution of the International Labour Organisation any categories which may have been excluded in pursuance of paragraph 1 of this Article, giving the reasons for such exclusion, and shall state in subsequent reports the position of its law and practice in respect of the categories excluded and the extent to which effect has been given or is proposed to be given to the Convention in respect of such categories.

3. Employment or work covered by Article 3 of this Convention shall not be excluded from the application of the Convention in pursuance of this Article.

Article 5

1. A Member whose economy and administrative facilities are insufficiently developed may, after consultation with the organisations of employers and workers concerned, where such exist, initially limit the scope of application of this Convention.

2. Each Member which, avails, itself of the provisions of paragraph 1 of this Article shall specify, in a declaration appended to its ratification, the branches of economic activity or types of undertakings to which it will apply the provisions of the Convention.

3. The provisions of the Convention shall be applicable as a minimum to the following mining and quarrying; manufacturing; construction; electricity, gas and water; sanitary services; transport, storage and communication; and plantations and other agricultural undertakings mainly producing for commercial purposes, but excluding family and small-small holdings producing for local consumption and not regularly employing hired workers.

4. Any Member which has limited the scope of application of this Convention in pursuance of this Article—

(a) shall indicate in its reports under article 22 of the Constitution of the International Labour Organisation the general position as regards the employment or work of young persons and children in the branches of activity which are excluded from the scope of application of this Convention and any progress which may have been made towards wider application of the provisions of the Convention;

(b) may at any time formally extend the scope of application by a declaration addressed to the Director-General of the International Labour Office.

Article 6

This Convention does not apply to work done by children and young persons in schools for general, vocational or technical education or in other training institutions, or to work done by persons at least 14 years of age in undertakings, where such work is carried out in accordance with conditions prescribed by the competent authority, after consultation with the organisations of employers and workers concerned, where such exist, and is an integral part of—

(a) a course of education or training for which a school or training institution is primarily responsible;

(b) a programme of training mainly or entirely in an undertaking, which programme has been approved by the competent authority; or

(c) a programme of guidance or orientation designed to facilitate the choice of an occupation or of a line of training.

Article 7

1. National laws or regulations may permit the employment or work of persons 13 to 15 years of age on light work which is—

(a) not likely to be harmful to their health or development; and

(b) not such as to prejudice their attendance at school, their participation in vocational orientation or training programmes approved by the competent authority or their capacity to benefit from the instruction received.

2. National laws or regulations may also permit the employment or work of persons who are at least 15 years of age but have not yet completed their compulsory schooling on work which meets the requirements set forth in subparagraphs (a) and (b) of paragraph 1 of this Article.

3. The competent authority shall determine the activities in which employment or work may be permitted under paragraphs 1 and 2 of this Article and shall prescribe the number of hours during which and the conditions in which such employment or work may be undertaken.

4. Notwithstanding the provisions of paragraphs 1 and 2 of this Article, a Member which has availed itself of the provisions of paragraph 4 of Article 2 may, for as long as it continues to do so, substitute the ages 12 and 14 for the ages 13 and 15 in paragraph 1 and the age 14 for the age 15 in paragraph 2 of this Article.

Article 8

1. After consultation with the organisations, of employers and workers concerned, where such exist, the competent authority may, be permits granted in individual cases, allow exceptions to the prohibition of employment or work provided for in Article 2 of this Convention, for such purposes as participation in artistic performances.

2. Permits so granted shall limit the number of hours during which and prescribe the conditions in which employment or work is allowed.

Article 9

1. All necessary measures, including the provision of appropriate penalties, shall be taken by the competent authority to ensure the effectively enforcement of the provisions of this Convention.

2. National laws or regulations or the competent authority shall define the persons responsible for compliance with the provisions giving effect to the Convention.

3. National laws or regulations or the competent authority shall prescribe the registers or other documents which shall be kept and made available by the employer; such registers or documents shall contain the names and ages or dates or birth, duly certified wherever possible, or persons whom he employes or who work for him and who less than 18 years of age.

Article 10

1. This Convention revises, on the terms set forth in this Article, the Minimum Age (Industry) Convention, 1919, the Minimum Age (Sea) Convention, 1920, the Minimum Age (Agriculture) Convention, 1921, the Minimum Age (Trimmers and Stokers) Convention, 1921, the Minimum Age (Non-Industrial Employment) Convention, 1932, the Minimum Age (Sea) Convention (Revised), 1936, the Minimum Age (Industry) Convention (Revised) 1937, the Minimum Age (Non-Industrial Employment) Convention (Revised), 1937, the Minimum Age (Fishermen) Convention, 1959, and the Minimum Age (Underground Work) Convention, 1965.

2. The coming into force of this convention shall not close the minimum Age (Sea) Convention (Revised), 1936, the Minimum Age (Industry) Convention, (Revised), 1937, the Minimum Age (Non-Industrial Employment) Convention (Revised), 1937, the Minimum Age (Fishermen) Convention, 1959, or the Minimum Age (Underground Work) Convention, 1965, to further ratification.

3. The Minimum Age (Industry) Convention, 1919, the Minimum Age (Sea) Convention, 1920, the Minimum Age (Agriculture) Convention, 1921, and the Minimum Age (Trimmers and Stokers) Convention, 1921, shall be closed to further ratification when all the parties thereto have consented to such closing by ratification of this Convention or by a declaration communicated to the Director-General of the International Labour Office.

4. When the obligations of this Convention are accepted—

(a) by a Member which is a party to the Minimum Age (Industry) Convention (Revised), 1937, and a minimum age of not less than 15 years is specified in pursuance of Article 2 of this Convention, this shall *ipso jure* involve the immediate denunciation of that Convention,

(b) in respect of non-industrial employment as defined in the Minimum Age (Non-Industrial Employment) Convention, 1932, by a Member which is a party to that Convention, this shall *ipso jure* involve the immediate denunciation of that Convention.

(c) in respect of non-industrial employment as defined in the Minimum Age (Non-Industrial Employment) Convention (Revised), 1937, by a Member which is a party to that Convention, and a minimum age of not less than 15 years is specified in pursuance of Article 2 of this Convention, this shall *ipso jure* involve the immediate denunciation of that Convention,

(d) in respect of maritime employment, by a Member which is a party to the Minimum Age (Sea) Convention (Revised), 1936, and a minimum age of not less than 15 years is specified in pursuance of Article 2 of this Convention or the Member specifies that Article 3 of this Convention applies to maritime employment, this shall *ipso jure* involve the immediate denunciation of that Convention,

(e) in respect of employment in maritime fishing, by a Member which is a party to the Minimum Age (Fishermen) Convention, 1959, and a minimum age of not less than 15 years is specified in pursuance of Article 2 of this Convention or the Member specifies that Article 3 of this Convention applies to employment in maritime fishing, this shall *ipso jure* involve the immediate denunciation of that Convention,

(f) by a Member which is a party to the Minimum Age (Underground Work) Convention, 1965, and a minimum age of not less than the age specified in pursuance of that Convention is specified in pursuance of Article 2 of this Convention or the Member specifies that such an age applies to employment underground in mines in virtue of Article 3 of this Convention, this shall *ipso jure* involve the immediate denunciation of that Convention,

if and when this Convention shall have come into force.

5. Acceptance of the obligation of the Convention—

(a) shall involve the denunciation of the Minimum Age (Industry) Convention, 1919, in accordance with Article 12 thereof,

(b) in respect of agriculture shall involve the denunciation of the Minimum Age (Agriculture) Convention, 1921, in accordance with Article 9 thereof,

(c) in respect of maritime employment shall involve the denunciation of the Minimum Age (Sea) Convention, 1920, in accordance with Article 10 thereof, and of the Minimum Age (Trimmers and Stokers) Convention, 1921, in accordance with Article 12 thereof,

if and when this Convention shall have come into force.

Article 11

The formal ratifications of this Convention shall be communicated to the Director-General of the International Labour Office for registration.

Article 12

1. This Convention shall be binding only upon those Members of the International Labour Organisation whose ratifications have been registered with the Director-General.

2. It shall come into force twelve months after the date on which the ratifications of two Members have been registered with the Director-General.

3. Thereafter, this Convention shall come into force for any Member twelve months after the date on which its ratification has been registered.

Article 13

1. A Member which has ratified this Convention may denounce it after the expiration of ten years from the date on which the Convention first comes into force, by an act communicated to the Director-General of the International Labour Office for registration. Such denunciation shall not take effect until one year after the date on which it is registered.

2. Each Member which has ratified this Convention and which does not, within the year following the expiration of the period of ten years mentioned in the preceding paragraph, exercise the right of denunciation provided for in this Article, will be bound for another period of ten years and, thereafter, may denounce this Convention at the expiration of each period of ten years under the terms provided for in this Article.

Article 14

1. The Director-General of the International Labour Office shall notify all Members of the International Labour Organisation of the registration of all ratifications and denunciations communicated to him by the Members of the Organisation.

2. When notifying the Members of the Organisation of the registration of the second ratification communicated to him, the Director-General shall draw the attention of the Members of the Organisation to the date upon which the Convention will come into force.

Article 15

The Director-General of the International Labour Office shall communicate to the Secretary-General of the United Nations for registration in accordance with Article 102 of the Charter of the United Nations full particulars of all ratifications and acts of denunciation registered by him in accordance with the provisions of the preceding Articles.

Article 16

At such times as it may consider necessary the Governing Body of the International Labour Office shall present to the General Conference a report on the working of this Convention and shall examine the desirability of placing on the agenda of the Conference the question of its revision in whole or in part.

Article 17

1. Should the Conference adopt a new Convention revising this Convention in while or in part, when unless the new Convention otherwise provides—

(a) the ratification by a Member of the new revising Convention shall *ipso jure* involve the immediate denunciation of this Convention, notwithstanding the provisions of Article 13 above, if and when the new revising Convention shall have come into force;

(b) as from the date when the new revising Convention comes into force this Convention shall cease to be open to ratification by the Members.

2. This Convention shall in case remain in force in its actual form and content for those Members which have ratified it but have not ratified the revising Convention.

Article 18

The English and French versions of the text of this Convention are equally authoritative.

RECOMMENDATION CONCERNING MINIMUM AGE FOR ADMISSION TO EMPLOYMENT*

The General Conference of the International Labour Organisation,

Having been convened at Geneva by the Governing Body of the International labour Office, and having met in its Fifty-eighty Session on 6 June 1973, and

Recognising that the effective abolition of child labour and the progressive raising of the minimum age for admission to employment constitute only one aspect of the protection and advancement of children and young persons, and

Noting the concern of the whole United Nations system with such protection and advancement, and

Having adopted the Minimum Age Convention, 1973, and

Desirous to define further certain elements of policy which are the concern of the International Labour Organisation, and

Having decided upon the adoption of certain proposals regarding minimum age for admission to employment, which is the fourth item on the agenda of the session, and

---

* Recommendation No. 146.

Having determined that these proposals shall take the form of a Recommendation supplementing the Minimum Age Convention, 1973.

adopts this twenty-sixth day of June of the year one thousand nine hundred and seventy-three the following Recommendation, which may be cited as the Minimum Age Recommendation, 1973:

I. National Policy

1. To ensure the success of the national policy provided for in Article 1 of the Minimum Age Convention, 1973, high priority should be given to planning for and meeting the needs of children and youth in national development policies and programmes and to the progressive extension of the inter-related measures necessary to provide the best possible conditions of physical and mental growth for children and young persons.

2. In the connection special attention should be given to such areas of planning and policy as the following:

(a) firm national commitment to full employment, in accordance with the Employment Policy Convention and Recommendation, 1964, and the taking of measures designed to promote employment-oriented development in rural and urban areas;

(b) the progressive extension of other economic and social measures to alleviate poverty wherever it exists and to ensure family living standards and income which are such as to make it unnecessary to have recourse to the economic activity of children;

(c) the development and progressive extension, without any discrimination, of social security and family welfare measures aimed at ensuring child maintenance, including children's allowances;

(d) the development and progressive extension of adequate facilities for education and vocational orientation and training appropriate in form and content to the needs of the children and young persons concerned;

(e) the development and progressive extension of appropriate facilities for the protection and welfare of children and young persons, including employed young persons, and for the promotion of their development.

3. Particular account should as necessary be taken of the needs of children and young persons who do not have families or do not live with their own families and of migrant children and young persons who live and travel with their families. Measures taken to that end should include the provision of fellowships and vocational training.

4. Full-time attendance at school or participation in approved vocational orientation or training programmes should be required and effectively ensured up to an age at least equal to that specified for admission to employment in accordance with Article 2 of the Minimum Age Convention, 1973.

5. (1) Consideration should be given to measures such as preparatory training, not involving hazards, for types of employment or work in respect of which the minimum age prescribed in accordance with Article 3 of the Minimum Age Convention, 1973, is higher than the age of completion of compulsory full-time schooling.

(2) Analogous measures should be envisaged where the professional exigencies of a particular occupation include a minimum age for admission which is higher than the age of completion of compulsory full-time schooling.

II. Minimum Age

6. The minimum age should be fixed at the same level for all sectors of economic activity.

7. (1) Members should take as their objective the progressive raising to 16 years of the minimum age for admission to employment or work specified in pursuance of Article 2 of the Minimum Age Convention, 1973.

(2) Where the minimum age for employment or work covered by Article 2 of the Minimum Age Convention, 1973, is still below 15 years, urgent steps should be taken to raise it to that level.

8. Where it is not immediately feasible to fix a minimum age for all employment in agriculture and in related activities in rural areas, a minimum age should be fixed at least for employment on plantations and in the other agricultural undertakings referred to in Article 5, paragraph 3, of the Minimum Age Convention, 1973.

III. Hazardous Employment or Work

9. Where the minimum age for admission to types of employment or work which are likely to jeopardise the health, safety or morals of young persons is still below 18 years, immediate steps should be taken to raise it to that level.

10 (1) In determining the types of employment or work to which Article 3 of the Minimum Age Convention, 1973, applies, full account should be taken of relevant international labour standards, such as those concerning dangerous substances, agents or processes (including ionising radiations), the lifting of heavy weights and underground work.

(2) The list of the types of employment or work in question should be re-examined periodically and revised as necessary, particularly in the light of advancing scientific and technological knowledge.

11. Where, by reference to Article 5 of the Minimum Age Convention, 1973, a minimum age is not immediately fixed for certain branches of economic activity or types of undertakings, appropriate minimum age provisions should be made applicable therein to types of employment or work presenting hazards for young persons.

IV. Conditions of Employment

12 (1) Measures should be taken to ensure that the conditions in which children and young persons under the age of 18 years are employed or work reach and are maintained at a satisfactory standard. These conditions should be supervised closely.

(2) Measures should likewise be taken to safeguard and supervise the conditions in which child and young persons undergo vocational orientation and training within undertakings, training institutions and schools for vocational or technical education and to formulate standards for their protection and development.

13. (1) In connection with the application of the preceding Paragraph, as well as in giving effect to Article 7, paragraph 3, of the Minimum Age Convention, 1973, special attention should be given to—

(a) the provision of fair remuneration and its protection, bearing in mind the principle of equal pay for equal work;

(b) the strict limitation of the hours spent at work in a day and in a week, and the prohibition of overtime, so as to allow enough time for education and training (including the time needed for homework related thereto), for rest during the day and for leisure activities;

(c) the granting, without possibility of exception save in genuine emergency, of a minimum consecutive period of 12 hours' night rest, and of customary weekly rest days;

(d) the granting of an annual holiday with pay of at least four weeks and, in any case, not shorter than that granted to adults;

(e) coverage by social security schemes, including employment injury, medical care and sickness benefit schemes, whatever the conditions of employment or work may be;

(f) the maintenance of satisfactory standards of safety and health and appropriate instruction and supervision.

(2) Subparagraph (1) of this Paragraph applies to young seafarers in so far as they are not covered in respect of the matters dealt with therein by international labour Conventions or Recommendations specifically concerned with maritime employment.

V. Enforcement

14. (1) Measures to ensure the effective application of the Minimum Age Convention, 1973, and of the Recommendation should include—

(a) the strengthening as necessary of labour inspection and related services, for instance by the special training of inspectors to detect abuses in the employment of work of children and young persons and to correct such abuses; and

(b) the strengthening of services for the improvement and inspection of training in undertakings.

(2) Emphasis should be placed on the role which can be played by inspectors in supplying information and advice on effective means of complying with relevant provisions as well as in securing their enforcement.

(3) Labour inspection and inspection of training in undertakings should be closely co-ordinated to provide the greatest economic efficiency and, generally, the labour administration services should work in close co-operation with the services responsible for the education, training, welfare and guidance of children and young persons.

15. Special attention should be paid—

(a) to the enforcement of provisions concerning employment in hazardous types of employment or work; and

(b) in so far as education or training is compulsory, to the prevention of the employment or work of children and young persons during the hours when instruction is available.

16. The following measures should be taken to facilitate the verification of ages:

(a) the public authorities should maintain an effective system of birth registration, which should include the issue of birth certificates;

(b) employers should be required to keep and to make available to the competent authority registers or other documents indicating the names and ages or dates of birth, duly certified wherever possible, not only of children and young persons employed by them but also of the those receiving vocational orientation or training in their undertakings;

(c) children and young persons working in the streets, in outside stalls, in public places, in itinerant occupations or in other circumstances which make the checking of employers' records impracticable should be issued licences or other documents indicating their eligibility for such work.

INTERNATIONAL YEAR OF THE CHILD (1979): INFORMATION RECEIVED FROM GOVERNMENTS OF MEMBER STATES ON ACTION IN RESPECT OF THE MINIMUM AGE CONVENTION (NO. 138) AND RECOMMENDATION (NO. 146), 1973[1]

1. At its 204th Session (November 1977) the Governing Body of the International Labour Office considered that the ILO's contribution to the International Year of the Child should include a special effort to promote the implementation of the ILO's most recent comprehensive standards on the minimum age for admission to employment. It accordingly decided to invite the governments of member States:

(a) to consider taking such further action as might be necessary to give effect to the provisions of the Minimum Age Convention (No. 138) and Recommendation (No. 146), 1973, and to consider the ratification of the Convention, if not yet ratified; and

(b) to inform the Director-General, by 31 July 1978, of any such action taken or contemplated and of any difficulties which in their view stand in the way of the implementation of the instruments in question and the ratification of the Convention.

The Governing Body requested the Director-General to submit to the Committee on Standing Orders and the Application of Conventions and Recommendations, in November 1978, a report summarising the information received, as a basis for consideration of any further action which might be called for at that stage.

2. The Governments of the following 58 States have supplied information: Argentina, Austria, Bahrain, Belgium, Bolivia, Brazil, Bulgaria, Burundi, Byelorussian SSR, Canada, Cuba, Cyprus, Czechoslovakia, Ethiopia, Finland, France, Gabon, German Democratic Republic, Federal Republic of Germany, Ghana, Guatemala, Hungary, India, Indonesia, Iran, Iraq, Ireland, Japan, Kenya , Libyan Arab Jamahiriya, Mali, Mauritius, Mexico, Morocco, New Zealand, Niger, Norway, Pakistan, Panama, Papua New Guinea, Paraguay, Philippines, Poland, Romania, Rwanda, Senegal, Spain, Sri Lanka, Suriname, Sweden, Switzerland, Tunisia, Ukrainian SSR, United Kingdom, Uruguay, Venezuela, Zaire, Zambia.

Ratification Position and Prospects with Respect to Convention No. 138

3. Convention No. 138 has so far been ratified by the following 13 countries: Cost Rica, Cuba, Finland, Federal Republic of Germany, Ireland, Libyan Arab Jamahiriya, Luxembourg, Netherlands, Poland, Romania, Spain Uruguay, Zambia.

4. In two countries—Bolivia and Iraq—the ratification of the Convention has been approved but not yet formally communicated to the ILO. The Government of Kenya proposes to ratify the Convention. In Burundi, Gabon, Italy and Zaire, a proposal for its ratification has been submitted to the legislature or the President. The Government of Tunisia, on the basis of a comparative study, has concluded that national legislation is in full conformity with the Convention; its ratification is being examined. The Government of Czechoslovakia considers that national legislation is in conformity with Convention No. 138 and Recommendation No. 146 and when certain minor points have been clarified, will examine the possibility of ratifying the Convention. Ratification is being considered in Rwanda. In Ghana, a recommendation in favour of ratification made by the tripartite Labour Advisory Committee is under consideration by the Government. The Governments of Mauritius and Norway have indicated that the implementation and rectification of the Convention are to be further considered by tripartite advisory bodies. The Government of the German Democratic Republic states that, on the occasion of the International Year of the Child, all ILO Conventions relating to the employment and training of children and young persons are being examined to decide whether they should be ratified or any other measures taken. In Cyprus a committee consisting of representatives of all the services concerned has been set up to consider the possibility

of taking such action as may be necessary to give effect to Convention No. 138 and Recommendation No. 146.

5. The Government of the Byelorussian SSR states that its legislation and practice fully meet, and in many respects go beyond, the standards laid down in Convention No. 138. The Government of the Ukrainian SSR has provided particulars of legislation and practice corresponding to those given by the Byelorussian SSR.

6. The Government of the Federal Republic of Germany, which has ratified Convention No. 138, indicates that its legislation was amended to make the ratification possible. A number of governments which consider that their country is not at present in a position to ratify the Convention also refer to measures which have been taken or are contemplated to improve the protection in employment of children and young persons. The Government of India has adopted a National Policy for Children and established a National Children's Board for planning, review and co-ordination (of which the Prime Minister of India is president); the Government is committed to the gradual elimination of child labour, and measures to raise the minimum age in certain sectors are contemplated or in course of adoption. In the Philippines a "Decade of the Filipino Child 1977-87" has been declared and a National Plan of Action adopted. In Canada it is proposed to include consideration of the application of Convention No. 138 and Recommendation No. 146 in the agenda of the next federal-provincial meeting of Deputy Ministers of Labour. The Austria Government has referred to the influence of Convention No. 138 on the raising of the minimum age for employment in agriculture and forestry. The Government of Suriname intends to raise the minimum age for employment of young persons as fishermen to 15 years, in conformity with Convention No. 112, and the Government of the United Kingdom is considering the adoption of regulations concerning minimum age for employment at sea which would make possible the ratification of Convention No. 58. Further particulars of measures contemplated are given below in the review of difficulties in the implementation of Convention No. 138 and Recommendation No. 146.

7. A number of governments, while providing some indications concerning their legislation on minimum age for employment, state that they are not in a position to ratify Convention No. 138. Many of them consider it difficult, at their country's present stage of development, to extend minimum age protection to all sectors of activity, to raise the minimum age to the required level, or to ensure general observance of minimum age standards. Problems of this kind are mentioned by the Governments of Argentina, Brazil, Ethiopia, India, Indonesia, Iran, Mali, Mexico, Morocco, Pakistan, Papua New Guinea, Paraguay, Sri Lanka, Suriname and Venezuela. It is not apparent from the replies whether, in all these cases, full account has been taken of the range of flexibility permitted by the Convention as regards the sectors to be covered by minimum age provisions, the possibility of excluding limited categories of employment, the fixing of the general minimum age at 14 years (instead of 15 years) in the case of developing countries, and the authorisation of employment in light work as from the age of 13 years

(or 12 years, for countries fixing the general minimum age at 14 years). More specific difficulties mentioned by government are analysed below.

Difficulties in the Implementation of Convention No. 138

Scope

8. The Convention, in contrast to earlier minimum age Conventions applicable to limited economic sectors (which it is designed gradually to replace), applies to all forms of employment or work. However, a State whose economic and administrative facilities are insufficiently developed may initially limit the scope of application of the Convention, but must apply it at least to mining and quarrying; manufacturing; construction; electricity, gas and water; sanitary services; transport, storage and communication; and plantations and other agricultural undertakings mainly producing for commercial purposes, but excluding family and small-scale holdings producing for local consumption and not regularly employing hired workers. In addition, limited categories of employment or work in respect of which special and substantial problems of application arise may be excluded, provided that they do not involve danger to health, safety or morals.

9. The Government of Canada indicates that, although school attendance is compulsory everywhere at least up to 15 years, it remains necessary to establish a minimum age for employment in agriculture; in addition, in two jurisdictions no minimum age exists for work in factories, hotels and restaurants. In Norway and Switzerland minimum age provisions do not at present apply to agriculture; in the former country it is proposed to extend them to that sector. In India minimum age legislation dos not cover all activities to which the Convention must be applied even under the special relaxation for developing countries. In Pakistan minimum age provisions do not apply in agriculture and the rural industrial sector. The reply from the Government of Bahrain mentions only legislation applicable to the private sector.

10. The Governments of Sweden and Switzerland indicate that the existing minimum are legislation applies only to persons working under an employment relationship, whereas the Convention is not confined to such persons.

Minimum Age

11. The Convention requires ratifying States to specify a minimum age which should not be less than the age of completion schooling, and in any case not less than 15 years. A country whole economy and educational facilities are insufficiently developed may, however, initially specify a minimum age of 14 years. Of the 13 countries which have so far ratified the Convention, all but two have specified a minimum age of 15 years; the Libyan Arab Jamahiriya and Romania specified 18 and 16 years respectively. Most of the non-ratifying States which have supplied information on their legislation appear to have set their general minimum age at a level consistent with the minimum standard of 15 years (or 14 years permitted initially for developing countries) laid down in the Convention.

12. The Belgian Government states that the only obstacle to ratification of the Convention is the fact that compulsory schooling ends at 14 years, whereas the Convention fixes a minimum age for employment of 15 years; the extension of compulsory schooling is contemplated. In Hungary compulsory schooling covers eight classes, which must children complete by the age of 14; however, more than 90 per cent continue their studies. The Government considers that it would be inappropriate to deprive the small number who do not continue their studies after the age of 14 of the possibility of entering employment, and refers to special conditions applicable to workers under 16 years (reduced hours, additional paid leave, prohibition of night work and of employment in arduous or unhealthy work). In Switzerland, in cantons where the school-leaving age is 14 years children who have completed their schooling may be employed, without limitation of such employment to light work. The Austrian Government mentions that, while in general children complete their compulsory education and can take up work only after they have reached the age of 15 years, exceptionally compulsory education may be completed and employment taken for a brief period before that age. The Canadian Government states that in one province with a school-leaving age of 16 years the minimum age for employment is 15.

13. A number of developing countries indicate that their legislation does not yet meet the 14-year minimum age standard which Convention No. 138 would permit them to apply initially. In Indonesia, Iran and Morocco the general minimum age for entry into employment is 12 years. The Government of Iran states that draft amending legislation now under consideration would raise this age to 14 years. The Government of Indonesia is examining the possibility of similar action. In Morocco a draft Labour Code would provide for a minimum age of 13 years. In India, while a minimum age of 14 or 15 years is laid down for employment in a wide range of industrial activities, rail and motor transport, merchant shipping, etc., the minimum age for work on plantations is 12 years and for employment in shops and commercial establishments it varies from 12 to 14 years (but was recently raised to 15 in one state). The raising of the minimum age under the Plantations Act to 14 years is to be examined when that Act is next amended, and state governments have been requested to raise the minimum age for shops and commercial establishments to 14 years, where this is not already the case; some state governments have already agreed to take such action. The Government of Pakistan reports that the minimum age under the Factories Act and the legislation on shops and commercial establishments was recently raised from 12 to 14 years. In Argentina children under 14 years may be permitted to work when this is necessary for their own or their family's subsistence. The Government of Venezuela states that, although the minimum age for employment is 14 years; economic factors frequently lead children to take up work before that age, and it considers that it would be justified to lower the minimum age to 13 years in such cases provided that it is limited to light work as permitted by the Convention.

14. In general, where the minimum age standard provided for in the Convention

cannot yet be fully attained, it would seem appropriate to re-examine the legislation with due regard to the provisions of the Convention relating to light work. In some cases the possibility of excluding limited categories of employment or work from the application of the Convention may also make it possible to overcome marginal problems.

Dangerous Work

15. The Convention provides that the minimum age for admission to employment or work dangerous to health, safety or morals shall be not less than 18 years or, under certain conditions, 16 years. It leaves the employments in question to be determined by each State after consultation with employers' and workers' organisations.

16. From the information supplied it would appear that the principle of setting the level for admission to dangerous work at 18 years is widely accepted, although the range of jobs to which that standard applies varies considerably. The Government of Canada, however, indicates that in general Canadian legislation does not contain a definition of "dangerous employment" and that, while the minimum age for underground work in mines is generally 18 years, it is 17 years in one province and the federal jurisdiction. In Mexico and Morocco the minimum age for dangerous work is in general 16 years. In Austria, for agriculture and forestry, there exists no list of employments prohibited for persons under 18 years. In France the application to employment in agriculture of the general provisions on dangerous work prohibited for young persons is dependent on the issue of a decree now under consideration. In Norway, where a number of specific prohibitions of employment in dangerous work of persons under 18 years are contained in the basic legislation, detailed regulations to supplement these provisions are being prepared. In Sweden measures to meet the requirements of Convention No. 138 as regards dangerous work on board ship are under consideration.

Light Work

17. The Convention leaves it open to ratifying States to permit the employment on light work which is not harmful to their health or development, and not prejudicial to attendance at school or participation in vocational orientation or training programmes, of children between 13 and 15 years (or between 12 and 14 years for States having specified a general minimum age of 14 years) and of children above that age who are still subject to compulsory schooling. From the information supplied it appears that most countries permit the employment on light work of children below the general minimum age. However, in several countries where the general minimum age is 15 (Austria, Japan) or 16 (France) light work is permitted as from the age of 12, instead of 13 as specified in the Convention. The Government of Sweden indicates that, while light work is permitted only in limited circumstances, there is no lower age limit for such work. The Government of New zealand indicates that children may be employed part-time on certain forms of light work, the prohibition of which would not have public support or appear necessary. The Government of Mauritius mentions the possibility for children under 15 to be employed in light work in agriculture and the construction

industry, without indicating whether this is subject to any minimum age condition.

18. The Convention also permits exceptions from minimum age standards to be made, by permits granted in individual cases, for such purposes as participation in artistic performances. The United Kingdom Government states that its legislation allows children to take part without permit in such performances subject to defined conditions, observance of which is subject to inspection and enforced by penal sanctions. The Government considers that the welfare of the children is safeguard and does not propose to alter the legislation.

Consultation

19. The Convention provides for the consultation of the employers' and workers' organisations concerned on various matters such as the determination of dangerous occupations and certain exclusions or exceptions. The Government of Brazil states that, while national legislation already contains provisions on child labour corresponding to those of the Convention, with due regard to conditions obtaining in developing countries, the system does not permit the consultation of employers' and workers' organisations in the form required by the Convention.

Enforcement

20. The Convention contains various provisions relating to the enforcement of its provisions, including the provision of appropriate penalties and the keeping of registers or other documents by employers. The United Kingdom Government indicates that its legislation requires the keeping of registers only in industrial employment and that the standard of record-keeping is poor especially among small employers. However, legislation on non-industrial employment of school children is being reviewed, and the making of regulations to require employers to keep records of children employed is contemplated. The Governments of several other countries (Indonesia, Mali, Pakistan, Venezuela) refer more generally to the difficulties encountered in enforcing existing minimum age legislation in view of prevailing economic conditions.

Comments Regarding the Implementation of Recommendation No. 146

21. Only relatively few replies refer specifically to the situation with regard to Recommendation No. 146. The Government of Ireland and Norway state that they have accepted this Recommendation. The Government of Sweden states that the aspirations expressed in the Recommendation are in general agreement with Swedish attitudes (although national legislation prescribes a night rest of 11 hours for young persons, as compared with the 12-hour rest provided for in the Recommendation). The Government of India, while giving particulars of its national policy to promote the welfare of children and of its efforts to raise the minimum age for employment, states that the objective of the progressive raising of the minimum age to 16 years stated in the Recommendation is not easy of attainment in developing countries like India. The Government of Kenya also states that it cannot at present ensure full-time education or

training of all children under 16 years. The Governments of the Byelorussian SSR, Czechoslovakia, France, Norway Romania, the Ukrainian SSR and the United Kingdom indicate that the general minimum age for employment in their countries is 16 years; in Spain the minimum age is being raised to this level in conjunction with the introduction of new educational and training measures. The Government of Japan considers that the raising of the minimum age from 15 to 16 years requires careful study, including its relation to the completion of compulsory education. It also mentions that national legislation does not ensure a night rest of 12 hours for young persons nor entitle them to a special annual holiday with pay. The Government of Austria and the United Kingdom refer to the difficulties mentioned in connection with the Convention. The latter Government also states that it cannot accept responsibility for application of certain provisions of the Recommendation relating to matters (hours of work, night rest, holidays with pay) which are normally dealt with by collective bargaining.

Conclusions

22. The information available indicates that the general principles underlying Convention No. 138 and recommendation No. 146 find a very wide measure of support and that the problem of child labour is receiving close attention from national policy makers, both within the framework of the International Year of the Child and as an important aspect of economic and social development planning. In many countries measures to improve the protection of children and young persons in regard to work have recently been taken or are under consideration. It would appear that Convention No. 138 and Recommendation No. 146, as a comprehensive and up-to-date statement of internationally agreed principles, are providing a direct source of inspiration and reference in this process. Their use in this connection is facilitated by the dynamic but flexible approach adopted in these instruments: they aim at a progressive raising of standards; they permit the gradual integration of young persons into active life on the basis of distinctions between light work, employment in general and dangerous occupations; and they make allowance for the varying possibilities of countries at different stages of development.

23. Nevertheless, the information so far available does not permit of a full or precise analysis of the situation with regard to the implementation of Convention No. 138 and Recommendation No. 146. Less than half the member States have provided information. The replies received vary considerably in volume and detail, and frequently they do not clearly identify the problems which may impede acceptance of these standards. In particular, while a number of developing counties express doubt as to their ability to ratify Convention No. 138, many of them do not provide any detailed analysis of the difficulties encountered or seek to accommodate these difficulties within the different flexibility devices embodied in the Convention. A more detailed examination of these questions would be useful, bearing in mind the relationship between the raising of minimum age standards and other aspects of social policy to which reference is made in Recommendation No. 146 (such as measures to combat youth unemployment and to

develop and adapt facilities for education and training). Furthermore, it has not been possible within the present context to analyse ways in which the various difficulties mentioned by governments might be resolved. This aspect also would merit further review.

24. To permit fuller study of national law and practice regarding the minimum age for admission to employment and to facilitate the application of the Convention and Recommendation of 1973, it would appear useful to obtain reports from member States under the provisions of article 19 of the Constitution (reports on unratified Conventions and Recommendations). This would provide a basis for a general survey of the situation by the Committee of Experts on the Application of Conventions and Recommendations. A proposal that Convention No. 138 and Recommendation No. 146 should be chosen for reports under this procedure in 1980 is made in another paper presented to the Committee.[2] The Committee, in considering that proposal, will no doubt wish to take into account the information and comments, contained in the represent paper.

Geneva, 1 Nov. 1978.

DECLARATION BY THE DIRECTOR-GENERAL OF THE ILO CONCERNING THE INTERNATIONAL YEAR OF THE CHILD*

Resolution 31/169 adopted by the General Assembly on 21 December 1976 proclaimed 1979 the International Year of the Child, with the general objectives of promoting the well-being of children, drawing attention to their special needs and encouraging national action on behalf of children, particularly for the least privileged and those who are at work.

This International Year is of special importance to the ILO, which, even since its foundation in 1919, has sought to restrict child labour and provide protection for children. In doing so, the ILO has acted in accordance with the principle set forth in the United Nations Declaration of the Rights of the Child—that a child has a right to protection against exploitation. Despite the efforts made by the ILO and by many countries which have laid down regulations on the minimum age for admission of children to employment and on the conditions of employment of children, child labour is still widespread and a disturbing problem in many parts of the world where poverty and tradition have precluded its elimination.

In the light of ILO standards, the International Year should enable governments and employers' and workers' organisations the world over to assess the situation of children at work and also give the competent national bodies and the ILO an opportunity and the means to strengthen their action programmes for children. For that purpose the ILO urgently appeals to them to apply its standards on the minimum age for admission to employment and the conditions of employment of children. Action should be based on

* Declaration endorsed by the ILO Governing Body at its 209th Session, February-March 1979.

the following principles: (a) a child is not a "small adult" but a person entitled to self-fulfilment through work at an early age; (b) governments should, in co-operation with all the national organisations concerned, take all necessary social and legislative action for the progressive elimination of child labour; (c) pending the elimination of child labour, it must be regulated the humanised.

I therefore declare the ILO's endorsement of the aims of the International Year of the Child and its pledge to make every effort and lend all support to member States for their earliest possible fulfilment.[

RESOLUTION CONCERNING THE INTERNATIONAL YEAR OF THE CHILD AND THE PROGRESSIVE ELIMINATION OF CHILD LABOUR AND TRANSITIONAL MEASURES*

The General Conference of the International Labour Organisation,

Recalling resolution 31/169 adopted by the United Nations General Assembly proclaiming 1979 as the International Year of the Child, with the general objectives of promoting the well-being of children, drawing attention to their special needs and encouraging national action on behalf of children, particularly for the least privileged and those who are at work,

Noting the activities that were undertaken at the national, regional and international levels in preparation for the International Year of the Child and the progress made since,

Convinced that the International Year of the Child provides for all member States an opportunity to review their economic and social policies concerning child welfare and to formulate guidelines in this sphere,

Considering that a new and fair international economic order would greatly contribute towards genuine economic and social development, primarily of benefit to children,

Recalling the endorsement by the ILO of the aims of the International Year of the Child and its pledge to make every effort and lend all support to member States for their earliest possible fulfilment,

Recalling the United Nations Declaration of the Rights of the Child, 1959, and particularly Principle 9, which stipulates that the child should be protected against all forms of neglect, cruelty and exploitation; that he should not be admitted to employment before an appropriate minimum age; and that he should in no case be caused or permitted to engage in any occupation or employment which would prejudice his health or education, or interfere with his physical, mental or moral development,

Considering that since its foundation the International Labour Organisation has sought to eliminate child labour and to provide protection of children,

---

* Adopted by the International Labour Conference, at its 65th Session in June 1979.

Noting with approval the Director-General's Declaration on the International Year of the Child,

Deeply concerned that child labour still remains widespread in many parts of the world and that working children frequently work under conditions including those of exploitation detrimental to their health and welfare,

Recognising the need to ensure that the health and strength and the tender age of children are not abused and that children are not permitted to enter avocations unsuited to their age or strength,

Considering that the International Year of the Child should be an occasion to reaffirm with practical measures and deeds that the well-being of today's children to the concern of all people everywhere.

Recalling the decision of the Governing Body of the International Labour office, taken at its 208th Session (November 1978), to request the member states to supply a report in 1980 under article 19 of the Constitution on the extent to which effect has been given or is proposed to be given to the Minimum age Convention (No. 138) and Recommendation (No. 146) of 1973:

1. Calls upon member States to strengthen their efforts for the elimination of child labour and for the protection of children, and in this context—

(a) to implement the provisions of the Minimum Age Convention, 1973 (No. 138), and, where they have not already done so, to ratify this Convention as early as practicable;

(b) to ensure in particular full recognition of the principle that any work undertaken by children who have not completed their compulsory education shall not be such as would prejudice their education or development;

(c) to apply the Minimum Age Recommendation, 1973 (No. 146), and the Minimum Age (Underground Work) Recommendation, 1965 (No. 124);

(d) to report in detail in 1980 under the procedure of article 19 of the Constitution on the progress reached in the implementation of the Minimum Age Convention (No. 138) and Recommendation (No. 146), 1973;

(e) pending the elimination of child labour, to take all necessary social and legislative action for the progressive elimination of child labour and, during the transitional period until the elimination of child labour, to regulate and humanise it and to give particular attention to the implementation of special standards for children relating to medical examination, night work, underground work, working hours, weekly rest, paid annual leave and certain types of hazardous and dangerous work embodied in a number of ILO instruments;

(f) to make every effort to extend the provisions of appropriate educational facilities, in order fully to apply compulsory education and to introduce it where it does not exist and, where education is compulsory, to make it effective;

(g) to ensure that appropriate protective labour legislation applies to all children at work in the sectors of activity in which they are employed;

(h) to ensure that special attention is given to the provision of fair remuneration and to its protection for the benefit of the child;

(i) to strengthen, where appropriate, labour inspection and to undertake all other measures conducive to the elimination of child labour;

(j) (i) to identify the special needs of children, to strengthen efforts to improve the general economic and social well-being of the family, and to launch a national campaign aimed at creating awareness among the general public of the adverse effects of child labour on his/her development;

(ii) to develop international solidarity and co-operation with the developing countries and to activate efforts to establish a new and fair international economic order so as to respond more effective to the basic measures undertaken by each State for better child protection.

2. Calls upon governments and employers' and workers' organisations to assess the situation of child work and to assist the competent bodies and the ILO to strengthen their action programme for children.

3. Invited the Governing Body of the International Labour Office to instruct the Director-General to continue and reinforce the ILO's action through such means as factual surveys of national situations and practices for the elimination of child labour and for the protection of children at work, and to make the necessary preparations for a global revision of the relevant ILO instruments.

NOTES

1. This appendix reproduces doc. GB.208/SC/2/11 of the Committee on Standing Orders and the Application of Conventions and Recommendations of the Governing Body of the ILO.
2. At its 208th Session (November 1978) the Governing Body decided to request governments to submit reports under article 19 of the Constitution in 1980 on the Minimum Age Convention, 1973 (No. 138), and Recommendation, 1973 (No. 146).

18

DETERMINANTS OF CHILD-LABOUR

This section presents in three sub-sections various facets of child-labour observed in the four locations taken up for study. The discussion in this Chapter is based on Primary data generated from these locations. Section (i) deals with certain general information on child-labourers and also their socio-economic conditions. Section (ii) presents familial and parental background, occupational pattern including tenurial conditions and also main determinants of child-labour besides a selected few important impact points of fertility to light up the relevance of child-wage-labour situation. Section (iii) mainly focuses on certain problems on general health and related aspects, wage and hours of work of child labourers. All these above said aspects are presented on the basis of micro-studies undertaken in four districts of Tamil Nadu viz., Anna district, Madurai district, Kamarajar district and Thanjavur district by studying four hundred samples—one hundred from each district—of both child-labourers and their respective parents.

Industry-wise distribution shows that in Anna district they are found working mostly in steel furniture making units, art silk weaving units, building construction units, shops, agriculture and animal husbandry and in a few non-district service units. In Madurai district the sample child-labourers are found working in match-box and fire-cracker making units, agriculture and domestic services. In Kamaraj district too most of the sample respondents work in match-box making units, service sectors like trading shops, selling different products and also in transporting articles. In Thanjavur district their main areas of activity include fishing, animal husbandry, agriculture, domestic units and different types of shops.

To get a better profile of the deeper aspects of micro-level analysis, location specific analysis of crucial factors is made separately besides making aggregate analysis of variables from the four locations. Facets of child-labour and parental fertility are analysed by projecting location-specific differences and similarities. Wherever possible location specific findings are compared with aggregate data pertaining to important variables.

The First Section relates to the characteristics and other related determinants of child labour in each study location and also in aggregate. Under general characteristics variables analysed include—place of origin, age and sex, perception of parents on age limit for child-work and perception of parents on merits and demerits of child-work.

Under economic background of child workers, variables like housing pattern, reported yearly income, expenditure savings and debt, utilisation of child-labour-wage and savings out of child labour wage are considered.

SECTION I

GENERAL CHARACTERISTICS OF CHILD-LABOURERS

(i) Place of Origin

Out of the four hundred child-labours studied, single largest proportion (55%) belongs to urban areas. The remaining (45%) belongs to villages. Location-wise disintegration of these figures shows an entirely different picture with only 21 to 23 per cent belonging to villages in Anna and Kamarajar districts respectively and 43 to 92 per cent belonging to villages in Madurai and Thanjavur districts respectively. While in Madurai district only 3 per cent of respondents reported their permanent residence being in village, in Thanjavur district 97 per cent belong to this category. Permanency of residence of four hundred working children shows that all the more they belong to different towns (69%) and as such children from villages got reduced further (31%). While further going deeper into their residential patterns in relation to temporary migrations, different patterns of migration emerges. Those living in the same village (20 to 86%) or in the same town (30 to 82 per cent) form a major segment in all the four localities. At the aggregate level too those living in the same town (44%) and in the same village (27%) constitute single largest segments. A third major group, migrated from their native villages to town followed by some migrating from native town to another town (8.5%) (See Table 18.1). Disaggregated data varied in their proportions in the four localities with nobody in Thanjavur district having migrated from their native villages to towns but as much as 30 per cent in Anna district marking high proportion of migration in this district. The pattern of those migrating from native town to another town is found only in Anna district (15%). Migration from native village to another village is very negligible in Anna (1 per cent) and Madurai (1%) district. Surprisingly in Thanjavur where majority live in villages (97%) only a small percentage is found to have migrated from a native village to another village (6%). On the other hand 5 per cent have migrated into this district from other districts and 3 per cent from other country but all these groups are found in coastal village. Aggregate picture shows that 16 per cent have migrated from native village to present place of residence.

The continuity of living in the same place was also a ascertained to know the duration of stay in the same place. The data from Table 18.1 Shows that most of the PARENTS (68%) of the child-labourers lived in the same place of birth over thirty years. The remaining parents lived for 10 years to 30 years in their place of birth. Location-wise data also show similar pattern.

Several reasons have been reported by parents who have migrated from their place of birth to different places. But the single largest proportion both at location and aggregate levels migrated to new place(s) through the normal course of marriage (20%). A small proportion of respondents (3.2%) migrated in search of employment and due to transfer. In Kamarajar district parents who are teachers and other government servants—have migrated from other places. Other less frequent reasons mentioned are, displacement due to Sri Lanka disturbances, to join the relatives in Thanjavur or to join spouse etc. Another reason cited was unemployment in their native places (19%). A lesser proportion did not work in their place of origin because of different types of difficulties they faced particularly financial problems. Some more related their shifting to political disturbances, routine transfers and so on. Nevertheless, an overwhelming proportion of parents could not attribute any specific reason at all. (See Table 18.1).

TABLE 18.1

Place of Origin and Present Place of Living Etc. of Parents and Child Labourers

Sl. No.	*Types*	*Thanjavur Dist.*		*Anna Dist.*		*Madurai Dist.*		*Kamarajar Dist.*		*Total Number*	*Percentage*
		No.	*%*	*No.*	*%*	*No.*	*%*	*No.*	*%*		
I.	*Place of birth of respondent*										
	1. Village	92	92	21	21	43	43	23	23	179	44.8
	2. Town/city	8	8	79	79	57	57	77	77	221	55.2
II.	*Place of permanent residence*										
	1. Village	97	97	24	24	3	3	—	—	124	31.0
	2. Town/city	3	3	76	76	97	97	100	100	276	69.0
III.	*Place of present living*										
	1. Same village	86	86	20	20	2	2	—	—	108	27.0
	2. Migrated from native village to village	6	6	1	1	1	1	—	—	8	2.0
	3. Migrated from native village to town	—	—	26	26	30	30	9	9	65	16.2
	4. Living in the same town	—	—	38	38	57	57	82	82	177	44.3
	5. Migrated from native town to another town	—	—	15	15	10	10	9	9	34	8.5
	6. Migrated from native district	5	5	—	—	—	—	—	—	5	1.2
	7. Migrated from other country	3	3	—	—	—	—	—	—	3	0.8

(ii) Age and Sex Child Workers

When they are classified sexwise, it was found that majority of families (58.3%) have one male child worker as against much less families and one female child worker (41.8%). As found in the State as well as in districts female child-workers are found less in the study areas too except in Madurai district where 50 per cent of the sample child workers are female. Only 8.5 per cent of the families reported to have two child-labourers per family, with Kamarajar and Madurai districts sharing equal numbers

(11 families each had two child-labourers) and in Anna district (3 families and Thanjavur district six family each have two child workers each. Only 12 families have 3 child-labourers per family. All are found in Kamarajar and Madurai and Thanjavur districts with the former sharing more i.e. Madurai have 5 and Thanjavur only one. Majority of these additional child workers are (both 2 and 3 per family) male.

The age-wise and sex-wise distribution of child labourers show that (Table 18.3) most of the male (99 out of 100) in Madurai district belong to 10 to 14 age group and in Kamarajar district it is 95 per cent. Over all average figures for this group is 56.5 per cent. Among female child workers all belong to this age group except in Kamarajar district where one female child alone belong to 5-9 age group. This is also true in the case of families with two more child labourers. Thus out of 400 child workers studied only a very negligible percentage of child-labourers—both male (1.5%) and female (0.2)—belong to age group of 5 to 9.

(iii) Past, Present and Prospects for Future of Child-labour

When the parents were asked to mention whether they had sent their elder children to work in the past—when they were young and also their intention of doing so in future, a significantly greater proportion answered affirmatively. In the individual districts, too, more or less similar pattern is seen with percentages varying between 40 to 48 with Anna district having the minimum and Kamarajar district having the maximum percentage. While only 3 per cent of parents did not send their elder children to work while young in Anna district, 12 per cent of the parents did not do so in Thanjavur district. Thus the overall picture shows that nearly 43 per cent of the parents sent their elder children for labour when they were young as against only a negligible, 7 per cent who did not do so. Regarding the future possibility of sending younger children to job, overwhelming proportion expressed in favour of it with varying proportions in different districts; 85 per cent in Thanjavur district but only 48 per cent in Kamarajar district. In aggregate, 64.5 per cent of the parents are willing to send their younger children to work. Many were unable to send as they had no younger children to be sent to work. Whereas in Kamarajar district as high as 43 per cent are under this category, Thanjavur district has only 9 per cent. In aggregate slightly more than a quarter of parents do not have younger children to be sent to work. But in all the four districts only a small percentage—varying from 6 to 10 do not want to send their younger children to work. The overall average shows that 8 per cent of the parents do not favour their younger children working. Thus, in the study area child labour seems to be an accepted way of life.

(iv) Preparation of Parents on the Age Limit for Child Work

Considerable variation in the opinion on sending boys and girls of a particular age for work had been reported by parents. Regarding the boys single largest proportion of parents want them to work till they become self-reliant in all the three districts except in Kamarajar where only 16 per cent of the parents feel so. In the other three districts 29 to 35 per cent of the parents feel it as important. Considering all the four districts, 27.5 per cent of the parents come under the category. Slightly a less than quarter of them (23.5%) would like to leave the choice of working to their own sons. Not much differences are noticed in this regard in different districts. Nevertheless 10 per cent of them do not delimit any age for their sons to work. Single largest proportion of parents do not prescribe any age limit in all the four districts for their daughters to stop working (29.5%) whereas 33 per cent of parents in Madurai district do not see any age limit; it is 27 per cent in Kamarajar district. However, second largest proportion of the total parents are democratic in their views and leave the choice to children themselves (21.5%). This percentage is less (20% each) in Madurai and Kamarajar districts and more (24%) in work till they get married and also as long as they get work. Thus parents have different views in allowing boys and girls to work till a particular age. (Table not given).

(v) Perception of Parents on Merits and Demerits of Child-work

When an open ended question was posed to parents to elicit their views on the merits and demerits of sending boys and girls to work, variation in perception has been observed on the basis of sex of the children. The single major merit of sending boys and girls to work happens to be additional income (25%). The second most important merit reported was to create a sense of responsibility among sons and daughters (13%). However, 10.8 per cent of them exclusively wanted sons to work so as to enable them to earn a living. Another group of parents wanted them to work in order to understand the difficulties of running a family. This group of parents gave higher priority to sons working (8.2%) than daughters (5%). In addition to these major reported merits, a few other less important merits exclusively mentioned for son's working are to strengthen family income base and to develop competitive spirit. For daughters, a group of parents felt that they should work in order to raise money to meet their own daily needs. These specific merits mentioned for committing the children to work are borne largely out of economic necessities for different purposes. Not much location specific differences are seen with regard to reported merits and demerits (Table not given).

It is surprising to note that an overwhelming proportion of parents see nothing wrong in allowing young boys (88%) and girls (92%) to work. Nevertheless, one single major adverse consequence of child-labour largely mentioned for boys (9.8%) is deprivation of education. But it is hardly mentioned by the parents for girls (1.56%). A set of parents, though they form a minority, feel loss of face in sending girls to work and also worried over their indulgence in seeing films often. The latter is reported as a problem relatively more among girls than boys. There are also other minor reported reasons like boys falling into bad company due to the economic independence, disobeying parents and late arrival of girls to home after work etc. (Table not given).

(vi) Economic Background of Child-labour-Families

As for the economic background the discussion is focussed on a few economic variables besides family-income perse. After completing these discussions, the economic benefits derived by child-labourer through wages and the pattern of expenditure and savings out of the same have been considered.

(a) House Pattern

The house patterns of most of the child-labour families are such that they live either in huts (52%) or in semi pucca type of houses (46%) and only very small proportion (1.8%) of the families live in pucca houses. District-wise variations are glaring. While in Thanjavur district as much as 77 per cent of respondents live in huts and 23 per cent live in pucca houses, a reverse pattern is found in Kamarajar district, where only 30 per cent live in huts, but 68 per cent live in semi pucca houses. Another notable feature is that while in other districts at least 2 to 3 have pucca houses, no one in Thanjavur has it. Regarding their ownership of houses again wide differences are noticed. Even though on an average 57 per cent in the study area are reported to live in rented house or shared a part of other's houses, location-wise the situation is different with only 12 per cent living in rented houses in Thanjavur and 14 per cent in Anna district. Almost half of the respondents, live in rented houses in the other two districts. The number of owned houses is also very less in the latter two districts, though the overall figures show that 43 per cent of the respondents live in their own houses, or shared a part of other's houses. Further only one per cent of parents has separate bedrooms other than a common bed room and it is found in Kamarajar district.

All these evidence bring out the poor economic status and living standards of the child-labour families. Among the four districts studied, housing condition in relatively better in Anna and Kamarajar districts (See Table 18.2).

(vii) Reported Yearly Family Income, Expenditure, Savings and Debt

Table 18.4 of Section (ii) presents income and expenditure pattern of the sample families. In a broad aggregate sense, it is encouraging to note that significantly large proportion of families (64.5%) have above Rs. 6,000 as income and only 35.5 per cent of them earn below Rs. 6000 per year. However, there are districtwise differences—while in Thanjavur and Kamarajar districts nearly 70 per cent of respondents earn more than Rs. 6,000 per year in Anna and Madurai districts 58 per cent and 60 per cent respectively belong to this category. Thus of among the four areas it is in Anna district that more respondents (42%) earn very low income. Those who earn Rs. 9,000 and above per year are very few especially in Anna district (16 per cent only) and are relatively more (26%) in Thanjavur. For the four areas together the percentage is 1975 only. Generally among those with more than Rs. 6,000 per annum nearly 50 per cent of them lead a poor quality of life; as observed in terms of dress, durable consumables used, movable productive assets possessed etc.

A simple correlation with 't' test between annual reported income and incidence of child labour in the four localities shows that values for the three locations namely Anna, Thanjavur and Madurai are significant enough to prove the hypothesis. (See correlation and 't' values in appendix). (Table 18.9).

Considering the annual expenditure pattern of these families, 39 per cent of the families lead a life similar to those who live below poverty line. Their percentage is slightly more than those who really belong and earn this income. In the four districts the pattern seems different. While in Kamarajar district only 32 per cent spend less than Rs. 6,000 per year in Madurai and Anna district the percentages are high. Those who spent more the Rs. 9,000 per year are very few (12%) in Kamarajar district compared to the other three districts. One noteworthy feature is that most of the income categories—except those with an annual income of Rs. 9,000 and above spend more than what they earn especially in Thanjavur district. This excessive consumption expenditure beyond their means is a major determinant of prompting them to send their children to work in the case of 39 per cent of families as stated earlier (See Table 18.5, item II.1) that financial motive was a major consideration for the continuance of child labour. *Hence, the hypothesis is confirmed that existing low level of income is a major determinant for continuing child labour in most of the families.* (See Table 18.5).

TABLE 18.2

Dwelling Pattern of Child Labour Families

Sl. No.	*Particulars*	*Thanjavur Dist.*	*Anna Dist.*	*Madurai Dist.*	*Kamarajar Dist.*	*Total Number*	*Percentage*
		Number	*Number*	*Number*	*Number*		
1.	*Type of House*						
	1. Huts	77	48	54	30	209	52.2
	2. Semi pucca	23	50	43	68	184	46.0
	3. Pucca	—	2	3	2	7	1.8
2.	*Ownership of House*						
	1. Not applicable	2	—	—	—	2	0.5
	2. Rented	12	14	56	47	129	32.3
	3. Sharing with another family	30	18	30	18	96	24.0
	4. Owned	56	68	14	35	173	43.2
3.	*Parents having separate bed-room*						
	1. No	—	—	—	—	396	99.0
	2. Yes	—	—	—	4	4	1.0

Data given in Table 18.5 further confirms the hypothesis given above. It relates to debt and savings of the child labour families. As stated earlier a significantly higher proportion (56%) of families have some debt; it ranges from less than Rs. 800 or less to more than Rs. 1,500 and above at the time of the study. However, the incidence of debt is not uniform in all the four districts. Where as in Thanjavur and Madurai districts 48 percentage of the respondents in each are reported to have no debt, in Kamarajar district; it is comparatively less with only 34 per cent. Therefore, economic liability, as stated above is clearly a determinant of child labour. Such economic problem was reported by 44 per cent of the parents. Since their economic level is low, demand for supplementary income will be there among these people which would be forthcoming through child labour. Further when savings is considered it again confirms the preceding conclusion. In other words, a significantly large proportion of families (63%) have no savings whatsoever especially in Anna district (86%) followed by Madurai district (71%). However the remaining 37% of the 400 families have some meagre reported savings. In Kamarajar district as much as 37 per cent of the families have reported savings of more than Rs. 2000. One reason for this is that parents of female child-labourers are very much interested in sending girls to work so that something is to be saved to meet their future marriage expenses. This idea is found to be very much deep-rooted in this area. Proportion of female child-workers is also highest (44%) in this study area (See Table 18.2 and also 18.5). Thus data from Table 18.5 fully confirm the hypothesis mentioned above.

(viii) Utilisation of Wage of Child Labourers

After studying the economic condition of families of child labourers it is logically appropriate to go into the details as to how their parents spend the amount earned by their children. A few questions were asked to the sample parents on the quantum of wages they get from their children, its sufficiency to them, regularity of payment, relationship between child wages and parental income and savings made out of child wages.

An overwhelming proportion of children—it is reported—handover their wages in full to their parents and 10 per cent, a part of wages. It is surprising to note that 53 per cent of the parents expressed that the wage their children give is sufficient. However, only 34 per cent of the parents would like to send their other younger children also to work, perhaps the wages of the existing earning child labourers are inadequate. District-wise disaggregated figures show that it is in Kamarajar district that 93 per cent of the parents get their working children's wage fully but in Thanjavur district only 83 per cent of the parents come under this category. Regarding the sufficiency of child wage to parents, it is seen that majority of parents in Kamarajar district (68 per cent) have reported the wage being sufficient, it is not so in the case of respondent parents in Thanjavur, where only 40 per cent felt it sufficient. Similarly in Anna district also, child wage is found insufficient for majority of the parents. Hence 44 per cent of parents in Thanjavur and 45 per cent parents in Anna district are willing to send their younger children too to work. But only 27 per cent of mothers are prepared to do so in Kamarajar district. To a question on the adequacy of children's wage to meet family's expenses, an overwhelming proportion of them (60%) in the four districts felt that it is insufficient if child labour is stopped. Nevertheless, 40 per cent of them are confident of meeting their requirements in such an eventuality. A large number of parents feel so in Thanjavur (76%) Madurai (63%) and Anna (60%) districts but only 41 per cent in Kamarajar district. A further prob revealed the reasons for the reported insufficiency. There are: (1) the existing total family income is inadequate (25%) (2) the present cost of the living is very high (22.5%) (3) they have a big family (10%) (4) parents do not earn etc.

Of the different reasons given, inadequate family income, high cost of living and presence of big family are reported as important ones in their order of importance.

Location wise also inadequate income has emerged as most important one in Madurai (28%) and Kamarajar (26%) districts, and cost of living is prominent (30% of cases) in Thanjavur followed by Anna (28%) districts. Big family has become second important one in Thanjavur (23%) only and in others its value is insignificant.

All these confirm that despite children's wage work most of the families do not get sufficient income to meet their overall requirements and economic value attached to child-labour is very high for them.

(ix) Savings Out of Child Labour Wage

As expected, an overwhelming proportion of respondents (69%) does not save anything out of the wages of children. A look at district-wise figures shows that majority of parents (90%) do not save any amount out of child-wage; in Anna district but only 43 per cent in Kamarajar district. But it is encouraging to note at the aggregate level that atleast a little less than 1/3rd of them (31.2%) save a portion of the amount of money out of child wages. Most of those who save would like the savings to be used for future uses like marriage expenses of their children especially for girls (13%) and also for meeting future unexpected needs (15%). Ensuing safe future of child-workers (15%) and preparing to meet marriage expenses especially of girls (13%) are the main reasons of parents. The former one is very important among parents in Anna (50%) followed by those in Thanjavur (47%), and it is least important in Kamarajar (32%) district, but latter one is very dominant among parents who saved out of child-wage in Kamarajar (59%) followed by in Madurai (48%) districts and least in Thanjavur (3%). Single largest proportion (10.5%) saves in the form of postal savings, chit funds and in jewels (6.8%). Postal Savings is especially reported, by parents of female child-labourers in Kamarajar district. Chit funds are very popular in Anna (80%) followed by in Madurai district (68%). In Thanjavur district whatever meagre saving made are mostly in the form of purchase of milch animal, land or building etc. Thus modes of savings differ in the study areas. A 10th of the parents in aggregate, of course deposited them in postal savings but in Kamarajar district (53%) and another 37% have invested in gold jewellery. These findings are encouraging to a certain extent because they save atleast a fraction of the amount for the benefit of their children (See Table 18.10 in Appendix).

SECTION II

FAMILIAL AND PARENTAL BACKGROUND OF CHILD LABOURERS

Under this section several determinants of child labour which stem out of parental background are considered. They are broadly classified under two sub-sections viz. (1) Socio-economic characteristics and (2) demographic characteristics. The social and economic characteristics include caste, religion, type of family, educational status of respondents and spouses, occupation of parents, tenurial pattern of occupations, number of members in the family and dependents famiiy income and expenditure and debt/savings. The demographic characteristics include the present age of mothers and their spouses, total number of living children—male and female.

While examining the case background of the child labourers certain differentials have been observed in the families having one and also more than one child labourer.

The single largest proportion of child-labourer families having only one child labourers is from Background Class (56.7%). Second highest proportion of single child labourer families is found among the Scheduled Caste families (35.5%). Only very negligible proportion of single child labourer families is drawn from Forward Class families (7.8%). Similar pattern emerges from the study locations except in Thanjavur where majority of the child-labour families is from scheduled caste. In all the four districts, Backward Caste is the dominating group, followed by Scheduled Caste. Forward caste forms only a microscopic minority. Naidu[1] in his study shows that child labourers are found more among scheduled caste. Besides this, all the elder girls from Schedule caste were found to be working. In the present study among the scheduled caste working children more are girls both in Anna, Kamarajar and Thanjavur. Among Backward Caste, girls are in majority (62%) in Madurai district and Forward Caste group is relatively more in Thanjavur; Girls are more in this group (57%) in Anna district. A further examination of number of child labourers in these communities reveals that two-child labourer families are found more among Forward Caste followed by Scheduled Caste and least among Backward Caste families.

But district-wise picture gives a mosaic pattern. Two child labour families are more in Backward Caste in Madurai district. But families having three child-labourers are found more in Kamarajar and Madurai districts (7 and 6 respectively) and found more in Forward Caste families (2 out of 4 and 1 out of 4 respectively). In Madurai district out of the total four Forward Caste families, two have two working children in each. Proportion of two and three child-labourer families is more in Kamarajar and Madurai districts (50% and 25% respectively). In Anna district all Forward Caste families have only single child-labourer per family.

(i) Religion

According to the 1981 Census, in Tamil Nadu's population 88.9 per cent constitute the Hindus, 5.8 per cent are Christians and 5.2 per cent are Muslims and 0.1 per cent are Jains. Out of the families studied, nearly universal proportion belong to Hindu religion (96.2%). In the single child-labour families also their number exceeds. All the Muslim families are found in Madurai and Kamarajar districts. Majority of the Christians are found in Thanjavur district. However, proportionately their number in two child-labourer families is somewhat less. Since most of the families studied are Hindus, there is limitation to identify and confirm their religion-wise variation in the sample for generalisation. (See Table 18.3).

(ii) Type of Family

Nuclear family is the most common feature noticed (96%) in the sample. Only very negligible percentage lives in joint families. They are found in districts other than Madurai with Anna district having majority (10%) and Kamarajar (2%) the least.

(iii) Education of Parents

An overwhelming proportion of mothers of child labourers is illiterate (96.2%). Only 3.8% of the mothers are literate, location-wise also the same pattern is seen except in Kamarajar district where illiterate mother respondents are comparatively less (93%). However, compared to mothers, slightly a higher percentage of fathers (16.8%) is literate especially in Anna district (23%). This figure is far lower compared to the literacy level among men in general in Tamil Nadu according to 1981 Census. Among the literates, 12.8 per cent of father's and 2.5 per cent of mothers have studied only upto primary level, location-wise figures are also not different. Those who studied upto middle school and above are 4 per cent among father and 1.3 per cent among mothers. They constitute only a very negligible proportion. As such, there is evidence to show that large illiteracy of the parents is one of the major factors that leads to the perpetuation of child labour in this population.[2]

(iv) Occupation of Fathers

Occupational background of fathers, shows that a high proportion of the (53%) is unskilled or semi-skilled non-agricultural labourers. The second highest category is 'agricultural labourers' (19.2%), and the third category is 'petty traders' (12.5%). Similar pattern is found in Naidu's[3] study also. All other occupational categories together constitute 12.5 per cent and they are weavers, brokers and salaried ones. A negligible percentage of fathers (3.8) is un-employed. However, disaggregated figures show that agricultural labourers are in majority in Thanjavur district (58%) and none of the self-employed or salaried categories are found here. Non-agricultural labourers are concentrated in Madurai (87%), and Anna (50%) districts respectively. Petty traders are in majority (37%) in Kamarajar district. Interesting none of their child labourers are reported to be in same occupation as that of their fathers. Among petty trader category of fathers majority are cooking-vessel merchants. Among self-employed, majority does brokerage. Such category is not found in other sample districts. Another surprising feature is that none of the fathers of the child-labourer in Kamarajar and Madurai district is reported to be working in match/fire-works industry, eventhough majority of the sample child labourers (80% of the respondents) of this area is found in this industry. This shows the fast occupational mobility taking place there. On the other hand in Thanjavur district, majority of non-agricultural workers is engaged in finishing in sea and related work and its working children are also found in the same work but in families where fathers are agricultural labourers—child workers are found in majority doing non-agricultural work. i.e. other services. Most of the salaried group is found in Kamarajar district. It is surprising to find even primary school teachers sending their young children for wage work.

(v) Occupation of Mothers

It is found that 36 per cent of sample mothers are reported as house-wives and

TABLE 18.3

Percentage Distribution of Respondents by Social Characteristics

Sl. No.	Social Characteristics	Thanjavur District No. of child labours[1]		Anna District No. of child labours[1]		Madurai District No. of child labours[1]		Kamarajar District No. of child labours[1]		Total Number	Percentage
		M	F	M	F	M	F	M	F		
1.	*Caste*										
	Scheduled Caste	10	16	35	15	27	16	7	16	142	35.50
	Backward Castes	44	14	29	14	20	33	46	27	227	56.75
	Forward Caste	11	5	3	4	3	1	3	1	31	7.75
										400	100.00
2.	*Religion*										
	Muslim	0	0	0	0	1	0	2	1	4	1.00
	Christian	1	0	3	3	0	2	1	1	11	2.75
	Hindu	59	40	64	30	49	48	53	42	385	96.25
										400	100.00
3.	*Type of Family*										
	Nuclear	60	36	60	30	50	50	55	43	384	96.00
	Joint	0	4	7	3	—	—	1	1	16	4.00
										400	100.00

4. *Educational Status of the Respondent*										
Illiterate	—	97	—	98	—	97	—	93	385	96.25
Primary	—	3	—	2	—	3	—	2	10	2.50
Middle	—	0	—	0	—	0	—	5	5	1.25
									400	100.00
5. *Educational Status of the Spouse*										
Illiterate	77	—	99	—	81	—	76	—	333	83.25
Primary	19	—	1	—	15	—	16	—	51	12.75
Middle +	4	—	0	—	4	—	8	—	16	4.00
									400	100.00

another 36 per cent as 'non-agricultural labourers'. Majority of the mother respondents (56%) in housewives' category is found in Anna district and also in Madurai district (46%), where this category is the second largest group. But in Thanjavur, this group is in minority (17%). 'Agricultural-worker' category is the single largest group in Thanjavur (49%) but none is found in Kamarajar district under this category. Non-agricultural category is found to be the single largest group (65%) in Kamarajar and in Madurai (50%) districts respectively while among those who come under non-agricultural category, almost all are found in match/fire works industry, in Madurai District. Next important category in this district is 'domestic workers'. Here occupational diversification is also seen that least. So, also in Thanjavur. Here, most of those belonging to non-agricultural category sell fish or do domestic work. Petty trade is another category of work found common among mothers. Weaving is another distinct work of mothers in Anna district (16%). Majority reported themselves as housewives. Those having female child-labourers are found to help their working children in weaving chair-seats with plastic wire at home to increase their child's earning. Only one is found to do salaried work and she is found in this district. Unlike in other districts mother in Anna District in most cases (except house wives) are observed to do the same type of work which their respective husbands are reported to do.

The aggregate data shows that while majority (36.75%) of mothers are 'house-wives', majority 'fathers' are non-agricultural labourers. Second important work of mothers is non-agricultural work. But their percentage is less.

Mothers working in 'other occupations' together constitute, 11.2 per cent which include 'petty trade' 'weaving' and wage work at home for different production units. More or less similar pattern is noticed with respect to the last category of occupation among fathers. Since the number of cases is small under the category of parents having two child labourers per family, discussion on this aspect is not rewarding. In most cases wherever mothers work, their working children are invariably, found in the same work unit especially in farming, match industry and hotel industry.

(vi) Occupation of Child Workers

Analysis shows that majority (44 per cent) is found in secondary sector—small scale and cottage industries—followed by in service sector (22.5%) and a small proportion is employed (15.25%) in agricultural sector and another smaller proportion is found in domestic services.

But location-wise analysis shows distinct features. Whereas overall pattern shows that majority works (secondary sector) in small scale industries none is found in this category in Thanjavur district but majority (44%) is found in the other service sector as shop assistants, maintaining mechanical boats, transporting fish products and as watch-men especially among boys. Another and big group (36%) also is engaged in activities, like fishing, irrigating paddy-fields and grazing animals. Majority of girls is reported (42.4%) to be working as 'domestic servants' and another 39 per cent as 'construction workers' and 'fish-sellers'. The rest of the girls (18%) are found in the primary sector as agricultural labourers doing weeding or transplanting of crops.

A comparison of employment pattern of sample respondents in the study area with that of the whole district data (as per 1981 census) shows a different picture. As per 1981 Census majority of the rural boys in Thanjavur district is found as artisans in metal work or jewellery making etc. Boys in the present study area are found more in fishing and related work. While majority of the rural female in the district is working as agricultural labourers, sample female workers are found more in the 'service sector' as domestic servants.

At the state level, unlike the sample respondents in Thanjavur District (17%) only a negligible percentage (3 per cent) is found as 'domestic servants' (1981). Majority of the rural boys and girls is found working as 'cultivator' and also as agricultural labourers at state level but cultivator category is not found in the study area. Thus in the study area of the district, much inter-sectoral and intra-sectoral mobility is noticed, i.e., boys from agriculture to fishing and related work and girls from agriculture to service sector. Again unlike in the state, (6.64%) more proportion of female (33%) children are found as child workers in the study area.

In Anna District majority of the child workers is found working in mostly (50%) in small scale units (steel furniture marking units).

Sex-wise analysis shows the 53 per cent of the boys and 45 per cent of girls are found in this sector. While boys are working in 'steel furniture making units', 'cloth dyeing units', and confectionery units—girls are found weaving chairseats with plastic wires, or winding cotton threads. Next main group (26 per cent) of boys is reported as shop assistants or helpers in hotels or tailor-shops while girls are found more in construction work. Hired 'petty trader' category is relatively more (10%) in this district. While boys working in the primary sector are mostly found grazing animals, girls are reported as 'agricultural workers'. Unlike in Thanjavur district (17 per cent) only a negligible percentage (3%) is found as domestic servants here. This pattern is not found at the state especially among the rural male child-workers.

More comparison of work pattern in the district and State is not possible due to the bifurcation of the Madurai district into Madurai and also Anna districts.

A comparison of data from the study area with State data also gives a different picture. Where as majority of working boys and girls in the state is found in the primary sector, in the study area in Anna district, majority found in secondary and also in tertiary sectors. Thus, in this area much inter-sector occupational mobility is seen. The proportion of female child worker is more (40%) in the study location, unlike that in the State pattern (6.64% in 1981).

Study area in Madurai district also gives some differential pattern. As seem from aggregate data, majority of child workers (42%) is found in the secondary sector, but within secondary sector only less number is found in cottage industry unlike in the study area in Anna district, where more are found (17 out of 50) in cottage industry. Again unlike in the state, 50 per cent of the sample child workers here are girls. Similarly unlike in the state pattern, less proportion of child workers (12%) in the study area is found in primary sector. More than half (54%) of the female child workers in Madurai district is found working as 'domestic servants'. This pattern too is not found in other study areas. This pattern is also not seen among girls at the state level. In the study area, majority is found (80%) in small scale sector. The second main activity here is 'domestic service'—where it is entirely a female domain. Unlike at the aggregate level, those working in 'other services' are very negligible here with no female child-labourers.

Here too like in other study areas, proportion of female child workers (44 per cent) is more compared to state pattern. Match and fire work are the two main industries which attract child labourers.

Comparison with district is not possible due to bifurcation of the district.

Thus on the whole, the sample child workers in the study are not found in the same sectoral and occupational divisions where majority of working children is found at the state level. Much occupational mobility is noticed here.

(vii) Tenurial Condition of Parental Occupation

The tenurial condition of occupation of the parents shows significant variations. More than one third of the mothers (36.8%) are reported as housewives and thus not engaged in remunerative work. Among the districts, Anna followed by Madurai district (38%) have larger proportion under this category. A very small proportion of fathers (3.8%) is also found to be not doing any work. This percentage was reported more (6%) in Kamaraj district but only two per cent in Madurai district. Among working fathers, majority (44.5%) is reported having work but not regularly. Among working mothers, 24 per cent come under this category. Area specific analysis shows that fathers who have temporary and irregular work are in majority (57%) in Thanjavur district and also in Anna district (52%) and comparatively less (23%) in Kamarajar district. Thus majority of main bread winners in the sample families not have regular income. Area-wise break-up figures for working mothers show that slightly more than one fifth have temporary or irregular work. Madurai (27%) and Kamarajar (26%) district respectively have comparatively higher proportion under this category. Next main category of work is also temporary, though regular in nature. *In total, only 24 per cent of fathers have temporarily regular work.* But there are area-wise difference; while in Kamaraj district 45 per cent come under this category, in Thanjavur district it is 2 per cent. As compared to fathers, a slightly less percentage (22.2%) is reported to have had regular work among mothers. Break-up figures for the four areas show that as in the case of fathers, it is in Kamarajar district that more mothers too have regular work (32%). In Anna district mothers working on regular basic are very less (11%).

In aggregate, nearly one fifth (19.5%) of the fathers in the sample area has only temporary seasonal work. Area-wise, Thanjavur has larger percentage (12%) under this category. Among mothers working on seasonal basis difference are seen in four areas with Thanjavur district having more percentage (27%) and Madurai having less (7%) followed by Kamarajar district (9%).

Among fathers only a small percentage (8.2%) has permanent work. None of the mothers is reported to have permanent work. Area-wise analysis shows that majority of permanently employed fathers is found in Kamarajar (14%) and Madurai (9%) districts and least (2%) in Anna district. They are mostly government servants. It is obvious that security of job for parents may reduce the need for child labour as found in Kerala. Child labour participation rate is very low there (See Table 18.15 in Appendix).

(viii) Tenurial Condition of Work of Child Labourers

Tenurial condition of work of parents shows that a large majority do not have permanent work. Thus, temporary nature of work would have encouraged them to send their children also to take up wage work to enable the family to earn some minimum income to meet its needs.

Analysis of working condition of child labourers also reveals that majority worked on temporary basis and also all worked in the informal sector. Only 26.75 per cent are reported permanently employed. Others (40.50 per cent) do regular works which are temporary in tenure in the sense that work is available if they are willing to work at the given wage condition. The rest are seasonally and irregularly employed. Those working in the agricultural sector and or those doing fishing, weaving or working in building construction and in certain services have seasonal irregular work.

Location specific data shows that those with very high fluctuation in job are found more in Anna district (42%), but no one in Kamarajar district. Those with seasonal employment are more (35 per cent) in the service sector, in domestic service with 27 out of 28 girls are found doing it. In 'Other service category' which is the third main work area of child workers in this study area, boys are mostly found as assistants in tea shops, tailor and cycle repair shops and girls are mostly reported as construction workers. *On the whole more proportion of child-workers are found in the 'service sector' (46%) when 'domestic' and 'other services' are taken together.*

A comparison of work pattern in the study area with that in Madurai district shows a different pattern. In the district, majority of the urban male child workers was recorded as 'sales-men' and 'shop assistant' and also as spinners, weavers and knitters etc. (secondary sector). But, majority of child workers in the study area is found in match/fire cracker making units. Whereas majority of urban female child workers in the state was found working in textile production industry and related works industry, in the study area, majority worked as 'domestic servants'.

Thus on the whole much occupational mobility across different sectors is seen in the study area too.

Study area in Kamarajar district shows an unique pattern. Nobody is found working in the 'primary sector'. Unlike in other study areas, least child work concentration is in Thanjavur district where agriculture and fishing are main activity of many. Those temporary though regularly employed formed 41 per cent of the 400 sample respondents. Mostly they work as domestic servants and also as helpers in hotels, repair shops, match box and fire crackers making units. Both in Thanjavur and Anna districts none is found to have permanently employed.

But in Kamarajar district a lion's share of the sample respondents are reported to be permanently employed.

Child-workers in the match and fire cracker making units are working on permanent basis and contribute towards Provident Fund. Since employment of children is prohibited by law, and there are frequent checking by Government officers, parents of child-labourers secure false birth-certificates (showing age 15 years and above) and see their children get employed, so that they get a regular income, besides making future of children safe in the midst of an uncertain labour market. *Thus in the four study areas majority of all the working children (40.5%) has temporarily regular work and income and 26.75% per cent have permanent work and income.*

Location-wise figures show that while irregularly employed children are in majority (42 per cent) in Anna district, seasonally employed are more (35%) in Thanjavur district, regulars are more (61.%) in Madurai followed by Thanjavur district and permanently employed are in largest majority (80%) in Kamarajar districts. None had permanent work in Thanjavur and Madurai districts. On the other hand none is seasonally or irregularly employed in Kamarajar district. Interestingly majority of the male sample child-workers is permanently employed here while only 1/5th of such category is found in Madurai district.

(ix) Reported Family Income, Expenditure, Savings and Debt

Please See discussion on Section I of this Chapter under this heading and Table 18.4.

(x) Dependents in The Family

The number of dependents in the family for financial and other supports is a factor encouraging children to take up wage work. In this study it is stated as one of the reasons for child labour by parents. Dependents constitute young children, adult but non-working unmarried girls and boys, aged-parents and other relatives who are in firm. The data in Table 18.5 support the above hypothesis and confirm that prevalence of one or more dependents would encourage parents to send their children to take-up wage work.

Families reporting to have one dependent is comparatively more in Kamarajar (20 per cent) followed by Madurai (12%) districts. Another note-worthy feature is that none of the sample families in Kamarajar district has more than four dependents per family, but 35 per cent of the sample families have more than four dependents in Thanjavur district.

The presence of more dependents leading to child labour has been strengthened further by the respondents themselves who reported the existence of dependents as a factor for sending their children to work (See Table 18.19). The existence of dependents as a reason for child labour is further supported by the data on number of members living in the family. In 88 per cent of the families, four and more number of members live together. Further break up of these families showed that in 39 per cent of the families six and more number of member live together. Areawise break-up figures show that sample families having six and more members are found in Thanjavur and Madurai district only. *Thus, the prevalence of large families with more number of younger children and other dependents along with poverty and low earnings together constitute factors encouraging parents in sending their children for wage work outside home.* (See Table 18.4).

(xi) Reported Major Reasons of Child Labour

When the parent respondents were asked to specify major reasons for sending children for wage work and to rank the reasons according to their relative importance, seven reasons have been cited by a good proportion of the respondents. They also mentioned the order of importance of reasons upto the third order. A single largest proportion (31.2%) mentioned the presence of more number of children at the single most first reason for sending children to wage work. It confirms the assumption that the existing high fertility is a major determinant of the prevalence of child labour in this sample population. It is further supported by the other two major reasons namely poverty (29.3%) and inadequate family income (21.3%). They together account for 50.6 per cent of those who encourage children to work largely due to their poor economic conditions. Thus, (50.60% plus 31.2%) 81.80 per cent of the respondents encouraged child labour for the twin major reasons viz. 'high fertility' and 'poverty'. Other reasons mentioned eventhough insignificant, do light up the main reasons, are 'number of earning members being less in the family,' 'number of more dependents;' 'children not attending school', 'employment opportunity exists', 'fear of children joining bad company' and 'children of neighbourhood are sent to work. Among these, most prominent one is children-dropping out of school (8.1%). It is also mentioned as the third most important reason (25.2%) and also one of the three reasons by 5.8 per cent of the respondents. In other words, 39 per cent of the respondents encourage children to work because their children dropped out of school. It is a very serious matter and deserve special attention to ensure their retention in the school, through mid-day meals programme and also through other welfare measures particularly for these poor children. Of course, the earlier mentioned two other reasons—poverty and high fertility—together exceed their proportion for beyond this reason. High fertility alone is mentioned by 41.8 per cent of the respondents who have large number of children. They mentioned it as first, second

TABLE 18.4

Economic, Background of Child Labour Families

Sl. No.	Economic background of respondent families	Thanjavur District		Anna District		Madurai District		Kamarajar District		Total	Percentage
		No. of child labour families	Percentage	No. of child labour families	Percentage	No. of child labour families	Percentage	No. of child labour families	Percentage		
I.	*Years family income (in Rs.)*										
	1. 6000	30	30	42	42	40	40	30	30	142	35.50
	2. 6001—9000	44	44	42	42	52	41	52	52	179	44.75
	3. 9000 +	26	26	16	16	18	19	18	18	79	19.75
	Total	100	100	100	100	100	100	100	100	400	100.00
II.	*Years family expenditure (in Rs.)*										
	1. 6000	40	40	41	41	44	44	32	32	157	39.25
	2. 6001—9000	44	44	43	43	40	40	56	56	183	45.75
	3. 9000 +	16	16	16	16	16	16	12	12	60	15.00
	Total	100	100	100	100	100	100	100	100	400	100.00
III.	*Out-standing debit (in Rs.)*										
	1. Not debt	48	48	46	46	48	48	34	34	176	44.00
	2. 500 or less	4	4	24	24	22	22	43	43	93	23.25
	3. 501—1500	25	25	18	18	15	15	13	13	71	17.75
	4. 1501 +	23	23	12	12	15	15	10	10	60	15.00
	Total	100	100	100	100	100	100	100	100	400	100.00

IV. *Present amount of savings (in Rs.)*										
1. No. savings	52	52	86	86	71	71	43	43	252	63.0
2. 2000	31	31	8	8	17	17	20	20	76	19.0
3. 2001 +	17	17	6	6	12	12	37	37	72	18.0
Total	100	100	100	100	100	100	100	100	400	100.00
V. *Total number of dependents*										
1.	5	5	10	10	12	12	20	20	47	11.75
2.	20	20	36	36	28	28	40	40	124	31.00
3.	18	18	30	30	26	26	24	24	98	24.50
4.	22	22	17	17	22	22	16	16	77	19.25
5.	28	28	7	7	5	5	—	—	40	10.00
6.	7	7	—	—	7	7	—	—	14	3.50
Total	100	100	100	100	100	100	100	100	400	100.00
VI. *Total numberof family members*										
1. 2-3	6	6	10	10	12	12	20	20	48	12.00
2. 4-5	50	50	58	58	49	49	40	40	197	49.25
3. 6-7	21	21	26	26	35	35	40	40	122	30.50
4. 8 +	23	23	6	6	4	4	0	—	33	8.25
Total	100	100	100	100	100	100	100	100	400	100.00

and third reasons in the order of importance, thus assuming dominant variable status. On the other hand 58.50 per cent of the respondents (more than the other two reasons) mentioned poverty as the first, second and third reasons in their order of importance. They are in fact having few numbers of children, still first child is a wage earner. Over and above this, inadequate family income is mentioned by 73.2 per cent as the first, second and third order of importance. Leaving these three major reasons, availability of employment opportunity is also mentioned as the fourth major reason by 37 per cent of respondents. Of course they give mostly second and third priority for this reason. This reason is also cited by Naidu,[4] as a determinant of child labour. Thus the preceding consolidated list of reasons conform that the control of child labour very much depend on four main factors namely: (1) improvement in additional source of income to the family, (2) poverty alleviation, and (3) control of high fertility and replacement of child labourers by adult labourers wherever such opportunity exist in future. Insistence on payment of equal wages for both adult and child workers for same type of work also has to be considered seriously wherever child labour is dominant (See Table 18.5).

Location-specific analysis shows that, of the reported reasons, poverty has been mentioned as the first important reason by majority of mothers in Thanjavur (39%), Kamarajar (28%) and Madurai (26%) districts. Of these three, it is in Thanjavur followed by in Kamarajar district, it is considered as major first reason.

Presence of more number of children is mentioned as first important reason by 37 per cent in Kamarajar and 31 per cent in Anna district. Thus presence of more number of children has emerged as first important reasons for child work in these districts. Interestingly child-labourers of third birth order are also found more in Thanjavur and Kamarajar districts. Average number of living children (more than three) are also found more in Thanjavur and also Kamarajar districts.

Inadequate family income has been reported as the first main reason by majority (31.%) of mothers in Madurai and in Anna (20%) districts. It is also reported as second main reason for child-labourer in Thanjavur (55%), Anna (51%) and Kamarajar (30%) districts. At the aggregate level as much as 42 per cent of mothers have mentioned it as second main reason.

Not attending school and also presence of employment opportunities are also reported as third main reason by more than 1/4th of the mothers at the aggregate level. Thus dropping out from school, has emerged as a determinant of child-labour in the study. 'Not attending School' has been reported as third main reason by as much as 46 per cent of mothers in Madurai and 30 per cent of mothers in Kamarajar district. Thus, it has become an important determinant of child-labour in these districts too. Availability of more employment opportunities for children is reported as third main important factor among 32 per cent of mothers in Kamarajar and 29 per cent of parents in Anna districts. At the aggregate level 24 per cent of the mothers have mentioned it as the third reason. Thus it also has became another determinant of child-labour in the study area.

Thus, poverty as first main reason in prominent in Thanjavur district, presence of more children is first main reason in Thanjavur and Kamarajar districts, whereas inadequate family income is very important as first main reason in Madurai district.

(xii) Demographic Characteristics of Parents

Under demographic characteristics of parents of child labourers, factors such as age, and total number of living children (male and female) have been considered. It is seen that most of the fathers belonged to middle age group. While 46.5 per cent of the fathers are in their forties and below 49.3 per cent of them belong to age group of 41-50 and only four per cent are above 50. Most of the mothers (60.5%) are aged 35 years and less. Data from the four selected districts show that fathers in the age group of 40 and below are single majority in Madurai (58%) and also in Kamarajar (52%) districts. But those within the age group of 41 to 50 are in majority (57%) and in Thanjavur districts. Those above fifty also though few in number are comparatively more in these two districts.

Among mothers, those in the age of 36 and above are comparatively the largest group in Thanjavur (76%) and in Anna districts (60%). Those who are 35 years and less are low (24%) in Thanjavur but relatively high in Kamarajar district. Majority of sample mothers (49.0%) in the study areas is of 1 to 50 age group (See Table 18.19 in Appendix).

Regarding the number of living children it is found that the single largest group (31.5%) has three children each. Another 22.2 per cent have five and more number of children. Only 27.5 per cent of the families have 2 or less number of children (small family). Area-wise, it is in Kamarajar district that majority (81%) has three or less children per family. It is lowest in Thanjavur (42%). Conversely it is here that majority (58%) has more than three children per family followed by Madurai district (50%). Anna district has the minimum (19%). *This support the discussion under the proceeding sub-section that existence of large members in family is a major factor influencing the parents to send their children for* wage work (See Table 18.19). Only a small percentage of families do not have male child (15%). The remaining have atleast one male child and 39.3 per cent of the families have one female child each. The prevalence of more number of sons (51.5%) and daughters (48.2%) definitely contribute to the desire or give a chance for sending children to work under the existing poor socio-economic conditions. *Thus availability of 3 or more number of children among an overwhelming proportion of families (72.5%) and also 3 and more number of male/female children existing in over 45 per cent of the families constitutes a major factor or encouraging child labour under the prevailing poor* socio-economic conditions (See Table 18.19 in Appendix).

(xiii) Birth Order of Child Labourers

Another demographic characteristics which is analysed is birth order of child-labourers. Majority (46 per cent) of the sample child labourers belong to first birth order and 1/4th of them (25.75 per cent) is of second birth order and the rest are of higher birth orders. Sex-wise analysis shows majority (53 per cent) of female child labourers belongs to first birth order but only 41 per cent of the boys belong to this category. On the other

TABLE 18.5

Reported Reasons for Child Labour

Reasons for Child Labour	*Thanjavur District*											
Chances	*Order of importance of reasons*											
	I			*II*			*III*			*IV*		
	Number of child labours/family											
Number of Child Labour	*1*	*2*	*3*	*1*	*2*	*3*	*1*	*2*	*3*	*1*	*2*	*3*
1. Poverty	38	0	1	7	1	0	18	1	0	63	2	1
2. More number of children	32	5	0	12	0	0	3	0	1	47	5	1
3. Inadequate family income	14	1	0	51	3	1	10	1	0	75	5	1
4. No. of earning memberless	3	0	0	5	2	0	7	0	0	15	2	0
5. Not attending school	0	0	0	0	0	0	19	1	0	19	1	0
6. No. of dependent more	2	0	0	4	0	0	5	3	0	11	3	0
7. Employment opportunities more	4	0	0	11	0	0	21	0	0	36	0	0
8. To following bad company	0	0	0	0	0	0	2	0	0	2	0	0
9. Neighbour's children are sent to work	0	0	0	3	0	0	8	0	0	11	0	0
Total	93	6	1	93	6	1	93	6	1	279	18	3

Reasons for Child Labour	Anna District												Madurai District											
Chances	Order of importance of reasons												Order of importance of reasons											
	I			II			III			Total			I			II			III			Total		
	Number of child labourers/family												Number of child labourers/family											
Number of Child Labour	1	2	3	1	2	3	1	2	3	1	2	3	1	2	3	1	2	3	1	2	3	1	2	3
1. Poverty	20	4	0	7	0	0	13	2	0	40	6	0	18	7	1	35	0	0	19	1	0	72	8	1
2. More number of children	27	4	0	8	0	0	1	1	0	36	5	0	17	3	4	3	0	0	1	2	1	21	5	5
3. Inadequate family income	20	0	0	46	5	0	17	1	0	83	6	0	30	1	0	22	7	1	0	1	1	52	9	2
4. No. of earning memberless	1	1	0	3	2	0	3	0	0	7	3	0	5	0	0	9	1	2	8	0	0	22	1	2
5. Not attending school	18	0	0	1	1	0	14	1	0	32	2	0	10	0	0	0	0	0	27	6	3	37	6	3
6. No. of dependent more	3	0	0	8	0	0	6	1	0	17	1	0	2	0	0	1	1	0	13	0	0	16	1	0
7. Employment opportunities more	1	0	0	14	1	0	26	3	0	41	4	0	2	0	0	11	2	2	12	1	0	25	3	2
8. To following bad company	0	0	0	4	0	0	6	0	0	10	0	0	0	0	0	2	0	0	2	0	0	4	0	0
9. Neighbourers children are sent to work	1	0	0	1	0	0	5	0	0	7	0	0	0	0	0	1	0	0	2	0	0	3	0	0
Total	91	9	0	91	9	0	91	9	0	273	27	0	84	11	5	84	11	5	84	11	5	252	33	15

Reasons for Child Labour	*Kamarajar District*												*Aggregate No. and Percentage*		
Chances	*Order of importance of reasons*												*Order of importance of reasons*		
	I			*II*			*III*			*Total*					
	Number of child labourers/family														
Number of Child Labour	*1*	*2*	*3*	*1*	*2*	*3*	*1*	*2*	*3*	*1*	*2*	*3*	*First*	*Second*	*Third*
1. Poverty	28	0	0	6	1	0	5	1	0	39	2	0	29.3 (117)	14.2 (57)	15.0 (60)
2. More number of children	20	7	6	4	0	0	5	0	0	29	7	6	31.2 (125)	6.8 (27)	3.8 (15)
3. Inadequate family income	18	1	0	25	3	2	4	3	3	47	7	5	21.3 (85)	41.7 (167)	10.2 (41)
4. No. of earning memberless	9	1	0	17	3	1	3	0	0	29	4	1	5.0 (20)	11.2 (45)	5.2 (21)
5. Not attending school	3	1	0	20	2	0	28	1	1	51	4	1	8.0 (32)	5.8 (23)	25.2 (101)
6. No. of dependent more	0	1	0	0	0	3	0	2	1	0	3	4	2.0 (8)	4.0 (16)	7.8 (31)
7. Employment opportunities more	2	1	0	4	2	0	31	1	0	37	4	0	2.5 (10)	11.8 (47)	23.8 (95)
8. To following bad company	2	0	0	5	1	0	6	2	1	13	3	1	0.5 (2)	3.0 (12)	4.8 (19)
9. Neighbour's children are sent to work	0	0	0	1	0	0	0	2	0	1	2	0	0.2 (1)	1.5 (6)	4.2 (17)
Total	82	12	6	82	12	6	82	12	6	246	36	18			

hand while slightly more than 1/4th of the male child workers (28.75 per cent) are of second birth order and 22 per cent of girls belong to similar category. Among those belonging to higher birth orders—though number of children are very negligible—more are female (2.3%) than male (1%).

Location-wise it is in Anna district that a large percentage (54 per cent) is of first birth order, followed by in Kamarajar district (49 per cent) but comparatively lesser percentage (31 per cent) is reported from Thanjavur district. Sex-wise, in all the districts, except in Madurai more girls belong to first birth order, with Anna district having the largest share (65 per cent followed by Kamarajar with 61 per cent and Thanjavur having the least 36 per cent). Child labourers of second birth order are more in Madurai and Kamarajar districts and less in Thanjavur district. Sex-wise distribution in the four localities shows that boys are more in the category of 1st birth order in all except in Kamarajar district. But percentage distribution within male-female group shows that while 43 per cent of respondent boys in Kamarajar are of second birth order, only 19 per cent of sample boys in Thanjavur came under this category. But, while 32 per cent of girls are of second birth order in Madurai district, only 15 per cent of girl are found under this category in Kamarajar district.

Higher birth order child labourers are generally less in all districts. While there is none in the 5th birth order in Madurai district, five each are found in Thanjavur and Kamarajar districts in the same category. All the sample child labourers of 6th birth order are found in Thanjavur district alone. Out of the total six, four children in this category are girls.

Thus, majority of the working children in the study area are of first and second order of births with more male children under this category than female. But, when boys and girls are considered separately, both at aggregate level and also locationwise percentage of girls are more among those under first order of birth except in Madurai district where boys are more (56 per cent) under the category. Those with higher birth order (two and above) are found more in Thanjavur and in Madurai districts (See Table 18.20 in Appendix).

SECTION-III

PROBLEMS OF CHILD LABOURERS

Section III of Chapter 11 focuses on several types of problems noticed among child labourers perhaps largely due to their teenage employment and other related aspects. The problems range from their personal grooming and health status including height and weight, school attendance, hours and days of work and wage. Certain amount of data on deficiencies children are identified through direct observation of their morbidity conditions. In fact the weight of the children may reveal the status of health resulting out of over work and other problems besides malnutrition.

(i) Personal Grooming and Appearance

A few indicators of physical appearance considered are the colour of the hair, presence of angular stomatitis, conditions of teeth and conditions of drees. It is encouraging to note that 55 per cent of the children have natural hair. Location wise data shows differences in the intensity of the problem. Those having natural colour of hair are more in Kamarajar district (67%) and less in Madurai district (49%). The remaining 45 per cent have hair with decolouration and matted type. This problem was found more (6%) in Thanjavur but nil in Madurai district. It perhaps gives a tentative clue that the above mentioned 55 per cent of children may have certain deficiencies or may be due to bad maintenance of hair. Another aspect observed is regarding the presence of angular stomatitis. This problem is noticed among 35.5 per cent of the children. Presence of angular stomatitis may be due to the food they consume which is not balanced perhaps due to poverty and ignorance. Another study conducted in India also shows presence of high incidence of severe protein caloric malnutrition, anaemia, tuberculosis and paralytic diseases among bonded child-labourers.[5] This problem of angular stomatitis is found more in Thanjavur district and less (29%) in Anna district.

Only 10 per cent of them have neat and good dress and another 23 per cent have fairly clean but very old dress. The remaining 67 per cent have unclean-torn dress. It is in Kamarajar district that nearly one third (31%) have neat and good dress but none has in Thanjavur district. In others only small percentage (7 to 11%) comes under this category with Madurai district having the least number. In the same district more children (33%) have clean but old dress. Only a small percentage (16%) have such dress in Anna district. Of the four districts, it is in Thanjavur district that a vast margin (89%) have unclean or old dress. The problem is found least (45%) in Kamarajar district. This shows the extent of poverty and neglect shown by parents and also children themselves for a clean living. Lack of concern for personal hygiene is also reported by Naidu[6] in her study conducted in Bombay. The type of work they do also has a bearing on the type of dress. For example those who are agricultural labourers herders of animals, fishermen and domestic servants have, generally unclean dress.

It is seen that 62 per cent of them have unclear but white teeth and another 31 per cent have unclear and stained teeth. Location wise pattern shows that Kamarajar and Madurai districts have largest percentage (70 and 64 per cent respectively) of child-labourers having unclean but white teeth. In Thanjavur large number have unclean and stained teeth (36%) and 1/4th of the children in Kamarajar district comes under this category. This reveals several factors resulting out of child-labour. First of all it may be due to their ignorance arising out of illiteracy followed by insufficient time available at their disposal and also lack of necessity for maintaining clean teeth in the work conditions in which they live in. For example those who work in match units, go out for fishing, take animals for grazing and working in cycle repair shops etc., due to their nature of work, do not seem to bother about personal hygiene (Table not given).

(ii) Health Problems

Under health problems, three aspects have been identified viz. types of illness during the study period (1986-87), ill health resulting out of the nature of work and steps taken to treat the diseases. A single largest proportion of respondents (63%) did not experience any major disease. Of those who suffered from certain ailments, fever was reported by many. Stomach-ache and measles were also reported besides certain unspecified diseases like-body-heat and head-ache. The presence of fits among a small fraction of children may be due to the stress and strain (2.5%) involved in work. Though negligible 1.5 per cent of the children suffered from itching especially in Thanjavur district. More cases of back paid are also reported from there.

Regarding health hazards they faced out of their work, 32 per cent of the sample children really suffered from cuts, burns, back-pain, body-heat diarrohea and head-ache. Out of them, body-heat back-ache, wounds/burns and head-ache are major ones. While body head was repeated mostly by children in Madurai and Kamarajar districts, (10 and 6 per cent respectively) back-pain and head-ache are reported by more in Thanjavur district. While head-ache was mostly reported by those who are herding animal, back pain was quoted mostly by boys who work in boats for fishing. Here, their main work is sitting in a forward stooping position and operating a wodden—ruddar to change the course of boat. Such long hours (more than 12 hours) of sitting is cited as reason by them. Occupational hazards like lead poisoning in jari industry, paralysis in naples due to toxic glue, sterility or laukamia due to exposure to radiation, presence of dermatitis among those handling chemicals and irritants are quoted by Shah[7] in his paper also.

Most of those suffered illness resorted to home remedies or medication by themselves (17%) especially in Thanjavur (20%) and Madurai (19%) districts. However, 12.5 per cent sought proper treatment from qualified doctors of PHC and Government hospitals mostly in Kamarajar (20%) and Madurai districts (16%). A few of them (2%) ignored ailments. Though reported morbidity cases constitute only 1/3rd of the child labourers studied, the affected persons may be more when we see their nutritional status and also the problems that might errupt in the near future based on the deteriorating conditions of their body.

(iii) Height and Weight of Working Children

Height and weight of these children have been assessed by classifying the height and weight into two broader categories. Item one is the subnormal category—upto 70 per cent level of the 'normal' and the other one is near normal height categories ranging from 80 to 90 per cent of the normal height—under Indian conditions. Only these two categories are made. In the aggregate, it is found that 19.74 per cent of male child workers were found to have deficiency in height i.e. 60 to 70 per cent of the standard height prescribed for different ages. Among girls 23.35 per cent came under this category.

Analysis of age-wise data shows that 50 per cent of the boys of 9 years of age come under this category but none among girls. Among ten years old, 23 per cent out of 27 were found deficient in height by 30 per cent and more and among girls, 30 per cent out of the 13 were found in this group. Among 11 years old children 3 out of 15 boys and one out of 10 girls are found deficient by 3% and more in height. Among 12 years old 16.4 per cent of male and 23.7 per cent of 61 females are deficient in height. Among 13 years old; 33% of 51 male and 26.3 per cent of 38 females are deficient in height. Among the 14 years old category 11.4 per cent of boys and 17.5 per cent of girls are found deficient in height by 30 per cent and more of the normal. *Thus it is among the higher age groups except in the case of 14 year old boys that those with more deficiency in height are found—male children are found to be more disadvantaged than females.* Comparison of weight of the respondents with that of standard weight prescribed for different age groups shows that a good number is more deficient in weight. *On an average 90 per cent of the boys and 64.67 per cent of girls were found to have deficiency in weight by 30 to 40 per cent of standard weight.*

In the nine year old age groups three out of 6 boys are found deficient in weight by 30 to 40 per cent but none among girls belonging to this age group. Among 10 years old, 56.52 per cent of boys an 13 per cent of girls are found in this category. Among 11 years old age group, 64.70 per cent of boys and 14.3 per cent of girls—are under this category. Among 13 years old group, 57.63 per cent of boys and 13.16 per cent of girls come under the category—among the 14 years old group 6.35 per cent of girls and 54.85 per cent of boys have such deficiency. *Thus with regard to weight more of boys than girls are found deficient.*

Location wise, not much differences noticed with regard to deficiency in height and weight of male and female child labourers.

(iv) Educational Attainment of Child Labourers

Educational attainment of child labourers is not disappointing. Table 18.2 reveals that 72.5 per cent of child labourers are semi-literate. But there are differences in the literacy levels in the districts studied. Whereas as 47 per cent of sample child-labourers are illiterate in Thanjavur district, it is least (11%) in Kamarajar district. While those having primary education are highest (72%) in Anna district closely followed by Kamarajar (70%) district, those having secondary and higher secondary education are comparatively much in the latter (13%). Only three per cent each belonged to this category in Madurai and Thanjavur districts. Among these total literates, 65 per cent have studied between 1 to 5 and only a negligible per cent have secondary education.

(a) Educational Deprivation

One of the prominent problems faced by the child labourers is the deprivation of education facilities due to lack of time. In the past it was all the more serious because not much facilities existed for non formal education. But it has improved during the last one decade. But even such facility does not benefit most of these children. Table 18.26 confirms this reality. A single largest proportion of (41%) of the children admitted that they could not attend school because they work during school time. Locationwise more children (46% uniformly) reported this reason in all districts except in Thanjavur (25%). Another 29 per cent expressed certain unspecified difficulty to study along with work. A still another 12 per cent considered it difficult to learn any more. This category is found relatively more in Thanjavur (38%) and Madurai (36%) districts. There is also problem in continuing learning because some are their family's sole bread winners.

Such cases are more in Madurai district. These problems are to be taken note of and suitable non formal education is to be introduced at close quarters in and around the work spot of children, to make use of education facility. In this context there is a need to re-examine the location of non-formal education institutions and their target group. The above reasons are further confirmed when a separate question was asked to know whether they are attending any non formal education. A near universal number of child workers (98.5%) did not make use of the facility. Hardly 1.5 per cent of them benefited out of this education and all are found in Kamarajar district. Here in one work unit classes are being held for working children during working time. But only very few attended it. Non attendance was mainly due to fear of loosing income. Those who attended had assurances of getting absorbed in higher posts after successful completion in the work unit itself. Even those attending these courses, all are not regularly doing so. (See Table 18.25).

(b) Dropout, Enrolment and Their Reasons

Further probes in to the details regarding (i) date of withdrawal (ii) reasons for withdrawal (iii) future plan for formal and non formal education (iv) reasons for not attending non formal education (v) reasons for not favouring continuance of education are made and recorded. It is noted that 47.30 per cent of sample children dropped out of school during the survey period (1986-87). The numbers are more in Kamarajar (60%) and Madurai (50%) districts. Another 24.50 per cent withdraw from school 3 to 5 years back. These informations question the validity of the claim that more enrolment of children into school as a result of mid-day meal scheme. If the noon meal scheme is an attraction for continuing in schools, how these children could drop out? The information given below partially explains the reasons for the same.

When further probed to know reasons for discontinuing their formal education, several interesting informations were obtained. Majority (56%) dropped out of school on account of different forms of economic difficulties. Out of these reasons poverty alone accounts for 22.5 per cent and the rest are due to other economic reasons like labour requirements in the family which accounted for 3.5 per cent and another 9.7 per cent due to discouragement by parents which again also may be for manpower requirements. Around 20 to 28 per cent of children in all districts except in Anna (15%) expressed 'difficulties in studies' as a reason. While poverty was a main reported reason in Thanjavur (30%) and Anna districts (28%) parents' discouragement had been the main factor in Kamarajar district (28%). A few less frequently cited reasons are; distance to school and harsh treatment by teachers (5.5%). When their future options for continuing education was sought—if opportunity is provided—most of them answered negatively (91%). It is a shocking information and further indepth study is needed to find out why they are not particular about future education. In this context certain information is also gathered here. Among the reasons cited the most prominent one is the 'difficulties faced in the family' which include financial and otherwise. Second reason again is exclusively financial (23%). However, 15 per cent of them are not interested in studies and another 11 per cent though interested, have no time to spare. The other less frequently mentioned reasons are 'absence of scope for better jobs in future', parents do not favour their further education and give priority for attending to domestic work. Timely interventions are thus very vital atleast of the benefit of avoiding future drop out of children from schools. In this context 1/5th of the children gave reasons for their future plan for education. They include the plan to earn more income, interest in education to get better jobs and gain improved skills. These findings could be effectively used for the promotion of universal education for children in future. (See Table 18.26 in Appendix).

(v) Wages Earned by Child-workers

The compulsion of receiving low wages is a problem highlighted by many other studies too (see review). In the present study also earnings are found to be low. Those who did not-agricultural work especially in match/fire works units, weaving, construction work, tailoring etc., are paid wages on piece-rate basis. Those in the service sector as general shop assistants, cycle repair shop assistants, domestic servants etc. got wages on a flat rate, some times based on experience, type of work and time involved. In match-box making units, wages are paid every week; in domestic work and shops etc. on monthly basis and in others on daily basis. In fishing, wage is paid in kind. In agriculture especially in Thanjavur district for farming, grazing of animals, payment is in kind. In farming it is a combined effort of family labour including that of child workers and hence in such cases there are problems in apportioning the share of child wage. Payments made to other children doing similar work has been used as yard-stick to measure child wage in the case joint work with family members. In the case of domestic servants and helpers in hotels and restaurants besides money wage, clothes, food etc. are also reported given.

Much locational variation exists in wages earned by child labourers. In Thanjavur district those engaged in fishing reported to earn as much as Rs. 50 per day during peak fishing seasons.

In total majority earned Rs. 4 to 5 per day. Kamarajar (50%) and Madurai (43%) districts have more number of child workers found under this category. Those earning Rs. 2.5 to 3.5 from second larger percentage in all the four districts with again Kamarajar district (32%) having more children under this category followed by Thanjavur district (30%). There are children who earn less than Rs. 2 in Madurai district 30 per cent of the sample children earned this amount. But only four children are found in this category in

Thanjavur district. A study in Madras city[8] also reports payment of such low wages to child labourers (Rs. 50 paise to maximum Rs. 2 only per day). Similar low wage payments were reported in carpet industry in U.P. and Kashmir. In Kamarajar district none are found to earn more than Rs. 7.5 per day where as in Madurai district two are found earning Rs. 10 to 11.5 per day. In Anna district eight children were found earning Rs. 8 to 11.5 and none earned more than this. In Thanjavur 21 per cent of sample child labourers earned Rs. 14 and more per day. (See Table 18.6).

Sex-wise differences in earning are noticed in all the four locations. Among those who earn Rs. 2.5 to 3.5 per day not much sex differences are found, but among those earn Rs. 2 and less, more are boys in Kamarajar and Thanjavur district. Similarly among those who earned Rs. 4 and 5, majority are male in all the four districts. Only one girl is found to earn higher amounts (Rs. 8 to 11.5 per day) in Anna district (See Table 18.6). One reason for the low wage earned by girls is due to less hour of work put in by them compared to boys. As in most cases wage is paid on piece rate, and hence wage discrimination is not noticed in the study areas. *Thus, majority earned less than Rs. 6 per day with the Madurai district having maximum (90%) followed by Kamarajar district (87%).*

Importance attached to child labour can be inferred from the share of child-wage in reported family income. In Madurai (24%) and Kamarajar districts it formed about 10 per cent of family income. In Anna district only 6 per cent came under this category. In majority of the cases child wage formed 11 to 20 per cent of family income. Whereas in Anna district in 50 per cent of families and in Kamarajar 49 per cent of families child wage forms 11-20 per cent of families income; almost one-third of the child-labourers in Anna district contributed 21 to 30 per cent family income. In Thanjavur, around one fourth contributed this percentage. However, in Thanjavur 21 per cent contributed 31 to 40 per cent of family income. In some cases child wage is the main source of income to families. As much as 8 families in total are found to depend heavily on child wage. In Thanjavur alone, in six families child-wage formed 51 to 70 per cent of family income. In Anna district, in one family child wage formed the only source of income (90%). *Thus on the whole, economic value attached to child labour seems to be considerable. Under such child labour syndrome, no amount of legislation to prevent child labour can change the situation. It calls for radical and feasible economic programmes for the elder members so as to augment their income in the immediate future itself. (See Table 18.7).*

(vi) Hours of Work

Another problem of child labourers is long hours of work which the young children do. Hamsa[9] reports that 20 per cent of the child-labours studied got no cash remuneration. They are reported to work for 12 to 18 hours/day against the provision of food only and 5 per cent earned between Rs. 21 to 30 per month and the highest income ranged between Rs. 75 to 100 per month. Only very negligible percentage of children (4%) reported to work for five hours and less per day. In the present study too a small percentage (9.5%) had to work for more than 12 hours per day; all of them are male

TABLE 18.6

Wages Earned Per Day by Child Labourers

Sl. No.	Wages per day (in Rs.)	Thanjavur District			Anna District			Madurai District			Kamarajar District			Aggregate Number	Per-centage
		Male	*Female*	*Total*	*Male*	*Female*	*Total*	*Male*	*Female*	*Total*	*Male*	*Female*	*Total*		
1.	2	4	—	4	4	6	10	10	20	30	5	2	7	51	12.75%
2.	2.5—3.5	6	24	30	20	7	27	10	7	17	12	20	32	106	26.5%
3.	4—5.5	27	8	35	17	20	37	20	23	43	29	21	50	165	41.25%
4.	6—7.5	7	1	8	13	5	18	8	—	8	10	1	11	45	11.25%
5.	8—9.5	—	—	—	2	1	3	—	—	—	—	—	—	3	0.75%
6.	10—11.5	—	—	—	4	1	5	2	—	2	—	—	—	7	1.75%
7.	12—13.5	2	—	2	—	—	—	—	—	—	—	—	—	2	0.5%
8.	14+	21	—	21	—	—	—	—	—	—	—	—	—	21	5.25%
	Total	67	33	100	60	40	100	50	50	100	56	44	100	400	100.00

children. Among them majority are from Thanjavur district especially those who go out in the sea for fishing. Atleast here, the long hours of work are compensated by higher wages. But grazing annuals is one work item which is time consuming but low paid. Among non-agricultural work, working in hotels, shops, tailor shops etc., also involve long hours of work. Majority (46%) in the present study are found to work for 8 to 9 hours per day. Among the locations, majority in this category (75%) are found in Anna district followed by in Kamarajar district (50%). Study by Mehta[10] et al, Singh[11] M. also shows instances of long hours work (11.5 to 12 hours/day) put forth by child labourers in their studies. In the present study too, 24 per cent of sample children in Kamarajar district and 1/5th in Thanjavur district are found to work for 10-11 hours per day. (See Table 18.29 in Appendix).

TABLE 18.7

Share of Child Wage in Family Income

Sl. No.	*Share of child wage in family income*	*Thanjavur District*	*Anna District*	*Madurai District*	*Kamarajar District*	*Total Number*	*Percen-tage*
1.	10%	11	6	24	20	61	15.25%
2.	11-20%	28	50	39	49	166	41.5%
3.	21-30%	26	31	20	18	95	23.75%
4.	31-40%	21	8	11	10	50	12.5%
5.	41-50%	8	3	5	3	19	4.75%
6.	51-61%	3	1	1	—	5	1.25%
7.	61-70%	3	—	—	—	3	0.75%
8.	71 +	—	1	—	—	1	0.25%
	Total	100	100	100	100	400	100.00

In general among those who work for more than 8 hours per day majority are boys. But as seen earlier, daily earning is less among majority of girls. Girls who work in domestic service have to work for long hours and receive low wages. *On the whole majority worked for more than 8 hours per day. But their daily earning is less. In general children reported that they felt their work being monotonous. Some found it hard too.*

(vii) Average Number of Working Days

Average number of working days of child labourers varied in the study areas. Besides working for long hours and earning low income, they are subject to work with very few holidays. *Nearly 3/4 of them worked for 21 to 30 days a month.* Slightly more than half of them worked for 26 days and more per month and nearly 1/4th has to work for all days in a month. They are domestic servants, assistants in hotels and tea shops, repair shops, stationary and provision shops, watchman etc. and also those grazing animals. Thus, nature of work is such that their presence is needed without break, day after day.

Location wise analysis shows that those who work for 20 days or less in a month are more in Anna (44%) and Thanjavur districts (43%) but none in Kamarajar district. On the other hand those who have to work on all days in a month are found more (59%) in Kamarajar district and least (3 per cent) in Anna district. Analysis based on sex, shows that among those who work on all days in month, female children are in large numbers in all except Kamarajar district where male children are more (60.5%) under this category. But in Madurai and Anna districts only female children are found under this category. Whereas in Thanjavur 42 per cent of girls worked on all days, only six per cent of their male counterparts worked throughout months. *Thus on the whole child workers had to work for more days in Kamarajar district having more percentage of both boys and girls who work on all days.*

NOTES

1. Naidu D.A., 'Micro-determinants of child labour—An evidence from rural South India—in *seminar report 'On Child Labour and Health'*, Tata Institute of Social Sciences, Bombay, p. 120, 1982.
2 Similar evidence is also found in Naidu's Study in Andhra Pradesh.
3. *Ibid.*, Naidu, p. 120.
4. Naidu, D.A., "Child-labour, Value of Children and Fertility Behaviour' Ph.D. Dissertation.
5. Meenakshi, N., Mehta et al, 'Types of Physical Health Problems in working children' in Seminar *Report on Child Labour and Health*—Tata Institute of Social Sciences Bombay 1982, p. 164.
6. Naidu, U.S. and Parasuraman S., *Health Situation of Youth in India*. Bombay: Tata Institute of Social Sciences.
7. Shah, P.M., Specific Health Problems of working children; Alternative Health Care in Seminar Paper on *Child labour and Health*, Tiss, Bombay, 1982.
8. Savithri, S., 'Prevalence of child labour in Tamil Nadu'—*Child Labour and Health*, Report of Seminar, Tata Institute of Social Sciences, Bombay, 1982, p. 111.
9. Hamsa N., 'Tackling the problem of child labour' *Yojana*--Vol. 32, No. 23, December 16-31, 1988, pp. 15-16.
10. See Meenakshi N. Mehta et al., 'Types of Physical Health Problem in Working Children'.
11. Singh, M. Kaira et al.,—*Working Children in Bombay: A Study*—Delhi University Press, 1980.

19

CHILD LABOUR: THE ILO PERSPECTIVE*

1. The Nature of the Problem

It is now over 81 years since the International Labour Conference adopted the Minimum Age (Industry) Convention, 1919 (No. 5) — the first in a long line of such Conventions—which fixed a minimum age of 14 for admission to employment in industry. It is ten years since the adoption of the more comprehensive Minimum Age Convention, 1973 (No. 138), a general instrument aimed at the total abolition of child labour. Over all this time, the progress made towards the elimination of child labour has been in many ways impressive. Yet the situation remains disquieting.

Child labour is still a widespread and perhaps even growing phenomenon in much of the world today. While many of the children who are working are engaged in activities permitted by national and international standards, many more are working in violation of these standards. Such is the case, for example, of;

- Young girls working in small industrial enterprises in tasks that involve handling microscopically fine wires, finally resulting in loss of the eyesight within five to eight years;
- shepherd boys subcontracted to owners of large estates to work for as long as 15 hours a day;
- children working underground in mines;
- bonded children;
- children employed as seasonal and cheap labour in pesticide-soaked fields;
- children working in numerous small industrial workshops and service establishments;
- children in street trades practically ubiquitous in the developing world.

That is child labour. Not teenagers working for a few hours to earn additional pocket money; not children helped on family farms; not youngsters doing household chores.

---

* This is extracted with minor modifications from ILO: Report of the Director-General, Part I: Child labour, International Labour Conference, 69th Session, Geneva, 1983.

But children prematurely leading adult lives, working long hours for low wages under conditions damaging to their health and to their physical and mental development, sometimes separated from their families, frequently deprived of meaningful educational and training opportunities that could open up for them a better future. Child labour of this kind is the object of national and international concern.

2. Causes and Forms of Child Labour

Children in almost all societies do one kind of work or another. But the extent and nature of their work are influenced mainly by the structure of the economy and the level and pace of development.

In agrarian societies work by children is an integral part of the socialisation process and a means of transmitting traditionally acquired skills from parent to child. Moreover, in societies at low levels of technological development the participation of all those who can contribute to domestic or non-domestic production is essential for meeting the consumption requirements of the household. Child work is therefore in essential part of the farm household's survival. This situation is still prevalent in many parts of rural Africa and Asia and, to some extent, Latin America. In such societies the division of labour is largely based on sex, age and physical capacity. Children, until they reach a certain age, are involved in light and time-intensive activities while adults usually take up effort-intensive activities.

To some extent, comparable patterns may be found in artisanal workshops and small-scale services. Children assist their parents in ancillary tasks, acquire skills and gradually become fully fledged workers in family establishments or trades.

Work of this kind is not without its problems, especially in relation to the health and safety of the children and to their schooling. But it is not what we usually mean by child labour.

Wage or quasi-wage employment is another matter altogether.

Historically, the growth of wage labour and industrial expansion are associated with a decline in child employment. The early stages of industrialisation, however, are marked by a high incidence of child employment, often under extremely poor and indeed exploitative conditions. This is the case in much of the developing world today.

Thus, in many developing countries, children are found working in all types of industrial and service establishments in urban areas in both the formal and the informal sectors and also in commercial agriculture. Often they are working for low wages and for excessively long hours. Vulnerable, flexible and unorganised child workers are used for reducing labour costs and maintaining competitive advantages and as a means of adapting and responding to economic uncertainties and fluctuations in demand.

The subordination of child workers to such pressures has been aggravated in many developing countries by the slow growth of urban employment. Urban unemployment rates of 20 to 25 per cent are not uncommon in many countries. In these circumstances, the employment of children becomes an essential means of generating or supplementing family income. The poverty or unemployment of their parents therefore forces children to work in households as domestic servants or in small enterprises or in street trades. At worst, they are drawn into such activities as beggary and prostitution.

The situation in the rural areas is in many respects similar. In a large number of developing countries technological innovations in agriculture have been accompanied by increasing landlessness and rural differentiation. This has led to the search for wage employment in commercial farms, especially plantations, as well as to a rapid migration way from rural areas. Children, especially from poor families, are forced into the labour market to work either individually or as part of contracted family labour. Given the need to met subsistence requirements on the one hand and growing pauperisation resulting from land alienation on the other, the pressure on rural households to find alternative sources of survival by all means, including the labour of their children, whether under family control or under contract to prospective employers and labour recruiters, becomes almost insurmountable.

A particularly disturbing situation may arise in agrarian societies where land tenure patterns impose on tenants, sharecroppers and similar categories of workers obligations over and above household consumption requirements. In some cases, these obligations may take the form of providing the landlord a share of the farmers' produce. But in others they might involve the provision of labour services, including those of children. The prevalence of such relations is known to lead to a severe and high incidence of debt bondage, giving rise to the phenomenon known as "bounded" labour which, while generally prohibited by law, is still found, for example, in parts of south and south-east Asia.

In short, the problem of child labour in both rural and urban areas is principally one of poverty and unemployment, themselves a result of unequal and low levels of development.

3. The Two Planks of ILO Policy

For the ILO, the abolition of child labour and more generally the protection of children and young persons against work of a character or under conditions unsuitable to their age have been constant concerns since its foundation.

A major part of the ILO's work in this area has been the adoption by the International Labour Conference of a series of Conventions and Recommendations dealing with the employment or work of children and young persons.

The first such Convention was adopted at the first session of the International Labour Conference, 1919. This instrument—the Minimum Age (Industry) Convention, 1919 (No. 5) — fixed at 14 years the minimum age for admission of children to industrial employment., Subsequently, many international labour Conventions and

Recommendations were adopted prohibiting the employment of children under a certain age and regulating their conditions of work in particular sectors or occupations—the most recent instruments on the subject being the Minimum Age Convention (No. 138) and Recommendation (No. 146), adopted by the Conference in 1973.

A further policy statement was issued by the Conference in 1979, the year designated as International Year of the Child, in the form of a resolution concerning the International Year of the Child. This resolution called on member States to ratify and implement the relevant international labour standards and, above all, to take measures to ensure the proper protection of children with regard to work. Recognising that the abolition of child labour in practice will take time, the resolution stresses the need—during the transitional period until its elimination — for measures to regulate and humanise it.

This affirmation of the elimination of child labour as an objective coupled with a commitment to action, pending its attainment, to improve the conditions of working children are the two planks of ILO policy. In the long run, the progressive elimination of child labour requires a general improvement of living standards, a reinforcement of the educational infrastructure and, perhaps most basically, a greater consciousness of the need for change. In the short run, the protection of working children requires practical measures that can improve their working and living conditions.

4. A General Framework for Policies on Child Labour

Effective policies aimed at the protection of children at work and the gradual elimination of child labour must be adjusted to the socio-economic situation of each country. Child labour cannot be approached as an isolated problem; its reduction and elimination will require a set of direct and indirect, albeit inter-related, measures.

Where work by children is truly part of the socialisation process and a means of transmitting skills from parent to child, it is hardly meaningful to speak of child labour. Nor can such work be divorced from the poverty and underdevelopment and the absence of alternatives to child work which together generate and sustain it. For the overwhelming majority who assist and work with their parents at home or on the farm, it is almost impossible to address their situation through formal measures as such; nor would such measures, if successful, necessarily be in the interest of many child workers and their families. Child labour is rooted in poverty: the progressive elimination of unacceptable labour by those too young to undertake it requires a general improvement in the economies of the countries concerned. In this context, the impact of policies or measures which may not be specifically addressed to children but which do try to bear on the causes of poverty and inequality can have a significant and even decisive impact on the incidence and extent of child labour. Such policies may include agrarian reforms, employment creation schemes, greater access by the poor to improved technologies, informal sector promotion policies, creation of co-operatives and social security programmes. These and similar measures can lead to broad-based growth, a more egalitarian structure and asset and income distribution and, consequently, a reduction in the incidence of child labour.

Another set of policies which can have a bearing on the incidence and extent of child labour relates to education, training and apprenticeship. The extension and application of universal compulsory education and the provision of training and apprenticeship schemes can have significant potential because they could not only reduce the number of children out of school but also provide opportunities for skill acquisition and later employment.

In addition, there is a third set of complementary policies which needs to be conceived parallel to these medium to long-term macro-economic and educational policies. This consists of measures which address the worst forms of child exploitation and lead to better working conditions.

Pending the improvement of economic conditions to the point where it will no longer be necessary or profitable for children to work, efforts must be made to complement long-term employment and development policies with progressive measures aimed at regulating and humanising child work so that children are provided with some protection against conditions that jeopardise their normal physical and mental development, deny them educational and skill development and block their lifetime opportunities. Such measures include the adoption and enforcement of protective labour laws, the implementation of improvements at the worksite and the provision of welfare facilities.

At this juncture, I should like to stress some points in respect of the role of labour laws in preventing or suppressing child labour, since they have been a subject of misunderstanding and even distortion in recent years.

The aim of such measures is not to supplant long-term structural reforms and anti-poverty-oriented policies but to reinforce and complement them wherever possible, to deal with the worst forms of child labour wherever they exist, and to provide minimum levels of protection where such labour is unavoidable. There is a risk that labour legislation, especially child labour laws, without supporting socio-economic changes may lead to greater Clandestine work and more exploitative work situations. Such laws must therefore never be conceived or implemented in isolation from the socio-economic setting.

By the same token, the dynamic character of child labour laws must also be recognised. Standards and laws must be based on specific country situations and must therefore taken into account the socio-economic realities of each country. At the same time, these standards should be raised progressively over time; hence, laws must be revised accordingly as the countries concerned develop their economies and institutions.

Yet it must also be stressed that there are certain absolutes arising from the inherent dignity of the human person and recognised in international convenants which nations, irrespective of their level of development, have accepted and should therefore adhere to both in the formulation of labour laws and in their subsequent enforcement. Every effort must be made at the national and international level to persuade and assist governments to adopt and enforce labour laws that can protect children at least from the worst forms or exploitation and dangerous working conditions. Such laws need not and should not await structural changes or significant improvements in general standards of living. To dismiss in a cavalier way, as some do, the potential role of child protective laws, or to invoke the pretext of poverty and underdevelopment for the continued transgression of universally accepted values is to accept the perpetuation of universally condemned abuses.

Child labour laws can play a catalytic and supportive role in efforts aiming at the establishment of a more humane socio-economic order. That is why the ILO, and indeed national governments, attach so much importance to the setting and implementation of international and national labour standards.

5. International Labour Standards

As I said earlier, the International Labour Conference has over the years adopted a series of Conventions and Recommendations dealing with the employment or work of children and young persons, starting with the adoption in 1919 of Convention No. 5, which fixed at 14 years the minimum age for admission of children to industrial employment. Since then, many such Conventions and Recommendations have been adopted regulating the employment of children in particular sectors and occupations. In 1973 the Conference re-examined the problem in depth and adopted the comprehensive standards laid down in Convention No. 138 and Recommendation No. 146 concerning minimum age for admission to employment.

Because of the fundamental importance of Convention No. 138 and Recommendation No. 146 as the basis for ILO policy aimed at the protection of working children and the gradual elimination of child labour it is worthwhile to spell out what, in the light of the provisions of those instruments, are the major elements that should inspire national policy and legislation.

First and foremost is a strong commitment to pursue a national policy designed to ensure the effective abolition of child labour and to raise progressively the minimum age for admission to employment or work to a level consistent with the fullest physical and mental development of young persons. The elements of such a policy may vary from country to country but should in general include:

(a) firm national commitment to full employment and measures designed promote employment-oriented development in rural and urban areas;
(b) the progressive extension of other economic and social measures alleviate poverty wherever it exists and to ensure family living standards and income

which are such as to make it unnecessary to have recourse to the economic activity of children;

(c) the development and progressive extension of social security and family welfare measures aimed at ensuring child maintenance;

(d) the development and progressive extension of adequate facilities for education and vocational orientation and training appropriate in from and content to the needs of the children and young persons concerned;

(e) the development and progressive extension of appropriate, facilities for the protection and welfare of children and young persons, including employed young persons.

Secondly, national laws or regulations should specify a minimum age for admission to employment or work. This minimum age should not be less than the age of completion of compulsory schooling and, in any case, according to the Convention, should not be less than 15 years. However, countries whose economy and educational facilities are insufficiently developed may initially specify a minimum age of 14 years.

The minimum age set for employment or work must also be linked to the nature of the work. Thus it is necessary to specify the ages of admission to heavy and light work. The Convention fixes at 18 the minimum age for admission to employment or work which is likely to jeopardise the health, safety or morals of young persons. However, this may be lowered to 16 on condition that the health, safety and morals of the young persons concerned are fully protected and that they have received adequate, specific instruction and training in the relevant branch of activity.

On the other hand, national laws or regulations may permit the employment or work of persons 13 to 15 years of age (or 12 to 14 if the basic minimum age is 14) on light work which is not likely to be harmful to their health or development and will not prejudice their attendance at school or their participation in vocational training programmes.

A third element that needs to be given special attention in legislation and indeed as a focus for national action relates to coverage. Although every effort must be made to provide protection in as many sectors as possible, the existence of serious constraints and hence the need for flexibility in coverage must be recognised. For these reasons, it may well be, and often is, necessary for national laws and regulations to exclude certain categories of employment or work where there could be special and substantial problems of application. Moreover, where the economy and administrative facilities are insufficiently developed, the scope of application of national laws and regulations may be initially limited to certain branches of economic activity or types of undertakings. Which activities or sectors should be included depends once again on the country's situation. But national laws should cover, as a minimum mining and quarrying , manufacturing, construction, electricity, gas and water, sanitary services, transport, storage and communication, and plantation and other agricultural undertakings mainly producing for commercial purposes. The Convention also provides for the possible exemption, under certain conditions, of work done in educational establishments for vocational training or won in undertakings if it is part of a training, guidance or orientation course.

A fourth important area for national policy is conditions of work. Given the fact that the total abolition of child labour is unattainable in the short run in many developing countries and that therefore millions of children will continue to be working, the conditions under which they work should be a focus of policy. Special efforts should be made to ensure that children are not employed under conditions involving use of dangerous substances, agents or processes, the lifting of heavy weights and underground work. Special attention should also be paid to the provision of fair remuneration and its protection, the strict limitation of daily and weekly hours of work and the prohibition of overtime, the granting of a minimum consecutive period of 12 hours' night rest and of customary weekly rest days, the granting of an annual holiday with pay of at least four weeks and, in any case, not shorter than that granted to adults, coverage by social security schemes, including employment injury, medical care and sickness benefits schemes, and the maintenance of satisfactory standards of safety and health.

Finally, an area that deserves to be conceived of as an integral part of national efforts is that of enforcement. Laws and regulations, if they are to be effective, must be backed by effective enforcement machinery. This therefore calls for the strengthening of labour inspection and related services, for instance by the special training of inspectors, so as to detect and correct abuses in the employment or work of children and young persons, especially in respect of employment in hazardous types of work. In order to facilitate the verification of ages, it is necessary (a) that the public authorities maintain an effective system of birth registration, (b) that employers be required to maintain registers and documents indicating the names and ages of all employed children and young persons and of all those receiving training, and (c) that children and young persons working in the streets, in outside stalls, in public places, etc., be licensed.

These are some of the elements that are at the heart of the international labour standards on minimum age of admission to employment and should serve as a guideline in the setting of national standards.

6. Conclusion

Although its extent and nature vary among countries and regions, child labour remains a widespread phenomenon. The magnitude of the problem, especially in developing countries, is great and the task of attacking it is urgent.

Not all work is harmful for children. Some types of activities under regulated conditions can have positive effects for the child and for society. Work experiences of the right sort can be a means of acquiring skills, of learning responsibility, of becoming a full member of the community-in short, a valuable part of growing up.

What gives cause for concern is work that places too heavy a burden on the child;

work that endangers his safety, health or welfare, work that takes advantage of the defencelessness of the child, work that exploits the child as a cheap substitute for adult labour, work that uses the child's effort but does nothing for his development, work that impedes the child's education or training and thus prejudices his future.

Child labour of this kind must be the target of national and international action.

To be effective, such action must be realistic. Children in the developing world work out of necessity. Without their earnings, however small, the already low living standards of their families would be still lower. Large numbers of them do not even have families or cannot count on their families for support: they must rely on their own efforts. For many children in the developing world the chances of receiving serious education and training are minimal. The facilities are inadequate, the direct and indirect costs are prohibitive and, perhaps most discouragingly, the relevance and practical value of the education offered are doubted by parents and by the children themselves. Many children do not go to school; many drop out very early; and many more attend but only sporadically and without drawing much benefit. In these circumstances, the alternative to work might be idleness, beggary or crime.

Thus the elimination of child labour and the progressive raising of the minimum age for admission to employment must be regarded as objectives to be attained gradually and as an integral part of a process of development designed to overcome the scourges of unemployment and destitution. Formal measures alone will not work; if applied in isolation from overall measures to improve the economic and social context, and especially in the absence of alternatives to work, they may even be harmful. Child labour is embedded in poverty and it is through sustained increases in standards of living that it will be abolished.

But recognition of this reality must not serve as a pretext for inaction. The problem of child labour is so grave and is often manifested in forms so unacceptable that it cannot be left aside until economic conditions and social structures are fundamentally improved.

I am convinced that, under existing conditions, direct action can be taken and significant progress can be made. Long-term development policies can be complemented by immediate measures aimed at regulating and humanising work by children so as to protect them against practices or conditions that jeopardise their normal physical and mental development, deny them the possibility of acquiring knowledge and skills and block their opportunities for the future.

I urge giving priority to:

— the review of existing legal standards on minimum age for admission to employment or work with the aim of identifying any significant gaps in coverage and, where possible, adopting laws or regulations for some or all of the sectors concerned;

- the adoption and strict enforcement of laws or regulations prohibiting the employment or work of children in hazardous activities;
- the promotion of occupational safety and health and the improvement of the physical environment at the workplace in sectors where children are known to be engaged;
- The regulation and improvement of other conditions of work of children, especially in respect of hours of work, night work, weekly rest and holidays;
- the regulation of levels and methods of remuneration and the protection of wages;
- the strengthening of labour inspection and other enforcement measures for the regulation of child labour;
- the provision of welfare facilities and services for children at or near the workplace;
- the expansion of educational facilities to permit the extension or more effective implementation of compulsory education;
- the introduction of schemes by which children who are obliged to work can combine remunerative activity with education or training;
- the encouragement of action by employers, trade unions and voluntary organisations to promote child welfare;
- the exposure of particularly abusive or exploitative practices;
- the dissemination of information designed to create greater public awareness of the adverse effects of child labour.

I reiterate the appeal made by the Conference during the International Year of the Child for member States to ratify the Minimum Age Convention, 1973 (No. 138), if they have not already done so, and to apply the provisions of that Convention and its supplementary recommendation (No. 146).

The protection of children at work and the ultimate abolition of child labour require concerted action by governments along many fronts, but they are not tasks for governments alone. They also require the commitment and the active co-operation of employers' and workers' organisations and indeed of the world community as a whole.

II. Child Labour: Questions and Answer

I. The Nature and Extent of the Problem

1. What is "child labour"?
2. Where do children work?
3. How many child workers are there in the world today?

4. Where are they mostly found?
5. Has it been decreasing or increasing?

II. What is to be done?

1. Why do children work?
2. What do they need?

III. ILO's Policy

1. Is the ILO opposed to all types of work?
2. What is ILO's policy on child labour?

IV. International Labour Standards: Principles and Relevance

1. Are there international norms and standards on child labour and the protection of working children?
2. What are Conventions and Recommendations?
3. What is the relevance of these international labour standards (or Conventions and Recommendations)?
4. What is the most important international labour Convention on the subject?
5. What are the major provisions of the Minimum Age Convention of 1973?
6. Does the minimum age limit of 15 apply for every country and for all types of work?
7. What is the real value of these international labour standards and for that matter national laws on child labour since, given the poverty of their families, children will continue to work at any rate?

I. THE NATURE AND EXTENT OF THE PROBLEM

1. What is "child labour"?

The concept of child labour is not as simple and straightforward as it may appear. Childhood can be defined in terms of age, but then different societies may have different age thresholds for demarcating childhood and adulthood. In some societies, age may not be a sufficient basis for defining "childhood." The fulfilment of certain social rites and traditional obligations may well be important requirements in defining "adult" and "child" status. In still others, the integration of children into socio-economic life may begin so early and the transition from childhood and adulthood may be so smooth and gradual that it may be virtually impossible to identify clearly the different life phases. We must therefore recognise that we are dealing with a concept which could mean different things in different societies and at different times.

However, in the context of child labour, a working definition of a "child" may be a person below the internationally agreed age limit of 15 years. We will come back to this point later in discussing international labour standards on the subject.

How about "labour"? Labour too can be a controversial concept to define, especially in the case of children. Children assist their families, for example, at home from early years on; they also assist in farms, in shops, etc. But this is not what we call child labour. Rather, we have in mind work or employment situation where children are engaged on a more or less regular basis to earn a livelihood for themselves or their families.

In short, the notion of child labour is intended to cover children under the age of 15 engaged in work or employment with the aim of earning a livelihood for themselves or for their families.

2. Where do Children Work?

On the land and in the village; in and around the home; on the streets; in crafts and trading; in plantations, in mines and factories. They are found almost everywhere under varying forms and terms of employment. Many work as unpaid family labour, but a growing number are also found working as wage labourers, casually hired, just as casually fired.

3. How Many Child Workers are There in the World Today?

Who knows? The honest truth is that nobody really knows. And this is not for lack of interest but because, among other reasons, child workers are statistically hidden even in the modern sector. Governments and employers deny that they exist—not everywhere but nearly so. We know, however, that it is a huge problem. Some years back, the ILO estimated the number of child workers at around 50 million. This is a significant figure but it is generally considered to be a serious underestimate. By some, it is felt that there are probably at least 100 million working children today and quite possibly nearly twice as many. All of this indicates that we know that the number is big, but how big it is, we don't know. But we need to know, and governments need to know if they, as well as the international community, are to respond effectively to the needs of children and child labourers.

4. Where are They Mostly Found?

Nearly everywhere. In Asia, Africa, Latin America, and, even in Europe and North America. Although we cannot rely too much on existing statistics, available estimates indicate that:

— child workers constitute as much as 7 per cent of the population under 15 years of age and as high a proportion as 11 per cent of the overall labour force in some Asian countries;

— in some African countries, as many as 20 per cent of the children are reported to be working, and child workers make up as much as 17 per cent of the workforce;

— as high a proportion as 12 to 26 per cent of children in some Latin American countries may well be working;
— in some industrialised countries hundreds of thousands and, by some accounts, millions of children under the age of 15 are known to work.

5. *Has it been Decreasing or Increasing?*

It is quite difficult to give a definite answer one way or the other. Statistics, as we said earlier, are quite difficult to come by and, even when available, are not altogether reliable or comparable. Moreover, the trend varies form one region to another and form one country to another.

But some tentative generalisations can be made:

— Firstly, in the industrialised countries the spread of compulsory schooling, the rapid and considerable improvement in levels of living and the enforcement of anti-child labour laws have all lead to a significant decline in child labour in both absolute and relative terms. In fact, in the vast majority of the countries in the industrialised countries, child labour has been virtually abolished, though it is still found in some.
— Secondly, in a large number of developing countries also there has been, say over the last five decades or so, a decline in the proportion of child workers, mainly because of the considerable expansion of schooling opportunities.
— Thirdly, the progress in many countries notwithstanding, the deterioration in living standards in some developing countries over the last decade or so is likely the have resulted in an increases both in the incidence and the number of child labourers.

Having said this, however, it should be recognised that the problem of child labour should be looked at not only in quantitative terms but also qualitatively. Unlike the pre-industrial period when children worked with their parents on farms or in family craft shops, today however many child workers are employed in wage or semi-wage employment in mines, factories, plantations, etc. Children are thus found working increasingly outside the orbit of the family. As a result, they are subjected to exploitative practices and, worse still, forced to work under conditions dangerous to their health, physical and mental development. As the Director-General said in his report to the 1983 International Labour Conference, "it is this radical transformation in the nature and forms of children's work with its concomitant harmful effects on the children concerned that makes child labour and even more pressing problem and a compelling cause for international concern."

II. WHAT IS TO BE DONE?

1. Why do Children Work

The are several reasons.

Is it because of the lack of legislation? This may be so in some exceptional cases. But as noted before, in the overwhelming majority of countries, legislation concerning minimum age for admission to employment and regulations on the employment of children do exist.

Is it then because of the ineffectiveness of enforcement of such legislation? Certainly, "yes," for in many countries the inspection system is not adequately developed; legislation often excludes traditional workshops, quasi-family undertakings, petty commerce, street trades and agriculture where the majority of children work and where the enforcement of legislation, if any takes place, is extremely difficult.

However, while part of the problem certainly derives from inadequate legislation and insufficient enforcement, a far more basic cause for child work is poverty. A child goes out to work in order to contribute to the family income. Also, another widespread cause for child labour is the low level of development of the countries concerned and the lack of educational facilities. The only alternative left for children in work in subsistence farming or fishing and petty commerce in which the family is engaged.

In some cases, ignorance, negligence or indifference towards the question of child labour could still be an explanation. It may be noted in this respect that reforms in the past, in many countries, originated in the recognition of the ill effects of child labour and the mobilisation of public opinion for the elimination of child labour and the protection of working children.

2. What Do They Need?

If children work, and they do, policies must be planned on how to meet their needs. What are their needs?

Firstly, they should certainly be protected from exploitation and from hazardous conditions of work which are likely to endanger their physical and mental development. They should be ensured of safety and health in their working place; they should be kept from night work; they should not carry heavy loads; they should be protected from excessively long working hours; they should have sufficient weekly rest periods and holidays. These call for adequate provisions in national legislation, in conformity with the standards set by the ILO, and their effective enforcement.

Children should also have access to educational opportunities, to get at least basic education and, it is to be hoped, basic vocational education to develop their potential as capable workers and responsible citizens. Where there are schools, the working hours should be so regulated that the children are able to attend classes. Where there are no schools, provision for some informal education should be made. Provision of such educational facilities falls naturally under public authorities but the responsibility for ensuring that children use such facilities naturally rests with parents and employers as well.

Further, there should be programmes to bring about a proper recognition of the needs of children among parents and the general public.

III. ILO's POLICY

1. Is the ILO Opposed to All Types of Work?

The simple answer is No. After all, child work takes many forms. In some cases, such as traditional agricultural or handicraft production, it is carried out under the supervision of parents. Work of this type is often an integral part of the socialisation process. It is a means of transmitting traditionally acquired skills from parent to child. Such work could also be a source of pride and satisfaction to the children themselves. This type of economic involvement is occasionally observed even in modern industrial societies where children may assist their families on a part-time basis or where teenagers may work for a few hours to earn additional pocket money. That is not what we are concerned about. Rather, the ILO is concerned about those situations where children are compelled to work on a regular or continuous basis to earn a living for themselves or for their families, and as a result are disadvantaged educationally and socially; where they work in conditions that are exploitative and damaging to their health and to their physical and mental development; where they are separated from their families, often deprived of educational and training opportunities; where they work as bonded labourers; where children are forced to lead prematurely adult lives, condemned to a cruel present and to a bleak future.

2. What is ILO's Policy on Child Labour?

The ILO's policy in the field of child labour derives from two inter-related but distinct objectives. The first is the effective abolition of child labour. The attainment of this objective requires countries to carry out a series of legal and socio-economic measures. Laws prohibiting admission to employment below a certain minimum age should be adopted and enforced. Socio-economic measures leading to improvements in living standards, fuller or higher levels of adult employment, and the application of compulsory schooling should be adopted in order to make child work economically unnecessary and to enhance the moral force and practical application of the law.

But the ILO recognises that the adoption and successful implementation of legal and socio-economic measures that could lead to the effective abolition of child labour will take time and that child labour will continue to be a persistent problem in large parts of the world. For this reason, its second policy objective is the protection of children at work. It therefore encourages countries to regulate the conditions under which they work, e.g. shorter hours of work, improved wages and remuneration, safer and less hazardous working conditions, etc.; it also encourages countries to provide working children with welfare facilities and services so that they can have minimum levels of education, nutrition and health protection.

IV. INTERNATIONAL LABOUR STANDARDS: PRINCIPLES AND PROTECTION OF WORKING CHILDREN?

1. Are There International Norms and Standards on Child Labour and Protection of Working Children?

Yes, there several norms and standards set up by the United Nations General Assembly as well as the International Labour Organisation to abolish child labour and to protect working children.

In 1959, for example, the United Nations General Assembly adopted the Declaration of the Rights of the Child which stressed that "mankind owes to the child the best it has to give." It also specified that "the child shall not be admitted to employment before an appropriate minimum age" and that "he shall in no case be caused or permitted to engage in any occupation or employment which would prejudice his health or education, or interfere with his physical, mental or moral development." These same principles were later reaffirmed in the International Covenant on Economic, Social and Cultural Rights adopted by the General Assembly in 1966.

But certainly the most extensive standards on the subject are those adopted by the International Labour Organisation in the from of Conventions and Recommendations defining the conditions, terms and areas of employment and work. These go as far back as 1919 and there are today well over 20 Conventions and Recommendations on the subject, the most recent and comprehensive being the Minimum Age Convention, 1973 (No. 138), and the accompanying Recommendation, 1973 (No. 146).

2. What are Conventions and Recommendations?

Conventions are comparable to multilateral international treaties: they are open to ratification by member States and, once ratified, create specific, binding obligations. A state that has ratified a Convention is expected to apply its provisions by legislation or other appropriate means as indicated in the text of the Convention. The Government is required to report regularly on the application of ratified Conventions; the extent of compliance is subject to examination and public comment by ILO machinery; complaints about alleged non-compliance may be made by the governments of their ratifying States or by employers' or workers' organisations and procedures exist for investigating and acting upon such complaints. Conventions that have not been ratified have the same value as Recommendations.

Recommendation are intended to offer guide-lines for action by member States. Often, a particular Recommendation will elaborate upon the provisions of a Convention on the same subject. Member States have certain important procedural obligations in respect of Recommendations — namely, to submit the texts to their legislative bodies, to report on the action result and to report occasionally at the request of the Governing Body on the measures takes or envisaged to give effect to the provisions. But no specific substantive obligations are entailed.

3. What is the Relevance of These International Labour Standards (or Conventions and Recommendations)?

ILO standards (i.e. Conventions and Recommendations) have a moral (political) and practical value, it is fair to say that ILO standards have exerted considerable influence on the laws and regulations of member States. Many texts have been modelled on the relevant provisions of ILO instruments; drafts of new legislation or amendments are often prepared with ILO standards in mind; trade unions use ILO standard to support arguments in bargaining and in promoting legislation; governments frequently consult the ILO, both formally and informally, about the compatibility of proposed texts with international labour standards.

The ILO's role is, however, more than that. It also exercises a supervisory role. The Office has the constitutional mandate to prepare detailed reports on the application of international standards and summarising national law and practice on specific subjects. Although the process can be slow, its observations often lead to changes in laws and regulations.

The extent to which national laws and regulations themselves are applied in practice is a more difficult question. The ILO's supervisory machinery does inquire as far as possible into practice as well as law. Governments must supply information on the practical implementation of ratified Conventions. Moreover, national employers' and workers' organisations have the right to participate in the supervisory process by receiving copies of reports sent to the ILO and submitting comments on the application of ratified Conventions. These comments often relate to the way in which the Conventions are applied in practice. On several occasions, pursuant to complaints or Conference resolutions and with the agreement of the government concerned, the ILO has sent special missions to various countries.

Clearly, a country's economic and social conditions, the government's material capacity for enforcement, the value that government places on national laws and regulations, and the vigilance of employers' and workers' organisations determine how those laws and regulations are applied. Even so, this qualification does not diminish the importance of ILO standards: they are a strong normative force; they have widely been reflected in national laws and regulations; and their implementation at least at the statutory level is effectively supervised by ILO machinery.

4. What is the Most Important International Labour Convention on the Subject?

As we said earlier, there are a number of ILO Conventions on the abolition of child labour and the protection of working children. But the most important of these is the Minimum Age Convention, 1973 (No. 138) and the accompanying Minimum Age Recommendation, 1973 (No. 146).

5. What are the Major Provisions of the Minimum Age Convention, 1973 (No. 138)?

The major elements of this Convention are described in Chapter 10 and 11. Briefly, however, the two most important ones are those that require member States:

(a) to specify a minimum age for admission to employment and to raise it progressively to a level consistent with the fullest physical and mental development of young persons; and

(b) to ensure that the minimum age for admission to employment shall not be less than the age of completion of compulsory schooling and, in any case, shall not be less than 15 years.

6. Does the Minimum age Limit of 15 Apply for every Country and for all Types of Work?

No. The Convention makes provisions for differences in levels of development and the nature of the work in which children are engaged. For example, a country whose economy and educational facilities are insufficiently developed may specify a minimum age of 14. In addition, the Convention sets a lower minimum age for light work, while it sets a higher age limit for heavy work. So while the Convention sets a minimum age of 15 for admission to employment, it has sufficient flexibility to accommodate the needs of countries at various levels of development and of children in different types of work situations.

7. What is the Real Value of These International Labour Standards and of National Laws on Child Labour Since, Given the Poverty of Their Families, Children will have to Continue to Work?

The first part of this question has already been answered indirectly under question IV. 3 above, where it was said that international labour standards provide both a common basis for international dialogue and a framework for drawing up national laws, regulations and programmes of practical action on labour and social matters. Take, for example, international standards on child labour. A survey of 107 countries conducted by the ILO, as part of its supervisory duties, concerning the application of the Minimum Age Convention, 1973 (No. 138), and Recommendation, 1973 (No. 146), showed that the principle of minimum age for admission to employment or work had been universally recognised. There was not a single State among all those which provided information which had not set some standards in this field. A number of countries have incorporated the ILO's Conventions on various aspects of the subject in their legislation.

But, even so, it may still be asked what the value of national laws and regulations is, given the poverty in large parts of the Third World and the difficulties of enforcing laws and regulations.

It must be stressed that child labour laws are not intended to supplant, or be carried out apart from, socio-economic changes; they are intended to reinforce and complement them wherever possible, to deal with the worst forms of the exploitation of children wherever they exist and to provide minimum levels of protection wherever such labour is unavoidable.

National legal standards also serve as a benchmark against which progress can be assessed. Far more importantly, they serve to provide minimum standards of protection. There are, after all, certain absolutes arising from the inherent dignity of the human person and recognised in international convenants which nations, irrespective of their level of development, have accepted and should adhere to, both in the formulation of labour laws and in their subsequent enforcement. Minimum standards enshrined in national laws help to provide the minimum protection to the human person; and such laws need not, or should not, await structural changes or significant improvements in general standards of living. As the Director-General said in his Report to the 1983 International labour Conference, "To dismiss in a cavalier way, as some do, the potential role of child labour protective laws, or to invoke the pretext of poverty and underdevelopment for the continued transgression of universally accepted values, is to accept the perpetuation of universally condemned abuses."

20

ILO'S CONCERN FOR THE CHILD

Abolition of child labour is one of the aims of the International Labour Organisation (ILO)—presently working as a specialised agency of the United Nations Organisations—which was created after the First World War, in 1919 through the Treaty of Versailles. Subsequently, when the defeated nations of the war began to challenge the validity and moral authority of this treaty itself on the ground that it had been imposed on them by the victorious nations, and the League of Nations—the Organisation which was created through the Treaty of Versailles for maintenance of world peace—began to get weakened, it was thought prudent to dissociate the International Labour Organisation with the treaty and the worldwide controversies raised because of it. It was wise indeed to do so. A Constitution was framed for the International Labour Organisation and it was reconstituted wedded to the cause of protecting the interests of the labour throughout the world.

As the basic aim of the International Labour Organisation is the betterment of labour by ensuring international cooperation for some minimum and uniform standards, the ultimate aim of abolition of child labour is not only consistent with its basic objectives and policies, it is an integral part of it. On this matter, a report[1] of the International Labour Conference has to state:

> "The abolition of child labour, one of the aims for which the International Labour Organisation was cresated, and the promotion of the well being of children in the fields within the ILO's competence have been the focal points of much of the Organisation's work throughout its existence".

Since the very beginning, the International Labour Organisation has been devoting its special attention to the various problems concerning child labour. It has been endeavouring for adoption and promulgation of measures by its member countries for providing the young persons and children, whether already in employment or seeking employment, with protection against exploitation, coercion, maltreatment and bondage. It has been forming conventions, making recommendations, or passing resolutions with this end in view. The member country has an obligation to adopt the International Labour Organisation's Conventions, but the recommendations are only the guide-lines for actions and are expected to be implemented progressive, whether in full or in parts.

In respect of children and young persons, the International Labour Organisation has adopted 18 conventions till recently, relating to the minimum age for their entrance into employment, the need for medical examination to ascertain their fitness to work and the imposition of ban or restrictions on taking night duty from them. In addition to these conventions, the International Labour Organisation has made nine sets of recommendations on these very subjects for the betterment of children and young persons.

The main provisions of the International Labour Organisation's Conventions and the position of India with regard to their ratification and implementation are stated herein below:

Minimum Age

The International Labour Organisation has so far adopted only ten conventions in respect to the minimum age for employment of children. There of them are confined to specified categories of work, while the other seven cover all other major sectors of economic activities.

The first convention on child labour was adopted by the International Labour Organisation in the very year of its inception and is known as the Minimum Age (Industry) Convention (No. 5) of 1919. According to this convention, children below 14 years of age should not be employed in any public or private industrial undertaking, other than the one in which only the family members may be employed. Under this convention, the term "Industrial Undertaking" includes mines, quarries, manufacturing industries, construction, maintenance and repair works, and the transportation of passengers or goods by road, rail or waterway. But, this convention does not apply to the work done by children in technical schools, provided or supervised by the prescribed public authority. However, for India, the convention contains an exclusive provision that children below 12 years should not be employed in manufacturing units driven by power and employing more than 10 persons; or the mines, quarries and other works for extraction of minerals; or in the transportation of passengers, goods or in jobs of handling goods at docks and quays, etc.

India has already ratified the Minimum Age (Industry) Convention (No. 5) and has fully implemented it.

The Convention No. 5 was partially revised by the Minimum Age (Industry) Convention (Revised) (No. 59), 1937, which raised the general minimum age for entry into employment in industrial establishments from 14 to 15 years. But, India, the convention continued to hold good the earlier provision that children below 12 years should not be employed or allowed to work in power-driven factories employing more than 10 persons. However, the minimum permissible age was raised to 13 years for employment in work connected with transportation of passengers or goods by rail and the handling of goods at docks, quays or wharves. Similarly, it was raised to 15 years for employment in mines and quarries, etc., and also for such occupations as have been specified in the Convention and 'scheduled' as dangerous or unhealthy by a competent authority. The Convention stipulates some more restrictions on the employment of children, for example, children between the age of 12 and 17 should not be employed in power-driven factories employing more than 10 persons without producing medical certificate of fitness for such employment. The same condition has been imposed on employment of children between 15 and 17 years of age in mines.

In India, the provisions relating to children and young persons as contained in the Factories Act, the Child Labour (Prohibition and Regulation) Act, the Motor Transport Workers Act, the Beedi and Cigar Workers (Conditions of Employment) Act and the Employment of Children Act (which was subsequently repeated by the Child Labour Act) do conform to those of the above mentioned Convention. However, the Mines Act falls short of it in as much as it does not provide for fitness certificate as stipulated by the Convention. Under this Act, such a certificate is only required for doing underground work in the mines. Consequently, India has not been able to ratify this Convention No. 59 because of the difficulties it finds itself faced with in amending the Mines Act due to variations in the nature of widely scattered mines and lack of effective system of medical examination.

In 1920, the International Labour Organisation had adopted another convention, namely, the Minimum Age (Sea) Convention (No. 7). It stipulates that no child below the age of 14 years should be allowed to work on any vessel except the one on which his family members may be employed. Vessels, under this Convention, include all public and private ships and boats of any nature whatsoever, engaged in maritime navigation, but it does not include ships of war. However, this prohibition does not cover also the work done by children on school ships or training ships, provided such work has the approval of, and is supervised by, the prescribed public authority. It also requires of every shipmaster to maintain a record, with relevant details, of all the persons below the age of 16 years employed on board.

India finds itself helpless in ratifying the Convention No. 7 also because, as a large number of Indian seamen are employed on foreign ships, it is felt that ratification by India would not be fruitful until the other countries also do not come around to ratify it.

In 1936, the International Labour Organisation revised the above mentioned Convention by the Minimum Age (Sea) Convention (Revised) (No. 58), raising thereby the minimum age for employment on vessels from 14 to 15 years. It also could not be ratified by India for the same reasons as given above.

In context of the agriculture sector, the International Labour Organisation had adopted the Minimum Age (Agriculture) Convention (No. 10) in 1921, which prohibited the employment of children below 14 years in public or private agricultural undertakings during the hours fixed for school attendance. Even if they are employed outside the school hours, it should not affect their attendance at school. Just as the other conventions, it also does not prohibit the work done by children in technical schools, provided such work is approved and supervised by some public authority. It does not contain any special provisions for India, and has also not been further revised so far. India could not ratify it also because of lack of resources which will be required for its implementation, as it related to a vast and unorganised field.

In the field of non-industrial sector, the International Labour Organisation had adopted a convention in 1932 which was known as the Minimum Age (Non-Industrial Employment) Convention (No. 33). It applied to any employment not dealt with in other Convention, that is, Nos. 5, 7 and 10, and laid down that children under the age of 14 years, or those over 14 years who were still required by the laws or regulations of the land to attend primary schools, should not be employed in any occupation to which the Convention applied. However, there were exceptions. It was not applicable to employment in sea-fishing, or work done in technical or professional school. In relation to India, the age for prohibition was below 10 years in place of 14 years with the exception that in the interests of art, science or education, the national laws or regulations, may, by permits granted in individual cases, allow children to appear in any public entertainment or film. It also had restricted the employment of children below 14 years of age in such non-industrial occupations which the competent authority may have declared to involve danger to life, health or morals. However, India did not ratify this Convention, and by this time it has been revised also.

The above revision took place in 1937 when the International Labour Organisation adopted a new convention, named as, the Minimum Age (Non-Industrial Employment) Convention (Revised) (No. 60), which also contains special provisions in relation to India, for example, that no child below 13 years of age should be employed in non-industrial establishments like shops, offices, hotels, restaurants, places of public entertainment and others referred to in this Convention. But, exceptions may be made in individual cases by the national laws and regulations in the interest of art, science or education. The revised Convention retains the provision that persons under 17 years of age should not be employed in any such occupation in a non-industrial establishment which the competent authority may declare to involve danger to life, health or morals. India has not ratified it as yet on the plea that the subject matter is primarily of the States' concern whose laws on shops and commercial establishments very with one another, and, therefore, a national consensus on the issues involved is called for.

The Minimum Age (Trimmers and Stokers) Convention (No. 15), 1921, lays down that young persons below 18 years of age should not be employed on vessels as trimmers or stokers. However, they can be allowed to work on school ships or training ships and on vessels mainly driven by means other than steam. India has ratified this Convention and its provisions have been implemented.

Regarding the minimum age for under-ground work in mines, the International Labour Organisation has adopted the Minimum Age (Under-ground Work) Convention

(No. 123), 1965, which states that minimum age of young persons for under-ground work in mines should be fixed in consultation with the organisations of employers and workmen, but in no case it should be less than 16 years. India ratified this convention in March, 1975.

The Minimum Age Convention (No. 138), 1973, also fixed the minimum age for entry into employment at 16 years but India has not been able to ratify this Convention as yet.

Here, it will be fruitful to mention two more Conventions adopted by the International Labour Organisation, which, though primarily deal with other subjects, contain provisions relating to minimum age for employment in certain specified occupations. One of them, the White Lead (Panting) Convention (No. 13), 1921, prohibits the employment of males under 18 and all females in the work of painting of an industrial nature involving the use of white lead, the sulphate of lead or any other product containing these pigments; and, the second one—the Radiation Protection Convention (No. 115), 1960—bans the employment of persons below 16 years of age in any work involving ionising radiations.

In addition to the above Conventions, the International Labour Conference has also adopted four recommendations solely in respect of fixation of minimum age for employment in different occupations, and two others containing specific provisions in respect to the same subject.

The Minimum Age (Non-Industrial Employment) Recommendation (No. 41), 1932, states the guidelines for member countries on application of the Minimum Age (Non-Industrial Employment) Convention (No. 33), 1932. This set of recommendations contains the examples of work which may be regarded as light work for making certain exceptions.

The other recommendation was adopted as a supplement to the Minimum Age (Industry) Convention (Revised) No. 59), 1937, and is known as the Minimum Age (Family Undertaking) Recommendation (No. 52) 1937. Through it the member countries have been called upon to make every effort to apply their minimum age legislations to all industrial undertakings, including the family undertakings.

The rest of the two recommendations on the subject are related to mines. The Minimum Age (Coal Mines) Recommendation, (No. 96), 1953, recommended prohibition of employment of children under 16 years of age in coal mines, but young persons between the age of 16 and 18 years may be employed under certain restrictive conditions. On the other hand, the Minimum Age (Under-ground Work) Recommendation, (No. 124), 1965, recommends that measures should be taken to raise the minimum age of employment in all mines and quarries to 18 years but, where the mining level may be low, it can be fixed at 16 years. It also recommends for adoption of measures to ensure the schooling of young persons falling below the minimum age prescribed for employment under-ground.

Besides, the Lead Poisoning (Women and Children) Recommendation (No. 4) recommends for the exclusion of women, and young persons under 18 years of age, from employment in certain processes, and calls for imposition of restrictions on their employment in certain others. Similarly, the Unemployment (Young Persons) Recommendation, (No. 45), 1935, has called upon the member countries to fix, as early as circumstances may permit, the minimum school leaving age for entry into employment but it should not be lower than 15 years.

Medical Examination

The International Labour Organisation has adopted a number of conventions for making the medical examination of young persons a condition precedent for entrance into employment.

The Medical Examination of Young Persons (Sea) Convention (No. 16), 1921, stipulates that no young person under 18 years of age shall be allowed to enter into employment on any vessel, other than the vessel on which only family members are employed, without a medical certificate of physical fitness by an authorised doctor. In case of continued employment of such a young person, the medical certificate of his physical fitness should be called for every year. India has ratified this Convention and its provisions are being fully implemented.

The Medical Examination (Sea Farers) Convention (No. 73), 1946, prohibits the entry of any person to whom the Convention applies, into employment on a vessel to which the Convention applies, without producing a medical certificate of his physical fitness for the given work. Every sea-faring commercial vessel, whether public or private, engaged in transportation of cargo or passengers, and registered in a territory to which this Convention applies, shall be treated as covered by this Convention. It has not been ratified by India in view of the fact that as the bulk of Indian seamen are employed on foreign ships, the ratification will be redundant.

The Medical Examination of Young Persons (Industry) Convention (No. 77) of 1946 requires that children and young persons under 18 years of age (16 years for India) should not be employed by any 'industrial undertaking' unless they have been found medically fit for the given work. Such a person should be put to medical test periodically till he attains the age of 18 years (16 years for India), but if the occupation involves high health hazards, till the age of 21 years (for India 19 years).

India had incorporated the provisions of this Convention in its Factories Act, 1948 and the Mines Act, 1952, except the provision for medical examination till 19 years of age.

The Medical Examination of Young Persons (Non-Industrial Occupation) Convention (No. 78), 1946, states that children and young persons below 18 years should not be allowed to work in occupations other than industrial, agricultural and maritime unless they have been found medically fit for the work in question. India has not been able to ratify this Convention because of its wide coverage.

The Medical Examination of Young Persons (Under-ground Work) Convention (No. 124), 1965, requires annual medical check-up of all young persons below the age of 21 years to ascertain their physical fitness for under-ground work in mines. But, in the Indian Mines Act, 1952, while incorporating the above provision, this age has been put at 18 years instead of 21 years.

Night Work

The International Labour Organisation is, in principle, against any night work being taken from children or young persons of tender age, on humanitarian and social grounds. In this connection it has adopted three Conventions. These are:

The Night Work of Young Persons (Industry) Convention (No. 6), 1919, prohibits children and young persons below 18 years of age from being employed during night hours in any public or private industrial undertaking. It has defined the term 'night' as a period of at least 11 consecutive hours, including an interval, between 10 p.m. and 5 a.m. The expression 'Industrial undertaking' includes manufacturing units, mines, quarries, construction work and transport. India has, fortunately, ratified this Convention.

The above Convention was partially revised by the Night Work of Young Persons (Industry) Convention (Revised) (No. 90) 1948, which has redefined 'night' as a consecutive period of at least 12 hours after sunset. It has also been made applicable to all industrial undertakings, such as, mines, quarries, manufacturing units, construction and repair work and transportation of passengers of goods by road or rail. For India, this Convention provides that the term 'industrial undertaking' shall mean to include only mines, factories, railways and ports, and that the prescribed age for young persons shall mean the age between 13 and 15 years India has ratified and implemented this Convention.

In the field of non-industrial sectors, the convention on the subject is the Night Work of Young Persons (Non-Industrial Occupations) Convention (No. 79), 1946, which prohibits night work by children and young persons employed for wages, or working directly or indirectly for gain, in non-industrial occupations. Under this Convention the term 'non-industrial occupation' includes all employments, except those specified by the competent authority, for industrial, agricultural or maritime purposes. In respect to India, it prohibits all sorts of employment during night hours, in non-industrial occupations, or children under 12 years of age who are eligible for full time or part time employment, children over 12 years of age who may or may not be subject to full time compulsory schooling, and of young persons between 12 and 15 years of age. Exceptions to the above may, however, be provided for by national laws or regulations for employment in public entertainments, or for working as actors or super numeraries in the making of films.

India has not ratified this Convention because it requires review at the national level of various State enactments relating to shops and commercial establishments.

Besides the above mentioned conventions and recommendations, the International Labour Organisation has adopted a number of resolutions relating to protection of children and young persons. The most important of them is the one of 1945 by which the International Labour Organisation has endeavoured to draw the attention towards the need of maintenance, health, education, employment, protection and general welfare of children and young persons.

India has been associated with the International Labour Organisation since its formation in 1919. Today, it is a permanent member of the Organisation, being one of the ten leading industrial countries of the world. Therefore, it has always tried to follow the standards set up by the International Labour Conferences despite of its poor economic conditions. The history of Indian Labour Legislation shows that there had been no labour statute worth the name upto 1919. All the major labour legislations had been enacted only after the birth of the International Labour Organisation. Even the Declaration of Philadelphia, adopted a the 26th Session of International Labour Conference held in May, 1944, had greatly influenced the drafting of the Indian Constitution. Moreover, India has ratified several Conventions adopted by the International Labour Organisation on child labour, though not all of them. An idea of its position regarding the ratification of the Conventions adopted by the International Labour Organisation so far can be had at a glance by Table 20.1

TABLE 20.1

Statement of India's Position with Regard to ILO's Conventions, and Ratification Thereof

Sl. No.	*No. of Conven-tion*	*Convention*	*Date of Ratification*	*Statutes which meet the requirements of Convention if any.*	*Reason for non-ratification, if any*
1	2	3	4	5	6
		Minimum Age—			
1.	5	(Industry) Convention, 1919	1955	Factories Act, Mines Act, Employment of Children Act (now repealed), Beedi and Cigar Workers (Conditions of Employment) Act, Motor Transport Workers Act, and Child Labour (Prohibition and Regulation) Act.	—
2.	7	(Sea) Convention, 1920	Not ratified.	—	Ratification will serve no useful purpose because most of the Indian seamen are employed on foreign ships.
3.	10	(Agriculture) Convention, 1921	-do-	—	Paucity of funds for implementation in vast unorganised areas.

1	2	3	4	5	6
4.	15	(Trimmers and (stokers) Convention, 1921	20.11.1922	Merchant Shipping Act.	—
5.	33	(Non-Industrial Employment) Convention, 1932	Not ratified	—	Ratification is open no more as a latter convention on the subject has come into force.
6.	58	(Sea) Convention, (Revised), 1937	-do-	—	Same as for Convention No. 7 (Sl. No. 2).
7.	59	(Industry) Convention (Revised), 1937	-do-	Factories Act, Employment of Children Act (now repeated), Beedi and Cigar Workers (Conditions of Employment) Act, Mines Act (only provides for underground work) and Child Labour (Prohibition and Regulation) Act.	Variations in the nature of wide spread mines and lack of effective system of medical examination.
8.	60	(Non-Industrial (Employment) Convention (Revised), 1937	-do-	—	Requires national consensus because of variations in States' Shops and Establishment Acts.
9.	123	(Under-ground Work) Convention, 1965	March, 1974	Mines Act,	—
10.	138	Min. Age Convention, 1973	Not ratified.	—	Due to prevailing economic condition.
		Medical Examination of Young Persons—			
11.	16	(Sea) Convention, 1921	20.11.1922	Merchant Shipping Act.	—
12.	73	(Sea Farers) Convention, 1946	Not ratified.	—	Same as for Convention No. 7 (Sl. No. 2).
13.	77	(Industry) Convention, 1946	-do-	Factories Act which fully satisfies the requirements.	Same as for Convention No. 59 (Sl. No. 7).
14.	78	(Non-Industrial occupations) Convention, 1946	-do-	—	Same as for Convention No. 10 (Sl. No. 3).
15.	124	(Under-ground work) Convention, 1965	-do-	—	Some legal deficiencies in the Mines Act. Ratification is possible only after their removal.
		Night Work of Young Persons—			

1	2	3	4	5	6
16.	6	(Industry) Convention, 1919	14.7.1921	Same as for Convention No. 5 (Sl. No. 1).	
17.	79	(Non-Industrial Occupation) Convention, 1946	Not ratified,	—	Same as for Convention No. 60 (Sl. No. 8).
18.	90	(Industry) Convention (Revised), 1948	—	Same as for Convention No. 5 (Sl. No. 1)	—

It would, thus, be obvious that though India could not go in for rigid standards through ratification of many of the International Labour Organisation's Conventions and adoption of its several recommendations and resolutions regarding child labour, and it could not prescribe through law some minimum universal age for employment in all occupations or the working conditions governing such employments, it has, nevertheless, imbibed the spirit and the principles behind those Conventions, etc., in its thinking which finds reflection in the formulation of its various legislative measures having a direct or indirect bearing on child labour.

NOTE

1. IV-1 Report of the 57th Session of the International Labour Conference, Geneva, 1972, p. 5.

21

THE INDIAN LEGAL UMBRELLA

Children are the future citizens of the country and therefore, it is on their proper brought up and training that the future of the country depends. In India, we are well aware of it and our law-makers have been trying to extend the legal umbrella of protection to poor and needy children who themselves cannot negotiate favourably the terms of their employment and are vulnerable to all sorts of exploitation because of their poverty, hunger and destitution.

Constitutional Provisions

Observations of the Whitley Commission and the Labour Investigation Committee of 1946, as well as the various statements of social reformers on the evils of child labour, which deprives the children of opportunities of education and good health, had vastly and deeply influenced the minds of the framers of our Constitution who had aimed at providing for socio-economic justice to children, the poor and the backward.

The preamble of our Constitution states:

"We, *The People of India,* having solemnly resolved to constitute India into a *Sovereign, Socialist, Secular, Democratic Republic* and to secure to all its citizens:

> *Justice,* Social, economic and political;
>
> *liberty* of thought, expression, belief, faith and worship;
>
> *Equality* of status and of opportunity; and to promote among them all
>
> *Fraternity* assuring the dignity of the individual, and the unity and integrity of the nation;"

Thus, the main aim of our Constitution is to secure justice, liberty, equality and fraternity for all the citizens, including children.

Article 15(3) of the Constitution lays down that "Nothing in this Article shall prevent the State from making any special provision for women and children." This clause constitutes an exception to the rule against discrimination. Thus, the State is unfettered to make provisions for free children, or to take all necessary and reasonable measures for prevention of their exploitation. In doing so, the State shall not be deemed to be contravening the provisions of Article 15.

The word 'for' has been used with 'women and children' in Article 15(3) of the Constitution to mean 'in favour of'. It is thus amply evident that the intention has been to safeguard the interests of women and children, which according to the framers of the Constitution, deserved protection. This view point was corroborated by judicial pronouncement in *Dhattatraya Motiram* vs. *State of Bombay,*[1] wherein Chagla C.J. of Bombay High Court had held that the state could discriminate in favour of women (and children) against men, but it could not discriminate in favour of men against women (and children). The words within brackets are mine).

Article 23 is also relevant for the present discussion. It states that traffic in human beings and 'begar' and other similar forms of forced labour are prohibited and any contravention thereof shall be treated as an offence punishable in accordance with law.

Thus, if a loan is extended on the condition that the debtor himself or one of his family members, including children, will work for him till the repayment of loan with interest, such an agreement will amount to contravention of Article 23 which prohibits 'begar'.

Again, if a custom makes it obligatory for every householder of a village to offer one day's free labor to the headman or mukhiya of the village, it will fall within the ambit of prohibited practices, being in contravention of Article 23.[2]

Further, if a person is forced to work against his will, no amount of compensation will be able to change its nature and convert it into something other than 'begar'. However, in *S. Vasudevan* vs. *S.D. Mittal,*[3] the Bombay High Court had held that what was prohibited by Clause (1) of Article 23 was imposing on the citizens forced labour, which was similar in form to 'begar'. In order to bring the case within the scope of Clause (1) of Article 23, it is necessary to show that a person was forced to work against his will and without payment. The Court further observed:[4]

> "... Every form of forced labour is not prohibited by... Clause (1) of Article 23. In fact, Clause (1) of Article 23 permits compulsory services for public purposes."

But, in a National Seminar, organised by the Aligarh Muslim University in February, 1989, one of the participants, Pro. S.C. Srivastava, expressed his disagreement with the above observation. According to him, "the extent to which the court's observation imply that Article 23 (1) permits some forms of forced labour, which 'forms' do not come within the purview of Article 23 (1) and are presumably, in addition to the forms covered by Article 23 (1), the observation must be rejected."[5]

As the above matter (*S. Vasudevan* vs. *S.D. Mittal*) does not appear to have reached the Supreme Court, we could not have the benefit of its verdict on the constitutional issues involved therein with regard to the interpretation and scope of Article 23.

However, there is no denying of fact that by now the Supreme Court has come up to be the guardian of the poor and weaker sections of the society, and as their protector from forced labour.

The Supreme Court has innovated new methods in the form of Public Interest Litigation to provide justice to the poor and weaker sections of the society who are denied basic rights and for whom liberty and freedom have no meaning.[6] Thus, the Supreme Court has assumed the role of the guardian of the weaker and poor sections of the country by becoming the court for the poor and struggling masses of the country.[7]

In *People Union for Democratic Rights* vs. *Union of India*[8] the Supreme Court not only created a history in the field of child labour laws but also played a role of the protector of the interests of the poverty ridden toiling masses of the society. The court has enlarged the scope of the legislations prohibiting 'traffic in human beings and forced labour' as laid down in Article 23 of the Constitution.

This case arose as a result of refusal of minimum wages to workmen engaged in construction work for the Asiad and non-enforcement of the Minimum Wages Act 1918, Equal Remuneration Act, 1976, Article 24 of the Constitution, Employment of Children Act, 1938 and the Contract Labour (Regulation and Abolition) Act, 1970. The Court's attention was not drawn in the usual form of a writ petition by the aggrieved workers, but a voluntary organisation had addressed a letter to Justice Bhagwati of the Supreme Court on the basis of the reports prepared by three social researchers after personal investigations and study.

The Supreme Court *inter alia* decided the issue as to what is the scope and meaning of the expression 'traffic in human beings' and 'begar' and other similar forms of forced labour, in view of Article 23. Bhagawati, J., observed:

> "What Article 23 prohibits is forced labour", that is, labour or service which a person is forced to provide, and 'force', which would make such labour or service 'forced labour', may arise in several ways. It may be physical force which may compel a person to provide labour or service to another or it may be force exerted through a legal provision, such as a provision for imprisonment or fine in case the employee fails to provide labour or service, or it may even be compulsion arising from hunger and poverty, want and destitution... The word 'force' must, therefore, be construed to include not only physical or legal force but also force arising from the compulsion of economic circumstances which leaves no choice or alternatives to a person in want and compels him to provide labour or services even though the remuneration received for it is less than the minimum wage."

The Court further added:

> "Where a person provides labour or service to another, remuneration for which is less than the minimum wage, the labour or service provided by him clearly falls

within the scope and ambit of the word 'forced labour' under Article 23. Such a person would be entitled to come to the court for enforcement of his fundamental right under Article 23 by asking the court to direct payments of the minimum wage to him so that the labour or service provided by him ceases to be 'forced labour' and the breach of Article 23 is remedied."[9]

The aforesaid observation was also followed in *Sanjit Ray* vs. *State of Rajasthan*[10] when a writ petition was filed by the Director of Social Work and Research Centre, a Social action group working in Tilonia village in Ajmer District of Rajasthan, to bring to the notice of the Supreme Court certain violations of the Minimum Wages Act, 1948. In the case Bhagwati, J. held:

> "Where a person provides labour or service to another for remuneration which is less than the minimum wage, the labour or service provided by him clearly falls within the scope and ambit of the word 'forced labour' and attracts the condemnation of Article 23."

The Supreme Court of India provided an umbrella of safeguards to the child labour employed in match industries of Sivakasi in *M.C. Mehta* vs. *State of Tamil Nadu.*[10a] The Court held that employment of children within the match factories directly connected with the manufacturing process up to final production of match sticks or fire works should not at all be permitted. However, the Supreme Court permitted the employment of children in the process of packing but packing should be done in an area away from the place of manufacture to avoid exposure to accident.

The Supreme Court of India has further stretched its protective arms against all the aspects of exploitation and made certain directions to the Central Government or the State Governments for identification, release and rehabilitation of bonded labour in *Bandhua Mukti Morcha* vs. *Union of India*[11] when miserable conditions of bonded labourers of stone quarries in Faridabad (Haryana) were brought to the notice of the Court by way of a letter. Bhagwati, J. observed:

> "When a complaint is made on behalf of workmen that they are held in bondage and are working and living in miserable conditions without any proper or adequate shelter over their heads, without any protection against sun and rain, without two square meals per day and with only dirty water from a nullah to drink, it is difficult to appreciate how such a complaint can be thrown out on the ground that it is not violative of the fundamental rights of the workmen. It is the fundamental right of every one in this country, assured under interpretation given to Article 21 by this Court in *Francies Mullin's Case*[12] to live with human dignity free from exploitation."

Again, in *Neeraja Chaudhary* vs. *State of Madhya Pradesh,*[13] the Supreme Court of India made directions not only for identification and release of bonded labour but also for their rehabilitation. The issue of rehabilitation of freed bonded labourers was raised before the court in this writ petition which was based upon a letter addressed to one of the judges of the Supreme Court by the petitioner who was a Civil Rights Correspondent of the Statesman, a leading newspaper. This letter was directed to be treated as a writ petition. The Supreme Court observed:[14]

> "It is not enough merely to identify and release bonded labourers but it is equally, perhaps more, important that after identification and release, they must be rehabilitated, because without rehabilitation, they would be driven by poverty, helplessness and despair into serfdom once again. Poverty and destitution are almost perennial features of Indian rural life for large numbers of unfortunate ill starred humans in this country and it would be nothing short of cruelty and heartlessness to identify and release bonded labourers merely to throw them at the mercy of the existing social and economic system which denies to them even the basic necessities of life, such as, food, shelter and clothing."

The Supreme Court, again, in *Mukesh Advani* vs. *State of Madhya Pradesh*[15] directed the Central Government to specify minimum wages for occupations in flag-stone mines as a first step against exploitation of workmen.

In a recent decision in *P. Sivaswamy* vs. *State of Andhra Pradesh,*[16] the Supreme Court took a serious note of the State Governments' failure to implement the provisions of the Bonded labour System (Abolition) Act, 1976, and the failure to provide effective rehabilitation of freed bonded labour.

Another Article in the protective umbrella of the Constitution is 24 which provides that, "No child below the age of 14 shall be employed to work in any factory or mine, or engaged in any other hazardous employment."

In the epoch-making judgement in the *People's Union for Democratic Rights* vs. *Union of India,*[17] the Supreme Court of India held that the employment of children below 14 years of age was, being hazardous, ultra virus of the Article 24 of the Constitution. The court took a serious note of the construction industry being kept out of the ambit of Employment of Children Act, 1938. In this judgement of Mr. Justice P.N. Bhagwati and Mr. Justice Bahrul Islam, it was observed:

> "... Construction industry does not find a place in the Schedule to the Employment of Children Act, 1938 and the prohibition enacted in Section 3, Sub-section (3) of that Act against the employment of a child who has not completed his fourteenth year cannot apply to employment in construction industry. This is a sad and deplorable omission which, we think, must be immediately set right by every State Government by amending the Schedule so as to include construction industry in it in exercise of the power conferred under section 3A of the Employment of Children Act, 1938."

The Court added:

> "... We have Article 24 of the Constitution which provides that no child below the age of 14 shall be employed to work in any factory or mine or engaged in any other hazardous employment. This is a constitutional prohibition which, even if not followed by appropriate legislation, must operate propriovigore and construction work being plainly and undoubtably a hazardous employment, it is clear that by reason of this constitutional prohibition, no child below the age of 14 years can be allowed to be engaged in construction work. There can, therefore, be no doubt that notwithstanding the absence of specification of construction industry in the Schedule to the Employment of Children At, 1938, no child below the age of 14 years can be employed in construction work and the Union of India as also every State Government must ensure that this constitutional mandate is not violated in any part of the country."

The aforesaid view was reiterated in *Labourers Working on Salal Hrdro-Project* vs. *State of Jammu and Kashmir*,[18] wherein the attention of the Supreme Court was drawn towards the denial of the benefits of the labour laws to workmen and non-enforcement of the Inter-state Mîgrant Workmen (Regulation of Employment and Condition of Service) Act, 1979, the Contract Labour (Regulation and Abolition) Act, 1970 and Article 24 of the Constitution.

In this case also, the action was not brought out by the aggrieved labourers working on Salal Hydro-Project, but by the People's Union for Democratic Rights by means of a letter to Mr. Justice D.A. Desai with a copy of the news item published in Indian Express dated August 26, 1982 carrying a report that a large number of migrated workmen from different States, including the State of Orissa, were working on the Hydro Electric Project in deplorable conditions and that they were denied the benefits of the labour laws. This letter was treated as a writ petition.

The Supreme court was, *inter alia,* called upon to decide the issue as to whether children under 14 years of age can be allowed to work in construction projects. The Court observed:

> "Construction work is a hazardous employment and no child below the age of 14 years can therefore be allowed to be employed in construction work by reason of the prohibition enacted in Article 24 and this Constitutional prohibition must be enforced by the Central Government."

Bhagwati, J., suggested:

> "The Central Government would do well to persuade the workmen to send their children to a nearby school and arrange not only for school fees to be paid but also provide, free of charge, books and other facilities, such as, transportation. We

would suggest that whenever the Central Government undertakes a construction project which is likely to last for some time, the Central Government should provide that children of construction workers, who are living at or near the project site, should be given facilities for schooling and this may be done either by the Central Government itself, or if the Central Government entrusts the project work or any part thereof to a contractor, necessary provision to this effect may be made in the contract with the contractor."

Again, the Supreme Court of India stretched its protective arms against exploitation in *Lakshmi Kant* vs. *Union of India*[19] wherein it laid down that the procedure which has been evolved by the High Courts of Bombay, Delhi and Gujarat is eminently desirable and it can help considerably to reduce, if not eliminate, the possibility of child being adopted by unsuitable or undesirable parents or being placed in a family where it may be neglected, maltreated or exploited by the adoptive parents.

A study of protection provided in the Constitution to children will not be conclusive without reference to the welfare provisions in relation to children under Part IV of the Constitution. This deals with the 'Directive Principles of State Policy'.

Article 39 of the Constitution provides that "the State shall, in particular, direct its policy towards securing:

(e) that the health and strength of workers, men and women, and the tender age of children are not abused and that citizens are not forced by economic necessity to enter avocations unsuited to their age or strength;

(f) that children are given opportunities and facilities to develop in a healthy manner and in conditions of freedom and dignity and childhood and youth are protected against exploitation and against moral and material abandonment."

Articles 41 of the Constitution provides that the "State shall, within the limits of its economic capacity and development, make effective provision for securing the right to work, to education and to public assistance in cases of unemployment, old age, sickness and disablement and in other cases of undeserved want."

Whereas Article 42 and 43 provide for securing just and humane conditions of work and hold a promise that the State shall endeavour to secure, by suitable legislation or economic organisation or in any other way, to all workers agricultural, industrial or otherwise, work, a living wage, conditions of work ensuring a decent standard of life and full enjoyment of leisure and social and cultural opportunities, etc.

Thus, the 'abuse' and 'exploitation' under Article 39 (e) and 39(f), respectively, show, that these Articles are wider in social context, than the Article 42. Article 42 relates only to working class. This Article will not cover the cases where a self-employed man takes the help of his family members, including children, for gainful activity because of economic compulsion. This problem can only be solved by a faster rate of economic growth and social justice.

Article 45 requires the State to endeavour to provide, within a period of ten years from the commencement of the Constitution, free and compulsory education for all children until they complete the age of fourteen years.

There is no doubt that the Articles in Part IV of the Constitution are not enforceable but they are still fundamental to governance of the country. When under Article 45 of the Constitution, the State has undertaken to provide compulsory education, it is a right which must be available to all on equal terms and cannot be denied to any body. The fact that the said right is not enforceable in courts ought not to make any difference.[20]

Legislative Enactments

As in many other fields of social justice and welfare, our Constitutional philosophy found concrete shape in our various legislative enactments in the field of child labour also.

Following are the enactments which either exclusively deal with, or contain provisions relating to, the child labour in India. These are:

(i) Children (Pledging of Labour) Act, 1933.
(ii) Minimum Wages Act, 1948, and the Rules made thereunder by the Central Government.
(iii) Factories Act, 1948.
(iv) Plantation Labour Act, 1951.
(v) Mines Act, 1952.
(vi) Merchant Shipping Act, 1951.
(vii) Motor Transport Workers Act, 1961.
(viii) Apprentices Act, 1961.
(ix) Atomic Energy Act, 1962.
(x) Beedi and Cigar Workers (Conditions of Employment) Act, 1966.
(xi) Child Labour (Prohibition and Regulation) Act, 1986.
(xii) Shops and Commercial Establishment Acts under different nomenclatures in various States.

Out of the above mentioned various Central Acts, two, namely, The Children (Pledging of Labour) Act, 1933, and The Apprentices Act, 1961, are related to employment in general. The Employment of Children Act, 1938, which was confined to certain specified employments, was repealed by The Child Labour (Prohibition and Regulation) Act, 1986. Though The Factories Act covers a wide range establishments, but even this Act cannot be said to be general law on child labour. The Plantation Labour Act, The Mines Act, The Merchant Shipping Act, Motor Transport Workers Act, The Atomic Energy Act and The Beedi and Cigar Workers (Conditions of Employment) Act are all the more narrower in their application. The Child Labour (Prohibition and Regulation) Act is applicable to certain specified employments. It either prohibits the employment of children in certain occupations or regulates the working conditions of children in other specified employment.

The main features of the different enactments are discussed briefly here-under:

The Children (Pledging of Labour) Act, 1933

Previously, the Act extended to the whole of India except Jammu and Kashmir, but since September 1. 1971, its application has been extended to Jammu and Kashmir also.[21]

Under this Act, 'child' means a person who has not completed his 15 years of age.[22]

Under this Act, any agreement by which a parent or guardian of child pledges its labour or services against consideration or the benefits to be received in lieu thereof, shall be null and void.[23]

However, any such agreement which is not detrimental to the child and has been made in consideration of any benefit, though other than reasonable wages, in lieu of the child's services, and is terminable at not more than a week's notice, shall not be deemed to be illegal under the Act.[24]

The penalty provided for breach of law is a fine upto Rs. 200 for the employer[25] and Rs. 50 for the parent.[26] Further, the employment of a child whose labour had already been pledged elsewhere has also been made an offence punishable with fine which may extend up to Rs. 200.[27]

The Minimum Wages Act, 1948

The Act extends to whole of India except the State of Jammu and Kashmir.[28] It provides for fixation of minimum rates of wages for employments specified in the Scheduled to the Act which can be enhanced through notification by the appropriate government.[29]

Under the Act, "Appropriate Government" means:

(i) in relation to any Scheduled employment carried on by or under the authority of the Central Government or a railway administration or in relation to a mine, oilfield or major port or any corporation established by a Central Act, the Central Government;

(ii) in relation to any other Scheduled employment, the State Government.[30]

According to this Act, 'child' means a person who has to completed his 14 years of age,[31] while 'adolescent' means a person who has completed his fourteenth year of age but has not completed his eighteenth year.[32] And, 'adult' means a person who has completed his eighteenth year of age.[33]

The Act does not contain any important prohibition in regulatory provisions applicable to child labour. But, it lays down that in fixing or revising minimum rates of wages, different minimum rates of wages may be fixed for adults, adolescents, children and apprentices.[34]

This Act empowers the Central Government to make rules for certain purposes, including the fixation of the 'normal working day'.[35] Rule 34 of the Minimum Wages (Central) Rules, 1950, made under this Act, provides, *inter alia,* that the number of hours which shall constitute a 'normal working day' in the case of child shall be 4½ hours. As a result of this, no child can be made to work for more than 4½ hours a day in the employments to which the present Act applies.

The Factories Act, 1947

This Act also excludes the state of Jammu and Kashmir from its jurisdiction.[36] The establishments employing 10 or more workers and using power, or 20 or more workers without using power are covered under this Act.[37]

According to this Act, 'child' means a person who has not completed the fourteenth year of age,[38] while a 'young person' means a person who is either a child or an adolescent.[39] An 'adolescent' is a person who has completed his fifteenth year but not the eighteenth year.[40] Thus 'young persons may be divided into three categories as given below:

(a) Persons who are under fourteen years of age;
(b) Person who are between 14 and 15 years of age; and
(b) Person who are between 15 and 18 years of age.

(a) *Persons under fourteen years:* The Act totally prohibits the employment in factories of persons who have not completed 14th year of age.[41]

In *Walker T. Ltd.* vs. *Martindale,*[42] it was held that the prohibition is absolute and not restricted to employment in one of the manufacturing processes. Thus, a child employed as a sweeper to clean the floor of a factory is in contravention of the provisions of the Act, even though he is not employed in any of the manufacturing processes.

The law courts have held that a child below 14 years of age cannot be taken into following employments:

(i) Sorting of groundnuts in a courtyard near the machinery room for decorating. *Ramanathan* vs. *K.E.*[43]
(ii) Plating straw in a workroom. (The mother was held liable to pay penalty because the benefits of employment of her 8 years old child went to her.)—*Beedon* vs. *Parrot.*[44]
(iii) Oiling of parts of machinery of the spinning mill during meal time.—*Prior* vs. *Slaithwaite Spinning Co.*[45]

(b) *Persons between 14 and 15 years:* The persons of this category can only be employed under certain conditions. These conditions are provided under Sections 68, 69 and 71 to 75 of the Act:

(i) Such a person should have a certificate of physical fitness for employment issued by a surgeon and should carry a token thereof.[46]

(ii) The certifying surgeon should follow procedure provided under Section 69 of the Act.

(iii) They should not work at night, that is, during twelve consecutive hours including the period from 10 p.m. to 6 a.m.[47]

(iv) They should not work for more than 4½ hours a day.[48]

(v) The working hours of the factory should be limited to two shifts.[49]

(vi) The shifts should not overlap.[50]

(vii) Each child has to be employed in one relay.[51]

(viii) The spread-over should not exceed five hours and should also not change except in 30 days.[52]

(ix) They should not be employed in two separate factories on the same day.[53]

(x) The employer should display a notice regarding the periods of work for such children.[54]

(xi) The manager of the factory should maintain a register in respect of such child workers.[55]

(xii) A child can be employed only for specified hours displayed through a notice and in accordance to the entries against his name in the register of child workers.[56]

The inspectors have been empowered by Section 75 of the Act to require any such person to go in for re-examination by a surgeon, and to prohibit his employment till then.

(c) *Persons between 15 and 18 years:* A person of this category can be employed as an adult provided he possesses a certificate of physical fitness issued by the certifying surgeon and carries with him a token of such certificate.[57] The adolescents below 17 years are not allowed to work at night.[58]

The Orissa High Court, in *Jhunjhunwalla* vs. *B.K. Patnaik,*[59] where the occupier of a glass factory was severely punished for employing 14 adolescents in the blowing section of the factory, which is a hazardous occupation, without any certificate of fitness as required under Sections 68 and 69 of the Factories Act, 1948, observed that the object of these statutory restrictions on the employment of young persons were made to prevent exploitation of young labourers and to provide for their safety.

The court further held that Section 69 deals with the procedure to be followed by the certifying surgeon when a young person is sent to him for medical examination. He has to decide whether a certificate of fitness should be issued to the young person to work in the factory as a child under Clause (a) of Section 69(2), or as an adult under Clause (b) of Section 69(2). Section 70(2) provides that if the certifying surgeon does not grant a certificate of fitness to a young person to work in a factory as 'an adult' that person shall be deemed to be ' child' for the purpose of the Act. By reading Sections 69 and 70 together, an inference may be drawn that if a young person is refused a certificate to work as an 'adult' by the certifying surgeon, the deeming provision, as contained in Sub-section (2) of Section 70, would automatically apply to him and he will get covered by the definition of 'child'. But, it is not so, because even a child who has completed his 14 years is prohibited by Section 68 from being employed in a factory unless he is granted a certificate of fitness by the certifying surgeon. The deeming provision is of no avail to him and he must present himself again before the certifying surgeon for the fitness certificate. Where thee was no evidence to show that in the instant case 14 workers were actually produced before the certifying surgeon by the petitioner (occupier), the court held that Sub-section (2) of Section 70 had no application and the petitioner was rightly convicted.[60]

Agains, in *Mechnitosh* vs. *First Brook Book Co.*[61] it was observed that it was the duty of the employer to ascertain through reasonable means that the applicant was of the requisite age and merely the statement of child about his age should not be treated as sufficient evidence of his age.

The Factories Act also provides that no young person should be allowed to clean, lubricate or adjust any part of a prime mover or transmission machinery in motion, or to clean, lubricate or adjust any part of any machine if the cleaning, lubrication or adjustment thereof would expose the young person to risk of injury from any moving part either of that machine or of any adjacent machinery.[62] The Act also lays down that no young person should work at any dangerous machine to which Section 23 applies, unless he has been fully instructed as to the risks involved and the precautions to be taken, and has received sufficient training in work at the machine, or is under adequate supervision of a person who has a thorough knowledge and experience of the machine.[63] The State of Uttar Pradesh, under special power, has declared power presses, other than the hydraulic milling machines used in the metal trades, guillotine machines, circular saws and platen-printing machines, as of a dangerous character.[64]

The Act further prohibits the employment of children in any such part of the factory for the job of pressing cotton in which a cotton opener is at work, except where the feed end of the cotton opener is in a room separated from the delivering end.[65]

The act empowers the State Governments to make rules prescribing the maximum weights which may be lifted by adolescents and children.[66]

Besides a weekly day of rest, every child-worker who has worked for a period of 240 days or more in a factory during a calendar year is entitled during the subsequent year for leave with wages at the rate of one day for eery 15 days of work as against every 20 days in the case of an adult worker.[67]

The Act also requires that there must be rest-shelters and canteens, etc. for all workers including children.[68]

The Act lays down penalty of imprisonment upto one month, or fine upto Rs. 50 or both for using a false certificate of fitness or a certificate granted to another person.[69] Parent or guardian shall also be liable to pay fine up to Rs. 50 for permitting double employment of a child.[70]

The penalty for employment of child in contravention of the provisions of Section 67 of the Factories Act, 1948, is imprisonment for a term which shall not be less than three months but which may extend to one year or with fine which shall not be less than ten thousand rupees but which may extend to twenty thousand rupees or with both. And the continuing offence shall be punishable with imprisonment for a term which shall not be less than six months but which may extend to two years.[71]

The Plantation Labour Act, 1951

The Act was enacted with the sole purpose of regulating the conditions of work in plantations and to provide welfare measures for them. This Act also extends to the whole of India except the State of Jammu and Kashmir.[72]

The Act covers all tea, coffee, rubber, cinchona and cardamory plantations, using areas of 10.117 hectares or more, in which 30 or more persons may be employed.[73]

The Act prohibits the employment of adolescent between 14 to 18 years of age without a certificate of fitness for employment issued by a surgeon.[74] Such certificates are valid only for one year.[75] The Act lays down penalty for using false certificate of fitness. The penalty being imprisonment which may extend to one month or fine or both.[76]

The Act makes the provision for education a responsibility of the employer and so is for the housing medical and recreational facilities.[77]

The Mines Act, 1952

The Act amended and consolidated the laws relating to the regulation of the working conditions of labour and safety of mines. This Act extends to the whole of India[87] and includes all excavations where any operation for the purpose of searching for or obtaining minerals is carried out.[79]

Under this Act, 'child' means a person who has not completed his fifteenth year.[80] This Act not only prohibits the employment of children in any part of a mine which is underground or in any open-cast working in which any mining operation is being carried on.[81]

An adolescent, a person between 16 years and 18 years of age, is allowed to work in any part of a mine which is underground, provided he has a certificate of physical fitness for working as an adult. However, no adolescent is allowed to work in any mine except between the hours 6 a.m. and 6 p.m. It means that he is not allowed to be employed between 10 p.m. and 5 a.m.[82] On the other hand, if and adolescent has no certificate of physical fitness, he may work in a mine above-ground for not more than 4½ hours a day, but shall not be employed between the hours 6 p.m. and 6 a.m.[83] The certificate of physical fitness is valid only for upto 12 months.[84] Like the Factories Act, the provisions of canteen, wholesome food and rest-shelters, etc., have also been made under this Act.[85]

The employer is liable to punishment of imprisonment upto 3 months, or with fine upto one thousand rupees, or with both, for contravening the provisions of the Act.[86] Double employment of young persons is also punishable.[87]

A person using a false certificate of fitness is punishable with imprisonment for a term which may extend upto one month, or with fine which may extend upto two thousand rupees, or with both.[88]

The penalty for employment of a child in contravention of the provisions of Section 40 of the Mines Act, 1952, is imprisonment for a term which shall not be less than three moths but which may extend upto one year, or with fine which shall not be less than ten thousand rupees but which may extend upto twenty thousand rupees, or with both. And the continuing offence shall be punishable with imprisonment for a term which shall not be less than six months, but which may extend upto two years.[89]

The Merchant Shipping Act, 1958

This Act applies to the ships registered in India. The provisions relating to young persons—persons who have not completed their 18th year of age—are contained in Sections 109 to 113 of the Act.

The Act prohibits the employment of children under fourteen[90] years of age, except:

(a) in a school ship, or training ship, in accordance with the prescribed conditions; or

(b) in a ship in which all persons employed are members of one family; or

(c) in a home-trade ship of less than two hundred tons gross; or

(d) where such a person is to be employed on nominal wages and will be in the charge of his father or some adult near male relative.[91]

However, children under 14 years are allowed to be employed as trimmers and stokers:

(i) in a school ship or training ship; or

(ii) in a ship which is mainly propelled otherwise than by steam.[92]

The Act also provides that where at any port, a trimmer or stoker is required for any ship, other than a coasting ship, and no person over eighteen years of age is available, two young persons over sixteen years of age may be engaged and carried to sea to do the work which would otherwise have been done by one person of over eighteen years of age.[93] Such persons, if employed, are required to produce a certificate of fitness.[94]

The Act also requires maintenance of a register of young persons employed in a ship.[95]

Further, the Act empowers the Government to make necessary rules in relation to the employment of young persons, as and when the occasion demands.[96]

The Act also imposes a fine upto rupees fifty on any person contravening the provisions of the Act.[97] However, the penalty for employment of a child in contravention of provisions of Sections 109 of the Merchant Shipping Act, 1958, is imprisonment for a term which shall not be less than three months but which may extend upto one year or with line which shall not be less than ten thousands rupees but which may extend upto twenty thousand rupees or with both. And the continuing offence shall be punishable with imprisonment for a term which shall not be less than six months, but which may extend upto two years.[98]

The Motor Transport Workers Act, 1961

The Act provides for the welfare of motor transport workers and seeks to regulate the conditions of their work. It applies to the whole of India[99] and covers every motor transport undertaking employing 5 or more transport workers. However, the State Governments are empowered to apply all or any of the provisions of the Act to any motor transport undertaking less than 5 workers.[100]

This Act prohibits the employment of children under fourteen[101] in any capacity in the motor transport undertaking.[102] An adolescent, that is, a person who has completed fourteen but not 18 years of age, is prohibited to work unless a certificate of fitness is granted to him.[103] The certificate of fitness will be valid only for 12 months.[104] The adolescent in not allowed to work for more than 6 hours a day, including a rest interval of half-an-hour, but cannot be employed between 10 p.m. to 6 a.m.[105]

The punishment for use of false certificate of fitness and for contravening the provision regarding employment of motor transport worker is also provided in the Act under Sections 30 and 31.

The penalty for employment of a child in contravention of provisions of Section 21 of the Act is imprisonment for a term which shall not be less than three months but which may extend upto one year, or with fine which shall not be less than ten thousand rupees but which may extend upto twenty thousand rupees, or with both. And the continuing offence shall be punishable with imprisonment for a term which shall not be less than six months, but which may extend upto two years.[106]

The Apprentices Act, 1961

The Act extends to the whole of India[107] and provides for the regulation and control of training of apprentices in trades and for matters connected therewith.[108]

According to the Act, no person shall be eligible for being engaged as an apprentice, or to undergo apprenticeship training in any designated trade unless he is atleast 14 years of age and satisfies such standards of education and physical fitness as may be prescribed.[109]

If he is a minor, a contract of apprenticeship has to be entered into by the guardian with the employer,[110] and it should be registered with the Apprenticeship Advisor.[111]

Rule 8 of Apprenticeship Rules, 1962, made under the Apprentices Act, 1961, provides that the weekly hours of work of an apprentice, while undergoing practical training, shall be as under:

(a) the total number of hours per week shall be 42 to 48, including the time spent on related instructions;

(b) apprentices undergoing basic training shall ordinarily work for 42 hours per week, including the time spent on the related instructions;

(c) apprentices during the second year of apprenticeship shall work for 42 to 45 hours per week, including the time spent on the related instructions;

(d) apprentices during the third and subsequent years of apprenticeship shall work for the same number of hours per week as the workers in trade in the establishment in which the apprentice is undergoing training, provided, however, that short-time apprentices may be engaged to work upto a timit of 48 hours a week.

The Atomic Energy, Act, 1962

The Act provides for development, control and use of atomic energy for the welfare of the people of India and for other peaceful purposes and for matters connected therewith.

The Central Government has made the Radiation Protection Rules, 1971, under Section 30 of this Act. Rules 5 of these Rules provides that a person below the age of 11 years cannot be employed as radiation worker, except with the prior permission in writing of the competent authority appointed under these Rules.

The Beedi and Cigar Workers (Conditions of Employment) Act, 1966

This Act also extends to the whole of India,[112] and provides that no child should be required or allowed to work in any industrial premises.[113] Under the Act, a 'child' means a person who has not completed his fourteen years of age.[114] The Act also prohibits the employment of young persons of 14 to 18 years between 7 p.m. and 6 a.m.[115]

The Act also defines the expression 'employee', so as to include any labour who is given raw material by an employer or a contractor for being made into beedi or cigar or both at home. A person who is not employed by an employer or a contractor, but who is working with the permission of, or under an agreement with, the employer or a contractor, also falls within this definition.[116]

The Supreme Court, in *M/s P.M. Patel and Sons* vs. *Union of India*[117] observed that the terms of the definition of 'employee' are wide. They include not only persons employed directly by the employer but also persons employed through a contractor. Moreover, they include not only persons employed in connection with the work of the factory. Accordingly, a home worker, by virtue of the fact that he rolls beedis, is involved in an activity connected with the work of the factory engaged in the task of rolling beedies. Therefore, the home worker rolling beedies is an employee under the Act.

The administration of the Beedi and Cigar Workers (Conditions of Employment) Act, 1966, rests with the State Governments, who appoint chief inspectors or inspectors for the purpose. The Act provides for contravention which may be imprisonment upto three months, or a fine upto Rs. 500 or both.[118]

The Act also contains provisions for the facilities of canteens,[119] first aid,[120] cleanliness,[121] and ventilation.[122]

The Child Labour (Prohibition and Regulation) Act, 1986

The Act was passed to prohibit the employment of children in certain employments and to regulate the conditions of work of children in certain other employments. The Act extends to the whole of India.[123]

Under this Act, 'child' means a person who has not completed his fourteenth year of age.[124] The Act prohibits the employment of children in specified occupations and processes. However, this prohibition is not applicable to any workshop wherein any process is carried on by the occupier with the aid of his family, or to any school established by, or receiving assistance or recognition, from the government.[125]

Prohibited occupations and processes have been enumerated in Parts A and B of the Schedule of the Act. The occupation enumerated in Part A of the Schedule are those connected with:

(i) Transport of passengers, goods or mail by railway;

(ii) Cinders picking, clearing of ash pits, or building operations in the railway premises;

(iii) Work in a catering establishment at a railway station, involving the movement of a vender, or any other employee of the establishment, from one platform to another, or into and out of a moving train;

(iv) Work relating to construction of a railway station or any other work or when such a work is done in close proximity to, or between, the railway lines; and

(v) A port authority within the limits of any port.

The Part B of the Schedule of the Act enlists the following processes:

(i) Bidi-making,

(ii) Carpet-weaving,

(iii) Cement manufacture, including the bagging of cement,

(iv) Cloth printing, dyeing and weaving,

(v) Manufacture of matches, explosive and fire works,

(vi) Mica cutting and splitting,

(vii) Shellac manufacture,

(viii) Soap manufacture,

(ix) Tanning,

(x) Wool-cleaning,

(xi) Building and construction industry.

The Act empowers the Central Government to add any occupation or process to the Schedule.[126] For purpose of addition and processes to the Schedule, the Central Government has been empowered to constitute a Child Labour Technical Advisory Committee, which should consist of a chairman and members not exceeding ten, to advise the Central Government on making additions to the Schedule.[127]

The Act regulates the working conditions of children in employment where they are not prohibited from working by Section 3 of the Act.[128] The hours and periods of work for such children are provided in Section 7 of the Act, which stipulates that no child shall work for more than three hours before he has had an interval for rest for at least one hour.[129] The period of work of a child shall be so arranged that, inclusive of his interval for rest and the time spent in waiting for work on any day, it shall not be spread over more than six hours.[130] The night work between 7 p.m. and 8 a.m.[131] and overtime[132] work are prohibited. The double employment of child has been banned.[133] The Act provides that the child employed in an establishment shall be allowed a holiday of one wholeday in each week.[134]

The inspector has been empowered to refer the matter for decision to the prescribed medical authority if a dispute arises between him and an occupier regarding the age of a child working in the establishment.[135]

The Act has imposed a duty upon every occupier to maintain a register in respect of children employed or permitted to work.[136]

The appropriate Governments are empowered to make rules for the health and safety of the children employed or permitted to work in any establishment or class of establishments. These rules may be regarding such matters as cleanliness, disposal of wastes, ventilation, dust, fighting, spittoons, protection of eyes, precautions against fire, etc.[137]

The Act lays down enhanced penalties for employment of children in violation of the provisions of Section 3 of this Act, Section 67 of the Factories Act, 1948, Section 40 of the Mines Act, 1952, Section 109 of the Merchant Shipping Act, 1958, and Section 21 of the Motor Transport Workers, Act, 1961.[138]

The punishment for violation of the above statutory provisions is imprisonment for a term which shall not be less than three months but which may extend to one year, or with fine which shall not be less than ten thousand rupees but which may extend to twenty thousand rupees, or with both. In case of a continuing offence, the punishment will be imprisonment for a term which shall not be less than six months but which may extend upto the years.[139]

The Act, repealed the Employment of Children Act, 1938.[140]

In order to obtain uniformity in the definition of 'child' in the related laws, the Act has amended the relative provisions of the Minimum Wages Act, 1948,[141] the Plantation Labour Act, 1951,[142] the Merchant Shipping Act, 1958[143] and the Motor Transport Workers Act, 1961.[144] As a result thereof, the expression 'child' now uniformally connotes a person who has not completed his fourteenth year of age.

The Shops and Establishments Acts

The Governments of various States and Union Territories have enacted their own Shops and Establishments Acts to regulate the conditions of work of employees, including child workers, in shops and commercial establishments. Time to time these Acts had been amended to meet the need of the situation. These provisions regulate the daily and weekly hours of work, rest intervals, payment of wages, overtime pay, holidays with pay, annual leave, employment of children and young persons, etc.

The minimum age of employment is 12 years in the States of Bihar, Goa, Gujarat, Jammu and Kashmir, Karnataka, Madhya Pradesh, Manipur, Orissa, Rajasthan, Tripura, Uttar Pradesh and West Bengal and in the Union Territory Chandigarh, Delhi and Pondicherry. Only in the State of Maharashtra the minimum prescribed age is 15 years.

The hours of work for young persons as fixed by various Shop and Commercial Establishments Acts of different States are seven hours a day in Andhra Pradesh, Bihar, Tamil Nadu, Tripura, West Bengal and Pondicherry; six hours a day in Gujarat, Jammu and Kashmir, Maharashtra, Uttar Pradesh, Karnataka, Madhya Pradesh, Orissa and Punjab; and three hours a day in Rajasthan.

All the States prohibit the employment of children and young person in shops and commercial establishments during night.

In the preceding pages, some of the important State Acts, which regulate the conditions of young persons employed in various establishments, had been discussed. The details of the provisions of different States Acts are given in Table 21.1

TABLE 21.1

State-wise Special Provisions for Time, Hours of Work, etc., for Young Persons Under The Shops and Commercial Establishments Acts

State/U.T.	*Age Definition*	*Permitted Employment*	*Hours of Work*		*Rest Interval*
			Per Day	*Per Week*	
1	2	3	4	5	6
Andhra Pradesh	14-17	6 a.m. to 7 p.m.	7	42	(Overtime work not allowed)
Bihar	12-18	7 a.m. to 7 p.m.	Children-5 Young Person-7	30 work	One hour after 4 hour
Gujarat	12-17	6 a.m. to 7 p.m.	6	—	½ an hour after 3 hours
J&K	12-18	7 a.m. to 9 p.m.	6	—	—
Karnataka	12-15	6 a.m. to 8 p.m.	6	6	—
Kerala	14-17	7 a.m. to 7 p.m.	—	—	—
Maharashtra	12-17	6 a.m. to 7 p.m.	6	—	—
Madhya Pradesh	12-17	7 a.m. to 9 p.m.	6	—	—
Orissa	12-15	Employment prohibited during night between 10 p.m. to 6 a.m.	5	—	—
Punjab	14-18	To be fixed by Government.	5	30	Half an hour after 3 hours
Rajasthan	12-15	Employment prohibited during night	3	—	—
Tamil Nadu	14-17	6 a.m. to 7 p.m.	7	42	—
U.P.	14-17	—	6	—	—
West Bengal	12-15	Not after 8 p.m.	7	40	1 hour after 4 hours work
Delhi	12-18	8 a.m. to 8 p.m. in winter and 7 a.m. to 9 p.m. in summer	6	—	½ an hour after 3½ hours work
Pondicherry	14-18	6 a.m. to 7 p.m.	7	42	one hour.

Source: Indian Labour Year Book, 1970, Labour Bureau, Shimla, 1973, p. 302.

A Comparative Study

The Indian laws relating to child labour mainly deal with following matters:

(i) Definition of child;

(ii) Minimum age of employment;

(iii) Medical examination;
(iv) Working hours.

Definition of Child

Under the following Acts, 'child' means a person who has not completed his fourteenth year of age:

(i) The Minimum Wages Act, 1948;
(ii) The Factories Act, 1948;
(iii) The Plantation Labour Act, 1951.
(iv) The Merchant Shipping Act, 1958;
(v) The Apprentices Act. 1961;
(vi) The Motor Transport Workers Act, 1961;
(vii) The Beedi and Cigar Workers (Conditions of Employment) Act, 1966; and
(viii) The Child Labour (Prohibition and Regulation) Act, 1986.

A 'child' under Children (Pledging of Labour) Act, 1933, and the Mines Act, 1952, means a person who has not completed his fifteenth year of age.

However, the definition of 'child' under various States' Shops and Establishments Acts varies from state to state. As it has already been shown, in some of the States a child is a person below the age of 12 years, in some other one who is below the age of 14 years, and in one State a person of less than 15 years of age.

Minimum Age of Employment

Under the following enactments, the minimum age of employment is fourteen years:

(i) The Factories Act, 1948;
(ii) The Plantation Labour Act, 1951;
(iii) The Apprentices, Act, 1961;
(iv) The Motor Transport Workers Act, 1961;
(v) The Beedi and Cigar Workers (Conditions of Employment) Act, 1966; and
(vi) The Child Labour (Prohibition and Regulation) Act. 1968.

The Children (Pledging of Labour) Act, 1933, prohibits the pledging of labour of children below 15 years.

Under the Factories Act, 1948, a 'child' (who has completed his fourteenth year) or an 'adolescent' (a person who has completed his fifteenth year but has not completed his eighteenth year) is permitted to work.[145]

The Mines Act specifies 16 years as the minimum age for a child to work underground, but an adolescent, who has completed his 15 years but not the 18th year, may be employed above ground in mines for certain specified hours.[146]

Whereas the Merchant Shipping Act lays down the minimum age of employment as 18 years, a lower age is permissible in respect of work specified in certain Sections.[147]

Rule 5 of the Radiation Protection Rules made under the Atomic Energy Act, 1962, prohibits the employment of a person below 18 years of age.

The minimum age limit under the Shops and commercial Establishments Acts of some of the States and Union Territories is 12 years, in some other States 14 years, but 15 years in the State of Maharashtra alone.

Medical Examination

Under the Factories Act, a certificate of fitness is required in respect of a "child' who has completed his 14th year of age and in respect of an adolescent, that is, a person between 15 and 18 years of age.[148]

However, under the Mines Act, no certificate is required for an 'adolescent' for working above-ground in a mine.[149] Medical certificate is required only for under-ground work in a mine.[150]

Under the Plantation Labour Act, a child or an adolescent may work after obtaining a certificate of fitness.[151]

Medical certificates are valid for twelve months under the following Acts:

(i) The Mines Act, under Section 41;
(ii) The Merchant Shipping Act, under Section 111 (3);
(iii) The Motor Workers Act, under Section 23 (2); and
(iv) The Plantation Labour Act, under Section 27 (2).

The following Acts also require renewal of medical certificates:

(i) The Plantation Labour Act, 1951;
(ii) The Mines Act, 1952; and
(iii) The Motor Transport Workers Act, 1961.

Working Hours

Under the Factories Act, children above 14 years are not allowed to work for more than 4½ hours a day, or during night hours (a period of at least twelve consecutive hours, which shall include an interval, between 10 p.m. and 6 a.m.).[152] Period of work has been limited to two shifts[153] and double employment has also been prohibited under the Act.[154]

The Minimum Wages (Central) Rules, 1950, made under the Minimum Wages Act, also restricts the working hours for children to 4½ hours as the maximum.

An adolescent under the Mines Act, 1952, if employed for above-ground work, shall not be allowed to work for more than 4½ hours a day, or during any time between 6 p.m. and 6 a.m.[155]

The Motor Transport Workers Act prohibits the adolescent from working for more than 6 hours a day, including rest interval of half an hour, and also prohibits work between 10 p.m. and 6 a.m.[156]

Similarly, the night work between 10 p.m. to 6 a.m. is prohibited for apprentice trainees under the Rules made under the Apprentices Act, 1961. The Beedi and Cigar Workers (Conditions of Employment) Act prohibits the employment of young persons during night between 7 p.m. to 6 a.m.[157] For them overtime work is also prohibited.[158]

Under the Plantation Labour Act, a child or an adolescent shall not be allowed to work for more than 40 hours a week.[159]

Under the Child Labour (Prohibition and Regulation) Act, 1916, no child is allowed to work for more than three hours before he has an interval for rest for at least one hour.[160] But, it shall not be spread over more than 6 hours, inclusive, of his interval for rest and the time spent in waiting for work.[161] Overtime work,[162] and night work between 7 p.m. and 8 a.m.[163] are prohibited under the Act.

The various States' Shops and Establishments Acts also prohibit the employment of child during night. However, the hours that constitute 'night' have been specified differently in different States.

At a glance, the working hours and the conditions of work for children and young persons under various enactments can be seen in Table 21.2.

TABLE 21.2

The Working Hours and Conditions for Children and Young Persons Under Different Acts

Act	*Age of Child (yrs.)*	*Age of Adolescent Young person (yrs.)*	*Minimum age for Employment*	*Permitted Employment*	*Night work*	*Overtime*	*Rest Interval*	*Spread over (Hrs.)*	*Max. Hours of work*		*Fitness Certificate*	*Validity period of fitness certificate*
									Daily (Hrs.)	*Weekly (Hrs.)*		
1	2	3	4	5	6	7	8	9	10	11	12	13
Children (Pledging of Labour) Act, 1933	15	—	—	—	—	—	—	—	—	—	—	—
Minimum Wages Act, 1948	14	14-15	14	—	—	—	—	—	4.1/2	—	—	—
Factories Act, 1948.	14	15-18	14	6 a.m. to 10 p.m.	Not allowed	Not allowed	1/2	5	5 in one shift	Not prescribed	Necessary	—
Plantation Labour Act, 1951.	14	15-18	14	—	Not allowed	Not allowed	1/2	5	6	40	Necessary	12 months
Miens Act, 1952	15	15-18	15-above ground 16-under ground	6 a.m. to 6 p.m.	Not allowed	Not allowed	1/2	5	5	Not prescribed	Necessary	12 months
Merchant Shipping Act, 1958.	14	14-18	18 (some time 15)	—	—	—	—	—	—	—	Necessary	12 months
Motor Transport Workers Act, 1961	14	15-18	15	6 a.m. to 10 p.m.	Not allowed	Not allowed	1/2	9	6	Not prescribed	Necessary	12 months
Apprentices Act, 1961.	14	—	14	6 a.m. to 10 p.m.	Not allowed	—	1/2	—	6	42.48	—	—

1	2	3	4	5	6	7	8	9	10	11	12	13
Atomic Energy Act, 1962 (Radiation Protection Rules), 1971.	—	—	18	—	—	—	—	—	—	—	—	—
Beedi and Cigar Workers (Conditions of Employment) Act, 1966.	14	14-18	14	7 a.m. to 7 p.m.	Not allowed	Not allowed	—	—	—	—	—	—
Child Labour (Prohibition and Regulation) Act, 1986.	14	—	14	8 a.m. to 7 p.m.	Not allowed	Not allowed	one	6	3	Not prescribed	—	—

NOTES

1. 55 BLR 323.
2. *Kahaosan Thangkhul* vs. *Simirei Shaili*, AIR 1961 Manipur 1.
3. AIR 1962 Bom. 53.
4. *Ibid.*
5. Srivastava, S.C., "Social Stratification and Protection of Bonded Labor in Nehru and Post Nehru Era", presented in National Seminar on 'Nehru: Law and Social Change' organised by Aligarh Muslim University on Feb. 25-27, 1989.
6. *S.P. Gupta* vs. *Union of India*, AIR 1982 SC 149.
7. *People's Union for Democratic Rights* vs. *Union of India*, AIR 1982 SC 1473.
8. AIR 1982 SC 1473.
9. *Ibid.*
10. AIR 1983 SC 328.

10A. AIR 1991 SC 417.

11. AIR 1982 SC 802.
12. AIR 1980 SC 849.
13. AIR 1982 SC 1099.
14. *Ibid.*
15. Air 1985 SC 1363.
16. 1988 Lab. IC 1680.
17. AIR 1982 SC 1473.
18. AIR 1984 SC 177.
19. AIR 1984 SC 469.
20. Mr. Justice E.S. Venkataramaiah's inaugural address at the Workshop on 'Child and Law' organised by the Delhi School of Social Work, University of Delhi, May 21-26, 1984.
21. The Children (Pledging of Labour) Act, 1933, Sec. 1(2).
22. *Ibid.*
23. *Ibid.*, Sec. 3.
24. *Ibid.*, Sec. 2.
25. *Ibid.*, Sec. 5.
26. *Ibid.*, Sec. 4.
27. *Ibid.*, Sec. 6.
28. The Minimum Wages Act, 1948, Sec. 1(2).
29. *Ibid.*, Sec. 27.
30. *Ibid.*, Sec. 2(b).
31. *Ibid.*, Sec. 2(bb).
32. *Ibid.*, Sec. 2(a).
33. *Ibid.*, Sec. 2(aa).

34. *Ibid.*, Sec. 3(3) (a).
35. *Ibid.*, Sec. 30(1) (g) read with Sec. 13.
36. The Factories Act, 1948, Sec. 1(2).
37. *Ibid.*, Sec. 2(m).
38. *Ibid.*, Sec. 2(c).
39. *Ibid.*, Sec. 2(d).
40. *Ibid.*, Sec. 2(b).
41. *Ibid.*, Sec. 67.
42. (1916) 85 JLKB 1543.
43. AIR 1927 Mad. 435.
44. (1871) LRQB 718.
45. (1898) IQB 881.
46. The Factories Act, 1948, Sec. 68.
47. *Ibid.*, Sec. 71(1) (b).
48. The Factories Act, 1948, Sec. 71(1) (a).
49. *Ibid.*, Sec. 71(2).
50. *Ibid.*
51. *Ibid.*
52. *Ibid.*
53. *Ibid.*, Sec. 71(4).
54. *Ibid.*, Sec. 72.
55. *Ibid.*, Sec. 73.
56. *Ibid.*, Sec. 74.
57. *Ibid.*, Sec. 68.
58. *Ibid.*, Sec. 70.
59. II LL J Orissa 551 (1964).
60. *Ibid.*
61. (1904) 34 CLT 370.
62. The Factories Act, 1948, Sec. 22(2).
63. *Ibid.*, Sec. 23.
64. U.P. Factories Rules, 1950, Rule 54.
65. The Factories Act, 1948, Sec. 27.
66. *Ibid.*, Sec. 34(2).
67. *Ibid.*, Sec. 79.
68. *Ibid.*, Chapter V.
69. *Ibid.*, Sec. 98.
70. *Ibid.*, Sec. 99.
71. The Child Labour (Prohibition and Regulation) Act, 1986, Sec. 15 read with Sec. 14.

72. The Plantation Labour Act, 1951, Sec. 1(2).
73. The Plantation Labour Act, 1951, Sec. 1(4).
74. *Ibid.*, Sec. 26.
75. *Ibid.*, Sec. 27(2).
76. *Ibid.*, Sec. 34.
77. *Ibid.*, Sections 5, 6 and 7.
78. The Mines Act, 1952, Sec. 1(2).
79. *Ibid.*, Sec. 2(j).
80. *Ibid.*, Sec. 2(e).
81. *Ibid.*, Sec. 45(1).
82. *Ibid.*, Sec. 49(1) and (2).
83. *Ibid.*, Sec. 44.
84. *Ibid.*, Sec. 41(1).
85. *Ibid.*, Chapter V.
86. *Ibid.*, Sec. 73.
87. *Ibid.*, Sec. 68.
88. *Ibid.*, Sec. 65.
89. The Child Labour (Prohibition and Regulation) Act, 1986, Sec. 15 read with Sec. 14.
90. Substituted for 'fifteen' by the Child Labour (Prohibition and Regulation) Act, 1986, Sec. 25.
91. The Merchant Shipping Act, 1958, Sec. 109.
92. *Ibid.*, Sec. 110.
93. *Ibid.*, Sec. 110(3).
94. *Ibid.*, Sec. 111.
95. *Ibid.*, Sec. 112.
96. *Ibid.*, Sec. 113.
97. *Ibid.* Sec. 436(2).
98. The Child Labour (Prohibition and Regulation) Act, 1986, Sec. 15 read with Sec. 14.
99. The Motor Transport Workers Act, 1961, Sec. 1(2).
100. *Ibid.*, Sec. 1(4).
101. Substituted for 'fifteen' by the Child Labour (Prohibition and Regulation) Act, 1986, Sec. 26.
102. The Motor Transport Workers Act, 1961, Sec. 21.
103. *Ibid.*, Sec. 22.
104. *Ibid.*, Sec. 23(2).
105. *Ibid.*, Sec. 14.
106. The Child Labour (Prohibition and Regulation) Act, 1986, Sec. 15 read with Sec. 14.
107. The Apprentices Act, 1961, Sec. 1(2).
108. *Ibid.*, Preamble.
109. *Ibid.*, Sec. 3.

110. *Ibid.*, Sec. 4(a).
111. *Ibid.*, Sec. 4(6).
112. The Beedi and Cigar Workers (Conditions of Employment) Act, 1966, Sec. 1(2).
113. *Ibid.*, Sec. 24(b).
114. *Ibid.*, Sec. 2(b).
115. *Ibid.*, Sec. 25.
116. *Ibid.*, Sec. 2(f).
117. AIR 1987 SC 447.
118. The Beedi and Cigar Workers (Conditions of Employment) Act, 1966, Sec. 32.
119. *Ibid.*, Sec. 16.
120. *Ibid.*, Sec. 15.
121. The Beedi and Cigar Workers (Conditions of Employment) Act, 1966, Sec. 8.
122. *Ibid.*, Sec. 2(II).
123. The Child Labour (Prohibition and Regulation) Act, 1986, Sec. 1(2).
124. *Ibid.*, Sec. 2 (II).
125. *Ibid.*, Sec. 3.
126. *Ibid.*, Sec. 4.
127. *Ibid.*, Sec. 5.
128. *Ibid.*, Sec. 6.
129. *Ibid.*, Sec. 7(2).
130. *Ibid.*, Sec. 7(3).
131. *Ibid.*, Sec. 7(4).
132. *Ibid.*, Sec. 7(5).
133. *Ibid.*, Sec. 7(6).
134. *Ibid.*, Sec. 8.
135. *Ibid.*, Sec. 10.
136. *Ibid.*, Sec. 11.
137. *Ibid.*, Sec. 13.
138. *Ibid.*, Sec. 15.
139. *Ibid.*, Sec. 14.
140. *Ibid.*, Sec. 22.
141. *Ibid.*, Sec. 23.
142. *Ibid.*, Sec. 24.
143. *Ibid.*, Sec. 25.
144. *Ibid.*, Sec. 26.
145. The Factories Act, 1948, See, 68.
146. The Mines Act, 1952, Sec. 44.
147. The Merchant Shipping Act. 1958, Sec. 109.

148. The Factories Act, 1948. Sections 68 and 70.
149. The Mines Act, 1982, Sec. 44.
150. *Ibid.*, Sec. 40(2).
151. The Plantation Labour Act, 1951, Sec. 26.
152. The Factories Act, 1941, Sec. 71.
153. *Ibid.*, Sec. 71(2).
154. *Ibid.*, Sec. 71(4).
155. The Mines Act, 1952, Sec. 44(1).
156. The Motor Transport Workers Act, 1961, Sec. 14.
157. The Beedi and Cigar Workers (Conditions of Employment) Act, 1966, Sec. 25.
158. *Ibid.*, Proviso to Sec. 17.
159. The Plantation Labour Act, 1951, Sec. 19.
160. The Child Labour (Prohibition and Regulation) Act, 1986, Sec. 7(2).
161. *Ibid.*, Sec. 7(3).
162. *Ibid.*, Sec. 7(5).
163. *Ibid.*, Sec. 7(4).

22

HISTORICAL PERSPECTIVE OF CHILD LABOUR

I. PRELUDE

The prevalence of child labour has been more or less in all periods of time, though varied in its nature and dimension, depending on the existing socio-economic structure of society.[1] In the past, child labour has been a part of the social organisation in which all members poled their labour to produce for the subsistence and survival.[2] This was particularly true of rural subsistence arming where the work of the child formed part of the labour necessary for the reproduction of the system and value of labour taken as part of child's socialisation for reproduction of labour power.[3] Child labour in the different periods has a chequred history and presents a vivid account of child's sad plight. It may be discussed under the following heads:

II. CHILD LABOUR IN ANCIENT INDIA

Though there is little evidence of the employment of children for wages, but if child slavery could be regarded as that, the existence on child labour in ancient India, can not be denied. Slaves of tender ages, often less than eight years of age, were owned for doing low and ignoble work. Children of slaves were born as slaves, lived as slaves and died also as slaves unless the master was pleased to monument them. It has been noticed that almost all the law-givers, with the solitary exception of Kautilya, were silent on this point, and did little to abolish this inhuman practice of keeping child slaves.[4]

As regard child labour in ancient India, it can be said that it existed in the form of child slaves. Child slaves could be purchased or sold like commodities. While dealing with slavery Kautilya stated that the purchase or sale of children as slaves was not forbidden amongst the Mlechches for they were backward and savage but an Aryan child could not in no case be allowed to remain a slave. In case a child born of an Arya (not of a slave) was sold or purchased or pledged with some one, both the parties to the deal were punished, even the witnesses to it were not spared punishment;[5] they were awarded various degrees of punishment.

Probably Kautilya also realised that slave children were not much different from Arya children and that they were not physically fit,[6] to carry out the ignoble duties of the slaves and that allowing the sale or purchase of slave children of less than 8 years of age would tantamount to inhumanity. Inspired by such feelings, he prohibited the purchase or sale of slave children of less than 8 years of age. This is how Kautilya sought to do away with the butchery of childhood which may have been rampant prior to his days. Though Kautilya had forbidden taking of ignoble and low work from slave children yet the treatment meted to them could not be discribed as exemplary, for freedom and equality of opportunity were often denied to them.[7]

According to Maine in the earliest period of history the Patriarchal system was in existence in all societies belonging to Indo-European stock, the Romans and the Hindus. As such the eldest male parent — the eldest ascendant—was absolutely supreme in his household. He had completely sway-over all the persons: male, female children, their property, cattle, slaves, etc. The flocks slaves and herds of the children were that of the father Law to them was parent's word.[8]

To some extent, parents obligations were very often involved in working for the landlord on such low wages that ti created conditions for the child to work on the farmer of wages and after remained as bonded labour in the landlords's house along with the parents to repay or to minimise the debt.[9] Children, however, helped their parents in house-hold activities and family crafts. They learnt the skills by observing and participating in such activities. A predominantly rural society is inevitable characterised by small and marginal economic units.[10]

In the age of Mauryas, the State had a monopoly in a number of industries and most of them were nationalised industries. Since state was a major participant in the economic and industrial activities, Kautilya prescribed standard wages for all types of workers.[11] The proper wages weaving cotton cloth was the equivalent money worth of cotton. The wages for weaving silken or woolen clothes were equal to one and half time and twice the value of silk and wool, respectively. Wages were payable according to time and work and according to contract, wages should be settled upon before the work was actually begun. If the workers failed to perform the allotted work at the time and place desired by the employer, nothing was payable to him. Workers could be made to work on holidays by payment of special wages. Cowherds and agricultural labourers were paid fixed wages. Kautilya did not favour the employment of children.[12] Inspite of that there was employment of children in agriculture and domestic service.

The labourers were not always entitled to a square meal and sometimes the diet actually varied according to labour. Wages paid in cash or kind were of a very low standard, the rates of share of profit were standardised by experts of the crop for the cultivator, of butter for the herdman, of the sale of proceeds for the herdman, of the sale of proceeds for the pedlar.[13] Labour legislation of the Dharmashastras shows that public conscience was not alive to the fundamental inequality in distribution of wealth because these protective laws were themselves derived form ancient tradition. The economic status of the slaves, hired labourers and unskilled workers was worse.[14] The same was the position of child when he was engaged in agricultural sector. It is revealed that child labour in ancient India was very common and could be witnessed in different occupations where they were engaged by the rich landlords to carry out activities directly or indirectly related to their agriculture sector.

III. CHILD LABOUR IN MEDIEVAL PERIOD

India, through its medieval period, was no exception. Increasing pressure on land led to fragmentation of holdings. Growing families had to look beyond personal cultivation for subsistence. A class of landless labourers came into existence, often bonded to the large landwoners. These labourers used their children to help in their economic activities. The rural artisan rarely worked alone. In fact, the entire family was a work unit with the 'peter familia' being the master craftsman. Occupations were determined largely on the basis of heredity and children were introduced to their traditional craft at a young age.[15]

Under the Mugul a labourer had no free will of his own. There was no difference between him and the commodities he produced. When ordered to move, he must move, and when ordered to stay he must stay. As to the work he might be, called upon to do, whatsoever the nature of the work might be, he had to do it. Remuneration was on the good old principle of giving as much to the labourer as would enable him to do the work and to keep him alive. It may be thought that the condition of labour were no better than slavery. It is revealed that there was a distinct and separate class of slavery of which we get frequent evidence in the Ain-i-Akbari, Bernier is Travels, etc. The difference between the two was this: Labourers could not be sold while slaves could be mortgaged and sold of as if they were a part of the movable property.[16]

The labour market was composed of labourers and of slaves. Slavery was the order of the day. Akbar freeing the slaves by not calling them Gulam (slaves) but calling them Chelas (disciples) did not in the least improve the lot of Chelas. In the decree of Akbar of 1594 A.D. It was laid down that, "A father or a mother might, if forced by hunger and extreme misery, sell their child, and afterwards when they had the means to pay, might buy it back again form servitude.[17]

Akbar realised the extremes to which a man may be forced and instead of trying to remove the cause (which affected his empire and incidentally his claim to greatness) responsible for several famines during his reign when cannibalism was practised near his capital, he mainly suggested hypothecation of children.[18]

In the province of Sylhet, which is a dependency of Bengal, it was the custom for the people of those parts to make eunuch of some of their sons and gives them to the Governor in place of revenue (mal-wajibi). This custom by degrees had been adopted in the provinces, and every year some children were thus ruined and cut-off from procreation. This practice had become common. At that time Jehangir issued an order that hereafter no one should follow this abominable custom, and that the traffic in young eunuch should be completely done away with.[19]

The position of child labour during the period of Jahangir did not improve at all. The supply of the child labour was more than demand and the demands was restricted mainly to the capital. Labourers could be taken by force and paid what ever the master liked to pay. In case the labourers objected which he would not do—there was corula (a whip of twisted card about a fathom long with a handle of about a cubit) to bring him to his senses.[20] there is not the slightest doubt that slavery was encouraged by the King and his Omrahs for two reasons, first, slaves—including eunuch slave girls, and concubines—met a real demand which then existed, and, second, the king enjoyed the monopoly of slaves. He made some money by traffic in slaves—and was himself royally served.[21]

Very ably Pelsaert sums up labour in *"Jehangir's India."* He says, "... a workman's children can follow no occupation other than that of their father, nor can they inter-marry with any other caste...." There were three classes of the people who are indeed normally free, but whose status differs very little form voluntary slavery—workmen, peons or servants, and shopkeepers.[22]

In the late 17th century the most significant change was the growth of organisations involving the employment of large number of artisans. The Dutch silk factory at Kasimbazar in Bengal, employed 700-800 weavers. But the characteristic unit of production was still the same unit. "The persistent dominance of family-based work units indicates that any disciplined organisation of an industrial society was not in sight."[23]

To sum-up, child labour in medieval India remained in existence on a large scale and even the rulers encourage it with an intention to make only traffic in child slaves. The child labour was found in the form of child slavery and rulers did not endeavour to weed out this practice and hence the result was that child was always exploited for this selfish ends.

IV. CHILD LABOUR IN MODERN ERA

Children have always been used in economic activities. In precapitalist societies including India, children had been employed in guild and in trade occupations. In these societies their workplace was an existension of the home and work relationship were informal relationship. The child grew up and found work within the family environment where the child was not given hazardous and difficult task. Work was a central aspects of their socialisation and training.[24] This conception, however, underwent a dynamic change with the advent of capitalism in the industrialisation during the 18th century and child labour began to be designated as a social problem.[25] the new economic forces unleashed by capitalism destroyed the family-based economy, a large number of labourers were displaced due to mechanisation of agriculture—the farmers were alienated form their home-based work place. They became wage-earning labourers. Extreme poverty made possible a situation in which the child had to be introduced in the labour market, lack of alternative employment of adults and lack of education for children reinforcing this process.[26]

This uneven development of industrialisation gave a new turn to the history of mankind and brought a change in the overall socio-economic order. Family-based economy continued to be destroyed and large number of people became wage-earning labourers and, as a result, the children were in a situation where they had to earn wages for themselves as well as for their families. The work-place was separated from the family environment and work now exposed the child to unhealthy environment. The hours of working started form morning to night but the earning remained quite meagre. The child's ability to grow and develop into a mentally and physically sound adult was severely restricted.[27] Further, the absence of any sponsored scheme of family allowances to enable poor parents to secure for their children an dequate and balanced diet and living conditions has also forced them to join the industrial establishments. Besides there was no compulsion on their part to get education upto a certain age limit and thus the children were left free to accept certain occupations even at tender age.[28]

Near the middle of 19th century, the mechanised large scale production came into existence. That time, state regulations were lacking over the conditions of employees in any industry. The employers were free to bargain with labour. Therefore, the labour in this country was exploited by the employers for their benefits. Many children were employed in cotton and jute mills and coal mines. They were even employed for underground work. With the advent of factory organisation, some public attention was drawn towards the existing evils of child labour in spite of active opposition for the employers.

First, protective legislation for child labour was enacted in 1881. This Act provided some protection of the children firstly forbidding employment of children under seven years of age in factories and also in two separate factories on same day, secondly, by limiting their working hours to nine hours a day and thirdly, by making it compulsory that four holidays in a month and rest intervals should be given to them. In addition, the Act made the provisions for safety such as fencing of dangerous machines.

However, this Act covered only factories employing 100 or more persons. The evils continued due to the lack of enforcement machinery. In addition to these defects, the coverage was quite inadequate as it did not pay any attention to the agriculture and unorganised sectors of industries. The result of this was that child labour continued as a means of cheap labour.

In 1891, the Indian Factories Act was enacted on the recommendations of a factory commission which was appointed by the government of India in 1890. This step was an advance over the Act of 1881. Under the Act, of 1891, the lower age was extended from 7 to 9 years. The upper age also exceeded from 12 to 14. Working hours were reduced from 9 to 7 hours per day. The children were not allowed to work at night. However, the exploitation increased because the attention was not paid due to the provisions of the Act due to the inadequate enforcing machinery.

Children's position in mines was also not different. Their condition was very bad. In 1901, about 5000 children were those child workers who had not completed their 12 years. In 1901, Mines Act was passed, which prohibited the employment of children under 12 years of age. The Chief Inspector of mine was empowered by the Act, to prohibit the employment of children to certain place, if he was satisfied that the employment conditions were dangerous to children's health and safety. This defective position continued because no improvement was made to the provisions of this Act till the next Mines Act.

Soon, the employers started work in factories for whole day and night, because they started to use electric power in their factories. In addition to this factor, the plaque which probe out for the first time in the industrial towns, also compelled the workers not to surrender to the old conditions of work. This position continued as there was no improvement inside the factories. But ultimately government felt that it was impossible to leave the matter in the hands of employers. It, therefore, appointed the Freer Smith Committee in 1906 and a factory Labour Commission in 1907 to make inquiries on labour conditions in factories. Thereafter, a New Factory Bill was introduced in 1909 which was enacted into law in 1911.

The Factories Act of 1911 reduced the working hours of children in factories to 6 hours a day. The Act further provided that all child workers should have in procession a certificate of age and fitness for employment. The children were not allowed to work at night, i.e., between 7 p.m. and 5.30 a.m. and they were also prohibited to work in certain dangerous process.

The next step in the history of child labour law was the Indian Factories (Amendment) Act of 1922 which was enacted to give effect to the International Labour Conventions on the minimum age for admission of children into employment, hours of work and night work of young persons and women. The scope of factory was extended to cover any premises where 20 or more persons were employed and mechanical power was used. The local Governments were empowered to extend the provisions to any premises where 10 or more persons were employed. For the purpose of this Act, child has been defined as a person who had not completed his 15 years of age. The children under 12 years were prohibited to enter into labour market. The children were required by this Act, to have a medical certificate as to their age and physical fitness for the employment. This working hours were fixed by this Act to 6 hours a day with an interval of half an hour to the children employed for more than 5½ hours. The inspectors were empowered to enquire form children a certificate of re-examination for continuing work. This Act also prohibited the employment of women and young person under 18 in certain processes. Some minor changes in this Act were introduced by an amendment in 1923.

The existing law in the area of mines was considered as inadequate and a new Mines Act was enacted in 1923 to give effect to the hours of work conventions of International Labour Organisation. This Act fixed the working hours for above ground work at 60 hours in a week, and for underground at 54 hours a week. This Act raised the minimum employment age from 12 to 13 years. Three years later the Indian Factories Act of 1911 was further amended in 1926 for some administrative purpose. After two years the mines Act, 1923 was amended for regulating the hours and working condition in mines.

Again, in 1931, the Indian Factories Act was further amended. This Act imposes certain penalties on the parents and guardians for allowing their children to work in two separate factories on the same day. Provincial governments were empowered under this Act, to make certain regulation of taking precautions against fire. In the same year the Indian Ports (Amendment) Act, 1931, provided a minimum age of 12 years for the employment of children in the handling of goods in ports. The year 1931, was also important in the Indian Legal History because in this year the report of Royal Commission on Labour was published. This commission was appointed under the compulsion of intensive agitation to improve the condition of labour, to investigate and report on the existing condition of labour in industrial undertaking and plantations, and on the health and standard of living of workers in British India. This Commission found that the children as young as five years were employed to do work for 10 to 12 hours daily for very few wages. They were not provided adequate meal interval or weekly rest. Therefore, the Commission recommended : that children under 15 years should not be allowed to work as adult without a certificate of physical fitness. It also recommended the fixation of minimum working-hours for children at 5 hours a day. It further recommended to limit the spread over for children at 7½ hours, and to prohibit work by children between 7 p.m. and 5.30 a.m.

The area of plantation was touched by the government of India only in 1933 when it enacted the Tea District Emigrant Labour Act. The only provision relating to children in the Act is one requiring that no child under 16 shall be employed and immigrated to the district unless accompanied by his parent or adult relative on whom the child is dependent. In 1933, one more step was taken to prevent the exploitation of child when children (Pledging of Labour) Act, 1933 was enacted by the Government of India on the recommendation of the Royal Commission on labour. The main aim of this act was to eliminate the evils arising from the pledging of the labour of young children by their parents for a loan or an advance.

One year after this Act, the Factories Act was completely overhauled on the basis of recommendation of Royal Commission on Labour. A new consolidated and amended Act was enacted in 1934, which was enforced from January 1, 1935. This Act prohibited the employment of children under 12 years. The children between 15 to 17 years were defined as adolescent. The maximum working hours for children between 12 and 15 years were five hours a day.

In 1935, Indian Mines (Amendment) Act, 1935 regulating the working conditions and hours of work in mines. This amendment prohibited the employment of children under 15 in mines. This Amendment Act further laid down that adolescent, i.e., the young between 15 and 17 years could be employed in underground work as adult on the production of certificate of physical fitness issued by recognised medical authorities. The working hours for such workers, according to this amendment, were 10 hours, a day and 54 hours a weak for above groundwork and 54 hours a week and 9 hours a day were fixed for underground work.

The Factories Act was subsequently amended by Factories Amendment Act, 1935 and Repealing and Amending Act, 1937 which did not alter the general provision of the Act.

In 1938, the Employment of children Act, 1938 was enacted in order to prevent the evils of employment of children in workshops which were not covered by Factories Act. The provision of this Act continues till now. This Act prohibits the employment of children under 15 in Railway and Port.[29] By the amendment of 1939 the children under 12 are prohibited to work in workshop connected with bidi-making, carpet-weaving, cement manufacturing, cloth printing, dying and weaving, manufacturing of matches, explosives and fire works, mica cutting and splitting, shallac manufacture, soap manufacture, tanning and wool cleaning.[30]

It is fruitful to note that before independence the law relating to the employment of children in various sectors failed to achieve its goal—the elimination of the evils of child labour. The labour investigating committee, in its report in 1946 pointed out that the main cause of this was the inadequacy of the inspecting staff to enforce the provisions of law.

V. CHILD LABOUR AFTER INDEPENDENCE

The first step after independence in this regard was the amendment of the Factories Act in 1948, which raised the minimum age for entering into employment in factories to 14 years. A new section was added which specifies that the provisions of chapter, dealing with employment of young persons, are in addition to and not in derogation of the employment of children Act, 1938.[31] The minimum age for admission to the employment in workshops was also raised from 12 to 14 by an amendment in the employment of Children Act, 1938. Regarding the verification of child's age in case of dispute between employer and the inspector, provisions[32] were introduced in 1949 under the employment of children Act.

The Indian Constitution, which came into force on January 26, 1950, laid down special protective measures,[33] for children, from exploitation. The International Labour Organisation Convention relating to night work for young person was responsible for an amendment in 1951 in the employment of children Act which prohibits the employment of children between 15 and 17 years at night in Railway and Port. The employers were required to maintain a register for children under 17 years. In 1951, Plantation Labour was passed in order to prevent the employment of children under 12 years in plantation.[34] Next year, the Mines Act, 1952 was enacted. This Act prohibits the employment of children under 15 years in mines.[35] Adolescent could be employed for underground as adult upon the satisfactory of two conditions—*firstly,* he must have completed his 16 years, and *secondly,* he must have a certificate of physical fitness from a Surgeon.[36]

In 1954, the Factories Act was again amended by the Factories (Amendment) Act, 1954 to prohibit the employment of adolescent under 17 years at night.[37] Night means, under this Act, a period of 12 consecutive hours which include hours between 10 p.m. to 7. a.m. Again the children under 15 are prohibited to be engaged or carried to sea to work in many capacity in any ship except in certain specific cases by an Act known as Merchant Shipping Act which was passed in 1958.

In 1961, two important Acts were passed in order to provide a large protection to children, *one,* the Motor Transport Workers Act, 1961. Prohibits the Employment of children under 15 in Motor Transport Undertakings.[38] *Second.* The Apprentice Act, 1961, provides for regulating and controlling of trainees.[39]

One of the important steps was taken in 1966 to protect the children in Bidi industries when the Bidi and Cigar Workers (Conditions of Employment), Act., 1966 was passed. This Act prohibits the employment of children under 14 years.[40] in any industrial premises young persons between 14 years and 18 years are also prohibited to work at night between 7 p.m. to 6. a.m.[41]

A report of National Commission Labour Published in 1969 observed that child labour persists in varying degree in the unorganised sector such as small plantations, restaurans and hotels, cotton ginning and weaving, carpet-weaving, stone-breaking, bricklaying, handicrafts and road building. To regulate the labour of unorganised sector as shown by National Commission on Labour the Government of India passed an Act in 1970, known as the Contract Labour (Regulation and Abolition) Act, 1970, the Act covers all the establishments and contractors employing 20 or more workers in the whole of India. As there is no specific provision relating to child work, many children can be seen in building the house, road, etc. under contractors.

In 1973, the Apprentice Act, 1961 was amended by Apprentice (Amendment) Act, 1973 to protect the rights of apprentice trainees.[42] The Act prohibited undergoing apprenticeship trainees of a person under 14 years. In addition to these legislative protective to child the sate passed various shops and commercial establishments Acts for their respective state. In these Acts the minimum age of employment on shops and commercial establishments under the respective state enactments is 12 years in Assam, Bihar, Gujarat, Madhya Pradesh, Maharashtra, Karnataka. Orissa, Rajasthan, West Bengal and Delhi and 14 years in Andhra Pradesh, Kerala, Tamilnadu, Punjab, Uttar Pradesh, Himachal Pradesh and Pondicherry.

The National Policy for Children Regulation, adopted in August, 1974 developed the idea that childhood and youth are to be protected against exploitation and no child below the age of 14 years shall be employed to work in any factory or mine or engaged in any other hazardous employment and set out a policy framework and measures aimed at providing adequate service for children. These were to form a prominent part of the Nation's Plan for development of human resources. The policy provides as one of its objectives that no child under the age of 14 years shall be permitted to be engaged in hazardous occupations or to be made to undertake heavy work.

The committee on child labour (Gurupadswamy Committee) which submitted its report in 1979, examined the problems of child labour in India. India is one of the country where the problems of child labour are quite openly manifest, and the widespread existence of child labour has been viewed by the government of India with Concern. The Gurupadswamy Committee recognised that a distinction had to be made between child labour and the exploitation of child labour as, though both are problem, they are of different orders. It has underlined that in all future action dealing with child labour this basic aspect would have to be taken note of i.e., that "Labour becomes an absolute evil in the case of child" when he is required to work beyond his physical capacity, when hours of employment interfere with his wages are not commensurate with the quantum of work done, and when the occupation he is engaged endangers his health and safety," i.e. when he is exploited.

Government has given consideration to these aspects of the problem of child labour from exploitation or from being subjected to work in hazardous conditions which endanger such children's physical and mental development, the need to ensure safety and ensure that children are not employed in factories or mines or in any other hazardous employment, and when they are employed in non-hazardous employment, or occupation, to ensure that the work is regulated in accordance with Part III of the Child Labour (Prohibition and Regulation) Act, 1986. Where it is necessary for the state governments to make rule under Child Labour Act, 1986 or under any other legislation so as to protect the interests of child labour, they will be so required to undertake reviews and frame rules as necessary.

The leaders of Indian movement for independence were aware of this history as also the sad plight of children in India. They knew very well that during colonial era legislative and other measures adopted for the welfare of children were wholly inadequate to improve their lot. That is why, as makers of constitution of free India, they incorporated a number of provisions therein for securing the well-being of children.

VI. SUM-UP

The detailed study of the foregoing chapter reveals that the evil of child labour in India has been in existence from the time immemorial. The study shows that even in the ancient India child labour was found in the form of child slavery. Child slaves could be purchased or sold like commodities. It is revealed from the study that the child labour in ancient India was very common, they were engaged in different occupations. Similarly, the notions of child labour in medieval period was no exception. It is revealed that increasing pressure on land led to fragmentation of holdings. During this period a class of landless labourers came into existence. These labourers used their children to help in their economic activities.

During the Mughal empire no serious efforts were made by the king to weed out the child labour. It was rather encouraged by them. The child was always used for their selfish ends. The study further reveals the fact that the uneven development of industrialisation gave a new turn to the overall socio-economic order in the 18th century. With the industrialisation the exploitation of children was increased. They had to work morning till night for a pitiful earning. Near the middle of 19th century, the employers were free to bargain with labour with the result that children were employed in cotton, jute mills and coal mines, etc. They were made to work mercilessly despite their tender age and were virtually converted into slaves.

The study discloses that first protective legislation for child labour was enacted in 1881. The Act prohibits the employment of children below the age of seven years, it limits their working hours to nine hours a day. The legislation aims at certain welfare measures for the welfare of child workers. In 1933, children (pledging of labour) Act, 1933 was enacted with an objective to eliminate the evils arising form the pledging of labour of young children by their parents for a loan taken in advance. It is clear form the study that various legislations were enacted even before independence to improve the working conditions of the child workers in our country. The study also discloses that a great attention has been paid by the government to improve their working conditions even after independence. Many legislations have been brought into existence in the light of child labour welfare philosophy contained in our National Charter. State governments are also equally concerned with the cause of the poor child workers and are busy to curb the arbitrary powers of the employers of the children in their establishment. Moreover, the National Policy for Child Labour, 1974 is a praiseworthy step initiated by the Government which aims at the welfare of the child workers so as to safeguard them against exploitation and enable them to grow into good citizens.

REFERENCES

1. See, U.C. Sahoo, "Child Labour in Surat Textile Industry," *Social Change*, Sept. 1990, Vol. 20. No. 3. p. 39.
2. See. N. Mitra. "The Slave Children of Mandsour," *Sunday*, 8, 19, Dec. 1980, pp. 10-17.
3. *Ibid.*
4. See, Jinesh Chandra Kulshrestha, *Child Labour in India*, (1978), p. 48.
5. *Ibid.*
6. *Ibid.*
7. *Ibid.*

8. See, Dr. S.N. Dhyani, *Jurisprudence: A Study of Indian Legal Theory*, (1985). p. 70.
9. See, Laiah-Eng. "The little workers: A study of child labour in small scale industries of Penang," *Development and Change*, Oct., 1992, Vol. 13, No. 4, pp. 565-70.
10. See, Manju Gutpa, "Child Labour: A Harsh Reality," *Child Labour in India* (1987), p. 1.
11. See, Radhakrishna Chaudhary, *Economic History of Ancient India* (1982), p. 131.
12. *Ibid.*
13. See, *Arthashastra*-III, IB.
14. See, *Supra* Note 11. p. 146.
15. See, *Supra* Note 10, p. 2.
16. See, Dr. Pant, *Economic History of India under the Mughals* (1990), p. 64.
17. See, Al-Badayuni *Murtakhabir-Tawarikh*, (Vol. II), p. 404.
18. *Supra* Note, 14, p. 66.
19. See, Rogers and Beveridge, *Tuzuk-i-Jahangiri*, Vol. I, pp. 150-51.
20. See, *Supra* Note 11, p. 131.
21. *Ibid.*
22. *Ibid.*
23. See, Ray Chaudhury, Tapan and Habib, Irfan, *The Cambridge Economic History of India* (1981), Vol. 1, p. 287.
24. See, Smitu Kothari, "There's Blood on those Matchsticks: Child Labour in Sivakasi, *Economic and Political Weekly*, Vol. XVIII, No. 27, July, 2, 1983, p. 1198.
25. See, Elias Menddelievitt, Child Labour, *International Labour Review*, 1979, Vol. 18, No. 5, Sept. -Oct. p. 212.
26. See, *Supra* Note 15.
27. *Ibid.*
28. See, *Supra* Note 11.
29. See, *The Employment of Children Act*, 1938, Section 3(i).
30. *Ibid.*, Section 3(3).
31. For detail see *Indian Factories Act*, 1948, Section 68.
32. *Ibid.*, Section 70(2).
33. See *Constitution of India Act* 15(3). Articles 23-24.
34. See, *Plantation of Labour Act*, 1951, Section 24.
35. See, *The Mines Act*, 1952, Section 2(j).
36. *Ibid.*, Section 40(i).
37. *Supra* Note, Section 70.
38. See, *The Motor Transport Workers Act*, 1961, Section 21.
39. See, *The Apprentices* Act, 1961, Preamble.
40. See *The Bidi and Cigar Workers (Condition of Employment) Act 1966*, Section 2(b).
41. *Ibid.*, Section 25.
42. See, *Report of National Commission or Labour* (1969), p. 386.

23

CHILD LABOUR WELFARE UNDER INDIAN CONSTITUTION

I. PRELUDE

The problem of child labour has been a world-wide problem. Industrialisation on a large scale leads to the employment of children in factories, workshops and their unregulated occupations.[1] It becomes a matter of deep concern to find out ways and means which may put an end to the employment and exploitation of children who are forced to join the labour steam. In recent decades, steady progress has been made in developing countries in the field of school education, resulting in a considerable improvement in the school enrolment of children.[2] This progress has especially helped in bringing down the indicence of child labour.

Of late, the United Nations Organisation and its organ, UNICEF, have organised convention on the rights of child with a view to elevating political and humanitarian obligations of nations towards children to the level of International law. For the protection of children there had been a number of international treaties and declarations, since the day of the League of Nations. Those international treaties and declarations did not touch all issues regarding the right of the child. Therefore, the comprehensive Human Rights Convention was drafted on the rights of the child which has binding effect on all member nations of the U.N., as the same has been ratified by the required number of member states.[3]

Adequate discussion on the status of children is significantly absent in the debates of the constitution.[4] The reason can be that this matter might have been taken for granted during deliberations. However, when the constitution was adopted, the preamble unequivocally states that social, economic and political justice, liberty of thought, expression, belief, faith and worship, equality of status and opportunity and fraternity assuring the dignity of the individual and the unity and integrity of the nation will be secured to all the citizens.[5] It recognises the need for granting special protection to children. The funding fathers were wise enough to provide that the children should also have their distributive justice in future in free India. Therefore, special provisions ensuring justice to children have been incorporated in Part-III with Fundamental Rights and Part IV devoted to Directive Principles of State Policy.

The constitutional provision dealing with welfare of children are explicit and are directly categorised into two categories. The explicit provisions dealing with the child welfare are:

1. Article 15(3), (It empowers the state to make special provisions for women and children).
2. Article 24, (It prohibits the employment of children in factories, etc.).
3. Article 39(e) and (f), (It obligates the state to safeguard the health of children and afford opportunities to grow with dignity), and
4. Article 45, (It provides for free and compulsory education for children).

The implicit provisions dealing with the welfare of children may be mentioned as under:

1. Article 14, (Equality before law).
2. Article 23, (Prohibition of Traffic in human beings and forced labour)
3. Article 38, (It endeavours to secure a social order for the protection of welfare of the people).
4. Article 41, (Right to work, to education and to public assistance in certain cases).
5. Article 42, (Provisions for Just and humane conditions of work and maternity relief).
6. Article 46. (Promotion of educational and economic interests of Schedule Castes, Schedule Tribes and other weaker sections), and
7. Article 47, (It obligates the state to raise the level of nutrition and the standard of living and to improve public health).

II. CHILD LABOUR WELFARE UNDER FUNDAMENTAL RIGHTS

Part III of Constitution of India contains a long list of fundamental rights. This chapter has very well been described as the Magna Carta of India.[6] Fundamental Rights are limitations upon all the powers of the Government, executive as well as legislative and they are essential to the preservation of public and private rights, notwithstanding the representative character of political institutions.[7] The rights are regarded as fundamentals because they are most essential for the individual for the development of his full intellectual, moral and spiritual potentialities. The negation of these rights will keep the individual's personality undeveloped. The declaration of fundamental rights in the constitution limits the range of government activity in appropriate directions in the interest of the liberty of the citizens.

The chapter on Fundamental Rights in Indian Constitution guarantees some fundamental rights only to the citizens[8] of India while the others are guaranteed to any persons[9] (i.e., for both citizens and non-citizens), within which the fundamental rights of the children are also implicitly included. The Children have rights to enjoy all the fundamental rights which are guaranteed to the citizens of India under Articles 15, 16, 19 and 29 of the Constitution because the children in India are also citizens of India.[10] The fundamental rights which are available only to the citizens are:

1. The right not to be discriminated against on the grounds of religion, race, caste, sex or place of birth (Art. 15).
2. The right to equality of opportunity in the matter of public employment (Art. 16).
3. The right to six freedoms enumerated in Art. 19, i.e. freedom of speech and expression, assembly, association, movement, residence and profession.
4. Cultural and educational rights conferred by Arts. 29 and 30.

There are also some fundamental rights expressly provided for children and some other fundamental rights which are also applicable for children. Article 14 guarantees equality before law and equal protection of laws to all persons within the territory of India and Article 15 prohibits discrimination on the grounds of religion, race, caste, sex, class or place of birth or any of them. But Article 15(3) enables the state to make special provisions in its laws for giving favourable treatment to children and women. Though, no ground is mentioned, preferential treatment is permitted on consideration of inherent weakness of children. Article 15(3) serves as an exception to Article 15(1) and 15(2). Article 15 in general prohibits the discrimination on the ground of religion, race, caste, sex or place of birth. Mr. H.M. Seervai is of the view that since Article 15(1) does not make age a prohibited ground of discrimination the reference to children in Article 15(3) appears to be pointless.[11]

It is submitted that a specific positive provision serves the purpose of avoiding any controversy and demonstrates the concern, however, inadequate of the framers of the Constitution that the state shall strive to promote the welfare of the people including children. Our solicitude for children and repulsion for the exploitation of children of tender age, impelled our founding fathers to make a specific mention of them,[12] the state can make law for welfare of children, given them preferential treatment over other persons in the society.

Article 21 is to provide for the protection of life and personal liberty of the people including children. "Right to Life" in the context has been held to be not a mere animal existence[13] but it is to be with human dignity and values.[14]

Article 23 of the constitution prohibits traffic in human beings, begar and other similar forms of forced labour and exploitation. Although this article does not specifically speak of children, yet it is applied to them and is more relevant in their context because children are the most valuable section of the society. It is a known fact that many children are exploited even by the parents who allows their exploitation because of their poverty. And in the absence of parents their exploitation by close relatives still deeper. They are deprived of education, made to do all sorts of work injurious to their health and personality.[15] In rural areas children are pledged by destitute parents to the landlords as full-time servant or part-time worker to look after both domestic and agricultural operation. In urban areas, the exploitation of children in myrid from exists such as helpers to artisans and skilled workers and also as domestic servants. Millions of children are exploited in violation of this fundamental right and no adequate legislature and administrative measures have been taken by the state.[16]

In reference to children the word "begar" can be given a wide connotation. Begar does not require total absence of payment. Even inadequate payment for the work rendered by the child amount to begar or forced labour. The most atrocious and heinous crime against helpless children is that they are captured and mained by criminal ganges to indulge them in begging business. Sometimes, the children of tender age are enticed for the flesh trade, thus all in violation of Article 23.[17]

Article 24 prohibits the employment of children below the age of 14 years in factories, mines or hazardous employment. But in the context of the prevailing poverty in the country it would be extremely difficult to implement the above provision.[18] Employment of children below a particular age is also prohibited so also hazardous or injurious work may be prohibited to children taking into consideration their physical structure.[19] This article does not create an absolute bar to the employment of children below the age of 14 years. Moreover, it does not prohibit their employment altogether. The employment is prohibited only in factory or mine or in any other hazardous occupation. However, this provision is to be understood in the light of realities and economic need of parents and children in our society. As Article 24 prohibits the employment of children below the age of 14 years, it is submitted that even with respect to children above the age of 14 years, all agreements either express or implied are avoidable and are of doubtful validity in case of exploitation.[20] Further, Article 24 is plainly and indubitably enforceable against every one and by reason of its compulsive mandate, no one can employ a child below the age of 14 years in a 'hazardous employment.'[21] This provision raises a question as to what are the 'hazardous' employment. Hazardous employment of children below 14 years is a constitutional prohibition which even if not followed up by the appropriate legislation, must operate propriovigore.[22] It is therefore, necessary to identify the employment which may be called 'hazards' employment. Thus Article 24 is an additional precautionary measures securing distributive justice to children.

There are also the fundamental rights which are available to any person.[23] Thus the question arises whether the fundamental rights which are available to a 'person' are also available to the child or not? The answer to this question finds in the answer to the question whether the word 'person' includes the child or not? The Indian Constitution does not define the word 'person' obviously for child a 'person' cannot include an 'artificial person.' But the question still remains whether an unborn child is included in the definition of 'person' as used in Articles 14, 17, 18(1), 20, 21, 22, 23, 25, 26, 27, 28 and 32 of the Indian Constitution. There is no direct decision of Indian Supreme Court on this point. The Allahabad High Court, however, held that for the purpose of Section 304-A(a) of Indian Penal Code, the word 'person' includes a child born or unborn. Child in Womb can be regarded as a living entity with a life of its own.[24] In Hindu law a child in Womb is deemed to be in existence as a person and is entitled to share the joint family property.[25] Thus, the fundamental rights which are variable to any 'person' may also be available to a child.

III. CHILD LABOUR WELFARE PHILOSOPHY UNDER DIRECTIVE PRINCIPLES OF STATE POLICY

The underlying principles of the Directive Principles of State Policy is "To fix certain social and economic goals for immediate attainment by bringing about a non-violent social revolution.[26] through such a social revolution the constitution also seeks to achieve the objectives of the child welfare. To achieve the goals of child welfare, the constitution has some provisions in Part IV. The Directive Principles of State Policy have been designed with an earnest zeal of strive to promote the welfare of people by securing and protecting as effectively as it may a social order in which justice, social, economical and political shall inform all the institutions of national life. Naturally, an effective implementation of this principle results, in promoting the welfare of the people through social, economic and political justice and in this turn its expected to promote proportionately, the child welfare also.[27]

Article 39(e) and (f) direct the state to evolve a policy eliminating the abuse of tender age and to free children from the circumstances forcing them to enter into avocations unsuited to their age or strength. The state is also directed to create social and economical conditions and infrastructure for the healthy development of children and to provide facilities and climate for exercise of freedoms and maintenance of dignity. The State is further directed to protect the children against exploitation and moral and material abandonment.[28]

Article 41 deals with the right to work, to education and public assistance in certain cases. Though it does not mention children, the ending words "..... and in other cases of, undeserved want." Article 41: Right to work, to education public assistance in certain cases: The state shall be within the limits of its economic capacity and development make effective provision for securing the right to work, to education and to public assistance in case of unemployment, old age, sickness and disablement, and in other cause of deserved want. It covers the children as the suffering children deserved the least fate as in no case they can be held responsible for their past sins. Hence it is the duty of state to provide social assistance to all the children who suffer for want of basic necessities of life. The implementation of this provision is also expected to promote the welfare of the children proportionately and to ensure distributive justice to them.

Article 42, requires the state to make provisions for securing just and humane conditions of work and for maternity relief. The measures for maternity relief are meant for expectant mothers and mothers during the period of pregnancy and after the child birth. These measures meant for providing proper health care and other facilities to the mothers before and after the child birth are expected to promote the health of children and to provide healthy environments for their bringing up.

Under Article 45 a duty is imposed upon the state to provide free and compulsory education within a period of ten years of the commencement of the constitution for all the children until they complete the age of 14 years. This Directive signifies that it is not only confined to primary education, but extends to free education whatever it may be upon the age of 14 years. Article 45 is the thus supplementary of Article 24 on the ground that when the child is not to be employed before the age of 14 years, he is to be kept occupied in some educational institutions. It is suggested that Article 24 in turn supplements the clauses (e) and (f) of Article 39, thus ensuring distributive justice to children in the matter of education. It is suggested that Articles 24 and 45 should be amended so as to raise that age limit from 14 to 16 years. By doing so the children's education atleast upto matriculation, would be ensured or the proper growth and development of their personality. There are various state Acts, which stipulate the upper age limit of 16 years.[29]

Article 46 provides that the state shall promote with special care, the educational and economic interests of the weaker section of the people, and in particular, of scheduled castes and the scheduled tribes, and shall protect them from social injustice and all forms of exploitation. The implementation of this principle, while promoting the economic and educational interests of the weaker section of the people particularly those of scheduled castes and scheduled tribes, will indirectly promote the welfare of the children of these sections of the society need the welfare measures most because of the appealing poverty and backwardness of their parents.

Article 47 imposes a primary duty upon the state to raise the level of nutrition and the standard of living of its people and improvement of public health.[30] Thus it is the responsibility of the state of provide nutritious food to the children as the world "people" includes not only adults but children as perhaps this provision becomes more relevant in case of children as the malnutrition can cause irreparable danger to the personality of the children through mental retardation and blindness.

Though these directives are not enforceable by the Court, yet these have been declared to be fundamental in the governance of the country.[31] it is the obligation of the state to apply these principles in making laws. If the government ignores them it will certainly have to answer for them before the electorate at the time of the election. Thus, it will not be correct to say that there is no sanction of enforceability behind these directives. In our democratic setup, vigilant public opinion is the real force behind the political institution which stands for the benefit of individual. The actions of the government are subject to scrutiny by the masses and distinguished leader of the different parties. If the government pursues a policy in accordance with the principles of the constitution, people tolerate it, otherwise they oust it in the next election. Since these directives relating to the welfare of children have also been embodied in the constitution, the government are apt to implement them. Though they do not have legal force behind them but the highest tribunal, i.e., public opinion behind them.[32]

Furthermore, Article 31-C gives precedence to all the directive principles over the fundamental rights. According to this Article, if a law is enacted for giving effect to any of the directive mentioned in Part IV its validity cannot be challenged in the courts of Law on the ground that it is inconsistent with or takes away or abridges any of the rights guaranteed by Article 14 or 19 of the constitution. This position has now been altered by the Supreme Court in *Minerva Mills*.[33] case in which the Court held that Article 31-C to the extent it was amended by 42nd amendment Act is unconstitutional. It is now confined to directives contained in Article 38(a) and (c) however, the court will have power to examine whether the law is really intended to give effect to directives or it is intended, in the guise of giving effect to directives. To achieve some other purpose.[34]

IV. SUM-UP

The foregoing study reveals that the very preamble of Indian constitution stands as a testimony to witness the presence of philosophy of socio-economic and political justice under our National charter. The opening words of the Preamble show beyond the shadow of doubt that the people of India have solemnly committed themselves to rescue all the citizens. *Justice,* social, economic and political, liberty of thought, expression belief, faith and worship, equality of status and opportunity, and to promote among them all; fraternity assured the dignity of the individual and unity and integrity of the nation.

In order to achieve goals of social, economical and political justice, the constitution of India guarantees special protection to the children against exploitation. To import justice to them, the state has been empowered to make special provisions to their welfare so as to bring them at par with other sections of the society. There are various provisions in the constitution which put the state under duty to ensure that the tender age of children is not abused and they are not exposed to economic necessity to enter avocation unsuited to their age and strength.

Article 15(3) of Indian Constitution empowers the state to make special provisions for women and children. In the same way Article 24 adopted by our wise founding fathers prohibits the employment of children below the age of 14 years in factories, mines or any other hazardous occupation. This article prohibits the employment of children who are below the age of 14 years, all agreements either express or implied are voidable at the option of these poor creatures. Article 24 is really an additional precautionary measure to securing distributive justice to children.

Similarly, Part IV of our National Charter envisages many important provisions with regard to the welfare of the child workers. The Directive Principles of State Policy have been designed with an earnest zeal to strive to protect and promote the overall growth of the child workers as effectively as it may. Consequently, an effective implementation of these principles is expected to promote the welfare of the child workers and render them justice; social, economic and political with a hope to enable them to grow as the good citizens of the country.

Article 39 (e) and (f) of the constitution obligates the state to evolve a policy eliminating the views of tender age and to free children from the circumstances forcing them into their age and strength. The state is also directed to crate social and economic conditions and infrastructure for the healthy development of children. It is also the fundamental duty of the state to safeguard the child workers against exploitation, moral and material abandonment. Moreover, the constitution of India has subjected the state under Article 45 to provide free and compulsory education to all the children until they complete the age of 14 years. Article 15 is thus supplementary to Article 24 on the ground that when the child is not to be employed before the age of 14 he is to be kept occupied in some educational institutions. Article 47 also imposes a primary duty upon the state to raise the level of nutrition and the standard of living of is people and improvement of public health.

To sum up, the deep analysis of various provisions contained in our National charter makes it abundantly crystal clear that is the duty of the state to promote the welfare of the child workers and help them to grow into good citizens of the country.

REFERENCES

1. See, T.N. Bhagoliwal, *Economics of Labour and Social Welfare*, (1976), p. 651.
2. See, B.M. Dinesh and P.H. Rayappa, "School and Work: Are they compatible?" *Indian Journal of Social Work,* Vol. XLVII. No. 2, July 1986, p. 117.
3. See, S. Roy, Hon'ble Judge of Patna High Court, "Constitutional Rights of the Child in India," *Social Change,* Sept. 1990, Vol. 20, No. 3, p. 3.
4. See, C.A.D., Vol. VIII, pp. 803-15.
5. The word, "Citizen," in the preamble includes the children as they acquire the citizenship by birth, see, Articles 5 to 11 of the Constitution.
6. See, the Declaration of the rights of the child, adopted by the General Assembly of the United Nations in 1959.
7. See, V.C. Ram Chandran, (1974), Fundamental Rights and Constitutional Remedies (1974), 2nd ed., p. 1.
8. See, The Constitution of India, Articles 15, 16, 19 and 29 which guarantee fundamental rights only for the citizen of India.
9. See, the Constitution of India, Articles, 14, 17, 18, 20 to 28 and 32 which guarantee fundamental rights for both the Indian citizens and non-citizen found in India.
10. See, Articles 5 to 11 of he Constitution of India and the Indian Citizenship Act, 1955.

11. See, H.M. Seervai, *Constitutional Law of India*, (1975), p. 293.
12. See, Paras Diwan, Indian *Constitution: A Document of People's* Faith (1981), p. 150.
13. See, *Francis Coralie* v. *Union Territory*. Delhi, AIR 1981 SC 746.
14. See, *Sheela Barse* v. *Union of India*, AIR 1986, SC 1773.
15. Article 23(1) reads: "Traffic in human beings and begar and other similar forms of forced labour are prohibited and any contravention of this provision shall be an offence punishable in accordance with law."
16. See, Sudesh Kumar Sharma, "Child and the Constitution: An Appraisal in Distributive Justice Prospective," *Supreme Court Journal*, 1989, Vol. II, p. 12.
17. *Ibid*.
18. Article 24 reads: "No child below the age of 14 years shall be employed to work in any factory or mine or engaged in any other hazardous employment."
19. Some of Laws which make special provision for children are: The Apprentices Act, 1850: Indian Majority Act, 1875. Guardians and Wards Apprentices Act, 1890. Child Marriage Restraint Act, 1929, employment of Children Act. 1938; the Mines Act, 1952; The Factory Act, 1948. The Hindu Marriage Act, 1955; the Hindu Minority and Guardianship Act, 1956; The Hindu Adoption and Maintenance Act, 1956.
20. See Constitution of India, Art, 23.
21. See, *Laksami Kant* v. *India*, AIR 1984, SC 469, upon the great importance of child welfare in the Country.
22. *People's Union for Democratic Rights* v. *Union of India*, AIR 1982, SC 1473.
23. See constitution of India, Articles 14, 17, 20, 21, 22, 23, 25, 26, 27, 28 and 32.
24. See, *Jabber v. State*, AIR 1966 All, 590.
25. See, D.F. Mulla, Principles of Hindu Law, (1974), p. 399.
26. See, K.S. Hegde, *The Directive Principles of State Policy; The Constitution of India* (National, 1972). p. 17.
27. See, Constitution of India, Part IV Article 38.
28. Article 39 the state is to see:
    (a) that the health and strength of workers, men and women and the tender age of children are not abused and that citizen's are not forced by economic necessity to enter avocations unsuited to their age or strength.
    (b) that children are given opportunities for facilities to develop in a healthy manner and in conditions of freedom of dignity and that childhood and youth are protected against exploitation and against moral and mental abandonment.
29. See, Madhya Pradesh Bal Adhiniyam, 1970. See. 2(1); Uttar Pradesh Children Act, 1952, Section 2(4).
30. According to a report of the Indian Council of Medical Research at least 60% of the children in India suffer from protein coloria malnutritional anaemia.
31. Constitution of India, Art, 37.
32. See, Chandra Pal, "Position of Child under the Indian Constitution: A critical appraisal of the fundamental rights of child and the Directive Principles for child welfare," Punjab University Law Review, Chief Edt. Paras Diwan, p. 459 (1980).
33. See Minerva Mills Ltd. v. Union of India, AIR 1980 SC 1789.
34. *Ibid*.